Administration

Units 1, 2, 3 and 4

Level 2

Carol Carysforth

www.heinemann.co.uk

✓ Free online support
✓ Useful weblinks
✓ 24 hour online ordering

Endorsed by OCR

01865 888058

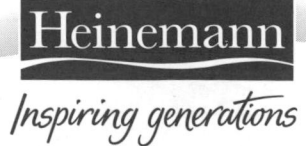

Inspiring generations

Heinemann Educational Publishers
Halley Court, Jordan Hill, Oxford OX2 8EJ
Part of Harcourt Education

Heinemann is the registered trademark of
Harcourt Education Limited

© Carol Carysforth 2003

First published 2003

07 06 05 04 03
10 9 8 7 6 5 4 3 2 1

British Library Cataloguing in Publication Data is available
from the British Library on request.

ISBN 0 435 46220 2

Designed by Kamae Design
Typeset and illustrated by J&L Composition

Original illustrations © Harcourt Education Limited, 2003

Cover design by Tony Richardson at the Wooden Ark Ltd

Printed in the UK by Scotprint

Every effort has been made to contact copyright holders of material reproduced in this book. Any omissions will be rectified in subsequent printings if notice is given to the publishers.

Websites

There are links to relevant websites in this book. In order to ensure that the links are up to date, that the links work, and that the sites are not inadvertently linked to sites that could be considered offensive, we have made the links available on the Heinemann website at www.heinemann.co.uk/hotlinks. When you access the site, the express code is 2202P.

Tel: 01865 888058 www.heinemann.co.uk

Contents

Acknowledgements   iv

Introduction   v

Dedication   vi

Unit 1   Preparing business communications   1

Unit 2   Maintaining effective working relationships   75

Unit 3   Working in business organisations   169

Unit 4   Following routine office procedures to complete tasks   309

Index   389

Please note:

The 'keys' to the Over to You questions in this book can be found on the Heinemann website, at www.heinemann.co.uk/hotlinks. The express code for accessing the keys, and for links to the websites described in this book, is 2202P.

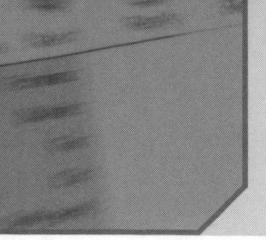

Acknowledgements

The author would like to thank all friends and colleagues who have contributed to this book by freely providing advice and information on a wide range of issues relating to current administrative practices. Special thanks are also due to Linda Mellor, for her careful editing; to Anna Fabrizio, commissioning editor, for her patience, support and encouragement; to Julia Sandford for her invaluable assistance in dealing with a myriad of changes and amendments at the eleventh hour; and to Margaret Berriman, publishing director, for too many reasons to list here!

The author and publishers would also like to thank the following organisations for providing permission to reproduce copyright material:

Amnesty International

The BSI Group

Cancer Research UK

The Copyright Licensing Agency

Greenpeace

Investors in People UK

News International

The Plain English Campaign

Richer Sounds

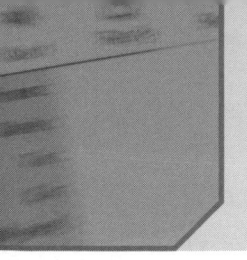

Introduction

Welcome to Administration level 2. Whether you are progressing from level 1, or starting out at this level, you are preparing to join nearly 5 million skilled professional administrators who work in a variety of organisations in the UK.

Administration is popular as a career option for several reasons. The need for skilled administrators is increasing every year, so jobs are plentiful. Whether you want to work for a small, local employer, a large international company or for your local council, hospital or college, you will normally find many opportunities available. Admin jobs are varied, too. Although almost all administrators use their IT skills on a daily basis, they can also choose to specialise in areas such as human resources (personnel), marketing, finance, law and medicine. Finally, promotion prospects for committed, enthusiastic administrators are considerable, with many becoming office managers, administration managers or PAs (personal assistants) when they have gained enough experience.

When you start to job hunt yourself, you will find that most employers insist that new administrators have a recognised qualification, such as the OCR Administration level 2 award you are about to start. This provides proof that your IT and communication skills are good, that you can carry out the basic tasks you will have to do to a competent level, and that you can understand and follow office procedures. It also shows that you understand business organisations and how they function, and – probably even more importantly to a prospective employer – you can work cooperatively with your colleagues and deal with customers in a professional way.

This book has been written to help you to learn all the skills you will need to achieve Units 1–4 of your OCR award. In addition to the basic skills, you will also learn other important skills that are valued by employers, such as planning your work to take account of the needs of other people, prioritising your work on a busy day and learning to use your own initiative to solve problems yourself. 'Real life' examples in each unit also show you how many of these areas relate to modern organisations.

After level 2 you will find that a range of opportunities exist for improving your skills to level 3 and beyond, whether you are working or studying full time. The more you learn, the greater your potential for taking on more responsibility and rising higher in the admin world. A 2003 survey by Office Team found that 83% of career-minded administrators felt that training and learning new skills was vital to progression. The award you are taking will enable you to get your foot very firmly on the ladder. Hopefully, this book will help to give you the interest and enthusiasm to keep climbing!

Carol Carysforth

August 2003

Dedication

To Margaret Berriman, with love and gratitude for being my supporter, mentor and friend from the outset of my writing career, and for learning to live with the fact that, whilst we think the same, neither of us always practises what the other preaches!

Preparing business communications

Introduction

Millions of communications are sent and received every day by businesses in the UK. Many go to other organisations or to private customers but many are also sent and received *within* a business – from one person to another.

The information in these documents is often very important and affects the decisions made by many people. A business communication may contain details of prices and discounts, or the date and time of a meeting or information about travel arrangements. If any information is incorrect, or missing, then this can create serious problems.

Businesses are judged on the quality of the documents they send – in terms of their layout, presentation and standards of English. A letter to a customer containing three spelling errors and sloppy punctuation gives a poor impression of the quality of service offered by the company as a whole – and can lead to a customer taking his or her business elsewhere.

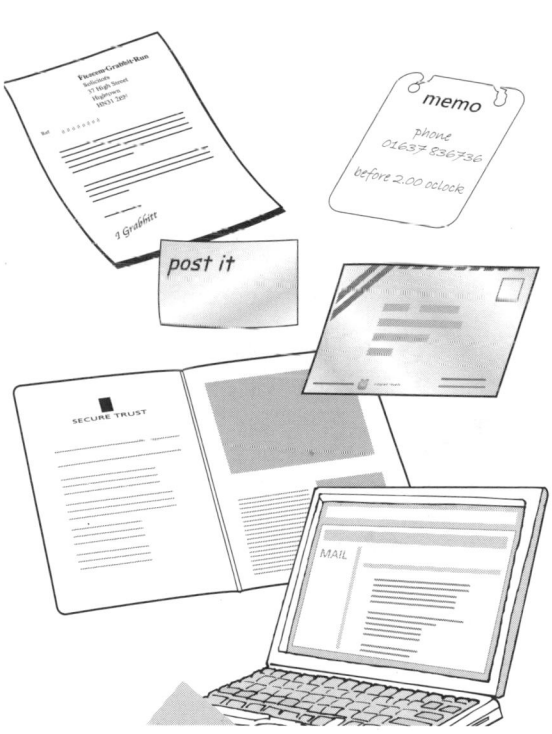

Wherever you work in business you will be involved in communicating with other people – both verbally and in writing. Your ability to do your job properly – and to help other people to do theirs – will often depend upon your communication skills. If you can be relied upon always to communicate clearly, accurately and promptly then you will be a valued employee.

This unit concentrates on developing your written communication skills. You will learn about verbal communication skills in Unit 2.

Unit summary

In this unit you will learn:

▶ **How to use accepted formats and conventions when you prepare routine business documents**. This relates to the layout of different documents and the items which must be included on each one.

▶ **How to analyse, extract and adapt information for a given purpose**. This helps you when you are given information or asked to read a detailed document to identify the key facts to use in a different document.

▶ **How to adjust the tone and style of your documents for different purposes**. An obvious example is the difference between a letter making a complaint and a personal request to a colleague for assistance. Even though both documents must be professional and use business language, the exact vocabulary and the phrases you use should be different.

▶ **How to improve your written English skills** in relation to spelling, punctuation and the structure of your sentences and paragraphs.

Assessment

Your assessment for this unit will consist of a written examination of two and a half hours. You also have an additional 10 minutes to read the paper before you start writing.

There will be four tasks on the examination paper which will test your ability to:

▶ compose business documents

▶ extract, adapt and present information

▶ use appropriate tone and style, bearing in mind the context of the document you are preparing

▶ use English accurately.

In the examination you will first read a scenario, or setting, under the heading 'General information applicable to all questions.' This describes your role and gives you information about the organisation where you are employed. For each question, you are also given background information relating to the document you will be asked to produce. The following points are very important:

▶ The tone and style of your documents *must* prove that you understand the context in which you are working as well as your own role. This also means carefully considering the purpose of each document: the recipient and the reason for sending it.

▶ All the information you need is given to you and you are not expected to invent any additional details. However, there are links between the questions and you will also need to refer back to the scenario for relevant information. You must therefore treat the examination paper as a series of tasks you would do when working in an organisation and *not* as a set of stand-alone questions.

▶ All errors are penalised – so this means that you must take extra care with your spelling, punctuation, and the structure of your sentences and paragraphs.

Special note

In this book, there are several references to word processing layout, which you will probably use at work to produce documents. In your examination, however, you may hand-write your answers. If you do, you should show, by the way you set out the document and your choice of capitals or underlining for headings, how you would present the document so that it is correct and looks professional.

Check the list of business documents you will learn about in the table below. Ask your tutor to explain if there are any descriptions you don't understand.

The A–Z of business documents

Advertisement	A short item promoting a product, service or event, usually stressing the benefits or main features.
Agenda	A list of items to be discussed during a business meeting.
Articles	A short written description of a specific item or event, often with graphics (such as a table or photograph). An example is a newspaper or magazine article.
Business letter	The traditional method of sending written information to people outside the organisation. It is used where a formal, written record is important.
Business notes	A short record of a particular matter or event. An example is notes (often called 'minutes') of a meeting stating who attended and the items discussed and agreed.
Email	A rapid method of communicating electronically either with a colleague or with someone outside the company. Both the sender and receiver need a computer and email software.
Fax	Another method of transmitting written information quickly. Both sender and receiver need a fax machine
Form	A document designed to enable a person to insert specific items of information and for the receiver to analyse the information quickly and easily.
Leaflet	A short document giving key information about an item or event. Leaflets are often folded.
Job description	A written document describing the main aspects of a job, such as the duties and responsibilities involved.
Message	A summary of the key points noted down for another person. An example is a telephone message.
Memo	An internal document which normally covers one topic. It is the internal equivalent of a business letter.
Notice	A document on which the main information about an item or event is displayed.
Report	An official written document describing an investigation into a specific topic and the result.
Summary	A shortened version of a longer document.

▲ He said it was his response to your 'Can I have a pay rise? XXX' email!

▼ PREPARING EMAILS

The greatest problems with email are caused by its main advantage, i.e. that emails are so easy to create and send that people are apt to send too many, too quickly. They type them rapidly, miss out punctuation, forget to check them and click on 'send' almost immediately. The result? Annoyed or confused recipients of the message – and senders who are quickly known for their terrible communication skills. No matter how efficient you are in other aspects of your work, if you send illiterate emails all around the company, then your name will be known for all the wrong reasons! It is important to take as much care over writing and checking emails as any other business document.

Email format

All emails have a 'header' at the top. This is normally set up by your software package and includes:

▶ the **sender's name** – usually inserted automatically

▶ the **recipient's name** – this is inserted automatically if you are replying to an email you have received. Otherwise you must enter the email address of your recipient here.

▶ the **date and time** – again inserted automatically

▶ the **subject** – this should be a brief title which indicates the content.

Options include:

▶ Selecting a recipient's name from your email address book. If the name is listed, then it will auto-complete once you start keying in the name.

▶ Sending a copy of your email to one, or more, other recipients. This is useful if you are contacting more than one person, or need to keep someone else informed about the action you have taken.

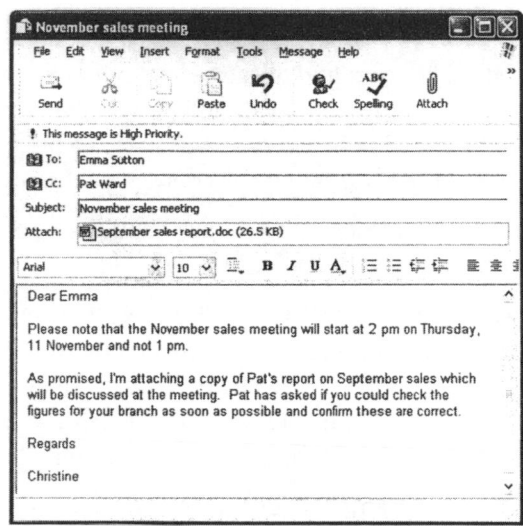

- Sending file attachments. These are electronic documents you have attached to the email, such as a word processed document or a spreadsheet.

- Identifying the priority level. If you indicate the message has high priority then a red exclamation mark is attached. Never abuse this facility – use it only for very important and urgent emails.

Email conventions

- If you are sending an email externally, some employers may expect you to start with a salutation. This is not usually the case with internal business emails and some people dislike any salutations on emails. At work, you should check the procedure used by other people in your organisation. In the examination, you do not need to start any email with a salutation.

- The text in your email should be in lower case with initial capitals at the beginning of sentences and for proper names (see page 7). Using ALL CAPITALS IS CALLED SHOUTING and is not acceptable. Using all lower case is just lazy.

- It is usual to close an external email with a brief, informal complimentary close such as 'Best wishes' or 'Regards' and then type your name. Many internal emails do not have a complimentary close and neither do you need to type your name – as it is already included on the header. However, many people prefer to add their name to give their email a personal touch. This is up to you.

- It is not usual to include emoticons (☺ ☹) on business emails.

- Abbreviations should be used only when they would be clearly understood. One of the most common is FYI (for your information) but even this is better restricted to internal emails.

The 'thread' of an email refers to the *sequence* of emails between two people. For example, you email someone and he or she replies. You should then click 'reply' if you want to respond again – and not start a new message. Then the other person does the same. If you print out at this point, you will see all four messages (in reverse order). This is very useful if you have forgotten what happened earlier and need to look back at what was discussed. The problem is that a lengthy exchange can result in a huge waste of paper every time you print out. For that reason, you may wish to delete some of the earlier messages before the final version becomes unmanageable.

Tone and style of emails

Emails should be short and to the point – but they must still be polite. They should be structured into proper sentences and paragraphs. You can also use bullets (as used in this book) or numbered points in an email so that a list of points is easy to read. The aim is to help the reader to understand the content quickly and without difficulty.

The content *must* relate to the subject heading. If you need to cover more than one topic, then either identify both topics in the subject heading or send separate emails for each one.

Do take care before you click on 'send'. It's all too easy to do this and then regret your actions! Many people confuse the ease and informality of email and say things in haste that they regret later. *Never* compose and send an email in anger. Either wait a day or save the email and look at it again 24 hours later, when you have calmed down. Never think that you can be more informal by email than you could be if you were speaking to that person.

Always check your email before you send it – for spelling (use the spell checker and then proofread it yourself), for punctuation, for content – and to make sure that any attachments you have mentioned are actually attached.

Finally, don't assume that because you have sent an email the recipient will read it quickly. Some people don't check their in-box every day, especially if they work away from the office a lot and others may be away on holiday. You can check if an email has been read on most internal systems but not if you send an email externally. If the matter is very urgent, or you don't receive a response quickly, then pick up the telephone.

> I've heard of flame mail but that's ridiculous!

▲ You should never compose and send an email in anger

Use of English

Proper sentences and punctuation should be used in all types of business communications – including emails.

▶ Start new sentences with an initial capital.

▶ Use capital letters for proper names (Bob, Paris, January) but not for seasons (spring, autumn) or general words (e.g. company, department).

▶ Finish normal sentences with a full stop and sentences that ask a direct question with a question mark, e.g. 'Will you be at the meeting?' A rhetorical question is one which doesn't expect a reply, e.g. 'I assume I will see you at the meeting.' This type of question *doesn't* need a question mark.

▶ Don't multiply question marks or exclamation marks for effect on any document – including emails, such as 'This is important!!!!'. People will take your email less seriously because it will look like the junk emails that everyone deletes almost immediately.

▶ Keep sentences short but make sure they have a subject (the person doing the action) and a verb (a 'doing word'). Therefore:

  – 'Can't be there' isn't a sentence (there is no subject)

  – 'Following your email yesterday' isn't a sentence (there is no verb).

KEY TIP – avoid starting any sentence with a word ending in 'ing'. This is because you will be in grave danger of not writing a proper sentence. Instead of 'Thanking you for your email' or 'Looking forward to meeting you' simply say 'Thank you for your email' or 'We look forward to meeting you'.

OVER TO YOU!

1 Jessica has sent two emails today. One is external – to a person in another business organisation. The other is internal – to a colleague in another office. Identify which is external and which is internal and give at least **two** reasons to support your choice.

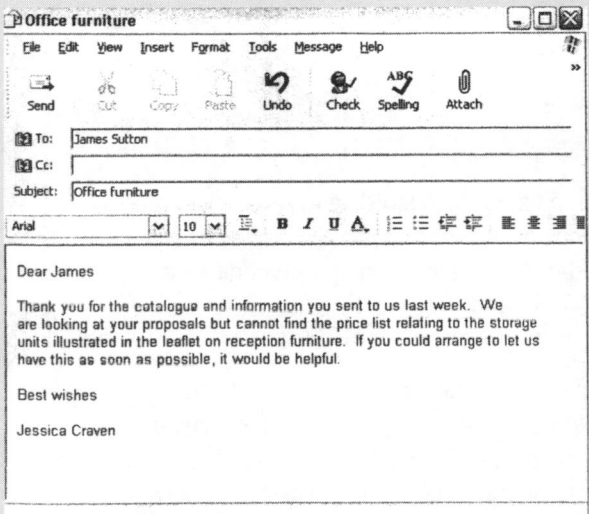

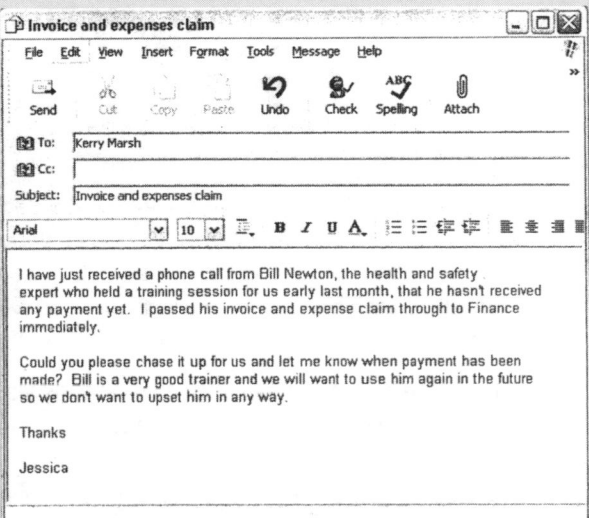

2 Joshua's English skills often let him down. He is worried that people will comment about his emails and has asked you to help him. Check the email Joshua has written below and identify the 12 mistakes he has made. Then rewrite it without any mistakes.

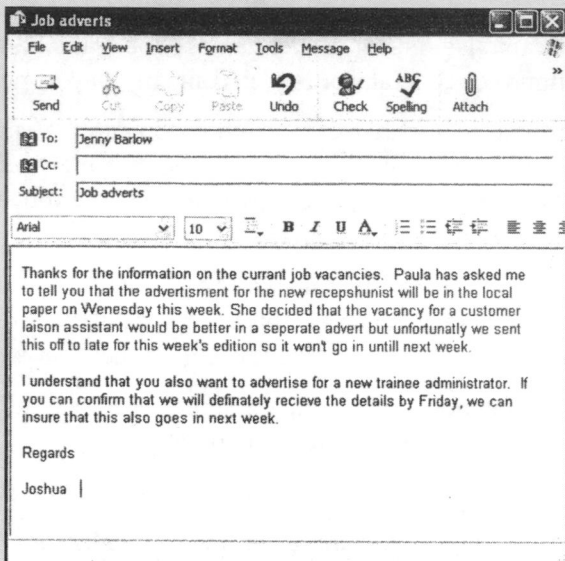

3 You are working for Lesley Abbott, Training Manager of Marlton Packaging Ltd.

a) Lesley wants to know how many new employees will be attending the induction programme to be held next Monday, so that she knows how many training packs are required. To find the answer you will have to email Mark Phillips, the Human Resources Administrator. Make sure you include next Monday's date in your email, so that there can be no confusion.

b) Marlton Packaging has trained first aiders in every department but recently two have left. Lesley has asked you to email all the staff (enter All Staff as your recipient) to state that there are two vacancies for first aiders and to ask all staff who are interested to contact the Training Office on extension 215. The first aid training will take place over 6 weeks and will be paid for by the company.

Check all your answers with your tutor.

COMMUNICATION IN BUSINESS

Email is the fastest growing method of communication at work. According to a survey carried out by Pitney Bowes, the average British worker sends or receives about 190 messages every day. In many companies, email use is now restricted to prevent staff being drowned in messages about second-hand cars, petitions for good causes, jokes and virus warnings. Workers are also reminded that if the recipient sits at the next desk, it's better to talk than email.

Email isn't new to most young employees, as many use Hotmail to contact their friends. However, research by ICM has shown that most people under the age of 25 never think about their punctuation, grammar or style when writing messages, and many sign off with love and kisses – even when they are writing to their boss! To help to improve email skills, numerous guides to email etiquette can be found on-line, so there are now no excuses for sloppy emails.

▼ ANALYSING, EXTRACTING AND ADAPTING INFORMATION (1)

At work you will often be expected to take and pass on messages for your colleagues. You may receive the information over the telephone, or from a visitor to your office. If you practise taking and recording messages this helps you to learn how to identify the important information which must be included and the irrelevant information which can be left out. You must also, of course, adapt the information for the recipient of the message.

Writing a message

Many organisations have a printed message form that you can complete. The headings will focus on the key facts that must *always* be included. If you work for an organisation that does not have printed message forms you can soon prepare your own version on a computer and save it. It is then a simple matter to enter the information on a blank form and print it out. This is better than handing someone a scribbled note, which may be difficult to read – and which may not contain all the information that is required.

On a form all the sections should be completed accurately and in full. If you are handwriting a form, make sure you write clearly. It is often better to print the names of people and places, so that there can be no mistakes.

It is important to think about the person you are writing to – and to phrase your message accordingly. You should be very careful when you are writing a message for someone who is senior to you – and make sure the tone is polite and courteous.

Selecting the information to include

In a message, all the facts must be accurate and complete. You may also need to convey the emotions of the person you spoke to, such as whether they were anxious, agitated, annoyed or impatient. This will help the person who receives the message to assess its importance and how to respond.

This does not mean, however, that you should include irrelevant information that has nothing to do with the message. You are likely to find that there are three types of people who give you information.

▶ Type A callers give you very little information and miss out some of the key facts. In this case you have to ask for the additional details you need.

▶ Type B are often business people who are used to giving clear, succinct messages. If you are really lucky, the information will also be in the right order. This group is relatively rare!

▶ Type C are people who like to talk and may include many details which are not part of the information you need to pass on – from the weather, to what they are doing this time next week. In this case you have to select the information you need – and discard the rest.

You can find out how to deal with each of these groups and the key facts to listen for by looking at the table below, which gives you the ten golden rules of taking a message.

10 golden rules when taking a message

1 Write out the message on a piece of paper, as you are listening, and *then* write out final message you will pass to the recipient. This gives you the opportunity to extract the correct information and put it in the right order.

2 Listen carefully. Be patient if someone is nervous. Ask someone who is speaking rapidly to repeat anything you do not hear properly.

3 Check you have all the **key facts** you need. These usually include
   ▶ **The name of the person** (check the spelling if you are unsure)
   ▶ **The name of the person's organisation or his/her private address**
   ▶ **The caller's telephone number and local dialling code**. Sometimes you may also be given a telephone extension number.
   ▶ **The main points relating to the message**, e.g.
      – The reason for the call
      – Details of any information requested
      – Details of any information given to you.

   With some callers you may have to ask a few questions to obtain all the information you need.

4 **Double-check** information given to you about dates, times, place names, product names or codes, prices, quantities – or any other numbers. You can never guess these afterwards!

5 If the message is long or complicated read it back to the caller to check you have understood everything correctly.

6 If the caller is annoyed then listen without interrupting – as this is likely to upset the caller even more. If the caller has been inconvenienced then apologise on behalf of your company for the problem. This is different from admitting a mistake has been made. Tell the caller you will pass on the information immediately and make sure the correct person contacts them as soon as possible.

7 Write out the message promptly, using simple, straightforward words that cannot be misunderstood. Include all the key facts in a logical order, even if the caller gave you the information in a random way. Be very specific about days and dates and always give *both* to be on the safe side. Never say 'today' or 'tomorrow' in case the message is read on a different day to that on which it was written.

8 Leave out any personal details or irrelevant information which won't help the reader to understand the message quickly.

9 Make sure you include **your own name** on the message and the **date and time of the call**.

10 If the message is urgent, pass it on *immediately*.

KEY TIP – Stating *both* the date and day in a business document helps to prevent any confusion.

He must be on to that Martha Jones again

▲ Some people like to give you more information than you need

OVER TO YOU!

1 Rebecca has been working in the sales department of Marlton Packaging for only two weeks when she receives a telephone call from an irritated customer. She becomes flustered during the conversation and struggles to write down a sensible message (see page 12).

Refer to the hints and tips on message taking on page 10 and then answer the following questions:

a) Identify the key facts which Rebecca has missed out from her message. As a group, suggest the problems this will cause for the recipient.

b) Again, as a group, suggest the questions Rebecca could have asked to find out this information.

c) What phrase did Rebecca hear and then repeat in the message that isn't very tactful? Decide whether you would have included this and, if so, how you would have worded it.

d) State the advice you would give Rebecca to help her to deal with any other difficult calls she receives.

e) Rebecca tells you that she hasn't passed the message on because Bill Griffiths, the Sales Manager, is on holiday this week. As a group, suggest what Rebecca should do.

f) You check in the files to help Rebecca and find out that the caller was John Brown from Hudson Construction in Birmingham. The order number is 30829, it was for polystyrene chips and it was placed 6 weeks ago. Rewrite the message correctly incorporating this information.

Message Form ☑URGENT ☐NON-URGENT

TO: Bill Griffiths   DEPT: Sales
DATE: (today)   TIME: 10.15 am

CALLER'S NAME John
ORGANISATION I think this was Hudicon something
TEL No: 208309   EXT No: 200

☑ Telephoned   ☐ Please return call
☐ Returned your call   ☐ Please arrange appointment
☐ Called to see you   ☑ Left a message

Message:
He phoned 'cos he was angry. He sent an order but the goods haven't arrived. He sent it quite a while ago. He spoke to someone else on Monday who said they'd ring him back but didn't. He says if they aren't delivered by tomorrow afternoon then to cancel the order and he'll get his supplies from somewhere else.

He said you must do something quickly if you want your firm to stay in business.

Taken by: Rebecca Scholes

---

2 Work in pairs for this activity. Work out a message you want to pass on to your tutor and assume your colleague answers the telephone when you ring to speak to your tutor, who is not available. Your message should contain at least three items of important information and one item of irrelevant information. (For example, you might want to check the date, time and room where a particular examination will be held and your irrelevant information may be that you are nervous about taking the exam.)

Hold a conversation with your colleague, who should prompt you for any important information you do not remember to provide. After your colleague has made notes for his/her message, reverse roles.

The crucial test is whether your tutor can understand the messages and whether they contain all the important information and don't include the irrelevancies.

3 Some telephone callers provide details which can be left out of the message. Paula works in the College library and one of her first jobs is to listen to any messages left on the answering machine. She then writes these out for the library staff. Below is a transcript of the first call on the machine this morning. Identify the important information and disregard anything that isn't relevant. Then write out a clear message for Margaret Edwards, the Librarian.

'Oh, hello, is that the library? I thought you'd be open, but obviously you're not. Anyway, it's 8.30 now and I'm calling about a book my son ordered weeks ago. He needs it for his coursework and his project must be finished in two weeks' time, so unless he gets it he'll have a real problem. He would have rung you himself but he's on work experience at the moment and can't use the phone for personal calls. His name is Jamie Douglas and he's on a business studies course. I don't know the proper title but his tutor's name is Sam Edwards, if that helps. It's Sam who asked him to get the book – it's called Business in Today's World *by Martin Keats. You only have a few and they were all on loan when he called in. Can you let me know if one has arrived yet? My name is Anne Douglas. Oh, my number is 02837–502803. I'll be out this morning but at home this afternoon. If someone can ring me, I'll pop in for the book straight away. Thanks.*

▼ PREPARING MEMOS

Memos – or memoranda to give them their full title – are internal documents used to send information from one department in a company to another. Today they are less common because so many people use email. However, memos are useful for longer, more complex or less urgent internal communications. Because they provide a hard (paper) copy which can be filed for future reference, they are more suitable than emails for giving detailed information or for describing the action taken about a particular matter.

Memo format

The design of memos is quite straightforward. There is always a header at the top which includes the main items of information, as you will see on page 15. These are

▷ The **sender's name** (and sometimes job title)

▷ The **recipient's name** (and sometimes job title)

▷ The **date**

▷ The **reference**. This may be the manager's initials followed by the creator's initials (e.g. AP/KL) or it may include a file number (e.g. Customer reference 392083).

▷ A **subject heading**. This helps the recipient to identify the content quickly. It is also helpful to anyone filing the memo.

Memo conventions

There is no salutation (e.g. Dear Martin) on a memo, nor is there any complimentary close (e.g. Kind regards or Yours sincerely). Because the memo has no external recipient, there is no need to write an address. Memos aren't usually signed but they are often initialled. This proves that the author has read and approved the memo if someone else has typed it.

Like other business documents, memos are kept simple. They consist of sentences which are grouped into paragraphs. If lengthy information is included it is often written as numbered or bullet points, so that it is easy to read.

Some organisations prefer that each memo only covers one topic, as this makes filing easier, but there are no fixed rules about this. On some occasions it may be necessary, and more practical, to include more than one topic.

If a copy is being sent to more than one person for information, the other names are usually included after 'cc' on the 'To' line. However, if you are sending several people copies of a memo, it is often easier to write a distribution list at the bottom which identifies all the recipients. In the 'To' line you can type 'See below'. Then tick off each person's name on their own copy of the document, to make sure you don't forget anyone. If you are sending a memo to everyone in a department or organisation, simply type 'All departmental staff' or 'All staff' after the word 'To' – but then make sure you send everyone a copy who should receive one.

Tone and style of memos

Memos are internal documents and may be formal or informal depending upon the recipient and the subject matter. A memo to a close colleague is likely to be worded rather differently from one to the Managing Director. Similarly, a memo about a Christmas party will be more informal than one about a serious customer complaint.

It is always better to avoid slang expressions although many organisations today use abbreviated words in informal memos (e.g. thanks, I'll, haven't). If you are asking someone to do something, remember to phrase your memo so that you are making a request – not giving an order!

If you are writing a long memo, always divide up your information into that which introduces the reader to the topic, that which gives further details and, finally, the outcome or result. It is usually better to have separate paragraphs for each of these. Therefore, if your boss told you that (1) one day there could be a break-in, (2) it is important in future that staff check windows are locked before they go home and (3) she found five windows left open last night, you should write about these in the order (3), (1) and then (2).

Use of English

You are likely to use many common business words in communications such as memos. Check you can spell each of the following:

receive	preferred	referred	efficient
relevant	responsible	unnecessary	regrettable
accommodation	appointment	fulfil	immediately

Check, too, that you can use plurals accurately.

▶ Basic plurals are formed by just adding an 's', e.g. computer/computers but some add 'es' e.g. potatoes, watches.

▶ In other cases you need to change a final 'f' or 'fe' to 'ves', e.g. half/halves, knife/knives.

▶ Sometimes a final 'y' converts to 'ies', e.g. company/companies, secretary/secretaries, money/monies.

▶ Other words have a different plural form, e.g. child/children, mouse/mice, woman/women – and some use the same word, e.g. salmon. As yet, no one seems to be quite sure whether more than one computer mouse is 'mouses' or 'mice'!

▶ An 'o' ending to a word can cause problems. Often you simply add an 's', e.g. radio/radios but some words always end 'oes' and you need to know these. They include potatoes, heroes, echoes and cargoes.

KEY TIP Never trust your spell-checker to find all your spelling errors. It can never help if you've typed a 'real' word by mistake, such as 'from' instead of 'form' or 'stationery' instead of 'stationary'. However, if you regularly misspell or mistype a word you can customise your Word spell-checker to correct it for you automatically by doing the following:

1 Type the word wrongly, e.g. voluntery.

2 Highlight the word.

3 Press your *right* mouse button.

4 *Left* click on AutoCorrect and select the option you want (voluntary).

5 From now on this word will automatically correct if you type it wrongly.

1 All the following words are spelled wrongly. Can you correct them?

awfull	citys	acceptible	competant
embarassed	privilegies	indispensible	succesful
budgetted	wierd	colleegues	desparate
permenant	payed	tomatos	shelfs
strategys	compatable	feesible	enviroment

2 Study the example of the memo below and identify all the items of information included in the header. Then check the content against the conventions listed above. Finally, identify who received a copy of this memo and how this was shown.

MEMO

TO: Alison Kemp   CC: Bob Scott

FROM: Bill Griffiths

DATE: 5 October 200-

REF: BG/LP

SUBJECT: SALES CONFERENCE

As you know, this year's sales conference will be held on Tuesday, 30 October at the Crown Plaza Hotel and, as always, all the representatives and sales staff will be there. We intend to have a special session on the new range of recyclable packaging materials we are introducing and this is scheduled for 2 pm in the afternoon.

I know your staff are busy preparing advertising and marketing materials to promote this packaging and it would be useful if these could be available on the day. I also thought it would be helpful if you could give a short talk, for about 20 minutes, which focuses on the special selling points of the packaging which are being highlighted in the marketing campaign. Then Bob Scott will follow you, to talk about the technical details of the materials.

If you are willing to do this, you may find it useful to join us on Monday, 17 October when we have arranged a planning meeting for the conference. The meeting starts at 11 am in my room - tea and coffee provided.

I'd be grateful if you could let me have your response within the next week.

BG

3 Sam Parsons is the Health and Safety Manager at Marlton Packaging. He has asked you to send a memo, addressed to all the staff (to do this, enter All staff after To in the header). He wants to notify them that the staff car park is being resurfaced this weekend. The car park will therefore be closed on Saturday and Sunday (give the dates) but will reopen at 7.30 am on Monday. Sam says to add that he is sorry for any inconvenience caused to staff working over the weekend, but that it is important to do the work quickly, as there have been several accidents recently because of the poor surface.

4 Your friend Rebecca has drafted out a memo to her boss, Bill Griffiths, because she wants to take a day off to attend a friend's wedding. She is worried because she knows the office is busy at the moment. She shows you the memo she has written; although it is very honest, you think it is unlikely to persuade Bill to agree to her request. Reword the memo to improve Rebecca's chances of going to the wedding.

MEMO

TO: Bill

FROM: Rebecca

DATE: (today)

Dear Mr Griffiths

I want to ask you a favour because I've got a problem. This guy I know, Ben, we've been friends since forever. Anyway, he's getting married soon and I've got an invite to the wedding and I'd really like to go.

I know it will be a pain if I'm off at the moment because we're up to our eyes in work but if you say 'yes' then I'll work extra hard. I don't mind working late for a few nights if that will help. I only need a day but it's a Friday which I know is our busiest day and it's next week which I know doesn't give you much time to think about it.

Please say I can go. Thanks a lot.

Yours truly

Rebecca Scholes

---

5 Alison Kemp is the Marketing Manager at Marlton Packaging. She was the recipient of the memo from the Sales Manager, Bill Griffiths on page 15. In response, Alison says the following to you.

'I'm free on the day of the conference and don't mind giving the talk – but I'm rather concerned that not all the marketing materials will be ready by then. I could take drafts of the press adverts and black and white copies of the leaflets but the colour copies won't be available until the second week in November.

'We're also producing a short video in Marketing, which will be ready by the date of the conference. I could take that along if there will be the facilities to show it but I'll need to know that the equipment will be available.

'I actually think that a major selling point is the fact that there are now strict laws on packaging materials and waste and these should be summarised at the conference – because the reps won't know them. Ashraf Khan, the Distribution Manager, is quite an expert and I think he would be the best person to talk to everyone. It would be useful if Bill could include him in the team.

'I can attend Bill's planning meeting but I've a previous appointment – we're interviewing for a new marketing assistant at 9.30. That's due to finish at 11.00 but could overrun. I probably won't be able to arrive at the meeting until about 11.15 am.'

a) Divide up the information into that which should be at the start of the memo, the more detailed information for the middle section and the information which should come at the end. Compare your ideas with other members of your group.

b) On your own, write the memo to Bill Griffiths, from Alison, which summarises the points she has made.

Would you understand a heading that said 'to install a component into the structural fabric'? Probably not. It was actually describing how to lay a brick in a wall! And what would you make of a letter which said 'I can confirm that you have not inform us a conservatory that has never been built and that you have not been charged any extra for one built'? If you are confused, so were other readers – so much so that both these written statements won Golden Bull awards in 2002. These are the annual awards for gobbledygook awarded by the Plain English Campaign.

For exceptionally good and clear communications, the Campaign allows organisations to use its Crystal Mark. It will also advise businesses how to write in plain English and – for a charge – will edit and correct draft documents and will approve clear websites. The Campaign stresses that it is pointless using long or fancy words or phrases if no one can understand what they are reading. Simple, straightforward English is far better.

You can find out more by following the link to their website at www.heinemann.co.uk/hotlinks. You can also see the winners of their awards for writing in clear, understandable English.

▼ PREPARING A BUSINESS LETTER

A business letter is one of the most important business communications you will write, as it is sent to people outside the organisation, such as customers, suppliers and other business contacts. A poorly written, sloppily typed or mis-spelt letter can send a stronger message about your organisation than the words you choose. It tells the reader that your firm is not very professional, is not interested in quality and can't be bothered to train its staff properly. No customer is likely to be very impressed with that type of business image!

Letter format

Business letters are always written on headed paper. This gives key information about the organisation – its name, address, telephone and fax number, website address and often the names of the directors and the address of the registered office. There may also be logos to illustrate any associations to which the business belongs or awards it has won.

Every letter contains certain specific items of information before the actual 'body' of the letter starts and after it ends. These are normally set out in a certain way, but this layout may vary a little from one organisation to another. The particular layout used is often known as the **house style** and can easily be checked by looking through past letters. If you practise using a standard format, you will find it very easy to adapt this if your eventual employer prefers a slightly different one.

Letter conventions

Today business documents are normally written using **open punctuation**. In a letter, this means that commas are used in the body of the letter only where they are inserted to help understanding. They are not used, for example, at the end of the address lines or in the date.

The main conventions are illustrated in the example below and then explained in more detail.

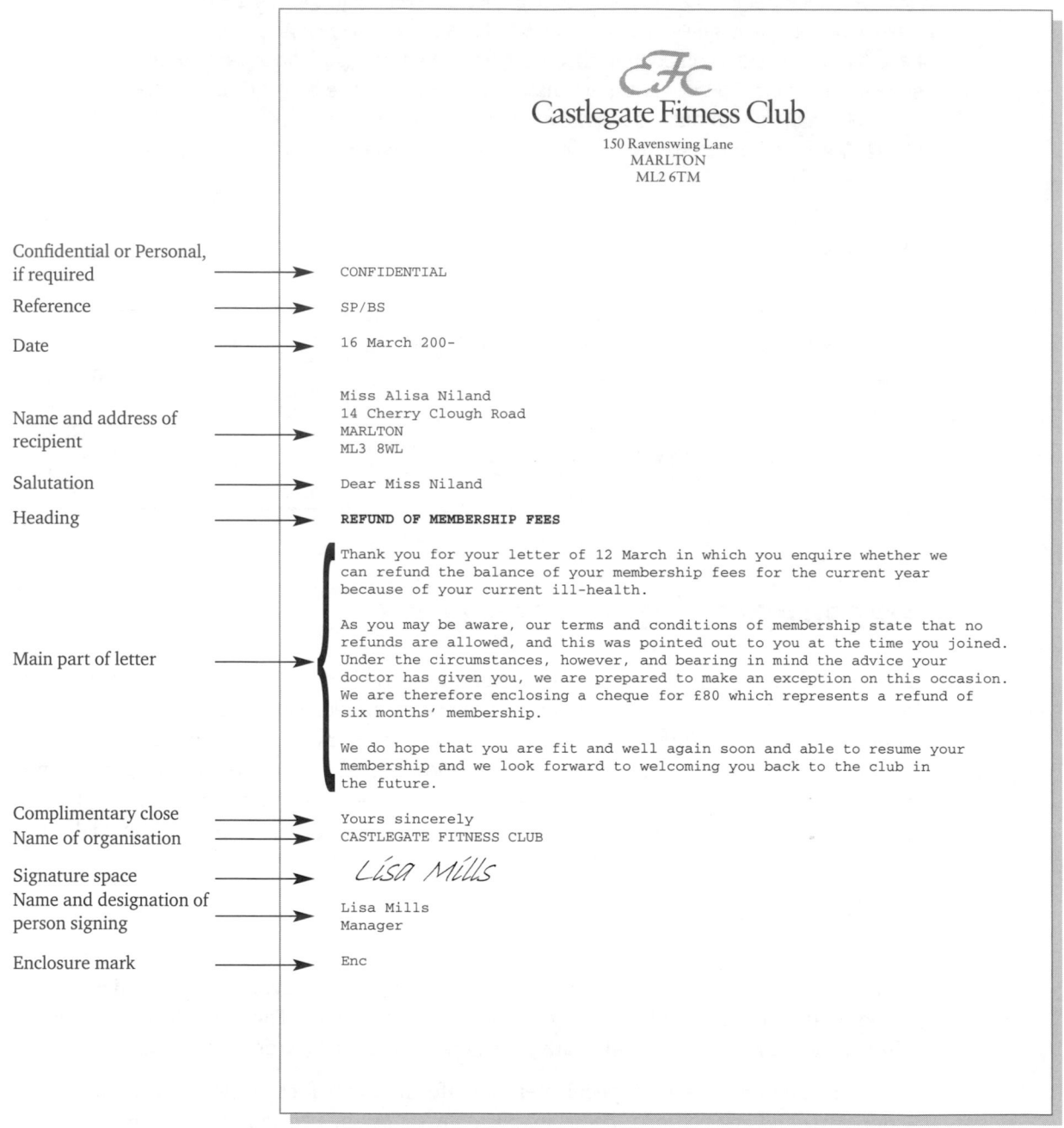

Confidential or Personal, if required → CONFIDENTIAL

Reference → SP/BS

Date → 16 March 200-

Name and address of recipient →
Miss Alisa Niland
14 Cherry Clough Road
MARLTON
ML3 8WL

Salutation → Dear Miss Niland

Heading → **REFUND OF MEMBERSHIP FEES**

Main part of letter →

Thank you for your letter of 12 March in which you enquire whether we can refund the balance of your membership fees for the current year because of your current ill-health.

As you may be aware, our terms and conditions of membership state that no refunds are allowed, and this was pointed out to you at the time you joined. Under the circumstances, however, and bearing in mind the advice your doctor has given you, we are prepared to make an exception on this occasion. We are therefore enclosing a cheque for £80 which represents a refund of six months' membership.

We do hope that you are fit and well again soon and able to resume your membership and we look forward to welcoming you back to the club in the future.

Complimentary close → Yours sincerely
Name of organisation → CASTLEGATE FITNESS CLUB

Signature space → *Lisa Mills*

Name and designation of person signing →
Lisa Mills
Manager

Enclosure mark → Enc

▷ If a letter is personal or confidential, then this is written first. It is also placed above the address on the envelope.

▷ Most letters contain a reference – either the initials of the writer followed by the person who prepared the document or a file reference number.

▷ All business letters are dated. The most usual style is 25 May 2004.

▶ The name of the recipient is given in full followed by the address. If you are writing to a business person, include his or her official title and the name and address of the organisation. Some organisations prefer you to omit the title and just put the name, e.g. John Hodson rather than Mr John Hodson. If you are using window envelopes then you will have to bear this in mind when you decide where to type the address, as it must show clearly when you fold the letter and put it in the envelope.

▶ Many letters have a heading. This isn't essential but can be useful for the reader. If you are word processing and use a heading, you can embolden it to make it stand out. If you are writing a heading, you can put it in capital letters.

▶ The salutation and the complimentary close must match. *Dear Sir* or *Dear Madam* = *Yours faithfully*. *Dear Mr Hodson* = *Yours sincerely*. *Dear Sir* isn't used very much today because it is so formal. If you use a first name then the ending may be more informal, so *Dear John* = *Yours truly*, *Kind regards* or *Best wishes*. Note that only the **first** word in the complimentary close starts with a capital letter.

▶ The name of the organisation may be written immediately after the complimentary close – to show that the writer is sending the letter on behalf of the company.

▶ You will need to leave sufficient space for the writer to sign the letter. This is usually 5 clear lines. Never sign a letter yourself unless you have been told you can do so.

▶ Enclosures are normally indicated by inserting the word Enc (for one) or Encs (for more than one) at the end of the letter.

▶ If a letter takes more than one page, you will need to continue to a new page. Try to do this between paragraphs or in the middle of a long paragraph. Some organisations simply put the page number at the top of the next page. Others like to include the name of the recipient and the date as well. This helps to identify the document if it becomes separated from the first page.

Tone and style of letters

Letters are normally more formal than internal communications, such as memos, simply because they are being sent to an external person. This doesn't mean using complicated words or elaborate phrases. Every letter must be clear, concise and easy to understand. You achieve formality by:

▶ never using abbreviations (such as isn't or don't)

▶ never using slang or words and expressions you would use with your friends (e.g. 'chill' or 'cool' – unless you are talking about an illness or the temperature)

▶ avoiding jargon and abbreviations your recipient won't understand (for example, 'our virtual guide on the web'. 'The on-line guide on our Internet website' is far more understandable.)

▶ avoiding Americanisms, no matter how many times you hear them on television (such as, 'you can get it for free if you call'. Instead say, 'You can obtain a copy of our free brochure if you telephone us.') Remember, too, that American spelling is different from English spelling (e.g. color and colour; theater and theatre). If you have an English employer then it is expected you will use English spellings. In the examination, both are acceptable unless you are inconsistent. If you use a mixture of spellings for the same word in a document then you will be penalised.

- being polite. Remember to say 'please' if you want something. You can avoid overusing the word 'please' with phrases like, 'we would be grateful if . . .' or 'it would help us if . . .'
- never ending a letter with 'thank you' on its own. You could say 'We appreciate your help in this matter.'

The exact tone is likely to be slightly different for particular types of letters. For example, a sales letter is usually lively and upbeat, a letter making a complaint should be factual and to the point, a letter in response to a justified complaint is likely to be apologetic.

You will need to write both routine and non-routine letters. Routine letters include those which are straightforward and where you can use many standard phrases to help you. They include letters which:

- confirm arrangements
- make an enquiry
- answer an enquiry.

Letters which are less routine deal with an individual situation. For example, letters which

- make a complaint
- reply to a complaint
- respond to a personal situation or problem
- promote a special event or product.

In these situations you may have to choose your words with extra care so that you are tactful, diplomatic, sympathetic or persuasive – depending upon the situation.

If you are writing a difficult letter, it's a good idea to save your letter and then re-read it a little while later – as if you were the recipient. Confusing sentences and silly mistakes are usually easier to spot then.

Use of English

When you use sentences of different lengths it makes any communication appear more professional and often more courteous. This is especially noticeable in a business letter.

Compare:

'Thank you for your letter of 25 March. We are enclosing our latest brochure. We are also enclosing a price list. If you have any queries, please telephone us.'

with:

'Thank you for your letter of 25 March asking for information on our range of office furniture. We are pleased to enclose a copy of our latest brochure and price list. If you have any queries, please do not hesitate to telephone us.'

You also need to be more careful about your word use in a business letter and make sure you don't confuse common words that you will have to use regularly. A list of common problem groups is given below. Learn these by writing them – not just reading them – and then test yourself!

Words that get confused

There – a place, 'he's over there'
Their – belonging to them, 'their company'
They're – short for 'they are', 'they're both going to the show'

Your – belonging to you, 'your office'
You're – short for 'you are', 'you're a good friend'

Whose – belonging to someone, 'whose coat is this?'
Who's – short for 'who is', 'who's going to the meeting?'

Accept – to agree or consent, 'she has accepted our offer'
Except – not including, 'they are all going except Brian'

Stationary – not moving, the car is stationary
Stationery – paper and related items, our stationery order

Personal – relating to one person, his personal needs
Personnel – relating to staff in a company, Personnel Department

Loose – not tight, 'the computer has a loose connection'
Lose – mislay, 'you will lose it if you don't keep it safely'

Principal – the chief or main one, the College Principal
Principle – a belief, he has strong principles

KEY TIP   Always remember that 'thank you' is *two* words, not one – and so is 'all right'.

1 Below are 6 sentences. Select the correct word from each pair that should be used. Use a dictionary to check the meaning of any you are unsure about.

a) I am confident/confidant that they will wave/waive the charge.

b) She produced a summary/summery for their/they're branch office.

c) He formally/formerly offered his resignation to the principle/principal.

d) We sent him three complimentary/complementary invitations but don't know yet if he will accept/except them.

e) She is the personal/personnel assistant to an eminent/imminent scientist.

f) It is impossible to simply lose/loose six packs of paper from the stationary/stationery cupboard.

2 Read the sample letter on page 18 and answer the following questions.

a) Why has this letter been headed 'Confidential'?

b) Would you consider this letter is 'routine' or 'non-routine'? Give a reason for your answer.

c) What is your impression of Castlegate Fitness Club from reading this letter? Identify at least two phrases to support your answer.

3 As a group, you are going to create the foundations of five good business letters, in stages, by working through the tasks below. The five letters you will be considering are:

a) a letter of confirmation

b) a letter of enquiry

c) a response to a letter of enquiry

d) a letter of invitation

e) a response to a complaint

Task A Match the different types of letters above with the opening sentences you think would be most suitable.

i)   We would like to invite you to our Open Day on Friday, 20 June 200-.

ii) Thank you for your letter of 10 June asking about our conference facilities.

iii) I refer to our telephone conversation this morning regarding the time of your interview with Mr James Birtwistle, our Personnel Director.

iv) Thank you for your letter of 10 June explaining the problems you experienced with your recent booking.

v) We are currently planning to redecorate our offices and understand you specialise in this type of work.

Task B Now decide which of the following endings would be most appropriate in each case.

i)   We look forward to hearing from you.

ii) Please let us know if you require any further information.

iii) We very much hope you will be able to attend.

iv) We look forward to meeting you.

v) We would apologise again for the inconvenience you have been caused and hope that you have a restful and enjoyable break.

Task C By arrangement with your tutor, so that all the letters are chosen by different groups, choose *one* type of letter and invent a suitable middle paragraph. Use your imagination to supply the details. If you are stuck, then discuss possible ideas with your tutor. Finally, compare your completed letters.

4 Tamasin Lorgat is an Administrator at Jentree Products Ltd, Livingstone Road, Marlton MR3 9DL. Tamasin is very annoyed with their stationery supplier, Stancliffe Stationery Supplies of Woodgate Street, Marlton MR2 7SP, which has repeatedly sent the wrong items – or forgotten to deliver anything at all! She has decided to write to the Sales Manager, Tim Ashton, to complain and has started to draft two replies.

a) Study them both carefully, decide which you think is more appropriate and give at least four reasons for your choice.

b) Write out (or word process) the letter you prefer using the correct business letter format.

Example A

I am really fed up with the service we are getting from you at the moment and I want to know what you are going to do about it.

Last week we ordered some stationery but only part of it was delivered. The week before that three items were damaged. The week before that, there was a problem because we received someone else's order. Now we are still waiting for photocopying paper and it looks like we're going to run out.

Unless you put things right straight away we will have to go somewhere else in the future.

Example B

We have been ordering our office stationery from your company for several months, but recently there have been several problems with the service we have received.

Three weeks ago, we received a delivery which was addressed to Fenton Chemicals and although we notified your office immediately it took three days for this to be collected and for our own order to be delivered. Two weeks ago, three boxes of envelopes were badly damaged and we are still waiting for replacements. Last week, photocopying paper was missing from the delivery. Again we notified you promptly but we have still not received it. The situation is now becoming critical because we urgently need further stocks.

Unless this situation improves rapidly, we will obviously have to consider changing to another supplier.

I should be grateful if you could let me have your comments as soon as possible.

5 You work for Tim Ashton, the Sales Manager of Stancliffe Stationery Supplies. Tim has received Tamasin's letter and has asked you to reply. He has said the following to you.

'This is all the fault of that temporary driver we had – the one who left us last week. Would you believe this is the third letter I've received like this! We need to thank her for her letter and to apologise for all the problems they've had there. Stress that this is very unusual and was unfortunately caused by a delivery driver who is no longer employed here. It's a good job – if he'd worked here any longer I doubt if we'd have had any customers left! Obviously we need to put things right as quickly as possible. Tell her that we are sending her the three boxes of envelopes and won't be charging her for these as a gesture of goodwill. We are also sending her the photocopying paper. Both items will be delivered tomorrow morning – give her the date. You'd better get this letter off today, then, or the stationery will arrive first! Don't forget to say that we hope that this solves the problem – add that we look forward to doing business with them in the future. I think that's important – we've had a good relationship in the past and I don't want to lose it. Oh, and finally tell her to contact me immediately if she has any further difficulties at all.

a) As a group, decide which of Tim's remarks should be included in the letter and which should not.

b) Draft out the letter to Tamasin, using the correct business format. The address of the company and other details you need were given in question 4, above. Check your final letter with your tutor.

▼ PREPARING A FAX

Fax machines are found in every office because they are used to transmit documents quickly all around the world. They are ideal for sending text, forms, drawings, photographs, maps – and any other type of graphical document. They can also be used to send authorised documents, such as signed purchase orders, which cannot be produced easily on a computer.

Fax messages have one other advantage over emails: their arrival is obvious and immediate. The recipient simply has to remove the fax from the machine and read it. There is no need to log into a computer, access email and take print-outs. For that reason faxes are a popular method of communicating with senior managers and executives, who may even have a fax machine at home, switched on 24 hours a day, to receive important messages.

You will learn more about using fax machines in Unit 4. In this Unit, you will find out how to compose fax messages.

Fax format

All faxes start with a printed header. This is inserted automatically by the fax machine. This identifies the date and time of transmission, the fax number of the sender, the organisation and the page number. This takes up the top few centimetres of the fax, so it is important that there is a clear top margin before the actual text starts.

The format of the fax message itself then depends upon the type of fax machine being used and the policy of the organisation. There are basically two options.

▶ A cover page can be sent. This is an option on virtually all machines. The amount of detail and the design depends upon the make and type of machine.

> A fax message can be sent *without* a cover page. This will often be on headed paper and set out to the organisation's own design. Often a memo heading is used on letter headed paper. This system was used before cover pages became common and is used rather less these days.

Information on a cover page

Faxes are often used to send standard or graphical documents to recipients, such as a map showing the location of a company, an urgent purchase order, a confirmation or a report. Often, too, agreement has been reached beforehand that the fax will be transmitted, so the recipient knows what to expect. For that reason, the actual message is frequently just short and courteous – to explain the document(s) that follows. This is where a cover page is ideal as it saves you having to prepare a front sheet yourself. An example of a cover page is shown here.

In this case, the cover page gives a considerable amount of information. On a more basic machine, you may only be able to send a cover page which identifies you as the sender and allows you to send a brief comment or message.

Fax message	
Date / Time:	05/10/200- 12:20
TO:	MARK ELLIS, CONWAY ELECTRONICS
FAX:	+44 1384 308972
FROM:	LIZ WEST, DALE AND WATSON
FAX:	+44 121 3798
TEL:	+44 121 4989
TO FOLLOW:	02 PAGES
MESSAGE:	COPY OF DIAGRAM AND MEETING AGENDA ATTACHED. PLEASE RING ME ON RECEIPT.

▲ A fax cover page

The telephone number is always shown with the international dialling code (+44 for the UK) followed by the regional code without the initial zero. This is because many fax messages are sent to overseas recipients.

Fax conventions

All the key items are included on a cover page. If you don't have this facility then you must remember to:

▶ identify both the company and the individual member of staff sending the fax

▶ identify the person to whom the fax is being sent – and the department if the organisation is large

▶ if there could be any confusion, include the designation of the sender and recipient

▶ state the number of pages you are sending. This is often shown on each page as 'Page 1 of 6', 'Page 2 of 6' and so on. This enables the recipient to check that no pages are missing when the transmission ends.

Because a fax machine can be used to transmit any type of document, the pages that follow the cover page should be in accordance with the standard conventions for that particular document. For example, a faxed letter would follow the normal conventions for a letter, as shown in the illustration on page 18.

Tone and style of fax messages

If you are asked to write a brief fax yourself remember that these messages are normally short and to the point. They are also, normally, *relatively* informal – especially if sender and recipient know each other quite well. This does not mean that a formal letter or document is never faxed. If speed of transmission is very important, this method may be best.

COMMUNICATION IN BUSINESS

Modern fax machines can be connected to a computer system. This enables them to be used for more than simply sending and receiving faxes. They can be used as a computer printer, or as a scanner or – probably their best use – to send and receive faxes direct from a computer. This means that you can word-process a message and then decide whether to send it by email or by fax. Although this means you can create cover sheets and messages easily, you would still have to use the fax machine in the traditional way if you wanted to send an urgent document which wasn't stored on your computer – such as a purchase order form for stationery which had been signed by your manager.

There are also fax services available for people who have a computer but no fax machine. The user sends an email message which is then forwarded to a fax machine. An alternative, or additional service, is that incoming faxes can be forwarded to an email address as an attachment. These services are ideal for business people who travel with a laptop and may need to receive or send urgent faxes as well as emails. You can find out more by accessing www.heinemann.co.uk/hotlinks and following the links to the efax website.

Use of English

On page 21 you saw apostrophes in use – for words such as they're, you're and who's – but you probably never gave them much thought. When it comes to written English, however, they probably cause more problems than all the other punctuation marks put together!

No matter how basic the document you are writing, or the method you are using to send it, if a word should have an apostrophe then this needs including – and in the right place!

If you usually try to ignore the existence of apostrophes (or worse, just guess when and where to put them) then the following rules should help.

Rule 1

Never use apostrophes in ordinary plural words, such as tomatoes or potatoes (no matter what you see in greengrocers' windows!) You also don't use them with ordinary plural abbreviations, e.g. MPs or VDUs, or numbers, e.g. 1940s.

Rule 2

Always use an apostrophe when you contract a word and put it at the point where the letters are missing, e.g. don't, can't, won't. The reason you put an apostrophe in o'clock is because this is really 'of the clock' with the middle letters omitted.

Rule 3

Always use an apostrophe to indicate possession, i.e. something belongs to something (or someone) else. If there is one owner, the apostrophe goes before the 's', for example the manager's office, the MP's secretary. If the world already ends in 's', just add an apostrophe, e.g. St James' Hospital. If there are several owners, the apostrophe goes after the 's', e.g. the managers' car park.

You can test if you have put any apostrophe in the correct place by simply turning round the phrase and adding the words 'belonging to'. The manager's office = the office of the manager – manager is one owner so the apostrophe comes before the 's'. The managers' car park = the car park belonging to the managers – several owners, so the apostrophe comes after the 's'.

The only exception is when you use a special plural word, such as 'children' or 'ladies' or 'companies'. In this case, if the word does not end in 's' then add an apostrophe plus s, e.g. 'they sell children's clothes'. If the word already ends in 's', then just add an apostrophe, e.g. 'they publish many companies' reports.'

Rule 4

Remember that time can also be possessive, eg a year's salary and three weeks' holiday. In this case, the same rules apply.

Rule 5

Remember that 'it's' is a special case. 'It's = it is. Possessive 'its' has no apostrophe, for example 'the fax machine has two major benefits – its speed and its ease of use'.

KEY TIP   Always use the 'belonging to' test to check if an apostrophe is needed. If you can turn the sentence around and it makes sense when you say 'belonging to' then an apostrophe is needed. This will help to stop you putting apostrophes where they are not required!

1 Katija has prepared her first fax message to send on behalf of her boss, Karen Sinclair, the Chief Designer at the company. She has prepared this from Karen's message on her voicemail.

a) Start by checking the *format* of Katija's fax. Karen didn't want a cover sheet attached so Katija tried to remember how to set out the fax. Look back at the key items listed on page 26 and check if she has included everything.

b) Katija has a problem. She is hopeless at using apostrophes! The ones she has included are wrong – and she has missed out nine! Correct all those she has put into the message – and then add all the rest properly.

JTL DESIGN CONSULTANTS
116 Waverley Road
MARLTON
MR7 4WW

FAX MESSAGE

TO   Bushra Rashid, Marketing Manager, Audio Express

FROM   Karen Sinclair, Chief Designer

DATE   10 February 200-

PAGE   1 of 4

NEW LOGO

I am attaching three design's for you to consider for your new logo. These all incorporate the suggestion's you made at our designer's meeting last Wednesday.

You asked for our recommendation, which is version 3.
It's major advantage is that it link's together your companys brand image in one design.

Ive talked to Alan about your deadline date and. hes of the opinion that its going to be difficult to meet that unless we have your MDs decision by 24 February.

Alan is going to Westchester in two days time and is staying at the Queens' Hotel. Hes happy to meet you if you have any queries.
Alans ideas impressed you, I know, so Im sure you would find his advice helpful.

Regards

Karen

---

2 You work for Jill Richardson, an IT consultant. Her fax number is +44 161 3798. Jill is flying to Dublin next week to give a presentation at an IT seminar. She has asked you to send three fax messages on her behalf. Use the fax format shown above unless you are specifically requested to prepare a cover page. In that case, prepare this according to the example on page 25.

Jill's instructions are as follows.

a) Please send a quick fax to the Liffey View Hotel – the fax number is 00353 1 660 2817. I rang them last night and booked a single room with bath for next Tuesday and Wednesday night at the rate of £120 a night. They asked for a fax confirmation. Please mention I won't arrive until about 7 pm on Tuesday. Don't forget to give the dates, either, will you? You can send this in your own name, on my behalf.

b) Can you fax the organiser, please. His name is Pat O'Connor and his official title is Technology Manager. His fax number is 00353 1 660 1187. Can you please send him these 6 pages of notes – just do a short cover page on the front with the message that these are my draft notes for the seminar and if he has any comments could he please telephone me as soon as possible.

c) Finally, can you please fax Chrissie Kent on 01865 484937. There's no job title because she works for herself. She will also be at the seminar next week – but I don't think she knows I'm going. The key points to mention – in no particular order are:

- ▶ Ask her to let me know where she's staying.
- ▶ Tell her I'll be at the seminar and say my session is scheduled for 3 pm on Wednesday
- ▶ Ask her if she can bring with her the web statistics she talked about on the telephone last week, as I'd be interested to see them.
- ▶ Tell her it will be good to see her again.
- ▶ Say I'd be delighted if she could join me for dinner on either Tuesday or Wednesday night.

Put these in a more logical order please and send the fax on my behalf, will you.

▼ ANALYSING, EXTRACTING AND ADAPTING INFORMATION (2)

When you are preparing written documents you may not be given all the information you need at the time. You may have to find some of this yourself or extract it from one or more other documents. These may be written documents, or they could be tables.

This section looks at analysing and extracting information that you have been asked to find. 'Analysing' simply means being able to make sense of it. In the examination, you will be given general information about the organisation you work for. You will also be given all the additional information you need from which you will have to select the exact information relevant to a task.

Here, you will practice doing this in a slightly different way. In this case you are working for Jill Richardson and she has already obtained a lot of information for her talk. She wants your help in finding and extracting the exact information she needs to use. Before you start, it is useful to look at the best method to find information you need when this is contained in several documents. The tips below should help.

▶ Make sure you know exactly what you are looking for, otherwise you can waste a lot of time! If someone is giving you instructions, write them down. If you have a list of questions to answer, start by reading them carefully.

▶ Next, read through the information. If you are allowed to mark the documents you are reading, then a highlighter pen is useful because you can use it to highlight relevant information

▶ Read numbers very carefully and check whether you are reading whole numbers or percentages (%). Large figures may be denoted by 'm' (for million) or 'b' (for billion). In a table, this may be shown at the top. Thousands, too, are often shown by '000' at the top of a column.

▶ Take your time. Don't panic if you can't find something immediately. It is unlikely that anyone will ask you to extract information if it isn't there! So if you can't find it, this means you have probably not looked properly.

▶ Work methodically, but don't worry if you are missing one or two items of information. Look for these at the end.

▶ Finally, check that you have found everything you need and that all your notes or answers make sense.

OVER TO YOU!

Look at the documents opposite and on page 32. These all relate to Internet usage in the UK – and Internet shopping.

1 See how good you are at extracting information by answering the following questions. The answers to all of them are contained in the documents opposite and on page 32.

a) What is the third most popular Internet shopping site in the UK?

b) How much was spent on Internet shopping at Christmas 2002?

c) What percentage of web users are aged between 25 and 34?

d) How many Internet users are there in the United States?

e) How many UK adults shopped on line at Christmas 2002?

f) How much did the highest spending group spend online in 2002?

g) How much do women spend online, on average, each visit?

h) Why are clothes not a popular item to buy online?

i) Identify three items which were bought online for Valentine's Day in 2003.

j) Between what times does most Internet shopping take place?

▲ '. . . so she told me I must do the shopping every Friday . . .'

2 Jill has to prepare a report about the growth of Internet shopping among women and older users in the UK. Find five relevant facts in the documents she could use in her report.

3 Jill has asked you to send a memo to a colleague, Jim Fornell, who is visiting a greetings card company next week to discuss their proposed website. She has said to you:

'Please refer to Jim's meeting with Neat Cards next week. Mention that I think the key facts he should mention to them are as follows.

▶ The number of people who now browse online to make a purchase

▶ The number of UK Internet users

▶ How many people came online worldwide last year.

▶ Why cards will be popular online – both because of the type of product and the success of other sites.

▶ Examples of popular Internet shopping sites

▶ How many more people shopped online in the UK at Christmas 2002 than at Christmas 1999

▶ How much is forecast to be spent online in the future – and the source, please.

You can find all the information to give him in the articles, so please be as specific as possible. Thanks.'

E-shopping

Seven out of ten Britons who browse online now make a purchase. About 670 million people worldwide had online access to the Internet at the end of 2002 with more than 110 million users coming online during that year. There are between 31 and 34 million users in the UK – surveys vary on the exact number. Most now have home access and many shop online. At Christmas 1999, only 1.5 million people shopped online. By Christmas 2002, this had risen to over 4.4 million UK adults who spent nearly £500 million. CDs, DVDs and books are the most popular as shoppers are familiar with these products. Items which customers like to see and touch before purchasing, such as clothes, are far less popular. One-third of all purchases are made between 6 pm and 9 am, showing that shopping online is popular with busy people who haven't time to shop during working hours.

Barclaycard estimates online shopping in the UK will soon reach £7 billion.

Top 5 Internet shopping sites in the UK

1 Ebay.co.uk
2 Amazon.co.uk
3 Tesco.co.uk
4 Ebay.com
5 Shopping.yahoo.com

Internet users per country, Dec 2002. (Forecast to be over one billion by 2005)

Country	Users (million)
US	160
Japan	60
China	55
Germany	35
UK	34

Women online

Today Internet use is split 50/50 between male and female. Fifty per cent of UK women now have Internet access and one in eight women regularly shops online and spends an average of £60 a visit. This helps working women to save time. They not only use online supermarket delivery and online banking, but book flights and holidays online as well. Men prefer using the Internet for multi use, such as visiting games sites.

Spenders online

Two surveys have destroyed the idea that the biggest Internet users are young and male. Jupiter MMXI found that 26% of web users are 35–49-year-olds, 20% are over 50 and 18.6% are aged 25–34. Younger users are more likely to be online at school or college rather than at home or at work.

According to Verdict Research, the highest spenders are aged between 35 and 44. In 2002 they spent over £1bn online and 44–54-year-olds spent £800 million. Together, these two age groups spent an average of £73 per visit. Younger age groups shop more often, but spend less when they do.

Online Valentine!

More Valentine gifts were purchased online in 2003 than ever before, according to Nielsen/NetRatings. Flowers, lingerie and animated greeting cards were the most popular. RiverSongs.com attracted the most visitors, closely followed by Americangreetings.com and Blue Mountain.

We are all familiar with completing forms. You filled in an enrolment form at College, you need to complete a form to obtain a passport or a driving licence or to open a bank account. Forms are popular because they enable the collection of key information in a standard way. At work, you will probably have to complete several forms every week yourself. You may also have to help customers to fill in forms. You can do this properly only if you are capable of completing one yourself, both neatly and accurately.

At work, you may have to design a form because an old form is out of date or you need to collect information which has never been requested before. If you have had to complete several forms yourself, you will soon realise that some are easier to follow than others. The best ones have clear instructions, introduce items in a logical order, are easy to follow and give you enough space. You therefore need to think carefully before you design a form yourself, so that it is as easy to follow as possible yet still gathers all the information you need.

Form format

Although the content of individual forms will vary, the format is generally the same. At the top is the name of the organisation and/or department. The address is normally included only if the form will be sent outside the organisation.

All forms have a title and this is shown at the top, followed by instructions on how to complete it. There must also be instructions to tell people where to send the completed form. Below are the sections to be filled in.

At the end of the form there is usually a space for the form to be signed and dated. An additional line may ask for the person's name to be printed in capitals, in case the signature is difficult to read. This is not required if the person's printed name can be found elsewhere on the form.

Form conventions

Most conventions have evolved because certain features help users to complete forms more easily. The main ones are given below.

▶ Clear instructions are essential. Most forms state if a black pen should be used. This is important if the form will be photocopied or scanned. They may also specify block capitals – because the form is then much easier to read.

▶ Today many forms include a space for a mobile phone number and email address. This is sensible if you may want to contact the person who completed it.

▶ Long forms are normally divided into sections, under headings, so that people can focus their minds on the different types of information that is required.

▶ Option choices are often given. There are three main ways in which you can ask someone to select an option:

  – by putting a tick or cross on a dotted line or in a box

  – by deleting the option that does not apply

  – by writing 'yes' or 'no' as appropriate.

Generally you should never mix these options on one form. Choose one method and stick to it – and put an appropriate instruction at the top of the form. An alternative is to put an asterisk (*) against all the options with the instruction at the bottom, e.g. *Delete as appropriate.

An example of a form with all these characteristics is shown below.

MARLTON PACKAGING PLC
APPLICATION TO ATTEND AN EXTERNAL TRAINING EVENT
Please complete this form in CAPITALS using black ink or biro and send it to The Training Manager, Human Resources Department.

PERSONAL DETAILS

Forename(s) .... Surname ....

Title (Ms/Miss/Mrs/Mr) .... Department ....

Pay reference number .... Job title ....

Tel: Work .... Home or mobile ....

Staff email address ....

PROPOSED TRAINING EVENT OR COURSE

Location	Date		Description	Cost
	From	To		

REASON FOR REQUEST
Please provide a brief explanation of why you wish to undertake this training.

Signed .... Date ....

MANAGER'S SUPPORT
I support this application for training.   It has high/medium/low* priority for my department.

Signed .... Date ....

FOR USE BY TRAINING DEPARTMENT

Date received .... Training agreed: Yes/No* ....

Start date .... End date .... Total cost ....

First review date .... Name of reviewer ....
*Delete as appropriate

Completing a form

If you ever have to look through a batch of forms as part of your job, you will realise how many people have difficulties filling in a form. You will frequently see people giving their date of birth as the current year, ignoring instructions, crossing out lines and forgetting to complete some sections.

This can create problems as well as giving a bad impression. If you make a mess of a form, or if it is difficult to read, it may well be put to the bottom of the pile. If you did this on a job application form you are unlikely to be offered an interview. If you do this at work, you will gain a reputation for being sloppy and inefficient and will probably have the form returned to you to be redone!

The golden rules for completing a form are shown below. Make sure that you follow them for every form you have to complete.

Form completion

▶ Read the form through *first*.

▶ Carefully study all the instructions. Make sure you have the right type of pen, know whether you must print everything and have identified any sections you should *not* complete.

▶ If the form is very important or very complicated, take a photocopy first – and practise on this copy.

▶ Study the address section carefully before you start as this can be the most confusing! There may be more lines than you need and the postcode may need to be written in a separate place.

▶ Identify any questions where you may have difficulty and need to ask someone for help or advice.

▶ If you are filling in the form for yourself and need to enter your date of birth, be very careful that you don't put the current year by mistake!

▶ Look up the spellings of any words if you are uncertain how to write them!

▶ Write neatly.

▶ Respond to every section. If one doesn't apply to you simply put 'Not applicable' (or N/A for short).

▶ If you have to include an explanation or comment at any point, draft this out first on a separate piece of paper. Then edit and correct it as necessary so that it is the best you can do in the space allowed.

▶ Check your form carefully at the end. Make sure you haven't missed anything out. This is particularly important if you have had to look up information from other sources to complete your form as you may still have one or two sections to complete.

▶ Sign it – but don't try a fancy flourish that no one can read!

If you use the Internet, you will find there are many sites where you are asked to register online. In this case you have to complete an electronic form. Designers of electronic forms have several benefits, they can provide instructions on the type of data which must be entered and the style – and then program the form so that inappropriate data is not accepted. They can also highlight the entries which *must* be made before the form can be submitted. Anyone trying to click 'submit' without entering their name or entering a date of birth in letters, not numbers, would immediately see an error message referring them back to these entries.

Even if a form is completed by hand, the details are often keyed in to a database. For this reason, database terms are often used when describing forms. Each entry is known as a **field** and the number of characters in each field may be restricted. Entering the information in a database means that a quick search of all the database records can be carried out under specific criteria, such as age, address, etc.

Computer software can also be purchased to help business organisations produce forms in-house. These result in more sophisticated forms than those produced on a word-processing package. You can see some of these if you follow the link from www.heinemann.co.uk/hotlinks, which shows examples of forms using this type of package.

Designing a form

The design and content of the form will depend upon:

▶ **why the form is needed** – this helps you to decide the title

▶ **who will be asked to complete it** – this will affect the design and the language you use when you write your instructions

▶ **what information will be required** – this helps you to decide the content

▶ **whether there are any specific formats you must use** because the information will be entered into a computer. For example, dates which are being keyed into a database must follow a specific format, such as 24/10/68. The form will normally show an example of items like this to avoid confusion.

It won't take long, Mr Hayes, just our new form to complete now.

Drafting your form

First, check if there is any similar, well-designed form you can use as a 'model'. This saves you a lot of work. If not, then the following tips should help.

▷ Start by listing all the data you need to collect, such as name, address, age, telephone number, etc.

▷ Arrange your data in a logical order and decide if you could group this into separate sections, such as personal details, financial information and so on. If so, each section should have a clear heading.

▷ Consider carefully the amount of space to leave for each entry, bearing in mind that the size of people's writing can vary considerably.

▷ Leave enough space between lines. Double spacing is normally preferred to single.

▷ If you are including boxes for people to tick, make these an appropriate size.

▷ If you are putting 'Yes/No' options, remember you will need to tell people what to do! This instruction is best at the end of the form.

▷ When you have drafted all your data items, write your instructions at the top. These should include whether a special pen must be used, whether block capitals are required, what to do with the form on completion. Make sure all your instructions are easy to understand.

▷ Remember to include space for the name and/or signature at the bottom and date of completion, if this is required.

▷ Check your form to make sure you haven't forgotten anything.

▷ Test the form yourself. Can you complete it easily and is there the correct amount of space for everything?

▷ Try out the form on a few volunteers, to see if they understand it and can complete it easily. Listen to any suggestions they make and be prepared to make amendments where required!

Use of English

Grammar is always important. Even on a short form, an ungrammatical sentence stands out. Common problems include the following.

▷ **Double negatives**. 'I have never had no experience of working in accounts' is incorrect. You should say 'I have never had *any* experience of working in accounts.' This is because the two negative words cancel each other out. Similarly, you can't say, 'I haven't seen nothing' because then you must have seen something!

▷ **Verb agreement**. Any verbs you use must agree with the subject of your sentence. If the subject is singular, the verb must also be singular (e.g. the car park is full). If the subject is plural, the verb must be plural (e.g. the car parks are full). Although this is straightforward, certain problem words can create difficulties:

  – An organisation is *one* body, so takes a singular verb, for example, the government *is* holding an election, the BBC *is* screening the Championship.

  – Singular pronouns (e.g. each, every, everybody, somebody, neither and nobody) also take a singular verb. It's often easier if you think of 'each one', 'every one'. So you would say, 'each of boxes *has* to be completed'.

- A collective noun can be either singular or plural, so long as you are consistent, e.g. 'the board is meeting to discuss its position next week' *or* 'the board are meeting to discuss their position next week.' You should *not* say, 'The board is meeting to discuss their position next week.'

▶ **Redundancy** This means using words unnecessarily. On a form, in particular, you may be short of space so redundant words should be removed. They also give a bad impression in other types of documents. For example 'I have never ever been there at all' can be reduced to 'I have never been there' without losing any of the meaning.

KEY TIP Be careful with your verbs if you insert a phrase in the middle of a sentence, for example, 'The trains *(plural)*, one of which was renamed last week, *were* held up at Crewe.' The secret is to identify the subject of the sentence and ignore the phrase. Because 'trains' is plural the verb is 'were', not 'was'.

OVER TO YOU!

1 Correct the errors in the following sentences.

a) I've never received no information about it.

b) He kept repeating himself by saying the same thing over and over again.

c) Marks and Spencer are publishing their results tomorrow.

d) Coldplay are a famous UK band which is often winning awards.

e) One of the children, scheduled to go on the trip, were ill yesterday.

f) Neither of them have signed the form and it's absolutely essential that they do.

2 As a group, collect about six or seven forms. You can collect actual forms, such as a holiday booking form, an application form to open a bank account or your college's accident report form *or* you could search for forms on the Internet using a good search engine such as www.google.com and print these out. As a group, score each one out of 15 as follows. (You may find this easier to do if you try to complete some of them!)

▶ Good design (max 5 points)

▶ Easy to understand (max 5 points)

▶ Appropriate space for all entries (max 5 points)

As a group, decide on the key features that make a good form.

3 Work in pairs for this exercise. A local taxi business has asked you to design a form which will enable them to record telephone bookings accurately. Decide what data you would need to collect from callers. Then design a suitable form which could be completed by the person receiving the call. Test the form between you – one person should make a 'call' whilst the other completes the form. Then do this with the other person making the call.

Finally, compare your final form with those produced by others and decide which one is the best.

4 Marlton College is planning an Open Evening and you will be helping on reception. You have been asked to design a form that tutors can complete when they are talking to visitors who are interested in starting on a course. They need to record the name of the interested person, address and other contact details. Other information needed is the course required, or area of interest. Tutors will also need to find out whether the visitor is still at school or at work and wants to attend on a full-time or part-time basis. Relevant previous qualifications or experience would also be useful. The tutor's name, signature and telephone extension should be recorded. When the forms are completed they should all be sent to the Senior Administrator in the Student Services Department.

▼ PREPARING MEETINGS DOCUMENTS

A large number of meetings are held in all business organisations. Some of these may be informal, with a small group of people meeting to discuss a problem or exchange ideas. Others are more formal – such as meetings of directors or senior managers. These have specific rules and procedures which must always be followed.

All meetings need to be well organised if they are to be successful. People need to know where the meeting is to be held, how long it will last or what will be discussed. Equally, once a meeting has ended it is easy to forget what was discussed and what each person agreed to do. Therefore, specific documents are usually prepared for all the participants both before and after the meeting.

▶ A **notice** and **agenda** is issued before the meeting. The notice says where and when the meeting will be held – and notification may be by email if the meeting is informal (see page 4). An agenda lists what will be discussed. Today, a notice and agenda is often issued as one document. You will not be asked to produce a notice for a meeting in the examination, but you could be asked to produce an agenda.

▶ **Notes of the meeting** are normally produced which record the key points that were discussed and actions agreed. These are circulated to everyone who attended. If the meeting is formal, these notes are often referred to as the **minutes** of the meeting.

Agenda format

There is a standard format for an agenda. The title of the meeting and the date must be stated, otherwise people who attend several meetings will not know to which one the agenda relates. The agenda items then follow. These are always listed numerically, normally in double spacing for clarity. Finally, the name of **the chairperson** (the person who is running the meeting) and the date the agenda is issued are shown at the end.

Agenda conventions

All agendas contain certain common items which relate to all meetings, apart from the very first one held by a group. These are as follows:

▶ **Apologies for absence**. Anyone who is invited to the meeting and cannot attend should have told the chairperson. This means that the chairperson can check at the start who is expected and who is not.

▶ **Minutes of the previous meeting**. If notes or minutes were taken at the last meeting, then the chairperson starts by checking that these are correct and there are no factual errors.

▶ **Matters arising**. This really means 'matters arising relevant to the last meeting and its notes'. Those present may want to comment on action they have taken since the last meeting or to query something which is in the notes.

▶ **Any other business (AOB)**. This item is for *minor* issues which are not on the agenda but may be of interest. Anything major would be left until the next meeting.

▶ **Date and time of next meeting**. It is sensible to agree this at the meeting itself, so that everyone can make a note in their diary when they will meet again.

In addition to these standard items, each meeting also has specific items to be discussed, i.e. why the meeting is being held in the first place! These specific items are always placed *after* 'matters arising' and *before* 'any other business' on the agenda, as you can see in the agenda that follows.

MARLTON COLLEGE

IT DEVELOPMENT GROUP – WEDNESDAY, 10 NOVEMBER 200-

Room T24 at 1400 hours

AGENDA

1 Apologies for absence
2 Minutes of the previous meeting
3 Matters arising
4 Email security
5 Database reports
6 Website improvements
7 Any other business
8 Date and time of next meeting

Tim Saunders
IT Manager

1 November 200-

Meeting notes format

The format for meeting notes is apt to vary from one organisation to another. When you start work, it is useful to check in the files to see how these are set out in your office. In some organisations, a specific template is designed for this and held on the computer system, so that everyone follows the same format.

There are some key items which are normally always included before the actual notes start. These are:

▶ **the title of the meeting**

▶ **the date it was held**

▶ **the names of the people who attended**. It is usual to put the chairperson's name first, then the names of the other participants in alphabetical order.

It is then normal (and easier!) to follow the headings of the agenda to write the actual notes. Many organisations like to have an action column, which shows the initials of the person alongside any action they agreed to take.

At the end, the notes must be signed and dated by the chairperson. This is normally done at the next meeting, once they have been agreed as being a correct record.

▲ 'Apparently he passed out when he saw the length of the agenda'

Meeting notes conventions

There are three main conventions you must follow.

▶ Because meeting notes always refer to what has already happened, they are written using the past tense. You must also use the third person (which means you never write 'I', 'you' or 'we'). For example, you would not write 'we are deciding' but 'it was decided'. You can gain further practice in developing this skill on pages 42 and 43.

▶ Meeting notes summarise only the key, relevant points that were discussed relating to the agenda items. A long discussion about whether the coffee is hot or cold is irrelevant and should be omitted. Even if a discussion is relevant, remember that you need to give only a summary. A useful phrase to use is 'after much discussion it was decided to'. This indicates that many people contributed to the discussion but it wasn't necessary to report everything that was said.

▶ Slang, strong adjectives and exaggerations are also omitted. If one participant, John Kent, gets annoyed and says 'I think they're all idiots in the Marketing Department, everything is always late. Those leaflets should have been ready weeks ago' no one would thank you for including that statement in the written notes! Instead you could put, 'John Kent queried the delay with the leaflets'.

Tone and style of meeting notes

Meeting notes are always formal. They are normally also quite short. The aim is to reflect the main business of the meeting and the decisions that were taken. This is so that they can be used for reference in the future.

One variation which often occurs is the way people are referred to in the notes. Because meeting notes are formal, it is unlikely you would just say 'Jack said . . .' If you need to identify people then you can use the full name 'Jack Wilkins said' or 'Mr Wilkins said'. An alternative, used by many organisations, is just to give the initials, e.g. 'JW said'. The major point is that each speaker should be clearly identifiable. If, therefore, you have *two* Mr Wilkins (or JWs) at the meeting, then you would have to differentiate between them in your notes.

Converting quite a long conversation into short, accurate notes is a skill you need to practise to do successfully. Don't expect your first set of notes to be superb! It helps if you read other meeting notes and use these as a guide to style; write in simple sentences and don't use any words you don't fully understand, apart from special terms discussed at the meeting which you have to include.

Writing notes will also test your ability to extract and adapt important information. In your examination you may have to read a conversation and then write notes. In this case, always start by identifying the key points that were raised and discussed, and the outcome. These are the important facts that you *must* include.

Use of English

If you read a novel or a report of an interview in a magazine, you will often see speech written in quotation marks. The correct term for this is **direct speech** and it is used when the words someone said are being quoted, for example:

'I think the new photocopier is being delivered here tomorrow. If it does not arrive, I will definitely telephone them,' said Kelly Watts.

Indirect or **reported speech** is the correct term used when you are saying what someone said earlier. Kelly's statement would therefore be written as follows:

> Kelly Watts said that she thought the new photocopier was being delivered to the Sales Department the following day. She stressed that she would telephone the supplier if it did not arrive.

Several things have changed and these are listed below.

▶ The quotation marks have been removed.

▶ The present tense verbs have been changed to the past tense, so 'think' becomes 'thought' and 'is being' becomes 'was being' and 'does' becomes 'did'. When you write notes, each statement moves one stage backwards in time. If someone refers to something in the past tense already, e.g. 'Bill Evans telephoned' you should write, 'Bill Evans had telephoned' – which moves it back one more step.

When Kelly referred to what she was going to do in the future 'will telephone' this is changed to the conditional 'would telephone'. This is because it was her intention to phone – but we don't know whether she has actually done so or not.

▶ The pronoun 'I' has been changed to 'she'. When you are talking about one person, never use 'I' or 'you' – instead use 'he' or 'she'. When you are talking about several people, never use 'we' or 'you' (plural) – instead use 'they'. Be careful, though that you make it clear who is being spoken about.

For example, if you had to convert:

'Margaret Foulds said she would do it,' said Paula Laird, then you should *not* write: Paula Laird said she would do it. This because Paula didn't say that! The correct report would say: Paula Laird said that Margaret Foulds would do it.

You also need to be careful with the word 'them'. Often the reader won't know what you mean, so you may need to be specific. That is why, in Kelly's statement on the previous page, 'them' was changed to 'the supplier'.

▷ The word 'tomorrow' has been changed to 'the following day'. This is because you don't know when someone will read the account. Therefore you need to change any words relating to time as follows:

now = then	today = on that day
yesterday = the previous day	tomorrow = the following day
last week = the previous week	next week = the following week

▷ References to places also need changing in a similar way so:

here = there	this = that	these = those

Again, if there is likely to be any confusion, specify the place. This is why, when Kelly referred to 'here' in her first sentence, this was changed to the Sales Department.

KEY TIP   Try not to overuse the word 'said' – otherwise your notes become very boring with PW said, JW said, VM said! Try using alternatives such as 'thought', 'felt', 'commented' and 'remarked'. See, too, how Kelly's second sentence was changed to avoid repeating the word 'said'.

COMMUNICATION IN BUSINESS

A new student dictionary has been produced by Bloomsbury, in liaison with teachers and lecturers who identified common mistakes their students made and focused on the advice and help they need. Frequent errors they reported included incomplete or poorly written sentences, the over-use of 'dull' words such as 'interesting' or 'good' and the inability to use commas. Very few knew the difference between 'there', 'their' and 'they're and regularly confused pairs of words which are pronounced the same but spelled differently and have a different meaning, e.g. 'faze' and 'phase', and 'pray' and 'prey'.

If this sounds like you, then you should perhaps rush to get a copy of the student edition of the Encarta Concise Dictionary as soon as you can. There are lists of commonly misspelled words and helpful usage notes to stop you making the same type of mistakes.

If you want to test your own abilities before you spend your money, check if you can immediately identify the differences between the words below:

▶ chilli and chilly
▶ breech and breach
▶ flare and flair
▶ hair, hare and heir
▶ peak, peek and pique
▶ vain, vein and vane
▶ pair, pear and pare
▶ site, sight and cite
▶ write, right, rite

1 Each of the versions of the verb 'to think' below has been matched up with an equivalent version in reported speech – but the second column is muddled up!

Copy out the table and the verbs listed in direct speech and then select the correct version from the second column you would use, each time, if you were writing it in reported speech.

Direct speech	Reported speech
We think	We should think
We are thinking	We should have thought
We thought	We had thought
We have been thinking	We had been thinking
We will think	We should be thinking
We will be thinking	We thought
We will have thought	We were thinking

2 Convert each of the following sentences into reported speech. Make sure you avoid any ambiguities or phrases which would cause confusion. If the speaker uses slang, change this to a standard expression that would be suitable in meeting notes and try to use the word 'said' only once throughout!

a) John Sinclair said 'I will see Peter Brent at the safety meeting next week.'

b) 'Yesterday, two more items were stolen,' said the security guard.

c) 'If it's pouring down again,' said Anna, 'we'll have to hold the show indoors.'

d) 'I'm sorry but I can't go to the conference,' said Hamida, 'I'm rushed off my feet this week.'

3 The IT development group meeting took place as arranged. Two members of the group were unable to attend, Karen Sheppard and Zulfiqar Khan. Neil Aspden, Emma Banks and Rhonda O'Sullivan did attend.

Tim Saunders opened the meeting, the minutes of the previous meeting were agreed and, under Matters Arising, Neil reported that all the new printers had now been installed.

The group then discussed email security. An extract from their discussion is given opposite.

Tim: We've had a problem with spam emails getting through our system. These are unwanted email messages which appear in the in-box. They can be a real nuisance.

Emma: I know everyone can delete these but that isn't enough. It wastes time going through them and reading them.

Tim: Quite. But it's even more important that we get rid of them because they may contain a virus in an attachment. For that reason we've installed new filters and a new security program to block all these messages as they arrive.

Rhonda: There's another problem related to email security. Some staff leave their computers switched on when they are away from their desk. If they are logged into email, this means anyone can send a message in their name.

Tim: Anyone who uses someone else's email address to send a message will be disciplined. It's against our Use of IT rules.

Neil: It may be a good idea if you remind all staff about this when you tell them about the new email security.

Tim: Good idea. Will do.

Tim went on to say that new database reports would soon be available for tutors who could search for key information on their students. He said that he needed tutors to let him know what type of information they would like to see on these. Emma said that she had been involved with these reports so she agreed to find out. Tim then said that he would have more information on the website improvements next week and as Zulfiqar was leading the development team, it would be better to talk about it when he was present.

Under Any Other Business, Rhonda said that several staff had complained about delays when they phoned the computer help desk. It was agreed that this would be put on the agenda for the next meeting, which would be at the same time and on the same day the following week.

a) Write a heading 'Email security' and then draft a note to go under this, summarising the discussion the group had.

b) Decide what specific information should be included at the top of the meeting notes.

c) Compare your answers to both with the complete set of notes on page 46. Then check how all the other items have been written. Use this as a future guide for writing notes of a meeting.

MARLTON COLLEGE

NOTES OF MEETING

A meeting of the IT Development Group was held in room T24 at 1400 hours on Wednesday, 10 November 200-.

PRESENT

Tim Saunders (Chair)
Neil Aspden
Emma Banks
Rhonda O'Sullivan

		ACTION
1	APOLOGIES FOR ABSENCE	

Apologies were received from Karen Sheppard and Zulfiqar Khan.

2   MINUTES OF PREVIOUS MEETING

These were agreed as a true and correct record and signed by the Chairperson.

3   MATTERS ARISING

Neil Aspden reported that all the new printers had now been installed.

4   EMAIL SECURITY

Tim Saunders said that new filters and a new security program had been installed to block 'spam' emails. This would also reduce the risk of viruses. Rhonda O'Sullivan mentioned that security was also jeopardised when staff did not log out of email when they left their desk. Tim Saunders agreed to remind staff about the College's Use of IT rules when he notified them about the new security measures.   TS

5   DATABASE REPORTS

Tim Saunders said that these would soon be available for tutors and he needed to know what key information tutors would need on their students. Emma Banks agreed to find out.   EB

6   WEBSITE IMPROVEMENTS

It was agreed to defer discussion on this item until the next meeting when Zulfiqar Khan would be present.

7   ANY OTHER BUSINESS

Rhonda O'Sullivan reported that she had received complaints from staff about delays when they telephoned the computer help desk. It was agreed this would be an agenda item at the next meeting.

8   TIME AND DATE OF NEXT MEETING

The next meeting will be held at 1400 hours on Wednesday, 17 November 200-.

Signed ………………….....…....…… (Chairperson)   Date ………………………..

▲ Example notes of a meeting

4 At Marlton College, three members of staff met today at 10 o'clock in the library meeting room to discuss one item – the design of the cover for the student diary for next year. A graphic artist, Sam Warren, has produced three possible designs for them to look at. The other members present are Yasmin Khan, Clare McIntyre and Nathan King – who is chairing the meeting. The meeting starts as follows.

Clare: Well, as a treat for you all, I've brought in some chocolate biscuits. My catering students made them this morning!

Nathan: Great! They look super.

Yasmin: I'm on a diet! You'll have to count me out. By the way, where's Sue O'Grady? I thought she was coming, too.

Nathan: She was, but I had a phone call this morning. Apparently she's off ill this week. Anyway, let's make a start. I've another meeting in half an hour. Sam, how far have you got?

Sam: I've done quite well. Here are the three designs. Two are based on photographs and one is text-based and highlights the key words relating to studying here.

(They all look at the designs)

Yasmin: I like the photograph of the students under the tree. It looks really summery.

Clare: Nathan – isn't that your group from last year?

Nathan: Yes, under protest I may add! It took me over an hour to persuade them.

Clare: I like that one, but I think I prefer the text one. It's jazzy and different.

Sam: That's my favourite too.

Nathan: I like it, but I think it should be more colourful. Could we have the text in lots of different colours?

Sam: Yes, I could do that, but you don't want too many or it'll start to look cheap and nasty. And we've to make a decision by Friday.

Nathan: Well, would it be possible to redo it before then so we could have a quick look? Do we all agree it's between that one and the summer photograph.

(Everyone agrees with this)

Sam: We could meet at 12 o'clock on Friday, if you want. I could have a more colourful version of the text cover done by then.

Yasmin: I can't come then, but I could come at 11 o'clock or 11.30.

Nathan: 11.30 everyone?

Sam: That's OK by me.

Clare: Fine, see you then.

---

a) Decide what information is relevant to writing a meetings note from this discussion and identify that which you should discard.

b) Write a meeting note to summarise what happened, using an appropriate format, and check your work with your tutor.

Business notes are prepared and used for many purposes – not just at meetings. You may need to prepare notes if :

▶ you are being given verbal instructions or information

▶ you need to find out or research information

▶ you have to attend a talk or other event and report back afterwards

▶ you are asked to prepare a facts sheet or other document which must contain only the key information required

▶ you are expected to re-arrange or summarise any relatively lengthy material into a shorter version.

A shortened version of a longer document is often called a **summary**. Business notes are a type of summary, because they focus on the important points.

Good notes and summaries

Good notes and summaries have a clear heading and are dated. This is very important at work because there may be several sets of notes on a topic and you may need to know which are the most recent. They are also:

▶ brief, and don't contain unnecessary or irrelevant information

▶ divided into sections, when they are long, under headings and sub-headings so that any information can be found easily

▶ clear and easy to read

▶ complete, in relation to all the key facts that must be included

▶ organised into a logical pattern.

▲ A good summary contains only essential information

The format of notes and summaries

There is a choice of styles you can use.

▷ Some written summaries are prepared under one heading, as continuous text. In this case you simply divide your information into appropriate paragraphs.

▷ Others need several headings and may also have sub-headings. These must be *consistent* throughout the document.

▷ You can separate the text with numbered or bullet points. The meeting notes on page 46 were prepared using numbered points. Bullet points are better if you don't want to imply a particular order. If you are indicating a sequence, then use numbered points.

If you think about why the notes or summary is required and how it will be used this will help you to choose the best style for that document.

Preparing notes or a summary from written material

If you do this methodically it will be easier.

Step 1 – identifying what is important

▷ Start by reading the document to get its overall meaning.

▷ Then read it again slowly. Highlight or identify each key point. Ignore examples of descriptions used just to illustrate something.

▷ Re-read the document, checking that you haven't missed out anything important.

▷ Write out the points you have identified. Use proper sentences – don't write in 'note' form. Don't worry about reorganising any information at this stage, just follow the original order.

Step 2 – reorganising the information

▷ Check if there is a particular sequence of events or sequence that people have to follow. This will indicate the best order.

▷ Group together any connected items of information.

▷ Decide on your main heading and where you will need any sub-headings.

▷ Draft out your information under these headings.

Step 3 – final checks

▷ Check that your use of English, spelling and punctuation are correct.

▷ Read the summary and check that it gives you the same meaning as the original document.

▷ Add the date at the bottom and, if you have to state the source of your summary, then add this, too. For example, if you are quoting from a handbook or a magazine, you should put the title and date of publication (if known).

1 Your boss, Oliver Jones, has arranged a programme of events for some French visitors who are coming to your company tomorrow. He has asked you to type these up from the following information.

'They will arrive at reception at 10 o'clock – I've told the receptionist to expect them. I will meet them and take them to the Board Room. At 10.15 we're having coffee with our MD, Ken Pickup, and Pierre Devereux will also meet us there. He's acting as interpreter all day as he speaks fluent French. At 10.30 I'll take them to Marketing.

Amanda and her team have prepared a great presentation – you should see it some time. At 12.00 we're going for lunch. I've booked a table at the Swan Hotel – I don't think we can run to a super meal here. They'll be leaving us at 4 pm – but before that at 2 pm I'm taking them over to meet Javeed Sadiq at Marlton District Council. We should be back for 3.30 pm for a final get-together in the Board Room with the MD again. By the way, the correct term for a 'final get-together' is a plenary session. Could you put that, please?

I think that's it. Can you just do a short, simple programme for us and use the 24-hour clock, so that there's no confusion about times.'

a) Decide on a suitable main heading for the programme.

b) List the items in time order, remember just to put the key information opposite each time you enter.

c) Check you haven't missed anything and end with the date at the bottom left-hand side.

Check your finished work with your tutor.

2 The senior administrator, Sally Cowan, is concerned about the number of photocopier breakdowns being experienced. Yesterday, the engineer said that the problem was because people were not using paper properly. Some were using the wrong paper or storing unused paper incorrectly. Others didn't know how to refill the paper tray. He said everyone should read the photocopier manual.

Sally thinks this is impractical, so she has given you an extract from the manual and also sent you a memo. She has asked you to draft a memo, from her to the staff, asking them to follow the correct procedures. She thinks this will be in everyone's interests as the number of breakdowns will be reduced..

a) *As a group*, decide the important information which must be included. If there are any words or terms you do not fully understand, discuss these with your tutor.

b) Then draft out a memo, summarising the key points and using appropriate headings so that staff can easily see what they have to do. Sally has also suggested that you use bullet points to explain how to refill the paper tray.

MEMO

TO: (You)

FROM: Sally Cowen

DATE: (Today)

SUBJECT: PHOTOCOPIER INSTRUCTIONS

Much of the information in the photocopying manual is too involved to put in a summary and not really relevant for staff. We always buy the recommended paper and this is kept in the main storeroom with a quantity next to the photocopier in the photocopying room. The problem seems to occur when the paper runs out in the room. Staff go to the storeroom and pick up the first packet they see! In future, I have told all administrators to keep the storeroom locked. If paper runs out in the photocopying room, then staff must go to the main office and ask the administrator for a further supply.

The other problem is that staff leave open packets lying around in the room and often remove the paper from its packaging even though they don't put it all into the machine. Or they try to put it into the wrong tray. Staff should only ever use paper tray 1 for A4 paper. We use paper tray 2 for A3 paper.

We have another problem when the heating is switched off at weekend. Any paper left inside the machine seems to get damp and then it jams on Monday. I've told the administrators to remove it last thing on Friday and put it back in the store cupboard. So far as the staff are concerned, please just tell them that the paper will be removed on Friday night from the machine and replaced on Monday morning.

I suggest you let me see your draft memo once you have prepared this.

SC

Extract from photocopying manual

There are two paper trays. The first holds A4 paper with a maximum capacity of 1600 sheets. The second paper tray can hold either A4 or A3 paper with a maximum capacity of 600 sheets. For tray 2, the paper size being used must be keyed into the machine. The bypass tray must be used for OHP transparencies, postcards and address labels. These items must never be placed in either of the paper trays.

Paper which has been already copied on must never be used as this will cause a misfeed. In addition, paper which is bent, folded, creased or torn should also not be used. Open reams of paper should be kept in the packaging until the paper is used.

When the paper runs out in a paper tray, this will be shown on the indicator panel. The paper tray should be pulled out until it stops (don't tug or force beyond this point). When the whole tray is pulled out the paper should be inserted flush with the paper guides. Paper should never be stacked above the red limit mark. The tray should then be pushed *gently* to return it to its correct position.

COMMUNICATION IN BUSINESS

Some organisations are becoming so concerned about bad spelling, punctuation and grammar in their written documents that they are starting to fine their employees! In 2002 a leading Swiss newspaper, *Le Temps*, announced that it was going to fine its journalists nearly three dollars for each mistake they made. In Britain, Nottingham City Council's leader challenged the chief executive and his staff to put £1 in the charity box every time a prepared document was found to contain an error. All the money goes in an 'apostrophe box' much to the delight of the Apostrophe Protection Society, which promotes the preservation and correct use of the apostrophe in written English.

Part of the problem is that many people today rely totally on word processor spell-checkers and grammar checkers. The first have serious limitations and will never highlight the fact that, in your haste, you typed 'further to your daft report' instead of 'further to your draft report'. The second are also far from perfect – and even if they highlight that a sentence is wrong, they may not be able to suggest a useful correction. In the US, some people use telephone hotlines to supplement their spell-checker. A far cheaper way is to learn the basic rules yourself and reach for the dictionary if you aren't sure and to customise your spell-checker where you can, using the key tip on page 14. If apostrophes are still a problem after you've read this book, follow the links from www.heinemann.co.uk/hotlinks to the website of the Apostrophe Protection Society.

▼ PREPARING A REPORT

Reports are a common business document in all organisations. Many reports are routine and are regularly completed, such as managers' reports on their departments, accident reports, safety reports, visit reports and financial reports. Others are written only for a particular reason. They may be required as the result of an investigation or to provide information on a certain matter. Examples could include a report summarising whether customer complaints have increased or decreased, with reasons; a report on security problems; a report on staff retention and the reasons why staff have left over the past 12 months or a report summarising current sales figures and trends.

If you have practised preparing business notes and know how to write a summary, then a report is the next step. This brings together the skills you have learned: to use clear headings, business English, and to summarise the main points that are required in a way that is easy to read.

Report format

A report may be written on plain paper with a clear heading. If you have to send it to someone inside the company, you can attach a short 'covering' memo. An alternative, if you are writing a short report, is to use a memo heading (see page 56).

There are usually three clear sections to a report.

1 An **introduction** – which states the reason for writing the report.

2 The **body of the report** – which gives the information that has been obtained. This is usually the longest section. Clear headings are essential and numbered points are often used to separate different items of information.

3 A **conclusion** – which sums up the information and indicates whether action is required or not. If you are asked to give your recommendations, then you should add your own suggestions about what should be done.

Clear headings are essential. Bold type will help your headings to stand out clearly but don't add underlining. Bold *plus* underlining simply looks too much. Another method is to use decimal numbering. This subdivides a main heading into sub-headings. You can see how this has been done in the example on page 56.

The most important aspect about headings is consistency. All your headings should be consistent in terms of style, size and numbering. Therefore, if you decide to type all your sub-headings in upper case bold, none of them should vary from this!

All reports should be signed and dated. If you have used a memo heading, the date and the name of the writer will be at the top. If you use plain paper, then put the date beneath the writer's name at the bottom.

Report conventions

All reports should be written objectively. This means you report the facts and not your opinions, unless you are specifically asked for these. You should use full, complete sentences and all the information should be in a logical order.

▲ Reports should not contain your opinions – only the facts

You will find it easier if you:

▶ **Start by drafting your introduction**. This is the shortest and easiest part as you simply say who asked for the report and why.

▶ **Organise all the main information** to be included into a logical order. Then decide how to separate these to keep it clear. This will depend upon the headings or numbering system you choose.

▶ **Finally, decide what your conclusions should be**. These should obviously link to the information you have given previously. For example, you can't investigate why 50 blank CDs went missing last week and conclude that there is no problem! Check whether you have been asked to make any recommendations yourself and, if so, add two or three suggestions. Don't try to tell your boss how to do his or her job! Simply suggest one or two appropriate solutions that you think would help to solve any problems you have identified.

Use of English

Commas are used in the middle of a sentence to denote a pause. They enable the reader to take a breath! However, where you put a comma can affect the sense of a sentence. Compare:

'She told me she was sick, and tired of working late.'

'She told me she was sick and tired of working late.'

Always read a sentence for sense when you are working out where to insert a comma. If you would pause if you were speaking, then it is likely a comma is needed.

Commas are also used:

▶ to separate a list of words (such as books, magazines, journals)

▶ to separate words such as 'therefore', 'however', 'unfortunately', 'interestingly' and 'consequently' from the rest of a sentence

▶ to separate a clause in the middle of a sentence. You can 'test' for a clause as the sentence would make sense without it; for example, 'we could introduce this idea, without any additional cost, by the end of January.' In this case you need a comma both *before* and *after* the clause.

You can also use a dash to indicate a pause or separate a clause. This denotes a longer pause, e.g. 'we can come to the meeting – if finance agrees to pay our travel costs.'

Brackets are rarely used in formal business documents – you are safer to use a dash instead. They can be useful at times to add additional information but if you do decide to do this, remember to close your brackets afterwards.

KEY TIP If you find you've written a very long sentence, always reread it so see whether it needs a comma or dash to indicate a pause. It's unlikely that you would read two or three lines of text without breathing!

1 Punctuate each of the following sentences and correct any spelling errors.

a) When you write to him please also send three sets of the leaflets two cattaloges four brochures and then tell mark sharples the sales manager that youve done this.

b) As agreed at the meeting this morning we will send the figures to you by wednesday next when we also hope to have completed the draught report on staff retention rates.

c) Joanna briggs formally Joanna kent until her marriage last march has gone down in history as the first employee of this company to complete the london marathon a feat she has been promising to achieve for the past two years.

d) On her trip she intended to visit several countries in europe including france belgum holland and italy but unfortunately because of a serious illness in the family she had to return after only two weeks.

e) We should be greatful therefore if you would arrange to send this to us at the above address marked for the attention of john osullivan.

2 Rehana's boss, Marie Wheatley, is horrified when she receives an invoice of more than £1,500 for one month's supply of printer cartridges because this is far more than the normal bill. She asks Rehana to find out why this has occurred and to send her a report.

a) Rehana's report is shown on page 56. Read this carefully and, in particular, note how Rehana has used suitable headings and how these are consistent throughout the report.

b) Marie is pleased with the report but then gives it back to Rehana and asks her to make three relevant suggestions and add these at the end. As a group, decide what suggestions you would make and then write these to end the report.

3 A week later, Marie has another idea. She likes the idea of recycling cartridges and giving these to charity. She has heard that there are various websites which advertise this scheme. She has asked you to find out about these and has given you two weeks to do it. Follow the links at www.heinemann.co.uk/hotlinks for some suggestions.

a) Working in small groups, investigate cartridge recycling schemes in the UK. Decide with your tutor which websites you should investigate and whether you should find out if any others exist by using a good search engine. If you take print-outs, restrict these to *relevant* pages for the site you are investigating.

b) In your group, prepare a short *verbal* report for your class, summarising what you found.

c) Exchange copies of print-outs with other groups and then, on your own, write a brief report to Marie summarising your investigation and including your own recommendations.

MEMO

TO: Marie Wheatley

FROM: Rehana Hussain

DATE: 20 March 200-

SUBJECT: **REPORT ON COST OF REPLACEMENT PRINTER CARTRIDGES**

1 INTRODUCTION

On Monday, 10 March, you asked me to investigate the use of printer cartridges in the department as the invoice we received for replacing these last month was over £1,500. I agreed to provide this information by Friday, 22 March.

2 STAFF INTERVIEWS

2.1 I spoke to the administrators who confirmed that last month they were involved in preparing several long documents for managers. First drafts were often returned with amendments and a request for a further print-out.

2.2 The marketing staff have recently prepared a number of coloured leaflets. Their work means that they cannot take advantage of draft print mode or greyscale to reduce cartridge use.

2.3 Senior staff said that many documents are printed without checking, which wastes both ink and paper. They felt that problems lay mainly with new administrative staff, especially during busy periods. They also felt that some staff did not know how to save cartridge use and routinely used best print mode, even for internal or draft documents.

3 STOCK PROCEDURES

3.1 The purchasing administrator is responsible for making out all orders. The orders can be approved by any member of the senior staff. This means there is no overall check on the number of orders submitted.

3.2 The cartridges are stored in the main stationery cupboard. There is sufficient room and the cartridges are stocked neatly.

3.3 There is no system in place to restrict the issue of cartridges. Staff simply help themselves from the cupboard. This could mean that staff with printers at home could be obtaining cartridges for this purpose.

3.4 In January we had a problem obtaining supplies and there was a concern that we would run out. To prevent this recurring, the purchasing administrator ordered an additional supply in February and obtained extra discount on this order. This has meant that we now have over 30 cartridges in stock, worth over £400.

4 CARTRIDGE SUPPLIES

4.1 We have recently changed our supplier to try to continue buying at a competitive price, but the price of cartridges has increased by over 10% in the last 12 months.

4.2 Many organisations offer to recycle cartridges. Some pay for used cartridges, others donate the money to charity. We could choose which we wanted to use. This action would be more environmentally friendly than simply throwing them away.

5 CONCLUSIONS

My conclusions are as follows.

5.1 Usage has been particularly high during the past two months but more could be done to prevent wastage.

5.2 Our stock procedures could be improved to monitor ordering, restrict access and check usage.

5.3 We could investigate further the benefits of recycling used cartridges.

Rehana Hussain

▼ PREPARING AN ARTICLE

If you read magazines or a daily newspaper, then you will see dozens of articles, written on a host of subjects. These are often accompanied by photographs or other graphics to attract the reader's attention.

At work, articles are often written for a staff newsletter or magazine. The editor will ask for contributions from all staff, particularly those who have been involved in an interesting event or activity. Articles, as well as press releases, are also prepared by marketing staff and sent to newspapers for publication. A press release normally covers an important event or development. The business hopes that the newspaper will print the information – which results in free publicity for the company.

Although you will not be expected to write press releases at this stage, you may be asked to write an interesting and informative article.

Article format

The format of a printed article is often different from the way it is prepared. You will normally see articles in magazines and newspapers divided into columns. The text flows continuously from the bottom of one column to the top of the next. Although this is possible on a modern word-processing package it can be quite complicated and there is no need for you to learn this for your examination. Most articles prepared internally and sent for publication are prepared as a normal word-processed document but may use one and a half or double line spacing. Editors often prefer this because then they can mark up amendments more easily.

Another feature you will see in many printed articles is a banner heading, which goes across a number of columns.

Finally, the location of any artwork or graphics is identified and then this is inserted. On a desk top publishing package, the text can be made to 'wrap' around the graphics so that it is continuous.

Article conventions

Articles are written in a different way from standard business documents because they aim to inform and interest the reader from the very beginning. For that reason, you divide up your information in a slightly different way.

▶ **An overview at the start**. The first section should say what the article is all about and include the key facts – such as **what** happened, **who** was there, **where** it was and **when** it occurred. Anyone who reads this section should understand what is going to follow.

▶ **Details in the middle**. The next section gives more information which builds on the summary. This may take several paragraphs. Normally paragraphs in an article are kept short and each relates to one specific aspect of the main theme.

▶ **A summary at the end**. The final section often summarises the article in a slightly different way from the overview at the start, because now the reader understands more about the topic. You will often find that writers refer back to a theme at the start when they end the article.

Most articles have a restricted number of words you can use – limited by the amount of available space when they are published. This is where word processing can be invaluable, as you can quickly do a word count at any stage and check you are not over the limit. If you are, then use the summarising techniques you learned on page 49 to shorten it!

Tone and style of an article

The tone and style should depend upon who your readers are and what you are writing about. For that reason an article about the business accounts would be written far more formally than an article about a staff night out!

It is always better to err on the side of caution – even if your article is for the staff magazine. You can write in a friendly way without being too informal and upsetting anyone. Obviously, if you are writing for an 'outside audience' – such as your customers – then you need to be careful to project the right image of the organisation. For that reason, it is always helpful to read similar articles that other people have written to see what style they have used. You will usually find that:

▶ Reported speech is normally used (see page 42) – so you write in the third person and past tense *unless* you are specifically asked to report on your own experience of something.

▶ There is a catchy title or headline to attract readers.

▶ There is a quotation or two to add personal interest.

▶ You can use an exclamation mark to emphasise a sentence which makes a strong statement or is surprising in some way – but don't overdo this. One or two *in the whole article* is plenty – and never in successive sentences.

▶ The writing style is upbeat, crisp and snappy (but not curt!).

Use of English

Pronouns can cause several problems in all communications. The four main ones are:

▶ Knowing when to use 'I' and when to say 'me'

▶ Confusing singular and plural pronouns

▶ Knowing when to use 'who' and when to say 'whom'

▶ Using the wrong pronouns.

Problem one

If you are talking about yourself and someone else, use 'I' when you would use the word 'we' and say 'me' when you would use the word 'us', for example:

Do you think Mary and I/me should go? = Do you think *we* should go?

Therefore = Do you think *Mary and I* should go?

Can you come to the meeting with Mary and I/me? = Can you come to the meeting with *us*? Therefore = Can you come to the meeting with *Mary and me*?

Remember, it is always polite to put yourself last.

Problem two

Mixing up singular and plural pronouns results in sentences such as:

I will investigate the matter and we will contact you again soon *or*
Each person must give their name on arrival.

In the first case you must say *either:*

We will investigate the matter and *we* will contact you again soon *or*
I will investigate and matter and *I* will contact you again soon.

In the second case you must say *either*:

Every person must give *their* name on arrival *or*
Each person must state *his or her* name on arrival.

Problem three

Use 'who' if a person is the subject of the sentence (the person carrying out the action) and 'whom' if the person is the object (the person being acted upon), for example:

Chloe *(subject)*, who works in Finance, is getting married next week.
When you *(subject)* tried to contact Chloe *(object)*, to whom did you speak?

If this seems really awkward, change the sentence around so that the object again becomes the subject. In this case you would just say, 'Who spoke to you when you tried to contact Chloe?

Problem four

The main pronouns which are wrongly used are:

▶ 'which' or 'that' when you are referring to people. *Always* use 'who' or 'whom', for example, 'It was Ken who was last', not 'It was Ken that was last.'

▶ 'what' instead of 'that' or 'which', for example, 'This is the bag that I want' *not* 'This is the bag what I want.'

KEY TIP Watch for sexist problems with pronouns. For example, don't say 'Each visitor must hand in his badge on departure' as this makes it seem as if all the visitors are male. It is easier to make everything plural and say 'All visitors must hand in their badges on departure.'

OVER TO YOU!

1 Correct each of the following sentences

a) Me and Paul will arrive at 9 am.

b) I regret that we were unable to write to you before now.

c) Anyone who forgets their log-in ID must contact the help desk.

d) There was only a handful of people that actually went on the trip.

e) Each member of staff has an annual appraisal with his line manager.

f) Whose the person you have to see?

2 Mark is the editor of the staff magazine and has written an article about a member of the sales staff who is leaving.

a) Read his article and note how he has done this to attract readers and how he has followed the 'rules' relating to format, convention, tone and style.

Lisa heads for a life down under

Sales staff took over Marco's Pizzeria last Friday for a farewell party for Lisa Eccles, our senior sales administrator. Lisa is moving to Sydney when she gets married next month to Jon, her beau from down under.

Insert photo of farewell party here. Thanks, Mark

Lisa joined us straight from college, when we were still in our old offices on Bold Street and, through hard work and dedication beyond the call of duty, rose steadily through the ranks. She stood out as being one of the few remarkable people who are just as happy and smiling on a Monday morning as they are on a Friday night!

Lisa met Jon two years ago, when she visited her uncle who lives in Melbourne. Twelve months ago, Jon came to England to work for software company Cybertronics, but has missed the outdoor Oz lifestyle. He and Lisa have therefore decided to return. Lisa says 'Life out there is incredible and Jon is pining for sun and surfing again. No matter how hard he has tried, he can't get used to the rain we have here.'

Colleagues presented Lisa with flowers, a farewell cheque and several requests for free board and lodging if they ever visit Australia themselves. Jack Bryant, Lisa's boss, said: 'Lisa will be sorely missed and I think everyone will agree with me that Jon's gain is our loss.'

Jon and Lisa get married on 10 March at Abingdale Lodge. Lisa's colleagues in Sales are now in training for another night out – this time at her evening celebrations!

b) Imagine you are Lisa. You have agreed to send Mark a short article on life in Australia after you've been there about a month. Invent any details you want – you could talk about settling in your new home or finding a new job. Remember that you don't have to use reported speech because you are talking about your own experiences. Try to keep it short, punchy and upbeat.

3 Your company, Kenton Plastics, has a football team which entered a 5-a-side indoor football tournament called the Challenge Trophy. They call themselves Kenton All Stars. Last Saturday they won the trophy in the final at Aversham Sports Stadium. You saw the match, which was exciting and close fought. The final score was 6 – 4. Afterwards you spoke to Max Edwards, the team captain, who gave you the following details. 'The Challenge is a knock-out competition. There were 32 teams when it started last September. Last year we were knocked out in the third round. It's incredible we've won. I think it's because Ken (my boss) kitted us all out in our new strip in the company colours! Pete Bryant, Bashir Ali, Glen Banks and Salim Ugrader make up the team. We were worried because Pete hurt his knee the week before and we were lucky he was fit enough to play. We can now have a good rest before we start training for next year – when we will have to defend our title as the best team in the region.'

Write a short article for your company newsletter based on this information. Remember to use reported speech this time. Indicate where you think any graphics could be positioned in the article and what these would be.

▼ PREPARING A JOB DESCRIPTION

A job description is a document which summarises all the basic facts about a particular job and the role of the job holder. It is often prepared or revised when a vacancy is created and before it is advertised. A copy may be sent to all the applicants so that they fully understand what type of work they will be asked to do.

Although companies may vary slightly in the way they set out these documents there are usually certain standard headings. Job descriptions can vary in length, too. Normally they are longer for more senior jobs.

Job description format

A common format is shown in the job description on page 63. After the title, there are separate headings with information alongside each one. Some organisations state only the department, the job title and purpose under the first section, others provide additional information such as hours of work, salary, the title of the job holder's line manager and any staff for whom the job holder would be responsible.

The 'duties and responsibilities' section is always the longest, and numbered points are used for this section because the duties are usually given in priority order, with the most important tasks listed first.

It is useful to include a date on all job descriptions so that anyone can check that they are referring to the most recent version.

Sometimes an additional document is sent out with a job description called a **person specification**. This states the essential and desirable criteria of the person required. To obtain an interview, the essential criteria *must* be met. The desirable criteria are more flexible.

Job description conventions

A job description is a list of facts, so it is kept brief and to the point. Each statement about the type of duties carried out is therefore a summary of an activity, not a full description.

The final item in the list is normally a general statement to cover additional duties which are not specifically mentioned. This is important because it prevents anyone claiming that they do not need to do something because it isn't included on their job description! The same applies to any general statement at the end relating to the fact that, from time to time, the job description may be amended. This, too, protects the organisation from any member of staff arguing that their job description cannot be changed.

Tone and style of job descriptions

The tone is factual and to the point. It is important, however, that all the statements under 'duties' are consistent in terms of their style. In the example on page 63, for example, it would have been incorrect to put 'receive and direct callers' in the first statement and then 'receiving telephone calls' in the second because you would have been using two versions of the verb 'receive' in different statements.

COMMUNICATION IN BUSINESS

Job descriptions are prepared as part of the recruitment process by most organisations and the content is often used as a basis for the job advertisement. Responses by prospective employees – whether by CV, application form or letter are *always* scrutinised carefully for both content and construction. This means that an application littered with grammatical or spelling errors is likely to result in your application being put straight into the waste bin.

Employers are becoming far more sensitive about this. According to the Learning and Skills Council (LSC) report *Skills in England 2002*, 61% of employers listed poor communication skills as one of the most frequent and persistent problems they faced when they recruited staff. Other skills shortages were identified in relation to customer handling, basic IT skills, practical skills, problem solving and team working. The key occupations where skills shortages are the greatest include customer services, support staff, and administrative or secretarial staff.

The good news, of course, is that those administrators who do possess high levels of skills in all these areas will be in great demand – a fact which should encourage you to persevere to achieve this qualification!

SYMMONDS AND COLE LTD: JOB DESCRIPTION

Department: Human Resources

Job Title: Receptionist/Administrator

Hours of work: 9 am – 5.30 pm Monday to Friday

Salary scale: £9,000 – £12,000

Responsible to: Human Resources Manager

Responsible for: Not applicable

Job purpose: To provide support for the human resource team in dealing with visitors, telephone calls and general enquiries.

Duties and responsibilities

1   Receive and direct callers to the Human Resources Department.

2   Receive telephone calls, deal with general enquiries and refer these to the correct person. Take telephone messages for staff as necessary.

3   Keep reception area neat and tidy and check heating and ventilation.

4   Make appointments for staff and visitors.

5   Receive and record all requests for application forms, training forms, accident forms, etc.

6   Receive and record all self-certification forms from staff and all departmental staff absence notifications.

7   Ensure an adequate supply of stationery and HR forms are available in the reception area and in relevant offices.

8   Attend any training course that may be considered appropriate by the personnel Administration Officer.

9   Maintain staff confidentiality at all times and be aware that breach of this could lead to instant dismissal.

10 Undertake any other relevant duties which may be identified.

This job description is not intended to be fully prescriptive and will be the subject of regular review and possible amendment. The post holder may be required to undertake related tasks which are not specifically mentioned above.

April 200-

SYMMONDS AND COLE LTD: PERSON SPECIFICATION

Department: Human Resources

Job title: Receptionist/Administrator

Personal attributes	Essential	Desirable
Qualifications	3 GCSEs grade C or above Level 1 Administration	GCSE English Level 2 Administration CLAIT or CLAIT Plus
Experience	None	Work experience/part-time work/dealing with people
Skills and abilities	Verbal communication skills Neat handwriting Good telephone manner Computer experience	Use of Microsoft Office
Personal attributes	Willing to undertake further study or training Neat and tidy appearance	Friendly personality

Use of English

Many words vary their spelling from a 'c' to an 's' when the word used changes from a noun to a verb. Several examples are given below.

practice/practise
licence/license
advice/advise
council/counsel
device/devise

How do you know which to use? Quite simply, every word with a 'c' is a noun and every word with an 's' is a verb. If you forget this, then you can still easily check which one is correct.

▶ If you can put 'a', 'an' or 'the' before the word, it is a noun, so use 'c'

▶ If you can put 'to' before the word, it is a verb, so use 's'

For example:

Tomorrow I want to apply for *a* driving licence.

He told me he has *to* be licensed to sell alcohol.

1 Decide which word is correct in each of the following sentences:

a) I have an appointment at the doctor's practice/practise at 2 pm.

b) On Tuesday I want to practice/practise for my driving test.

c) I must pay my television licence/license fee next week.

d) There is a meeting of the town council/counsel today.

e) I need you to advice/advise me about this.

f) She has to council/counsel a client at 5 pm.

g) This is a new device/devise but it doesn't work properly.

h) I think I need your advise/advice.

i) Can you device/devise a new way of doing this?

2 Work through the job description on page 63 and check with your tutor if there are any terms or words you do not understand. Check that you understand the format and the style of the document.

3 Tilly has worked as junior administrator in the Student Services department at Hogarth College for twelve months and is now being promoted. Her boss, Julia Richards, has asked Tilly to help prepare the job description for her replacement by listing all the tasks she carries out under the heading 'Duties and Responsibilities'. Tilly isn't exactly sure what to write and has asked you for help.

Look at Tilly's list below and decide which items should be included, which should not and which should be split into two items. Then reword each one so that it could be included on a job description. Finally, help Tilly by writing out a correct version of the list for Julia Richards.

Duties and responsibilities

I keep the racks of careers leaflets tidy and check that we're not running out of any. If we are, I order some more.

I do photocopying for the staff. I also have to check the forms we use regularly and photocopy more when stocks are low.

I keep the appointments diary for the Student Welfare Officer so if a student calls in to see her, I can make the appointment.

I keep my desk tidy and put things I've been using away before I go home at night.

I clean out the stationery cupboard if it gets dirty.

I answer the telephone and take messages for people. I also try to help everyone who calls in to see us.

I get coffee or other drinks for everyone when it's my turn.

I file all the leaflets on different courses and careers information and keep these files tidy. I also file any other documents Julia Richards asks me to file.

I use my computer a lot – mainly to prepare documents using word processing but I also have to enter and find information on the student database.

I research information on the Internet. Mainly about careers but also about gap year work, student grants and other things students need.

I keep the part-time jobs board up-to-date and tidy.

4 Karen Andrews is the supervisor of a very busy business administration team at Calibre Insurance. She has been asking for another member of staff for ages. Yesterday, her boss agreed – and told her to prepare a job description.

Karen has consulted her team to see what they think and has summarised their comments below. She has also noted down her own ideas. From the information provided, draft out a job description for the new job role.

Team comments

Jane: I think a junior administrator would be better, to learn all aspects of the job. I need help coping with visitors on reception as it often gets very busy.

Sam: We need someone who knows about IT – to help keep the customer database up-to-date and do word processing – given all the documents we have to prepare.

Gretchen: We need the most help with general duties, such as reception, answering the telephone, filing and photocopying. Someone who is willing to learn.

Julie: I need help with the post – delivering it in the morning and getting it ready to be despatched each evening. It's a rush on my own when there's a lot of mail.

Sadia: The new person will have to learn to use the fax and the photocopier. It would also be good if he or she could be responsible for keeping the stationery stocks neat and tidy, checking the stock against the record cards, issuing stock to staff and updating the record cards.

Karen's notes

▶ Definitely require junior administrator. Correct title is Trainee Administrator. Salary scale for this job is £9,250 – £11,500. She will report to me.

▶ Will give one day a week off for training. Must be willing to undergo training as arranged.

▶ Working hours will be as normal: 8.45 am – 5.15 pm.

▶ Purpose of job is to provide administration support.

▶ Key aspect of job is answering telephone and taking telephone messages.

▶ Agree with team's comments but must add 'to carry out any other appropriate duties as required' – in case things change in the future.

▼ PREPARING LEAFLETS, NOTICES AND ADVERTISEMENTS

All organisations prepare promotional material to advertise products, services and events. Many are intended for customers but others are produced to inform staff about internal functions or changes. Organisations also advertise to prospective employees when they need new or replacement staff.

Large organisations may employ an advertising agency to prepare professional advertisements for customers, but this is very expensive. Smaller firms often produce their own, and desk top publishing and graphics packages have made it much easier for businesses to produce a range of well-designed and printed promotional materials in-house. In all organisations, internal notices and advertisements for staff vacancies are usually prepared internally.

Promotional formats

All promotional materials should follow the **AIDA** principle:

▶ **Attention** – capture the attention of the readers

▶ **Interest** – gain and hold their interest

▶ **Desire** – make them desire what you are offering

▶ **Action** – tell them how to take action to obtain it.

If you look at well-designed leaflets, notices and advertisements yourself, you should be able to see how this technique is used. First, it is used in relation to the format. The design or layout *must* be eye-catching so that the most important selling point or piece of information is the first item that the reader sees. The other key points to remember are shown in the table below.

Creating promotional documents

Do	Don't
Use bold, large letters and colour for effect	Use more than 3 sizes of text, 2 styles of typeface or 3 colours in any one document – and *never* all of these at once!
Leave plenty of white space	
Use one large graphic rather than lots of small ones	Underline emboldened words
Use headings to break up text if appropriate	Try to make it fancy! Plain is best
Use bullet points to separate items	Clutter up the document with too much text or too many images
Use words which all your readers will understand	Go into too much detail – stick to the key selling points

Conventions of promotional material

You need to ensure that you have a catchy or interesting heading, that you have included all the relevant details of **what, where, when** and **how** and that there are no grammar, punctuation or spelling errors. Other conventions will depend upon the type of document you are creating and the amount of information you have to communicate.

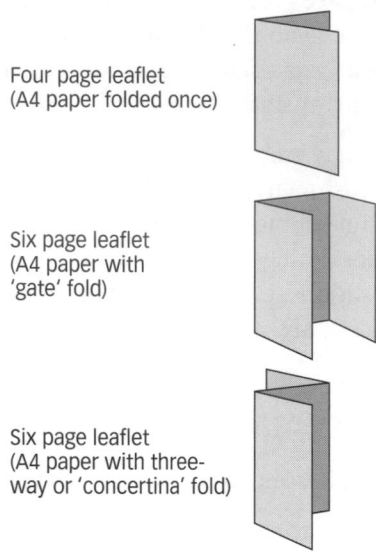

Four page leaflet
(A4 paper folded once)

Six page leaflet
(A4 paper with
'gate' fold)

Six page leaflet
(A4 paper with three-
way or 'concertina' fold)

▷ **A leaflet** can be folded in several different ways. For this reason, if you are creating the whole leaflet, you need to start by dividing up your information into different pages. It is normal for the first page to show the main selling points, the centre pages to contain the additional information and the 'action to be taken' is left until last. The back page should contain the least important information. In some cases this is even left blank, or the organisation's name and address, logo and telephone number are inserted in the centre and towards the bottom of the page.

▷ A **notice** is only one page – usually A4 if it is for a staff noticeboard. It is usual to put the date on the bottom of a notice so you can tell when it is out-of-date. An external notice would include the same organisational details as a leaflet.

▷ An **advertisement** is much smaller than an A4 page, especially if it is for a newspaper. The size of the advert determines its cost, so you need to keep it quite short. Many organisations have a specific style for job advertisements and always include their logo and an equal opportunities policy statement. At work, you would need to check any specific conventions you must follow.

require

RECEPTIONIST/ADMINISTRATOR

Playaway is a new learning and play centre for
children under 10 years.
We need a lively and energetic administrator
to join our new team.

**The successful applicant will possess the following
qualities and skills:**

- Good customer service and communication skills
- Attention to detail
- The ability to work to deadlines
- A pleasant and flexible attitude to work
- Fully conversant with Microsoft Office
- Smart appearance

Please apply In writing enclosing your current CV to
Maria Hancock, Manager, Playaway Ltd,
Whitecliffe Road, Marlton MR2 4MM

Closing date for applications is Thursday, 16 March.

Tone and style of promotional material

The tone of all promotional materials is positive and upbeat, often with eye-catching words or phrases. The style of a leaflet or a notice may be quite informal. Obviously this depends, to some degree, on the content. A notice about vacancies of interest to internal applicants will be more formal than one about a charity fun run.

The tone of an advertisement also varies. An advert for a staff vacancy, is formal and factual (and reflects the tone of the job description you read on page 63). An advert for a product, service or event is always written with the age and type of customer in mind. You will see this if you glance through any magazine or newspaper. Some adverts are informational, such as those in office equipment magazines for fax machines and photocopiers. In this case the advert will include product details. Other adverts are promotional, such as those for perfume and cars, where the advertisers are selling a life-style or an image rather than the product itself. Writing promotional adverts is a specialist job and you will not be expected to design one of these yourself in your examination.

Use of English

Adjectives are often used in promotional material. They describe nouns and pronouns and enable you to say something in a more appealing or persuasive way. For example:

Visit our café bar is factual, but not interesting or persuasive.

Visit our new, fully air-conditioned café bar is more tempting, especially during a long, hot summer.

You can also use adjectives to compare one thing to another.

▶ If you are comparing two people or objects then use '-er' or 'more', for example:

Our prices are *cheaper* than theirs *or*
We offer more *choice* than they do.

▶ If you are comparing more than two, use 'est' or 'most', for example:

Our prices are the *cheapest* in the country *or*
We offer the *most* choice in town.

▶ Remember that some adjectives change their form when you are comparing two or more than two, for example:

This is good. That is better. This one is the best.
He is old. She is the elder. He is the eldest.
This is bad. This one is worse. That is the worst of all.

▶ Finally, some adjectives are called 'absolute'. This means they stand alone and you shouldn't add another adjective to them. Examples include the words perfect, excellent and unique. So you can't say 'this is absolutely perfect' because perfection is as good as you get!

KEY TIP Don't think that the words less and fewer are interchangeable – because they're not. Use 'less' if you can't count the number and 'fewer' if you can. So you should say 'there is less space in this office' *but* 'there are fewer members of staff'.

COMMUNICATION IN BUSINESS

According to research by the Royal Mail, spelling mistakes and poor grammar cost UK business over £700 million a year in lost customers. Almost a third of consumers have stopped dealing with a company because they are weary of receiving sloppy or over-familiar communications or random emails, text messages and letters. The Royal Mail calculated the total cost of all these communication errors at £4 billion a year.

To improve communication skills, some companies are now insisting that their staff improve their spelling, grammar and written English by attending in-house training courses. At the directory enquiry company The Number 118118, all staff have to do a spelling test each week and at the PR company WhiteOaks, employees have a grammar and writing lesson every Friday morning so that press releases are accurately written. One of the first things staff learn is never to rely on computer spell-checkers and grammar checkers!

1. Adjectives can be confused if you're not sure of the exact meaning. Select the right option for each of the sentences below and then say what the *other* word means.

   a) The adverse/averse weather ruined our holiday.

   b) He works in a 10-story/storey building

   c) The book has faint/feint lines.

   d) He is practising his speech for the oral/aural examination.

   e) He is not a rational/rationale person.

   f) Tomorrow is the official/officious opening.

2. As a group, collect a selection of leaflets and compare the styles and designs. You will find these freely available at tourist information centres, at exhibitions, museums and in some supermarkets, as well as through the post and in newspapers and magazines. Assess these against the AIDA principles for their ability to attract your attention and interest you.

3. Last month, you applied for the Receptionist/Administrator's job at Playaway (see page 69) and were successful. You started work there last Monday. Playaway is currently planning its grand opening and Maria Hancock has drafted out a one-page notice advertising the event. She also wants to prepare a leaflet which can be distributed to households in the area. She likes the idea of a folded A4 leaflet.

   Maria has also decided to hold a balloon race to launch the grand opening. Each child who attends the opening will be given a balloon and tag, on which to write his or her name and address. A Playaway pass, which entitles the holder to free admission for 3 months, will be given to the ten children whose balloons travel the furthest.

   Decide on the type of folded leaflet you would prefer, and use the notice Maria has prepared (on page 72), and the information on the balloon race, to plan out an attractive leaflet to advertise the event. Indicate where you think graphics should be placed, if any.

4. Playaway is a huge success and, six months later, Maria decides she needs an accounts administrator. She tells you that she needs someone who is well organised, with good typing skills and a sound knowledge of Microsoft Office, especially word processing and spreadsheets. The successful applicant must also be able to work as a member of a team and be able to use his or her own initiative. Excellent numeracy skills are essential and previous accounts experience would be an advantage. All applications should be sent to Maria by Friday, 14 October at the Playaway address.

   Draft an advertisement for the vacancy.

PLAYAWAY

New learning and play centre for children under 10 years

GRAND OPENING

Saturday 21 April 9 am–9 pm

We provide high-quality child care with a wide range of play facilities

- ROSPA-approved play area
- Vetted staff
- Permanently staffed reception
- Interactive activities
- Parent and toddler sessions
- Tea room and ice cream parlour
- Party palace

Plus much more!

Playaway Ltd, Whitecliffe Road, Marlton MR2 4MM
Telephone (01787) 660881   Fax (01787) 660882
www.playaway.co.uk

5 The play organisers at Playaway have recently held a meeting with the staff at Marlton leisure complex. This focused on holding special water sessions for Playaway children, called Splashaway. Splashaway sessions will be held every Wednesday and Thursday from 2 pm to 3 pm and every Friday from 4 pm to 5 pm. During Splashaway sessions, parents go into the water with their children. Children must be aged between 2 and 6. There are toys, floats, nursery rhymes and fun play to help to build confidence in the water. All the supervisors are swimming coaches and hold ASA teacher's qualifications. The price per session is £3 and the sessions start during the first week of next month. Interested parents can book the sessions at the Playaway reception desk.

You have been asked to design a suitable notice for reception which advertises the Splashaway sessions. Indicate on your notice where you think a suitable graphic could be included.

Maintaining effective working relationships with colleagues and customers

Introduction

'People skills' are a key requirement in most organisations today. It is not enough to be able to carry out efficiently all the tasks you are given; you also have to be able to deal with other people in a professional manner. Two of the main groups of people you will deal with regularly are your colleagues and your customers. You will be expected to work with your colleagues to achieve common objectives and to provide assistance and information to your customers when required. You will also need to communicate with both groups regularly as an integral part of your job.

There is, however, a huge difference between a person who provides only a minimal service and someone who is well informed, friendly and helpful. It is very off-putting to deal with someone who is distracted, curt or surly. Similarly, you soon learn which of your colleagues are easy to work with, because they are cooperative, positive and willing to lend a hand when needed.

Of course, you cannot choose your colleagues any more than you can choose your customers, and this fact alone can create difficulties. Arguably, anyone can get on with people they like and enjoy being with. The hard part is learning how to develop and maintain good working relationships with people you find less easy to handle.

Studying this unit will not make you into a paragon of virtue, who never puts a foot wrong. As a normal human being you have good days and bad days just like everyone else. You also have strengths which other people admire – together with a few weaknesses that your friends and family have probably learned to tolerate! At work, people will be less inclined to do this. Therefore, the aim of this unit is to help you to understand about 'people skills' so that you can develop your own skills in this area and also learn some strategies for coping when things go wrong.

Unit summary

This unit is divided into two separate elements.

▶ **Element 1 – Working with colleagues**. This element focuses on working with your colleagues, particularly as a member of a team.

▶ **Element 2 – Working with customers**. This element covers the different situations you are likely to encounter when you are working with customers.

The skills you will learn in this unit will give you the ability to deal with other people thoughtfully, positively and effectively, so that you are able to develop and maintain effective working relationships with both your work colleagues and the customers you deal with.

Element 1: Working with colleagues

In this element you will learn how to:

▶ **Contribute to the work of a team**. This is about the importance of teamwork and the most important aspects of team working.

▶ **Confirm own responsibilities including working arrangements**. To be an effective team member yourself, you need to be clear about your own responsibilities.

▶ **Carry out tasks allocated**. Many of your colleagues – and certainly other members of your team, will need to depend upon you to do your job properly and as agreed.

▶ **Work with others to complete tasks**. This is about the importance of cooperating with other people and what to do if you are having difficulties.

▶ **Communicate effectively with others**. Your communication skills can help to create team harmony – or destroy it. To communicate effectively means learning many skills, including tact and diplomacy!

▶ **Maintain effective working relationships**. The relationships you have with your colleagues help you all to achieve your objectives more easily. Maintaining this with everyone, all the time, can be difficult if not impossible. In this section you learn what to do when things start to go wrong.

▶ **Review your contribution to the team activity**. A key way of developing your own skills is to look back at something you have done and analyse what went well and what did not – and your own contribution to this.

▶ **Review the overall performance of the team**. A team is more than a group of individuals so you will need to review the team's performance as a whole. This is the only way that the team itself can learn how to improve.

Assessment

Your assessment for Element 1 will involve you working as a member of a team on **two** separate occasions. Your tutor will set a substantial task for your team, which will involve a number of activities. For example, your team could be asked to prepare materials and arrange a special event, or research and select information from various sources and then create a leaflet or booklet. On each occasion you will be responsible for doing a series of activities on *your own*. You must also liaise with other members of your team when you are planning the work and to give regular progress reports. You will be expected to make a positive contribution when the team is discussing the work or asking for suggestions. Finally, you must produce a report on the team and its performance and explain how you overcame any difficulties you experienced in relation to the way the team worked together.

Your tutor will assess you in relation to *all* the aspects of teamwork you have learned. These are the items in bold, in the list above.

Element 2: Working with customers

In this element you will learn how to:

▶ **Present a positive image to customers.** This is about the importance of presenting a positive image to all your customers and why providing effective customer service is so vital.

▶ **Follow company procedures for communicating with customers.** All organisations have procedures for dealing with customers both face-to-face and on the telephone, to help their staff deal with a range of situations.

▶ **Interact effectively with customers.** This covers your communications with customers and how to develop your skills to deal with both routine and problem situations.

▶ **Use appropriate tone and manner.** It is pointless being smartly dressed and knowledgeable if your tone and manner with customers upsets or irritates them. This section looks at the importance of using the correct tone and manner in a variety of situations.

▶ **Convey information clearly and accurately.** This covers the importance of this skill and some of the problems that can occur if you are inaccurate, unclear or indiscreet – from minor difficulties to serious complaints!

▶ **Resolve difficulties using organisational procedures.** Not all customer relationships go smoothly. You may have complaints, difficult queries or problems to deal with. How to cope with these is dealt with here.

▶ **Record information accurately.** Your colleagues will often rely upon your written records about a customer. You will learn about the importance of keeping such records and why they are used.

▶ **Ensure customer requirements can be met.** Here you will learn how to check that your customers are satisfied that all their needs have been met.

Assessment

Your assessment for Element 2 will consists of practical activities. You will communicate with customers on **two** separate occasions. These will involve dealing with customers by telephone and face-to-face, finding out or checking information for a customer and identifying an initiating follow-up action.

On both occasions you will be assessed in relation to the first five aspects of customer service and the last two items in bold in the list above. On at least one occasion you will be assessed on your ability to resolve difficulties using organisational procedures.

▼ELEMENT 1 – WORKING WITH COLLEAGUES

You work with your colleagues every day, often as a member of a team. If you relate to other members of your team in a positive way then both you and the team as a whole will be more productive. In addition, your working relationships will be better, which means work is far more enjoyable. For these reasons, there are many benefits in knowing what to do – and what not to do – when you are working with your colleagues.

▼ CONTRIBUTE TO THE WORK OF A TEAM

Some people think that teams have little to do with administration or working in an office. They associate teams more with sporting activities. Traditionally this was true, but the benefits of teamwork are so great that today many organisations group their staff into teams, as you can see in many job advertisements. An administrator may work in a team of administrators or may provide support to, and be a part of, a separate team of people, such as the sales team or the marketing team.

Teamwork also benefits the members of the teams themselves, because they feel a key part of a small group, rather than one individual trying to cope alone. So, because of the emphasis on teamwork today, it is important to understand the skills that are required to be a good team member, which is one key focus of this unit.

The importance of teamwork and how it benefits the organisation

A good example of teamwork in a working environment is the emergency services. In the police, the fire service and the ambulance service, no one can operate individually, especially in an emergency. At a basic level, two paramedics simply moving a patient will do so with coordinated and skilled movements. At a more complex level, such as the scene of a road accident, all the different emergency services know their own role and how it fits with the other teams there. This type of skilled coordination means that the incident is dealt with as speedily as possible and nothing is overlooked. People don't get in each other's way, there are no arguments about who does what. The teams have complementary skills, so that each aspect of the problem is dealt with – releasing and treating injured people, redirecting traffic, clearing the area and removing any hazards. They work together, in harmony, to achieve a common objective as quickly and professionally as possible.

▲ Teamwork in action

A definition of a team is therefore:

A group of people who possess complementary skills and who work together to accomplish a common goal.

A famous writer about teams, Meredith Belbin, argued that a major benefit of teams is that the members, collectively, possess more strengths, i.e. a greater range of skills, than one individual. Belbin wasn't just referring to job skills. He also included other skills, such as problem solving, communications and an eye for detail. If you are good at setting up spreadsheets but poor at proof-reading, and your colleague is the opposite, then 'sharing' your skills brings you both mutual benefits. A team simply does this on a larger scale.

Most organisations encourage and promote team working because of this. The benefits they gain – and the benefits for individual members – are shown in the table below. Together these are more than sufficient to justify the continued emphasis on teamwork as an essential skill required by all administrators.

Benefits of teamwork

Benefits to the organisation	Benefits to the members
A greater range of skills and abilities	Social benefits, as members know they belong to a defined group of people and are not left to cope on their own
Work standards higher, as individual strengths and skills can be maximised	
Work completed more quickly	Practical and emotional support from other team members
Greater flexibility – team members can be multi-skilled to 'cover' for each other	Opportunities to share and exchange information and ideas
Less duplication of work or effort	
Improved communications because team members consult each other	Help and advice available when needed
Better cooperation between people within the organisation.	Greater job satisfaction as more work is produced more quickly and to a high standard
More motivated staff because of benefits to team members (see opposite)	Assistance during busy periods
	Joint problem solving when difficulties are encountered

Functions of the team and the roles of individual team members

The functions of the team will depend upon its key areas of responsibility. Its functions can be described in the same way that individual jobs can be said to comprise a list of separate tasks or duties – as shown in the job description on page 63. The difference is that the functions are not the responsibility of one person, but of the whole team.

For example, two functions of a marketing team may be to produce a customer catalogue and a staff newsletter each month. Producing the catalogue would mean photographing products, writing descriptions, writing any special features, designing the cover, preparing all the pages and arranging for printing and distribution. Producing the newsletter would involve writing articles, obtaining photographs or graphics as well as design, printing and distribution. The team would divide up the tasks to take account of the skills of each team member. One member of the team may be responsible for photographs and graphics, another for writing descriptions and articles, a third for preparing pages using a desk top publishing package and so on. Therefore each team member would have an individual, specialist role which contributed to the achievement of the functions for which the team is responsible.

A slightly separate role is that of team leader. The team leader is a member of the team but also has responsibility for the team as a whole and its performance. The team leader will allocate jobs amongst the team, discuss difficulties with them and be responsible for making certain that all the tasks undertaken by the team are carried out to the right standard and by the required deadline.

Important aspects of team working

Some teams are highly skilled and work together very effectively. Others are less so. Generally, teams become more effective if they are well managed and work together regularly, because the members know and understand each other's strengths and weaknesses better. A good example is in the world of football. Club players know each other well and are used to playing alongside each other. The England manager has a greater problem, however. The England team plays far less frequently, and comprises members from many different clubs. To help to compensate for this, before an important tournament such as the World Cup, the team will go away beforehand to practise together. This is not to improve individual skills, but to help to develop team working skills and to concentrate on the key aspects of team working, which are listed below.

▶ **Target setting and planning**   A team works towards a common aim or goal. For a specific project or task this is often defined as a target. Frequently, targets are set which are quantifiable. In plain English, this means they include figures – such as the date by when something will be completed, the number of items that will be produced and so on. For example, a football team may have the target of winning the UEFA Champions League next year and the marketing team mentioned above may have the target to produce 25,000 specially illustrated Christmas catalogues to be despatched to all customers on the mailing list by 12 November. Sensibly, targets should be planned well in advance to allow for all the preparatory work to be carried out in good time for the target to be achieved.

▶ **Clarifying objectives**   Objectives are 'steps along the way' towards achieving the target. A football team would know the matches they must win in advance to win a particular cup or league. The marketing team would have to work out exactly what tasks comprise the overall task they have to do. These sub-tasks are then shared out among the team with different members being responsible for particular jobs, either working with each other or on their own.

▶ **Identifying resources and timescales**   The next stage is to identify the resources required in terms of equipment, materials and human skills. Equipment availability can determine which type of tasks can be done internally and which may need to be undertaken by an outside company. Many materials may be kept in stock but others may need to be specially ordered. Some tasks may require specialist skills, which are possessed by only one member of the team, and this must also be taken into account.

All these factors affect the timescale by which a job can be completed. Extra time needs to be allowed if an outside company must do part of a job, if there will be a delay until certain materials arrive or if a specific member of the team can work on a specialist task only at a certain time.

▶ **Exchanging information**   This is essential both during the planning process of a team activity and when the work is being carried out. At the planning stage, ideas and suggestions should be put forward by everyone. This normally results in a better and more achievable plan than if the plan is devised by the team leader – who may have only limited knowledge of some aspects of the work.

When the work is being done, all members of the team must be kept up-to-date with developments, changes or other aspects of the overall task which will affect their own contribution. For that reason, it is normal to hold regular team discussions and, in addition, for team members to exchange information between them informally in relation to the tasks they are doing together.

▶ **Cooperating with others**   Working in a team means that the team objective comes above individual or personal objectives. This may mean readjusting the way you work or what you do next, to fit in with other people. For example, if you have two tasks to do, and you know that another member of your team is depending upon you to complete one of these quickly, then this should take priority. Cooperation, of course, is not a one-way street. If the team is to be effective, then you should be able to depend upon your team members to cooperate with you, too.

These are the most important aspects of team working. Other aspects which particularly relate to overall team effectiveness are identified below.

Team effectiveness

All team members

fully understand and are committed towards achieving the target	✓
are willing to put the team's aims above their personal aims	✓
understand their own role in the team and how this 'fits' with the roles of other team members	✓
take collective responsibility for the quality and quantity of the work produced	✓
feel they have equal status within the team	✓
respect the views of other team members, even though these may differ from their own	✓
are reliable and dependable	✓
feel their own contribution to the team is useful and valued	✓

PEOPLE IN BUSINESS

Developing team working skills is a major focus of many training activities run by organisations. These can be short events, held in-house, where teams get together, away from their desks, to discuss how they operate together and how this can be improved. Alternatively, they may be more elaborate events which are hosted by specialist training companies. In this case, the teams are usually faced with a challenge and have to overcome various obstacles. These are specially designed to test the team as a whole, rather than individual members. A key part of the activity is when the team evaluates its own performance at the end. This enables them to look back at their experience and suggest how they might have worked together better. Normally, the most successful teams are those that have good communications skills and those where the team members trust each other.

A new type of team today is a **virtual team**. These are teams which work on a project together from a distance, using computers to communicate with each other. To match this trend, some training companies are now providing on-line training for virtual teams – so that they, too, can develop their team working skills and abilities.

OVER TO YOU!

1 Three of the groups below work as a team, and three do not. Decide which are teams and which are not and give a reason for your decision in each case.

a) a band of musicians

b) check-out operators in a superstore

c) the pilot and co-pilot on an aircraft

d) the air traffic controllers in the control tower

e) solicitors in a group practice

f) nurses on a hospital ward.

She said he was sacked if she didn't get down safely

▲ Outdoor activities can help to develop team skills

2 A team of administrators holds a meeting to discuss a task they are doing together. They have to help to prepare a presentation that the sales director will be giving to some important prospective customers in two weeks' time. The team leader, Maria, asks Sara to research the information required, Tamira to prepare the graphs and pie charts and Max to produce the PowerPoint slides, because he is excellent at this. Maria will work with Suzie to prepare and photocopy all the literature to be given to the customers. She will also book the meeting room, arrange refreshments and check all the equipment is in working order.

a) What is the target of Maria's team?

b) Identify four objectives related to this target.

c) Suggest three resources the team will require.

d) If Sara is struggling to obtain the information, why is it important that she tells Maria?

e) Max needs Tamira to finish the graphs and pie charts before he can put these into the presentation, but – despite several promises – Tamira still hasn't completed these. How could Tamira's actions affect the overall effectiveness of the group?

f) Maria's boss, the sales director, has now suggested that the literature should be produced in full colour, but the company has only a black and white photocopier. The local print shop can do the job but needs three days' notice.

  i) Why would it have been better for this to have been decided at the outset?

  ii) What do you think Maria should do to ensure that the overall target is still achieved on time?

3 Each of the following people is talking about their team. Identify those who work in an effective team and those who do not. For each person who works in an ineffective team, suggest at least one key aspect of team working that is missing.

a) Jake: 'Team meetings are supposed to be a discussion but our team leader listens only to the people she likes. I've given up saying much these days.'

b) Alana: 'Judy is responsible for making sure we have the resources we need. Even when there are problems she seems to be able to find a solution and help us out.'

c) Joanne: 'Rebecca is a good laugh but she's so scatterbrained. A job takes twice as long if you're working with her.'

d) Soraya: 'Jon's very ambitious and sees himself as team leader next. I don't think he deserves it because he will do anything to suit the boss, even if it means letting us down.'

e) Nick: 'Our team leader has encouraged us to develop our own skills but insists that we are all multi-skilled, so that we can help each other out when necessary.'

▼ CONFIRM YOUR OWN RESPONSIBILITIES, INCLUDING WORKING ARRANGEMENTS

To be a dependable member of the team you need to understand *exactly* your own role and responsibilities. Therefore you must confirm:

▶ which tasks you have to do

▶ the resources you can use

▶ the timescales by which your work must be done

▶ the procedures you must follow if you encounter a problem.

You also need to identify:

▶ whom you will be working with

▶ what resources you will require for each stage of the task and their availability

▶ any limits which apply to your role.

The tasks you have to do

Working in a team means that you are rarely responsible for every aspect of an overall task. You may be allocated specific tasks to do on your own and/or certain tasks to do with other people. It is not sensible to rely on your memory – especially if you are given these tasks verbally. Sometimes, if there is a meeting of the team, you may be issued with a printed list of jobs with your name alongside those you must do. If not, then you should make your own notes and check that you have written everything down correctly. One way is to make out a checklist which contains all the information you need. An example is shown on page 84. You then have a constant reference source if you need to remind yourself what was agreed.

TEAMWORK CHECKLIST

Overall task . . . .

Purpose of the task . . . .

Deadline date for completion . . . .

Activities	Team member(s) responsible	Resources req'd	Deadline dates

Special notes on resources (e.g. quality of materials/equipment availability/allowable sources of reference)

Additional notes (on reporting back, limits of role, etc)

Some tasks may be familiar to you, in which case you will feel confident about doing them. Others may be new. If you are nervous about anything, then find out who can help you if you have any difficulties.

Normally tasks are allocated fairly between team members, bearing in mind people's skills and areas of interest. If you are unhappy about the tasks you have been given – either because you do not understand something or feel you have been given more to do than someone else – it is sensible to ask to speak to your team leader in private afterwards, rather than challenge the list in front of other people. There may be a very good reason why your team leader wants you to do something, so you need to find out if this is the case.

The resources you can use

Resources relate to materials and equipment. For many administrative jobs you will need stationery supplies, but these can vary greatly. Most organisations keep a range of stocks from top-quality items to standard ones. You would not be popular if you used the most expensive paper or folders, which have been kept back for a special event, just for a routine job. It is therefore important to check:

▶ **the type** of materials you require – plain or headed paper, envelopes, card, folders, etc.

▶ **the quantity** you are allowed to use – no one will expect you to use three packets of paper to produce 20 copies!

▶ **the quality** that is most appropriate for the task – as a rough guide, best-quality items are normally used for external jobs, such as a report to a customer, whereas standard items are used for internal jobs.

Using the correct equipment is also important. For example, you may have the option of more than one photocopier, more than one type of stapler or more than one type of hole punch. You need to select the one that is most suitable for the task in hand. If you used a small desktop photocopier for a large copying job, then it will take you much longer than if you used a larger, faster machine with a greater range of features (see page 338). If you used a small desktop stapler to fasten a thick batch of documents then you will have problems, because you should have used a heavy-duty one. Similarly, you can punch only a small quantity of documents at once with a normal hole punch. To punch a thick document you need a heavy-duty punch. Therefore it is not enough just to check the items of equipment you need, but that you have also selected the most appropriate for the task in hand.

The timescale by which your work must be done

There are two timescales you need to bear in mind.

▶ The deadline for separate tasks you have to complete.

▶ The deadline for the overall task.

As you saw on page 81, you have less freedom with timescales if other member(s) of the team need you to finish a particular task before they can start their own. If you cause a delay at this point then you will affect everyone else and there will be the danger that the job itself can no longer be completed on time.

Deciding which jobs must be done first is known as **prioritising**. You can read more about this on page 90.

The procedures you must follow if you encounter a problem

Problems can occur in several areas – but hopefully not all at the same time! For example:

▶ a task that you felt you could do easily may be more complicated or more difficult than you thought

▶ you may be unable to complete a task because you are waiting for information or help from someone else

- you may have a problem working with someone else in the team
- you may not be able to find the materials you are told to use or find there are not enough in stock
- you may have difficulties accessing or obtaining the equipment you need, or it may not be working properly
- you may take longer to do a task than you thought
- a complication may put the deadline for the whole job in jeopardy.

Until you become more experienced, it can be difficult to find the right balance between keeping your team leader informed of important difficulties – yet not panicking unnecessarily every time there is a slight hiccup. You may not want your team leader to think that you are incapable of coping on your own. On the other hand, it is important that you report back promptly if there is a serious problem. As a guide, it will help if you consider the consequences of a particular problem and then assess your own ability to sort things out on your own. You can also usefully divide problems into two main areas:

- task-based problems
- people problems.

You can try to sort out some task-based problems on your own first. If a task is complicated or is taking longer than you first thought, can another team member help you? This is where the support of other team members can be really valuable. If you are waiting for something from someone else, can you give that person a hand to help to speed things up? If, however, you have a problem with shortage of materials or access to equipment then you will probably have to ask your team leader for help.

▲ It is important to decide if a problem is serious and should be reported

People problems relate to difficulties working with other people in the team. As your people skills improve, you should get better at dealing with minor problems on your own (see page 109–121). If there is a serious problem, your team leader needs to be informed.

At this stage of your career, it is sensible to discuss at the outset what action your team leader would expect you to take on your own. Finally, if you are in any doubt, err on the side of caution. It is always better to consult your team leader if you are worried rather than overstep the limits of your role (see below). It is also important to give your team leader sufficient warning about a serious problem so that there is still time to take remedial action.

Who you will be working with

If you are working with someone else (or other people) to do certain tasks, then you will need to arrange a time when you are both available to do the work. You may also be expected to organise the work between you. To keep harmony in the team it is useful to remember to:

▶ share the work out as equally as possible

▶ *discuss* the options with your team members – don't tell them what to do!

▶ try to play to people's strengths – including your own

▶ don't expect someone else to do something you wouldn't be prepared to do.

Resource availability for each stage of the task

Planning ahead means checking that you have the resources you require *before* you start a task. This is also quicker, in the long run, than having to keep breaking off to find something. Occasionally, if many people use an item of equipment, you may have to arrange a specific time to use it, in advance. The same is true if you are asking someone to do you a favour or do a specialist task for you. You would have to work around their work schedule, not the other way round.

The limits of your own role

These define the actions you can take on your own and those you can't. For example, if you are finding out information you may have access to some files, but not to others. You may be expected to find out information on the Internet but not to phone a customer without prior agreement. You may be allowed open access to certain resources but have to obtain authorisation for others.

When you first start work, it is sensible to check with a more experienced colleague before you take any action that may not be allowed, if you are unsure of the limits of your own role. The golden rule is to ask whenever you are unsure. This is far better than overstepping the limit and then having to apologise afterwards or jeopardising the whole task.

▲ Knowing the limits of your role is vital

OVER TO YOU!

Jan Fielding is briefing Dawn, Tara and Nadia on a task she wants them to carry out. Jan is a member of an IT group in the college. The group has decided to produce a health and safety booklet for all students on the use of IT equipment. At the briefing she gives them the following instructions:

'Today is Monday and we've two weeks to do this job. First, we need to find out the key points to include in the booklet. Dawn, you're good at IT, can you please look at the HSE site on the Internet – that's the Health and Safety Executive site. See what you can find. Tara and Nadia, please can you visit the library and see if they've anything available – try both the college and the town libraries. When you've done that, look through everything together and highlight the points you think are most important. I think we need to cover posture, use of equipment and the Display Screen Equipment Regulations. We can all get together at 10 am on Friday to see how far you've got, so you'll need all your information by then. We'll then decide what to include on each page.

'I think the booklet should be about four pages, if it's any longer people won't read it. It would be good to have an appropriate illustration on the front. Nadia, you're excellent at graphics, so could you please do that. Tara and Dawn, can you word process the text on the pages and then let me see your draft pages for checking by next Wednesday. Use white A4 paper at this stage. By the way, I've arranged for you to use the computers in the IT office, it will be easier for you to concentrate there. They will be available from Monday to Wednesday. Finally, we can print out the booklet using the large photocopier next to the Admin office. That way, we can automatically collate and staple the booklets. We've some blue A4 paper in the stockroom that will be ideal. To save paper, I think we'll reduce the size so that the booklet is actually A4 folded into A5. As you haven't done this before, I'll show you what to do when you start photocopying on Thursday morning. We have until next Friday to complete the booklets because we have said we will have 3,000 ready to give out the following Monday.'

1 Working in groups of two or three, copy out the form on page 84 and complete it as if you were a member of Jan's team.

2 a) How many times has Jan arranged for the team to check back to her?

b) Why do you think she has done this?

3 When the team starts work, the following problems occur. In each case, state what action you think they should take.

a) On Tuesday, Nadia arranges to meet Tara to go to the library, but Tara is away ill that day.

b) On Thursday morning, Dawn loses her bag which contains the printouts she has taken from the HSE website.

c) On Friday, Nadia has a dentist's appointment for the time that Jan has suggested they meet together.

d) On the following Tuesday, there is a fault with the college network and they cannot use the computers.

e) On Wednesday, Nadia is still drafting out the illustration and isn't happy with it.

f) On Thursday, the team find that the photocopier is out of order and they cannot use it until it has been repaired.

4 The team are keen to use their own initiative when they can, but this can mean they sometimes overstep the limits of their role. For each of the following, state whether the action taken is acceptable or not. In each case give a reason for your answer.

a) Nadia's brother suggests he can obtain information for her from his workplace that might be useful, because they have a similar booklet there. Nadia asks him to do this.

b) Dawn finds three other useful sites on the Internet and prints out additional information.

c) Tara doesn't like the information that Jan has agreed for her page so decides to change it.

d) Nadia thinks the blue paper doesn't look as good as white, so changes the paper in the photocopier.

e) Dawn decides that it is too complicated creating A5 booklets and changes the photocopier setting to A4.

▼ CARRY OUT TASKS ALLOCATED

Once the overall task has been planned and the resources and timescales agreed at a team briefing, it is then up to individual members of the team to do the tasks they have been allocated. As you saw in the *Over to You* section above, sometimes things will go smoothly and at other times they won't. However, there are certain actions you can take to try to minimise the difficulties you might encounter.

Planning and prioritising

During the average day we all have several tasks to carry out. We may have also made arrangements to see people, telephone them or meet them at a certain time. At work, you will be expected to juggle a considerable number of tasks and arrangements so that you fulfil all your responsibilities. If there is a crisis, then you may have to select the key tasks to do and either leave the rest until another day or ask your team leader if someone else can help you.

It is never a good idea to trust to luck that you will remember everything. This is why, in every office, people use special systems to help them to remember what they need to do. Some, or even all, of the following may be used:

▶ a **diary** in which important jobs, meetings and appointments are listed

▶ an **action** and/or **pending tray** on the desk with all the 'to do' items stacked in order of priority

▶ an **action folder** with important documents inside

▶ a **'to do' list** of all the tasks to be done that day. As jobs are carried out they are crossed out and at the end of the day all outstanding jobs are listed for the next day

▶ a **wall planner** identifying important events and specific deadlines for tasks.

You can read more about planning aids in Unit 3, page 238.

Most administrators like a personal 'to do' list, even if they use other systems as well. Each morning they look through the list to see what must be done first. In other words, they put the list into priority order.

Prioritising is very important. You cannot simply do jobs in the order in which they were given to you. To prioritise you need to separate tasks into different categories, according to their urgency and importance.

Prioritising

CLASS A
Urgent and important – do these jobs FIRST.

CLASS B
Urgent but not important – do these jobs NEXT.

CLASS C
Important but not urgent. Remember, these jobs may be urgent tomorrow!

CLASS D
Neither urgent nor important. These are routine jobs which can be done last.

▶ **Class A** jobs are both urgent and important. These are the ones you should do first because the consequences of leaving them until later would be serious.

▶ **Class B** jobs are urgent but not important. In this case, the tasks *should* be done today but the consequences would be less serious.

▶ **Class C** jobs are important but not urgent. The problem with this category is that, if you leave these tasks long enough, you have to move them into class A.

▶ **Class D** are routine jobs which you should do because they are your responsibility. However, unless you leave them too long, there should be few problems if you put them to one side if you are very busy.

This may sound simple enough, but you have three other aspects of prioritising to consider.

The first is the temptation to be human, and to do the jobs you like, rather than the jobs you really should do! There may be a routine job you enjoy and there is a danger you will indulge yourself rather than concentrating on a less pleasant task which is more urgent. The secret here is self-discipline and sometimes the trick is to do the job first that you dislike the most! Then, once it's out of the way, life suddenly becomes more pleasant again.

The second aspect is that not all jobs take the same length of time. You may have six tasks which are 'class A', four of which would take you 10 minutes and two which would take much longer. Again the secret is to do the quicker ones first. This takes some of the pressure away and allows you to concentrate better on the remaining two, which are probably more involved.

The final aspect concerns how to classify your jobs if you simply cannot decide which tasks to do first. In this case, ask yourself:

▶ How serious would the consequences be if the job wasn't done today?

▶ Are you holding anyone else up if you don't do this job?

▶ How important is the person who gave you the job?

▶ How long will it take you if you concentrate on it?

▶ Is the deadline absolutely fixed – or could it be altered in a crisis?

Using this guide, you can then see that if a senior member of staff asks you to produce an important document to give to a customer who must leave in five minutes, this is absolutely top of your priority list.

Following instructions and agreed working practices

In every organisation there are agreed ways of doing particular tasks – from greeting visitors in reception to ordering stationery. These are often called organisational procedures and you will learn more about these in Unit 4. In a new job, you need to learn about the procedures used by your new employer. This is why the first week or two in a new job is always the worst!

When you are given a task to do, therefore, you have to abide by

▶ the specific instructions for that particular job

▶ the agreed working practices that operate in that organisation.

The specific instructions will be given to you at a team briefing, such as the one held by Jan Fielding and described on page 88. However, if you look back at this, you will see that Jan did not specify any working practices. These could include following specific procedures to obtain paper from the stockroom and to log the copies made on the photocopier.

When you first use equipment or do a task for the first time, you should be shown the specific procedures or working practices you must follow. If not, then ask someone to tell you what these are. It is always better to check first than to risk doing the wrong thing.

Working safely

No team leader is going to tell you that you should work safely each time you are given a task to do. It will be taken for granted that you will do this because it is in your own interest. You will learn more about health and safety in Unit 3, but in relation to carrying out tasks you are allocated, the key points to remember are as follows.

▶ Only use materials and equipment for the purpose for which they are designed.

▶ Don't use equipment you are not trained to operate or which you have been told not to use because it is faulty.

▶ Never poke about inside or try to repair equipment that isn't working properly.

▶ Never try to move an item of equipment without permission.

▶ If you are using something for the first time, read the instructions *first* – not later!

▶ Never take unnecessary risks which could endanger yourself or other people – such as running or leaving boxes where someone could fall over them.

▶ Work in a tidy manner and put your personal belongings out of the way.

▶ Close drawers in desks and filing cabinets immediately you have removed what you need.

▶ Never lift anything too heavy or carry anything which would block your vision.

▶ If you spill anything, wipe it up immediately; if you break anything, clear it up. Never put anything hazardous (such as broken glass) in the waste bin without wrapping it up first.

▶ Stack items safely.

▶ Use safety equipment where this is provided, such as a kick stool for reaching up to a high shelf.

▶ Wear protective clothing when you are told to do so.

▶ Follow *all* the instructions you have been given, regardless of whether you agree with them or not!

▶ Remember that even routine items in an office can be hazardous. Paper can give you a nasty cut, for example; a staple in your finger rather than in the page is extremely unpleasant.

▶ If you are using a computer, adjust the chair properly to support your back, sit straight and tilt the screen or keyboard to suit you. Take regular short breaks if you are doing a long job.

Respecting confidentiality and security issues

Many administrative tasks involve handling confidential information, for example:

▶ personal details about members of staff or customers (such as home address, telephone number, date of birth or age)

▶ payroll details

▶ work and health records of staff

▶ product information, plans for the future and financial information which would be of interest to competitors

▶ plans relating to internal changes which are still under discussion and have not yet been announced to staff.

All this type of information is classed as 'sensitive' – even if it does not have the word 'confidential' stamped on it. This means that you have to take special precautions if you are handling it.

▶ If you are photocopying, always remember to remove the original documents from the glass or the document exit tray afterwards.

▶ If you are looking in a file, keep the papers neatly together and put them away again immediately afterwards. Never take the file into a public area or leave it open on a desk.

▶ If you are sending a document to someone, put it in a sealed envelope.

▶ If you are throwing away a document, shred it.

You will also want your team leader to trust you! This means that you can be relied upon not to disclose information you are told in confidence or read in the process of doing a task. Discretion is an important skill to learn. If you love to gossip at work, this will severely limit the type of tasks you will be given – and your eventual career progression!

Security is closely linked to confidentiality, as you will know if you use a computer system. You will need to log in, with your user ID, and enter a password. Even then, the amount of information you would be able to access at work would be restricted. Supervisors and managers would have a higher level of access. This is to protect computer records relating to financial information, salaries and so on. Similarly, there may be special security systems in relation to access to certain areas (where a code has to be entered on a keypad on the door) and access to certain filing cabinets.

You must abide by all security restrictions and regulations which are in place. Never try to be creative and find a way around them. At work, this could result in disciplinary action being taken against you (see page 301). If you find that security restrictions prevent you from carrying out a task you have been allocated, then tell your team leader.

Meeting deadlines

Deadlines have already been discussed on page 85 – and so have some of the strategies to use to help you to meet them, such as prioritising. Sometimes, however, you may be asked to suggest a deadline yourself – or you may find that problems are arising which seriously threaten your ability to meet a deadline. This can easily happen if you underestimate the time it will take you to do something.

If you are asked to specify a deadline remember that this needs to be realistic. You can't ask for three days to type one page! However, a useful trick is to slightly over-estimate how long it might take you. This allows for interruptions and minor difficulties. It also gives you the opportunity to surprise your team leader by completing a task earlier than expected.

Some deadlines are non-negotiable. This means that, if there are problems, your team leader must know so that additional help can be given to you if you are running out of time. Other deadlines may be slightly more flexible. You can spot the difference if you think, again, about the consequences of the deadline not being met. If it would be disastrous, then this is very different from the fact that someone may be slightly inconvenienced for a day. If a deadline is renegotiated, then – out of courtesy – you should contact anyone who is likely to be disappointed by the delay, and apologise. Then focus on meeting the new deadline without delay!

Using your initiative to solve problems

Good administrators take a personal pride in always meeting their deadlines first time, unless the reason for the delay is completely out of their control. Even then, they will have taken all steps possible to try to solve the problem themselves.

Learning to use your initiative is a very important skill, and one which is highly valued by employers. It separates the excellent administrators from the average ones. You use your initiative when you solve routine difficulties by thinking of a way around them. For example:

▶ You have been told to research information on the Internet but the site you were given is 'down'. You use your initiative if you use a good search engine, such as Google, to see if there are other suitable sites.

▶ You are told to obtain information from someone who is away ill. You then think who else might have a copy and contact them instead.

▶ The printer linked to your computer is faulty – so you copy a document onto a floppy disk and log on to another computer to take a printout.

▶ You are told to contact a customer urgently but when you ring their home phone you get the answer phone. You therefore leave a message and then check in the file to see if there is a mobile number listed.

▶ An important file you need is missing from the cabinet – so you check the filing trays and any records which list borrowed files to try to trace it.

In all these cases, a possible delay which might have affected a deadline has been avoided. If you put these together over the course of a month or year at work, you can soon see why administrators who use their initiative are so highly sought after!

OVER TO YOU!

1 The following tasks are on Gemma's 'to do' list for today, Monday.

a) Classify these into A, B, C or D tasks.

b) Decide in which order she should do all the Class A jobs.

c) If Gemma had to abandon one urgent job altogether, which should it be and why?

Gemma's 'to do' list

Check email for today
Send out catalogues to two prospective customers
Get filing up to date
Photocopy sales report for meeting, Wednesday
Send email to say tomorrow's team meeting cancelled
Book restaurant table for customer meeting, tomorrow lunch
Research train times on Internet for Brian's trip next week
Order presentation folders for Friday (supplier needs three days' notice)
Finish article for staff magazine, deadline today
Log last week's sales visits on database
Type letters to candidates for Friday's interviews
Type up answerphone messages from over the weekend
Tidy stationery cupboard
Fax location map to customers for tomorrow's meeting

2 Gemma is involved with the customers who are visiting the company tomorrow. Identify which of the following are her specific instructions for doing this task and which are agreed working practices in Gemma's organisation. For each working practice, suggest *why* this is a requirement.

a) All visitors reporting to reception on arrival must be issued with name badges.

b) When the visitors arrive at reception at 10 am, Gemma will meet them.

c) All car parking for visitors must be booked in advance, with the senior administrator.

d) Visitors must not be allowed to walk around the building unaccompanied.

e) Tomorrow's visitors will be taken, by Gemma, to the MD's office.

3 You are working with three colleagues to carry out some tasks for your tutor in the Admin office. Explain the action you would take in each of the following situations bearing in mind that you are working as a member of a *team*.

a) The paper jams in the photocopier. Although none of you have yet been trained to rectify this, your friend says she can manage and starts to peer around inside it.

b) A visitor arrives and says he urgently needs to contact your tutor that evening and asks for her home telephone number.

c) You have been asked to send a very urgent fax message but every time you try the number it is engaged. You have now been trying for over half an hour.

d) You decide to work through your break to finish your section of an urgent document and put down a can of drink next to your keyboard. Two minutes later you knock it over. Now your keyboard won't work.

e) You agreed to prepare a spreadsheet but are having problems with the formulas. You said you could do it in an hour but after 45 minutes you are nowhere near finishing it and the numbers still look wrong.

▼ WORK WITH OTHERS TO COMPLETE TASKS

The whole purpose of being a member of a team is that you work together cooperatively to complete a task. This benefits everyone. You have support and help when you need it – and so do they. However, some teams are **dysfunctional**. In other words, they don't work well together. Team members may argue, hold each other up, play silly games with each other (such as deliberately keeping a team member waiting for something), not communicate with each other – or all of these. In this situation, working in a team can rapidly become a nightmare.

Cooperation doesn't just happen, as if by magic, and sometimes it can be hard to cooperate with someone you find difficult to work with. If all team members know the main points to bear in mind, and respect each other's feelings, then there is a far greater chance the team will function well together.

A key aspect of cooperation is communication, which you will read more about on pages 100–108. You are not, for example, being cooperative if you withhold important information from someone who needs it. Good communication is also required for other reasons, as you will see below.

Reporting progress

If you are doing a task that involves other people it is both courteous and sensible to let them know whether you are on schedule, working ahead of time or are having problems meeting the deadline. This means talking to your team leader as well as to other members of your team.

If you are on schedule, then everyone knows there is no need to be concerned about your contribution. If you are ahead of time, then you may be able to help someone else who is having difficulties. If you are having problems, then you may need help.

Remember that there are two aspects to reporting progress. One is the information that you give and the other is the way that you do it! You won't be popular with your team if you brag when you are doing well and whinge or moan whenever you have a problem, or blame other people. Remember that you will be judged on how well the *team as a whole* did the task and worked together. If the task was done well and ahead of time – but none of the team is speaking to each other at the end – this is a very poor team performance overall!

Identifying and conveying essential information

Essential information affects *any* part of *any* task being carried out by *any* member of the team. If you fail to pass it on promptly (or pass it on inaccurately) then you would create serious problems for someone else. It is infuriating to be given a critical piece of information too late – such as someone saying, just after you skipped lunch to finish typing an urgent document, 'Oh, didn't you know? Kelly's had to go out and said it would do tomorrow.'

At first, you may be uncertain which information is essential and which is not. In this situation, you are still better to say something. If the information doesn't affect anyone very much, they will probably just shrug and carry on – but you haven't created any problems. Always pass information on promptly, too, otherwise you are in danger of forgetting it. If you find out something when some of the team are not around, write it down so that you won't forget.

The final point is to make sure you pass on information *accurately*. Only pass on facts – not rumours or 'best guesses'. If you are not sure whether your information is correct then either check it yourself or tell your team that you are not sure and make a joint decision what to do. The consequences of passing on inaccurate information can be as bad as keeping information to yourself, and could even result in one of your team making a serious mistake as a result.

Asking for help and offering help

Everyone likes to think they are helpful, but we all know that we regard some people as more helpful than others. You can test how helpful you really are by answering this question. One team member is struggling to complete a really boring job (that you hate doing) and you are doing an interesting one. At your current rate of working you will finish before she does. How tempted would you be to slow down, so that you don't have to help her to finish it?

There is an old saying 'what goes around, comes round'. In this context, it is true that normally the more often you offer help yourself, the more willing other people will be to help you. You probably know yourself that it is far harder to turn down a request from someone who often helps you out. Many people at work deliberately try to 'build up' favours from other people, on the basis that, when they need a favour themselves, they have several people they can ask.

If you need to ask for help yourself, then you will improve your chances if:

▶ you have a reputation for being helpful yourself and good to work with

▶ you ask positively and remember to say 'please' and 'thank you'

▶ you explain exactly what you want help with and how long the job is likely to take

▶ you are wise enough to include a compliment in your request, for example, 'Shahida, I'm sorry, I know you're busy, but I'd really appreciate your help checking these figures. You've a far better eye for detail than me, so I would know they'll be right.'

▶ you are prepared to accept a refusal graciously, i.e. without sulking or getting angry, especially if that person is genuinely too busy or doesn't know enough to help you.

You should offer help yourself when you see someone is struggling or if you have spare time on your hands. Volunteering is always better than waiting to be asked, but do this positively (and tactfully) too. Saying brightly: 'Can I give you a hand?' is much better than muttering, 'You look as though you've got a problem. I suppose I'd better help you to get it finished in time.'

Identifying difficulties

Difficulties may occur when

▶ you are trying your best to communicate with your team, but other people are letting you down

▶ someone else regularly doesn't pass on essential information

▶ you desperately need help urgently, and everyone else is busy

▶ someone asks for your help, but you are too busy to comply.

Team communications and working relationships are dealt with in the next two sections. Fundamentally, however, the important point is that the *more* the team communicates in a positive and tactful manner, the less likely it is that problems will arise. This is because you can raise your concerns, at the time, without upsetting anyone. You will find out how to do this on page 107.

If you need help to meet a deadline but everyone is genuinely very busy, then see your team leader – not to complain about the others but to say that there is a problem.

If someone asks for your help when you are too busy, so that you cannot comply without jeopardising your own work, then aim to give an explanation followed by a suggestion, such as 'I'm really sorry I can't help you at the moment because I have to finish this report for Ken. Why don't you try Carla? I think she's just finished the photocopying she was doing.' This is always better than a flat refusal!

▲ Cooperation is a key aspect of team work

OVER TO YOU!

Jen, Damian and Fiona work in a team. Their team leader is called Marie. They are all working hard to prepare for a sales conference to be held at a nearby hotel in two weeks' time. Jen is preparing the PowerPoint presentation, Damian is preparing spreadsheets and liaising with Finance about these, Fiona is preparing marketing materials. There are a series of progress meetings being held and the next one is tomorrow afternoon. At these meetings, Marie checks that all the work is going smoothly and that there are no problems.

1 The following events happen on Monday. In each case, state the correct action the team member should take and identify the consequences if they don't.

a) Finance ring at lunchtime and speak to Jen. They say the sales figures for last year have been amended.

b) Fiona hears a rumour that the computer network might be 'down' for maintenance later today.

c) The hotel phones and tells Damian that their data projector for the presentation has broken and won't be available on the day.

d) Marie sees Jen in the corridor and tells her that the next progress meeting has been rescheduled for Wednesday.

e) Damian puts the marketing folders Fiona has prepared into a cupboard whilst she is at lunch, because they are in his way.

2 At the progress meeting, each member has to report back on progress. Jen is struggling, because she has only just learned PowerPoint, but doesn't like to say anything. Damian is on schedule and says he will complete the spreadsheets by the end of the week. Fiona is boasting to Marie that she has almost finished the marketing materials and telling her about all the difficulties she has overcome.

a) Why do you think it is important that Marie holds progress meetings?

b) Identify two dangers of Jen not being honest about her problem.

c) Why is Fiona's attitude not helpful to the team?

d) Suggest four way(s) in which the lack of communication skills and trust between the team members could threaten the overall task *and* relationships between them?

3 On Wednesday afternoon, Marie is very busy and has put a 'Do Not Disturb' sign on her door. Jen receives a call from the Managing Director's office asking if Marie can attend a special meeting at 9 am tomorrow related to the conference. What do you think Jen should do, and why?

▼ COMMUNICATE EFFECTIVELY WITH OTHERS

As you have just seen, communication skills between team members are very important. Some communications are formal – such as the meetings with Marie. Others are informal – such as when a team is working together on a task and talking between themselves.

Team members also have to communicate with other people – their boss, or team leader, other people in the organisation and external people. In the example above, the team communicated with Marie, Damian is liaising with Finance and they received a telephone call from the hotel.

Effective communications are:

▶ accurate in every detail

▶ easy to understand

▶ sent in good time for the proper response to be made

▶ prepared with the recipient and the situation in mind – in terms of their style, tone and wording

▶ sent using the most appropriate method, for example face-to-face discussion, telephone or email. The key points to bear in mind when choosing the best method are shown opposite.

Basically you can choose to talk to someone or write to them. In Unit 1, you learned about written communications so this section simply summarises the main points to remember. The main focus of this section is your verbal communication skills with other people.

Choosing the best method of communication

Communicate verbally		Communicate in writing	
Face-to-face if	**Telephone** if	**On paper** if	**By email** if
The information is confidential or personal	You are busy and it would take time to see someone in person	You need a written record for the file	The matter is urgent
The matter is urgent and you see the person regularly	The matter is urgent and the person is some distance away	You are contacting someone who hasn't got email	The person is difficult to contact by phone
You are giving really bad news	You need a rapid response to a query	You are contacting someone who rarely reads email	You are busy and want to pass the information on quickly
You need to have a discussion	The information is quite straight-forward	Your team leader has asked for this method	The information is too long or complex to be said over the telephone
You want to ask someone to do you a favour		You are giving a copy to everyone at a meeting	You need to send an attachment
			You want a written record that you passed on the information

Verbal communication skills

You speak to people every day, mainly in a very informal way. At work you may have to change your style, especially in more formal situations or if you are talking to someone who is senior to you or important to the business. This doesn't mean you cannot be pleasant and friendly, it's just that the words and phrases you choose should be different. This applies whether you are speaking to someone face-to-face or over the telephone.

Face-to-face communications

You communicate with people face to face informally all the time – such as speaking to the person at the next desk or to someone standing next to you. Formal examples of face-to-face communication are when you have a review meeting with your boss about your work or attend an interview. You also communicate face-to-face as a member of a group if you attend a meeting. Because you will be contributing to a general discussion, the communication skills you need here are slightly different again.

Whenever you are communicating face-to-face you give and receive information in three ways. First, through the words that you speak and hear, second through your tone of voice and third by means of body language. These are the unspoken signals you send when you shrug your shoulders, frown, smile, nod or even slouch! You receive the same type of signals from other people – from their posture, facial expression, gestures and eye contact (or lack of it).

With your friends, it is normal for your words and body language to match. If you say you are fed up then you probably look as though you are! If you and a close friend are approached by someone neither of you like very much then your body language will reflect this. You will probably stand closer together, not look at the newcomer and keep your body turned away from them – even if you turn your head to acknowledge them. On the other hand, if you are approached by someone you like, you will turn fully towards them (or even move towards them), smile and perhaps even touch them.

At work, either of these approaches may be considered rather extreme – especially if the person is senior to you. Your boss would not expect to be virtually ignored but could be quite alarmed to be suddenly grabbed by the arm! People therefore modify both the words they use and their body language at work. However, sometimes they don't get this quite right. A good example is the person who sweetly agrees to retype a document for the boss and then sighs heavily or bangs things around on the desk; or people who offer to help and then look annoyed when their offer is accepted. And everyone steers clear of a colleague who is obviously in a foul mood even though not a word has been spoken!

For all these reasons, it is important that you are aware of your body language at work, as well as the words that you speak.

In many cases, talking to other people is simply a case of thinking before you start to speak and remembering your manners. The golden rules to follow are shown in the table opposite.

Communicating by telephone

Taking a telephone message was covered in Unit 1, page 10. This section looks at your verbal communication skills in this situation.

The major difference between communicating with someone by telephone rather than face-to-face is that they cannot see your body language – and you cannot see theirs. You therefore have fewer clues to guide you about their feelings and attitude and their response to what you are saying.

For these reasons, the emphasis is more on what you say – so accuracy and clarity become more important. You will create problems unless:

▶ you think carefully about what you are going to say in advance

▶ you make certain that you have a list of the key points you must mention

▶ you identify yourself clearly

▶ you speak clearly and don't use words or jargon the listener won't understand

▶ you concentrate on what is being said in reply

▶ you take notes so that you don't forget what you are told

▶ you pass on only information that you are certain about. If you don't know something then say so!

▶ you check words or phrases that you don't understand

▶ you 'sum up' the conversation at the end, to check there are no misunderstandings.

These are key points to remember, regardless of whether you are speaking to a colleague in the next office, a senior manager or an external contact. However, there are one or two other useful guidelines to bear in mind in relation to the *differences* between speaking to someone you know well – such as a team member – and someone you do not.

Face-to-face communications – the golden rules

1 Look pleasant and smile at people. It doesn't cost you anything!

2 Choose the right time to approach someone. Don't try to pass on important information if someone is very busy or distracted.

3 If you must interrupt someone, say 'Excuse me, I'm sorry to interrupt but . . .'

4 Think first, then speak – not the other way round!

5 Speak to people clearly and using the right volume – don't shout (or mutter).

6 Look at the person you are speaking to – if you don't make eye contact then you look as if you're trying to hide something. If you carry on with what you are doing (e.g. reading, typing) then you will look as if you are ignoring them.

7 Use an appropriate tone of voice and choice of words for the person you are talking to. Generally, the phrases you would use to a close friend or colleague aren't the same as those you would use with a senior or much older member of staff.

8 Get to the point and keep to it. Don't take 10 minutes to say something which could be said in two.

9 *Listen* when someone is speaking to you. Don't interrupt and don't be so impatient for them to finish that you can't remember what they said afterwards.

10 Make sure your body language matches the words you say!

11 Watch the other person's body language to check that their reaction to what you are saying is positive. Otherwise, think about changing your own tone and style.

12 Pass on confidential information only when you are alone with the person who needs to receive it.

13 Give people 'thinking time' if you are passing on something complicated or which needs a decision.

14 If you are shy then try to forget yourself and focus on the information you are communicating. This is especially important if you struggle to speak to someone senior or talk when you are in a group.

15 If you are in a group and are trying to make yourself heard, don't shout over everyone else. Instead, lean forward and try to get the attention of the person running the meeting by making eye contact.

16 If you are bored when someone is talking to you then watch your body language. Checking your watch, leaning back or looking out of the window will give you away. So will doodling in a meeting!

With your team remember:

▶ to be as courteous, clear and concise as you would be with anyone else. If you are annoyed with a team member then don't express your feelings over the telephone – and *never* slam down the receiver in anger! In a conflict situation, you are much better talking face-to-face (see page 115).

▶ to take messages with as much care as you would for your boss. Don't make extra work for your colleagues by forgetting to write down important points.

- to keep your call business-like. Exchanging gossip or information about your social lives should be done at lunchtime!

- to help out by answering the telephone if someone is very busy or away from their desk

- to find out who is calling if you answer the telephone for someone else.

With other callers remember:

- if you answer the telephone state your name (and department in a large organisation)

- if you are making the call on behalf of someone else, then say so; for example, 'Joanne Barnes asked me to ring you about . . .'

With all callers note that:

- making jokes or light-hearted conversation on the telephone is unwise unless you know the person *very* well. Because your body language cannot be seen, the listener cannot tell whether you are serious or not – and may not share your sense of humour either!

- you should always guard against giving confidential or sensitive information without specific permission from your team leader (see page 93).

▲ It is not normally a good idea to make jokes during business phone calls

Written communication skills

All verbal communications are over quickly. If you say something tactless or insensitive in a conversation and spot an adverse reaction, then you can apologise. If you say something you later regret, then you can hope that people have forgotten about it. If you do this in writing then the evidence is there forever and, if it is filed, for everyone to see! For that reason, it is very important that you take great care with your written communications. Always 'think before you write', even if the document is only for internal use.

It is also not acceptable to think that, because you are communicating in writing to a team member, you can scribble down anything. No one wants to receive a message they cannot read or understand, or to find a scrawled or scruffy note on their desk. It is also important to:

- keep to the point and not to add personal remarks or opinions, unless you have been asked for these
- check you have included all the key points
- check that your punctuation, spelling and grammar is correct
- make sure that your tone and wording is appropriate, bearing in mind the situation and the recipient(see below)
- avoid writing anything you wouldn't be happy to read in six months' time!

PEOPLE IN BUSINESS

Wired Magazine's website recently carried a business news report about people who had seriously jeopardised a relationship, or their job, by sending an email to the wrong person. The worst examples were people who had bad-mouthed their colleagues (or their boss) and then sent the email to that very person, rather than the one they intended. Some have even been sacked as a result. A link to the website can be found at www.heinemann.co.uk/hotlinks.

The perils of email are so great that they have even triggered a television programme, 'Emails you wish you hadn't sent'. It is all too easy to write something you could regret later – and press 'send' too quickly – perhaps whilst you're still thinking about the person you're writing about so you type their name in the address line.

It is also dangerous to rely too heavily on your email address book! One team member had a nasty shock when he nearly sent an email intended for a colleague called John (whom he knew well) to an important customer – also called John. His email started with the words 'I reckon you're an idle, good-for-nothing layabout!' The moral of this story is to check the address line carefully – particularly as email 'auto-completes' with the surname if it *thinks* it knows the name of the recipient!

Styles and manner of address

The styles and manner of address you should use in written communications were covered in Unit 1, under the different types of documents you might prepare. In verbal communications, they will depend upon the person you are communicating with and the organisation you work for. Some organisations are quite formal and senior staff are addressed by their surname. In others, even the Managing Director may prefer to be addressed by his or her first name. Until you are sure, err on the side of formality. You will quickly be corrected if the situation is different.

The same is true with external contacts, as you will see on page 136.

If you are involved in a meeting, bear in mind that:

▶ the way you should act and talk to the chairperson who is running it will depend on its formality. In a formal meeting you may hear this person actually addressed as 'Mr (or Madam) Chairman (or Chairperson)'. Obviously you won't find this happening in an informal group discussion.

▶ in most cases it is usual to 'talk through the chair'. In other words, you don't address remarks directly to other people in the group, unless there is an open discussion on a topic. This is to help the person running the meeting to control it as it prevents interruptions and people talking together about something instead of addressing the whole group.

Language and tone

In Unit 1 you saw that language and tone should vary in written communications depending upon the person, the situation and the type of document you are preparing. Language and tone is also important when you are speaking to people.

▶ **Language** refers to the words and phrases you use. You shouldn't use slang or the current expressions you would use with your friends if you are speaking to someone older, more senior or external to the organisation.

▶ **Tone** refers to the way you say something, which is reflected in your tone of voice. It is quite possible to say a simple statement like 'thank you very much' in a variety of ways – ranging from obvious gratitude to outright anger!

A useful tip, if you are in a new or unknown situation, is to watch, listen and copy other people who are more experienced. Otherwise, if you are on your own, then remember the golden rules you read on page 103.

Diplomacy and tact

This means phrasing your words carefully so that you don't cause offence or upset anyone, even when you are telling them something they would rather not hear. There is a story about a tactful assistant in a shoe shop who, rather than saying, 'Madam, your left foot is larger than your right' would say, 'Madam, your right foot is smaller than your left.' Both statements mean the same thing, but you can guess which the customer would prefer to hear!

You may need to be diplomatic when you are giving someone bad news or are 'interpreting' a remark that someone else has said to you. For example, a visitor arrives in your office and asks to see your team leader. If her response, when you tell her is: 'Oh, heavens, not him again. I've got tons to do today. Get rid of him, will you?' then you can hardly repeat this to the visitor! A tactful interpretation would be 'I'm very sorry but Jan is really busy at the moment. Can I help you at all?'

▲ It is helpful to be diplomatic sometimes

You also need to be diplomatic when you are talking about your team to someone senior or about any of your colleagues to external contacts. It is doubtful that any team member would thank you for mentioning a mistake they have made or a problem they struggled to overcome to anyone outside the group – no matter how amusing you thought it was.

If you want to practise your diplomatic skills, remember that tactful people:

▶ always think about a person's reaction to what they might say *before* they say it

▶ don't lie – but may omit details that someone would find hurtful or embarrassing

▶ always try to communicate in a positive way

▶ are never rude or sarcastic

▶ make neutral or factual statements that are unlikely to cause offence, even when they are disagreeing with someone. They also help other people to 'save face' by putting the responsibility on themselves, for example, 'I'm sorry, but according to my notes yesterday, we agreed to meet on Tuesday. Is this still the case?' *not*, 'What on earth are you talking about? Yesterday you said it was Tuesday!'

1 As a group, decide how you would interpret each of the following body language 'signals'.

a) When you are talking to your boss she glances at the clock and starts to drum her fingers on the desk.

b) You see a close friend sitting with her head in her hands.

c) You watch a young man in reception smoothing his hair and then straightening his tie before he approaches you.

d) When you are giving a complicated message to a colleague he never looks up from the document he is reading.

e) You see a manager talking to one of your colleagues. He is stabbing his finger in the air and she is shaking her head frantically.

2 Decide a more tactful way to say each of the following:

a) 'You must be joking!'

b) 'I suppose so.'

c) 'If you take anything else off my desk without asking first, I'll swing for you.'

d) 'Haven't you got the hang of that yet?'

e) 'I wish you'd shut up. Some of us have work to do around here.'

f) 'No, we can't deliver it this week. I told you before we need ten days' notice.'

g) 'How old are you?'

h) 'I haven't had time yet, have I?'

3 As a group, decide how you would phrase each of the following messages to cause the least offence, both verbally and in writing. Then prepare a short *written* message for each one.

a) A message to your boss that the reason no one turned up for her meeting was because she forgot to put the date it would be held on her email.

b) A message to your team leader saying that you can't stay late tomorrow night, as requested, because you have already made arrangements to go out.

c) A message to a team member from your team leader, Jo, that you are to take over the work your colleague has been doing updating the customer database. Instead, she must help out in the mailroom tomorrow. You know this is because she is making a mess of the database and taking too long – and you need the files to do the work. You also know she doesn't like working in the mailroom.

d) A message to a customer who was confused about a bill and has paid the wrong amount. He paid £750 last week by cheque but still owes your firm £100.

e) A message to a senior manager that you can't let him have the file he said he needed urgently because your team leader, Jo, is working on it at home today.

Most of us like to work in a pleasant environment. People want to do their jobs to the best of their ability, to be appreciated and to enjoy the company of their colleagues. They don't want to be kept guessing, ignored, told off or insulted. Most organisations appreciate this and work hard to develop good relationships both with and between the staff. They know that, if they do, then their staff will concentrate all their efforts on doing their jobs – rather than spend valuable time and energy squabbling or being upset.

Even if you work for a superb organisation which regards its staff very highly, you will still have to make an effort to develop and maintain your own working relationships with your colleagues. This is quite easy if you like everyone you work with and have a relatively easy-going personality. It is less so if there are some people you find more difficult or if you sometimes have problems controlling your own emotions. In addition, at work you cannot choose your colleagues. Therefore, it is unlikely that you will automatically get on well with everyone you have to deal with. How to cope with different personalities or if you are in conflict with someone else is covered on page 115. In this first part we look at some of the types of behaviour that will help you to develop and maintain good working relationships with the majority of people you work with, including other people in your team.

The nature of business relationships

Most business relationships are different from your social relationships. You may make some close friends at work, start to see them socially, and stay in contact with them over many years. This is the exception. In most cases you will find the following.

▶ The only common interest you have with your colleagues is the organisation, the managers and your respective jobs. This means that whilst you can talk to them at length whilst you are working together, on a social evening you may struggle to find much to talk about unless they are your own age and have the same interests as you.

▶ Colleagues at work can become quite friendly, quite quickly – mainly because of the number of hours they spend together each week. However, if someone leaves, they are forgotten very quickly.

▶ Because people work closely together – and are often under pressure – minor incidents can get blown up quite quickly, and rumours and gossip can cause strong reactions.

▶ Most organisations are hierarchical. This means that you are working with people at different levels. Senior, older and more experienced staff will expect you to comply with their instructions and give them respect for their seniority and status – regardless of your personal opinions.

▶ You are paid to do a job and to act professionally with everyone else. This means that you cannot behave in ways that might be quite acceptable with your friends or family.

Both the style of organisation and the behaviour of individuals affect relationships within the business. In an organisation where there is good management and staff harmony, working relationships will be effective and productive. The other key aspects that denote the difference between good and poor relationships are shown in the table on page 110.

Effective and ineffective working relationships

Effective working relationships
- ▶ People cooperate with each other
- ▶ Communications are good
- ▶ People consider each other's feelings
- ▶ People focus on the job, not on internal politics or gossip
- ▶ Everyone is courteous to each other
- ▶ There is loyalty and camaraderie
- ▶ People are respected and supported, even when things go wrong
- ▶ People are praised for effort
- ▶ Decisions are fair and the reasons are explained
- ▶ People listen to each other and value each other's views and opinions
- ▶ Differences of opinion are openly discussed in a positive manner

Ineffective working relationships
- ▶ People blame each other when something goes wrong.
- ▶ Communications are poor
- ▶ No one trusts anyone else
- ▶ There is obvious favouritism
- ▶ People take each other for granted
- ▶ Instructions are poor or muddled
- ▶ There are constant arguments
- ▶ There is open conflict
- ▶ Some people obviously work less hard than others – but nothing is done about it
- ▶ Some decisions seem unfair but no explanations are given
- ▶ Some people are self-opinionated or arrogant and ignore the feelings of others
- ▶ People are 'shown up' in front of their colleagues

PEOPLE IN BUSINESS

Each year, the *Sunday Times* publishes the *100 Best Companies to Work For* list in the UK. This is compiled from the opinions of employees who answer a complex survey, in confidence, and send their comments to the organisers. The survey includes questions on overall leadership in the business, day-to-day management, personal growth of individuals, wellbeing of staff, team relationships, giving back to society and the local community, the way the company treats its staff and pay/benefits.

In 2003, the top ranked company was Microsoft with 1,595 staff – 89% of whom said they loved working there. Second was Richer Sounds, the hi-fi retailer with less than 500 staff, 90% of whom reported that their teams were 'fun to work with'. 90% liked the fact that they can have a laugh with their colleagues. Teams also scored highly with the third ranked employer, Flight Centre, a travel agency, where over 90% of staff also said their teams are great to work with.

If you want to find out more, and check out the remaining 97 winners, go to www.heinemann.co.uk/hotlinks and follow the links – but remember that if you are reading this after 2003 the winners' names may be different!

Rights and responsibilities in the workplace

By law, every employee in the UK has specific rights and responsibilities both to their employer and to their colleagues. Equally, employers also have rights and responsibilities to their staff. You will read more about these in Unit 3 (pages 294–306) but in this section it is important to know how they affect your working relationships with other people.

An important area is **equality**. **Discrimination** against anyone is illegal if it is on the grounds of gender or race or because of a disability. Discrimination simply means treating someone differently and unfairly.

Many organisations have **equal opportunities policies**, in which they claim that they treat everyone equally and fairly all the time. A problem often arises when individuals within the organisation don't abide by these policies. It doesn't matter whether this is through ignorance or because they don't care – so far as the law is concerned neither is an excuse.

It is also an offence to victimise, harass or bully someone else, so that their lives are made a misery. **Victimisation** is when one person is singled out for unfair treatment by someone else. **Harassment** is 'unwelcome behaviour' which upsets, offends or frightens someone. It is sexual harassment if the behaviour is linked to gender and racial harassment if it is linked to ethnic origin or culture. Because bullying is also unwelcome behaviour, it is virtually the same as harassment in the eyes of the law.

You have the right not to be subjected to discrimination nor should you ever be made miserable by anyone else. If you are ever unfortunate enough to work for (or with) someone who operates like this then you should report the matter to your boss or another senior member of staff immediately (see page 302–304). If you are working in a very small company, and the problem is the manager, the only answer may be to leave – as quickly as possible. Even though you may be able to take legal action, it is usually far simpler – and less traumatic – to put the episode behind you and move on.

The main point is that *no one* should ever have to tolerate this type of behaviour. This means that everyone has to take care that their own actions do not upset other people at work – either accidentally or deliberately. Whether it's an email that pokes fun at a member of staff or spreads malicious rumours, a racist joke told in front of all the office or a team that deliberately ignores or is unpleasant to one member (for whatever reason) – all the perpetrators are living very dangerously. They are disregarding the legal rights of their colleagues and not abiding by their own responsibilities. The likelihood is that serious disciplinary action will be taken against them, as you will see on page 301.

Personal qualities of effective team members

Ironically, the personal qualities that your boss or team leader values the most may not be exactly the same as those valued by team members. It is, however, quite possible to do a 'balancing act' if you are certain in your own mind about what you think is the right course of action in a situation. This does not mean being obsequious (smarmy!) to the boss – a trait which is despised by most people in an organisation.

What your team leader will expect

Your team leader will have certain expectations about you. These include:

▶ always giving a positive image of the business and your own team

▶ a willingness to cooperate and to have the same priorities about the work which must be done

▶ appreciating the pressures team leaders may be under and how this may affect them

▶ respect for their seniority and status

▶ a cheerful and positive attitude to work

▶ good communication skills, so that you report problems and difficulties in good time and factually. Don't gain a reputation for making a drama out of a crisis!

What your team members will expect

Your team members will want you to be a committed member of the team. This means putting the team's goals before your own. They will also want you to be:

▶ fair – so that you treat them all in the same way

▶ loyal – so that you don't talk about people behind their backs or give away personal information they have told you

▶ diplomatic – so that you don't hurt people unnecessarily

▶ kind and considerate – especially if they are having a bad day or personal problems

▶ reliable – so that they can depend upon you never to let them down

▶ friendly and positive – so that they enjoy working with you

▶ tolerant – if they have different opinions from your own. Don't think you have failed if people don't always do what you want – you can't be right all the time!

▶ honest and prepared to admit your mistakes. This isn't easy but a simple apology is much better than trying to fudge the issue or – even worse – blaming someone else for the problem

▶ generous enough to give praise when it's due and to share the credit if someone else has helped you to achieve something

▶ a good listener, so that you don't have to be told things twice and understand how people feel about a situation

▶ a prompt, accurate and reliable communicator

▶ prepared to help out if there is a problem or a crisis, without making a fuss about it

▶ consistent with your moods and attitude. No one likes moody people!

What all your colleagues will expect

Most of the qualities above are so important to good working relationships that they are essential no matter who you deal with. It is no use being loyal to your team, positive with your team leader and then tetchy or irritable with everyone else! In addition, everyone you work with will hope that you are:

- courteous and polite to everyone – saying 'please' and 'thank you' costs nothing but their importance is often forgotten

- friendly to work with but not intrusive or too personal with people who would rather keep themselves to themselves.

Finally, when you first start work, remember that you cannot rush working relationships any more than you can rush friendships. Don't make judgements about anyone when you first meet them and don't expect them to treat you like a long-lost friend after five minutes! If you are naturally enthusiastic, then hold back a little in the early days until you get to know people better. If you are naturally shy, then make an effort to respond to people positively. This way, you start to build your working relationships on more secure foundations.

The importance of negotiation and democratic agreement

It is often the case that when you are working in a team, a joint decision must be made about something. Reaching agreement can be easy if you all think the same way, or if the issue is straightforward. On many occasions, however, this is not the case. People have different views and opinions and somehow a consensus must be reached.

Problems will arise if:

- one team member always shouts everyone else down

- the team bicker and squabble between themselves without getting anywhere

- people start to hurl insults at each other.

It is much easier to move forward if you *expect* other people to have different ideas and you don't see a discussion as a personal challenge which you have to win. It is much easier if you take a different approach and think of the issue as a challenge to the team as a whole – so that you are all debating it to reach the best solution you can *all* think of. Often, in this way, a simple suggestion by one person can be refined or improved by the others, so that the end result is better than anyone would have thought of on their own.

This is where negotiation comes in. You negotiate if you are prepared to:

- listen to other people's viewpoints

- contribute to the discussion in a thoughtful way

- modify or change your own ideas during a discussion

- make suggestions rather than tell everyone what to do.

Democratic agreement means that everyone's views are treated with the same courtesy. It also means that a group vote may be held to decide the best way forward, especially if there is stalemate. You will be expected to abide by the wishes of the majority – and not moan and groan afterwards about how they are bunch of idiots!

▲ Other people's viewpoints also need to be considered

The importance of cooperation with others

Cooperating with others means sometimes putting your own interests second. At times, this may be a nuisance. There are very few people who, if they are in the middle of something, may not mutter a little if they are asked to drop what they are doing to help someone else.

You will find it easier to be cooperative if you:

▶ naturally prefer to work in a group, and be a member of a team, than to work on your own

▶ are not instinctively competitive and always want to be better than anyone else

▶ are flexible and relatively easy-going

▶ are prepared to share the work – and the glory

▶ don't expect other people to be perfect

▶ have a natural tendency to roll up your sleeves and give practical assistance in a crisis

▶ enjoy meeting challenges faced by the whole team

▶ don't like letting people down.

Cooperation is important because it enables the team to be more effective as a whole. This means the work produced – and the decisions that are reached – are better and time is saved. At the end of the day, this benefits everyone.

Dealing with different personalities in a team

A 'dream team' would be one where all the skills and the personalities of the members were complementary, so that every job could be tackled with ease and everyone would always see eye to eye. Unfortunately, dream teams rarely exist! Where skills are lacking, people can be trained. So far as personalities are concerned, you cannot just send a shy person on a training course to make them an extrovert, or turn a competitive person easily into a team player. People's personalities are a combination of their genes, upbringing, education and experiences. Whilst people may adapt in the course of their lives, they rarely change very much. This means that, in all team, allowances have to be made and differences tolerated. In the best teams, personality differences are actually seen as a strength, because this gives the team a better 'mix' of attributes and abilities.

Different specialists have studied personalities and looked at how they affect a team. One expert, Professor Cary Cooper, has identified three that are absolutely essential:

▶ There must be at least one **Social Emotional Leader**. This doesn't have to be the official team leader. This person has a caring personality and stops potential arguments before they begin, arranges social activities and helps to balance a hard-working team.

▶ There must be **Task People** who are keen to complete the job in hand. Otherwise the team won't do the work it is given and meet its responsibilities.

▶ There must be at least one **Communicator**, who makes sure that everyone knows what is going on and who keeps people informed, both within and outside the team.

Other experts, such as Dr Meredith Belbin, who did extensive research on teams, identified other roles linked to personalities. He argued there should be one 'leader', keen on pushing the team forward, a 'people person' who cares about the wellbeing of the team, a 'detail' person who makes sure that tasks are finished properly, a 'creative' person who has good ideas and a 'coordinator' who brings things together. This means that in a small team, some people must take on more than one role, otherwise important aspects of teamwork will be overlooked.

The important point, as a team member, is to identify the personalities of your colleagues and then realise the roles they can take on with ease – and the roles they can't. Don't expect people to do more than they feel comfortable with, and use individual strengths to the best advantage. If the team as a whole realises an important role is missing because of their mix of personalities, then the team must solve that problem by working together to cover this area.

Strategies for handling conflict

Conflict occurs when two (or more) people fundamentally disagree. At times this can be very healthy because it can lead to some lively debates – and trigger some excellent and creative thinking. The danger, however, is that conflict becomes destructive. Something that starts as a minor difference can quickly escalate if no one will back down, consider the other person's point of view or if they start making personal and insulting remarks. All these actions are like fanning a smouldering bonfire.

With most people, destructive conflict is something to be avoided. It is upsetting and disturbing for those involved and, at work, can affect working relationships in a wide area – particularly if people start taking 'sides'. At this point, even those not directly involved are likely to spend more time gossiping and speculating than working. For these reasons it is important to recognise when and why conflict is likely to occur and to learn how to handle it.

Conflict can occur for many reasons, including:

▶ Personality differences – we all have traits that annoy other people. If these are very different you may hear people talk about a 'personality clash' – where they just cannot understand the other person at all.

▷ Pressure of work. In a crisis one person may panic, another may become short-tempered or irritable. Because they are stressed, they both blame each other for the situation.

▷ Differences of opinion between very strong-minded people.

▷ Misunderstandings and poor communications which mean people are poorly informed, jump to conclusions and react accordingly.

However, most types of conflict can be divided into two categories. As a first step, you should try to identify the category and then take unofficial action to try to sort it out yourself.

Category 1 – conflicts over issues

Conflicts over issues are those which occur when two people can't agree about a way of working or another aspect of their work. There is a clear issue. Normally they get on, but on this issue they disagree. For example, a new photocopier is being delivered and there is an argument about where it should go or you have to agree to share a job with a colleague and you have different views about who should do what.

▲ Sharing is all part of team work

These types of conflict are the easiest to resolve but it helps if you bear in mind the following.

▷ Remember that a decision has to be made eventually – so it might as well be now, rather than later. This is especially important if there is a deadline involved!

- Think about how important the issue really is to you, personally. It is easy to get upset about something very minor, but rarely worth it in the long run. Ask yourself how much it would really affect the quality of your life if you agreed, for the sake of peace.

- Develop a reputation for being reasonable and prepared to compromise normally. In this case, if you do feel quite strongly about something then people may be happier to listen.

- Put your views forward calmly and logically. State what you think and support it with *good* reasons.

- Avoid making it a personal issue. Stick to the facts and don't make it personal, i.e. 'I honestly think if we did it this way, we would finish more quickly' *not,* 'It was your fault we had to work late last week and you wouldn't listen to me that time, either.'

- Try to avoid raising your voice or interrupting. This means you are still talking, not trying to shout someone down!

- Never 'paint yourself into a corner'. This means taking a stand where you leave yourself no way out. In this case, if people still ignore you then you will look foolish. A typical example is, 'If you put it there, I'm *never* going to use it and that's for sure.' The bottom line is that you still have to do your job. So don't make silly and meaningless threats.

Category 2 – personality problems

Personality clashes are usually more serious than conflicts over issues because there is no clear focus for the argument. You normally have a personality clash with someone if they constantly make you feel bad about yourself, for example:

- they are constantly critical and even criticise you in front of other people. Nothing you do pleases them

- they disregard all your suggestions – or even ridicule them

- they are sarcastic if you try to explain something

- they make it clear they don't like you and may even try to exclude you

- they make hurtful remarks

- they deliberately try to make life difficult for you (e.g. by withholding information, sulking or even making fun of you)

- they have such a different way of working or thinking to you, that you dread being involved with them in any way, because there's always trouble.

In this situation, you may want to run away or retaliate, depending upon your nature. At work, you can't do either, particularly if the person is more senior than yourself. So, what should you do?

Start by trying to work out:

a whether their behaviour is accidental or deliberate. It is more annoying if we think it is done on purpose but often it isn't. This might help you see the problem more objectively.

b How many other people feel like you? If there are several then this person isn't targeting you personally. Their behaviour may be caused by pressure or serious worries and may be affecting several people.

Whatever your conclusions, but certainly if you are convinced their behaviour is both intentional and personal, then you need to take action. You do this by changing *your own* behaviour. This is because, no matter what you do or how strongly you feel about something, you can *never* ever force another human being to change theirs!

Strategies to try include the following:

▶ Watching how someone else responds to this person (preferably someone who gets on well with them) and taking a lead from them.

▶ Approaching the person who is upsetting you and saying how their behaviour makes you feel. Don't be accusatory – keep the focus on how you feel, i.e. 'I know you probably don't mean it, but when you say things like that, especially in front of other people, it really upsets me. If you want to comment on my work, please could you speak to me in private' *not,* 'You're always criticising me and everything I say, and I'm fed up with being made to look a fool.' Always remember to say such remarks in private. In front of an audience the other person may feel they have to defend themselves to save face.

▶ Be patient if you don't know someone very well. They may feel insecure or be finding it difficult to settle in. Avoid them when you can and just be neutral when you can't. Keep all conversations strictly business-like.

▶ If you are constantly trying to please them without success, stop and give them more space. Let them come to you for a change.

▶ Talk over the problem with someone you trust, or with an older or more experienced person – preferably someone who knows the other person. This is far more productive than moaning about the situation to a friend who can't do anything positive to help. Listen – and act on – the suggestions you receive.

▶ If you are still unsuccessful, talk to your team leader or another senior person, preferably someone you think is understanding and easy to talk to. Even if you don't like the sound of some of the ideas put forward it is still important that you try to cooperate as much as you can. This is very important if the conflict becomes any worse and the situation becomes serious.

▶ The final step is to make a formal complaint. Both at work and at college you will find official grievance procedures exist. This protects people against serious problems, such as victimisation and harassment, which you read about on page 111. Normally, conflicts about minor matters are sorted out informally without taking this type of action, particularly if you have tried all the strategies listed above. You will learn more about grievance procedures in Unit 3 (see page 300).

PEOPLE IN BUSINESS

Many people in business attend training courses which teach **assertiveness** skills. These focus on people's rights and on developing the verbal skills needed to express your own point of view calmly and rationally.

Everyone has the right to consider their own needs, to refuse to do something without feeling guilty or selfish, to make mistakes and to express themselves. No one has the right to upset other people or to think that other people's rights are less important than their own.

Therefore it is just as wrong to be a perpetual 'doormat' than it is to rant and rave. People who agree to anything for peace (even if they are unhappy about it afterwards) are known as **passive**; those who get annoyed quickly may be **aggressive** – and quite scary to be with if they are in a rage. At work, both these extremes are inappropriate.

If you are assertive then you state your case calmly, are prepared to give a reason for what you are saying and get to the point quickly without lots of explanations. You start statements with the word 'I' rather than 'you' – which would put the other person on the defensive. You take the balanced view that whilst anyone has the right to ask you something, you also have the right to your own views and to state your case pleasantly and unemotionally. The benefit is increased control over your own life and priorities.

OVER TO YOU!

1 What team qualities do you possess? And how good are your assertiveness skills? Answer the quiz below to find out!

Teamwork quiz

Select one answer from each of the options below.

1 Your team leader tells you that she needs one person to help her to do a very interesting job but she knows you are busy at the moment. Do you
   a) tell her there's nothing you can't sort out and volunteer immediately. Then tell the team you've been called away unexpectedly
   b) agree and say you'll talk to the team and decide who would be best
   c) say that you can give your work to the others so there isn't a problem

2 Your team is running late to complete a long, boring and complicated task. Do you
   a) sigh heavily and say you're sorry to leave them to it, but you are going out that night
   b) suggest that you stick at it and then have a pizza together afterwards
   c) find yourself staying late on your own, because all the others have said they can't stay

3 Your team leader is hopping mad because some work your team were doing is wrong and the deadline was missed. You know *your* contribution was fine and done to time. Do you

a) see your team leader in private to make sure she knows it wasn't your fault

b) tell the others exactly what you think of them

c) suggest you have a team discussion to identify what went wrong and how it can be avoided in the future

4 You are trying to finish an important job on which you need to concentrate. The others have finished and are distracting you by chatting. Do you

a) try to ignore them and press on regardless

b) tell them to shut up because you can't think when they're talking

c) ask them to help you or go somewhere else to talk

5 You inadvertently tell a team member to deliver some documents to the wrong building. It's pouring with rain and you know she'll be annoyed when she returns. Do you

a) prepare your apology in advance – and put the kettle on

b) tell her that it's not your fault – you were given the wrong information

c) put your coat on to go and find her

6 You find out that there is a much easier way of doing a job than you thought. Do you

a) keep this to yourself, so that you'll seem the most efficient member of your team

b) tell your closest friend, but no one else

c) share it with the team as soon as you can

7 A member of your team is always challenging your ideas and suggestions. Do you

a) stop making any

b) tell her she's getting on your nerves

c) talk to her on her own and tell her how you feel

8 You have made a silly mistake which the others think is funny. Do you

a) try hard to see the funny side yourself, even if it's difficult

b) get upset, because they are picking on you

c) get annoyed and point out a few mistakes they have made recently

9 You work in a team with several lively and quite forthright members. Do you

a) find it a nightmare and say as little as possible

b) try to hold your own, because open discussion is healthy

c) prove that you can be as forthright as anyone else

10 You are doing a job you find difficult when a team member keeps suggesting a better way of doing it. Do you

a) listen to see if she is right

b) tell her to be quiet because you can't concentrate

c) tell her to do it herself, if she's so clever

Now check your answers with the key on page 127.

2   Each of the following problems has occurred in Lisa's team. In each case, as a group, decide how they might be resolved.

   a) Because of mistaken communications, both Tim and Jessica have both prepared a poster to advertise an event being held next month. There is space for only one of them. Tim's is the best but Jessica has put in a lot of work and is now upset.

   b) Paula is a perfectionist. Her desk is neat and tidy and so are all her belongings. Jason is far less fussy, is constantly losing things and then helps himself to other people's – which drives Paula mad. Yesterday a major row broke out and now neither of them is speaking to the other.

   c) The team are responsible for collecting the mail each morning and afternoon from the main office. Whenever it is raining Fatima always finds something else to do. The others have started to resent this and have now refused to help Fatima out when she is stuck.

   d) Yesterday, Mark was giving information to a visitor which was incorrect and Jenny corrected him. He is furious she did this in public. Jenny says that if she hadn't said anything, the whole team would have looked stupid.

3   In a group of three or four, decide on a *team response* to the following problem – with reasons. Your decision should be reached by means of discussion and negotiation so that each one feels that his or her views have been heard and considered.

   You have been asked to suggest 3 charities that would benefit from funds raised by students this year, which will probably amount to about £10,000 in total. You must also state the percentage you think each charity should receive. You have the following options plus 1 of the group's own choice:

   a) a national animal charity, such as the RSPCA or Guide Dogs for the Blind

   b) a national children's charity, such as the NSPCC or Barnardos

   c) a charity which focuses on medical issues, e.g. Cancer Research or the British Heart Foundation

   d) a charity which helps the homeless, such as Shelter or the Salvation Army

   e) an international charity, like Oxfam or Save the Children

   f) a local or regional charity (e.g. for a hospice or local cause)

▼ REVIEWING THE TEAM ACTIVITY

Throughout our lives we all make mistakes, often through lack of experience and sometimes through lack of preparation. Even if we don't actually make a mistake, we often realise that we could have done something better, quicker or more easily. This thought normally occurs afterwards, when it is too late to do much about it – and is generally known as hindsight. The important point is that you learn from it. Otherwise, the next time, you will simply make the same mistakes and cause the same problems all over again.

Therefore it is vital to review your own performance and that of the team. Unless you are prepared to do this, and to think carefully about the result, you will never improve – in terms of performance, experience or attitude.

As part of your assessment you will have to write a review of your experiences of working in a team for both activities you have to carry out. This section helps you to do that.

Reviewing your own performance

You need to start by looking back over the tasks you carried out, and write your review using each of the following headings:

▶ **The purpose of the team activities in which I took part**. You need to start by describing these and stating what the overall purpose was, for example:

'Our team was given the task of researching information on "Going Green in the Office" and to find out the ways in which offices can be environmentally friendly. We were told we could talk to college staff and research information on the Internet and in the library. Then we had to prepare a presentation to give to the rest of our group and 20 copies of a summarised page of information.'

▶ **The tasks I performed**. It helps if you explain exactly how you did these tasks, for example:

'I researched information on the Internet and also visited the college library. I talked to the office staff and found out about the recycling boxes and why they were used. They also told me about recycled paper and stationery and other actions they take to save paper – such as reusing internal envelopes and jiffy bags. I typed this information and shared it with the team so that we could agree a final list. I worked with Sean to prepare visual aids for our presentation. Then I worked with the others to decide what we were going to say.'

▶ **How well I feel I performed the tasks.**

This is the most difficult part, but the most important. Even if you did the task successfully, you may be able to suggest what you would do next time to save time or to do it more professionally. Before you answer this, you need to consider different aspects:

– Did you complete every task accurately first time, or did you have to make amendments and changes?

– Did you carry out all the instructions correctly without having to be reminded at all?

– Did you meet every deadline? Sometimes there may be a good reason for not meeting a deadline, such as an unavoidable problem you couldn't do anything about. In this case, what did you do? Could you have used your own initiative at any stage to improve matters?

– Did you work in the most effective way? With hindsight, would you do anything differently next time?

If you think about all these aspects, this helps you to give a more complete review, for example:

'I researched the information but it took me some time to identify the best sites on the Internet. At times I had difficulties deciding which information to use and which to discard and took more print-outs than we needed.

We wanted to include an illustration on our information page but I wasn't sure how to cut and paste this properly so that it was in the best place. There were also several mistakes on our first print-out so I could have been better at proof-reading. I had no problems helping with the visual aids and I enjoyed doing these.'

Reviewing your contribution to the work of the team

For this section you should consider:

▶ the planning discussions you were involved in and any progress meetings

▶ the tasks you were allocated, as part of the overall job

▶ the help and assistance that you gave to other members of the team

▶ any other relevant factors, such as encouraging other people, staying positive and suggesting how to overcome difficulties.

Then write your review using the following headings:

▶ **The ways in which I feel I contributed to the work of the team**. For example:

'I contributed to team discussions at the beginning when we were planning how to do the work and I suggested that Jacqui would be best at checking our final document because her English skills are very good. We all agreed to research different aspects of information and this worked well. When Jacqui was trying to find out about 'eco-friendly cleaning materials' I offered to talk to the cleaning supervisor who was very helpful. When we were preparing our talk, I showed the others how to do 'prompt cards' so that we wouldn't forget what to say. I knew how to do this because I did it on my course last year.'

▶ **Could I have contributed more**? Here you should think about both the way you approached the tasks you were given *and* about your own attitude and behaviour as a member of the team. You can identify other things you could have done or ways in which you could have changed your behaviour to help. You can say that you couldn't have done any more but you must give a reason for your opinion. For example:

'I could have contributed more by helping Sean when he was finding out about how toner cartridges could be recycled. I had seen a notice in the office about this but forgot to tell him. Also, at our meetings, I was so busy thinking up ideas and concentrating on what I wanted to say that I didn't listen properly to what the others were saying. I was also a bit stubborn at times and was annoyed if my suggestions were turned down. I think it would have helped if I'd been more willing to compromise.'

or

'I don't think I could have contributed more because we met regularly and we all helped each other out whenever it was needed. We all worked hard and no one person was ever expected to do more than the others. We also had very friendly and lively meetings and we all took into account all the ideas and suggestions that were made. I think we worked hard to try to ensure that no one was left out and everyone's views were discussed properly.'

▶ **How well I feel I related to the other members of the team**.

This is often difficult to review because you are trying to explain your own relationship with the other members of your team. You may find it hard to be critical if you have worked with your close friends and prefer to forget any minor squabbles or disagreements.

Alternatively, if you have had a nightmare experience, then it is difficult to assess your own contribution to the problem and very tempting to blame everyone else! As a tip, you may find it easier to be objective if you don't name other people when you are assessing your own relationship with any member of the team you found it hard to work with. A positive review may say:

'Overall our team worked well together. I have worked with Sean before and so we understand each other quite well even if we don't always agree. Jacqui was very supportive of me and I tried to help her when I could. I therefore think I related well to both Sean and Jacqui.'

If you had a problem relating to one or more people in the team, then your review could say:

'I found it really difficult to relate to one member of our team. I have strong opinions and so does she, so we found it difficult to work together. It also irritated me that she always thought she was right and she sulked if anyone disagreed with her. I didn't have any problems with the other members. They were friendly and helpful and good fun to work with.'

▶ **Whether I encountered difficulties with others and if so how I overcame them**.

Even good teams encounter difficulties at times but work together to overcome them. If a team relationship is poor, then it may be that one or two people tried to overcome any difficulties but struggled to get other people to cooperate. Remember that in this section you are identifying difficulties with the *team relationship* – it is not relevant to say that the photocopier wasn't working or that there was a paper shortage! For example:

'Jacqui and I had a few minor disagreements when we tried to identify the best information to include. We were told to keep it to one A4 page but we couldn't agree on which information was the best at first. In the end we decided to rank the information as essential, useful and not very important and this helped a lot. Although we met regularly, one person was often late, which was annoying. However, we tried to discuss problems we were having at the time and this helped us to fit in with each other and take account of each other's views.'

or

'At the start, we all agreed what to find out but then we couldn't agree on how to reduce the information so that it fit on one A4 page. We had a problem, too, when one member of the team wanted to do a presentation using PowerPoint but the others didn't feel confident enough to do this. In the end, when we agreed to give a simple presentation using our own visual aids, that person wouldn't join in, which spoiled things.'

Reviewing the performance of the team

For this final part of your review you are not focusing just upon yourself but on the team as a whole. You need to consider whether the task you were given was completed successfully and whether you met all your objectives and the strengths and weaknesses of other members of the team.

You will need to write your comments under the following headings:

▶ **Was the team successful in meeting its objectives?**

Before you start this, think about the overall task and the objectives you were given. Then say whether or not you achieved these, for example:

'Our team was given the task of researching and preparing a presentation and handout on recycling in the office. The objectives we identified were to research alternatives, prepare a handout and prepare a presentation. We had seven days in which to do this. We met our objectives because we obtained the information required, then decided the information to include on our handout and prepared a presentation which we gave to the rest of the group seven days after being given the task.'

or

'Our team had the task of researching and preparing a presentation and handout on recycling in the office. We knew we had to research alternatives, prepare a handout and also give a presentation to our group within seven days. We did not meet all of our objectives. Our research took longer than expected and there were difficulties deciding which information to include in our handout so we didn't have our draft handout ready for the deadline date. It also contained some errors so we had to redo this. We had to arrange to give our presentation a week later than originally planned.'

How did the other members of the team perform? Strengths and weaknesses

For this section try to be a little charitable! If someone helped you on several occasions but let you down once, don't focus on the negative – even though this may still rankle! If you are feeling negative, leave it a day or two until you write your review.

▶ Start by thinking about the strengths of each member of the team. How did they help you, what were they good at, what benefits did they bring to the team as a whole?

▶ Consider their weaknesses but keep these in perspective. No one is perfect – including you!

▲ Everyone has their weaknesses but no one is perfect!

Finally, write your comments. These can be positive or negative but, in either case, you need to provide evidence for your opinion; for example:

'Our team had many strengths but a few weaknesses. Communication was very good, we all exchanged information regularly and we felt we could speak freely to one another. This helped a lot. Sean was excellent because he always had time for everyone and, although his IT skills were better than ours and he would have preferred to prepare a PowerPoint presentation, he was quite happy to accept that we were worried about this. He made an excellent leader during the main presentation and was clear and witty as well. Jacqui has a good eye for detail and this prevented us from making several mistakes. We enjoyed working together.

or

'Our team had several strengths but also some weaknesses. We struggled to communicate at first and this hampered our work. We also argued quite a lot. We couldn't agree on the information to include and both Sean and Jacqui weren't prepared to change their minds over this. I was the same, so overall we couldn't reach agreement. Then we disagreed about the presentation. I think we all have very fixed views and this is a weakness of our team – no one is prepared to give way. I don't think we were a total failure because we did produce a good handout and gave a presentation to our group, as agreed. However, I think it would have been better if we had been able to negotiate a compromise when it was necessary.'

OVER TO YOU!

Ruksana, Ryan and Ailsa's group are planning a day out at the end of term and their team has been given the task of finding out about different travel alternatives and the cost. They must then recommend, to their group, the best option; report back to their tutor and then make and confirm the booking and arrange for payment. The group will be visiting a large city, 100 miles away. It has been agreed that private transport is not an option. They can hire a coach, travel by train or use a regular bus service.

At their planning metting, Ruksana agrees to telephone several coach companies in the area whilst Ryan goes to the station and finds out about train times and fares. Ailsa finds out about standard coach times and the cost. They then meet to compare their findings. The standard coach cost is the lowest but they all agree the times aren't suitable. Ryan and Ruksana then argue about which is best – going by train or hiring a coach. Hiring a coach is more expensive but Ruksana and Ailsa both think it would be more fun to do this. Ryan is dubious. He also says Ruksana should have telephoned at least four or five coach companies – rather than just the two she contacted. The following day he arrives triumphant, because he has rung two more and obtained a cheaper quote than either of Ruksana's. This annoys Ruksana who said that finding out about coach fares was her job. By the time the team are ready to tell the rest of the group, Ruksana and Ryan aren't speaking and Ailsa is pleading with them both to be sensible. Ailsa hurriedly calculates the cost of Ryan's cheapest coach option for each person. She says that as there isn't time to put this on paper, they will just have to tell the group verbally what they have found out.

At the group meeting, it is agreed to hire the coach, because the times will be more flexible. With their tutor's agreement, Ailsa tells everyone the cost and it is agreed that the money will be collected the following week. Ryan agrees to telephone the coach company and confirm the booking.

A week later, when the team check the money, they find to their horror that they haven't enough. When Ruksana checks the figures she points out that the calculation was wrong and they really need an extra £2 from each person. Ailsa is horrified and blames Ryan, who was supposed to have checked her calculation before she told the group. Ryan argues that it was agreed that the money would be Ailsa's responsibility. Ruksana says that it doesn't matter how much they argue, it won't solve the problem. She then adds that if Ryan hadn't come rushing in bragging about his cheaper quotes at the last minute, the problem would never have occurred. Ryan says that if she'd done her job properly, he wouldn't have had to.

None of them like the idea of telling the rest of the group what has happened and are stuck, trying to find a solution to their problem.

1. What was the purpose of the team activity in which Ruksana, Ailsa and Ryan took part?

2. a) What tasks did Ailsa perform?
   b) How well do you think she carried out these tasks? Give a reason for your answer.

3. a) What tasks did Ryan perform?
   b) How well do you think he contributed to the work of the team? Give a reason for your answer.

4. a) How did Ruksana contribute to the work of the team?
   b) Do you think she could have contributed more? Give a reason for your answer.

5. How well did Ryan relate to the other members of the team?

6. a) What difficulties did the team experience?
   b) How well do you think they overcame these difficulties?

7. Was the team successful or unsuccessful in meeting its objectives? Give a reason for your answer.

8. What do you think were the strengths and weaknesses of each member of the team?

9. What do you think the team should now do to solve their problem?

10. Select a member of the team and, from that person's point of view, prepare your own review. Start with the title 'Review of my team activities – activity 1'. Then write your comments under each of the headings shown above. Compare your completed review with those written by other members of your group. You may find it interesting to see whether your comments match those of other people who chose to be the same person as you! Finally, check with your tutor that your comments would have been acceptable if you were writing an OCR review as a member of this team.

Key to quiz on page 119

1b) 2b) 3c) 4c) 5a) 6c) 7c) 8a) 9b) 10a)

▼ ELEMENT 2 – WORKING WITH CUSTOMERS

All organisations need customers in order to survive. Private businesses need to make a profit – and this comes from selling their goods and services to customers. Organisations in the public sector (see Unit 3, page 180), such as hospitals and schools, also have customers to whom they provide a service – although they may be called by a different name, such as patients or pupils.

No organisation wants its customers to be dissatisfied or unhappy. A private business will be concerned that it will lose customers to its competitors and public sector organisations will want to avoid complaints and bad reports in the press.

For that reason, working with customers effectively is important for all staff. You will be expected to do all you can to help your organisation to retain its current customers and attract new ones.

▼ PRESENT A POSITIVE IMAGE TO CUSTOMERS

Customer loyalty is cherished by all businesses. This is because it costs money to attract customers and to gain their trust. Gaining customers is likely to be the main responsibility of the sales and marketing department but keeping them is the responsibility of everyone. One sharp or dismissive word on the telephone, or one rude encounter with an employee, can convince a customer that it is better to go elsewhere in the future. Therefore presenting a positive image to customers is very important and must be done every hour of every day.

Your possible range of customers – internal and external

Who are your customers when you are at work? If you work in administration or in an area like finance you may see few customers face-to-face during the day. Today, the idea of customers includes any other person to whom you offer a service. As an example, the army catering corps refer to the soldiers for whom they make meals as their 'customers'.

All administrators have two types of customers, external and internal.

▶ **External customers** are easy to understand. They are all the private individuals or other businesses which buy goods and services from the organisation. As an administrator you may be involved in responding to customer queries, dealing with customers on the telephone and greeting visitors to your organisation. Remember too that as well as existing external customers there will be prospective customers. This group is very important as your employer will want to convert prospective customers into actual customers.

A rather different type of 'customers' are the other people who rely upon you for help and assistance – such as anyone making a delivery or providing a maintenance service. Keeping busy people waiting whilst you finish something unimportant is unacceptable. They have a job to do just like you!

▶ **Internal customers** are a little different. They are all your colleagues who need you to do something for them. This may be because they are directly answering a customer enquiry themselves. For example, if you worked as a finance administrator and sales were querying a customer account, your sales colleague would need you to provide the right information in order to help the customer. In this case, the sales person is your internal customer.

Remember, too, that your internal customers may not all be important in terms of status. However, even the office cleaner is a 'customer' and shouldn't be held up because you can't be bothered to move something!

You have a responsibility to give all your customers equal importance. You may think it obvious that you would have to give good service to an external customer, but if you let your internal customer down this may also affect an external customer. And it won't enhance your reputation in the eyes of your colleagues!

The importance of your impact on other people

Everyone is influenced by 'first impressions'. The first time you visit a new place or start a new job you are particularly aware of your surroundings. The first time you meet someone you have a similar reaction. This time, however, you are aware of their appearance and attitude. This influences your opinion as to what type of person they are. In business, because that person represents the organisation, it also influences your opinion of the company as well.

For example, imagine for a moment you have walked into a new clothes store. The assistant is scruffy, ignores you for a while and then slouches over and says 'Yeah?' Or the assistant is haughty and dismissive, so that you feel unwelcome. In either case you would form a bad impression about the store – and this may easily put you off visiting it again.

In an office, you will be judged not just on your personal appearance and attitude but also on the tidiness of your work area, the way you treat your colleagues in front of customers, the way you speak on the telephone (and how long it takes you to answer it) and the way you communicate in writing. The main factors that influence your customers are so important that each is described in more detail below.

Personal presentation

In some organisations, the presentation of customer service staff is so important that they are issued with uniforms or told what they can and cannot wear as part of the company dress code guidelines. In administration you are less likely to find yourself issued with a uniform and many employers will not have an official dress code. They will simply expect you to look businesslike and use your common sense. In simple terms, this means:

▶ They will expect you to be clean and tidy at all times. This includes your hair, fingernails and shoes – as well as your clothes.

▶ They will expect you to wear suitable work clothes. This normally excludes jeans, trainers, Doc Martens, crop tops and shorts.

▶ Your jewellery should be restrained – especially in relation to body jewellery. Twelve earrings and a nose ring is a definite no-no!

▶ If you are female, your make-up should also be restrained – very dark lipstick and black nail varnish are not appropriate at work.

▶ For both sexes, you need a hairstyle that conforms to the organisational image. Therefore punk styles (or male ponytails) are likely to be frowned upon.

▶ Watch what you eat and drink during working hours. Some organisations specifically ban certain foods, such as onions, curry and garlic, within 12 hours of dealing with customers – for fairly obvious reasons.

Manner and attitude

Everyone's manner and attitude is influenced by the way they think. If someone is depressed, they will act in a negative way. If they are fed up then their attitude will reflect boredom. Conversely, if they enjoy being with other people, they will act in a friendly way. If you are dealing with customers then being friendly can be useful – but it isn't the best you can do. Customer service professionals argue that the best attribute is to have a positive attitude. There are several reasons for this.

▶ People prefer being with others who radiate positive vibes. They are open, approachable and easy to be with. They make other people feel better!

▶ Positive people always think 'yes' (whereas negative people think 'no'). Therefore someone with a positive attitude looks at problems or difficulties as a challenge. They see opportunities more easily than negative people.

▶ If you are positive about your work and your customers then you are also giving a positive and up-beat image of the organisation. You reflect commitment and interest in every customer.

▶ Positive people usually have high personal standards and always want to do their best. They also believe they are capable of doing this.

You only have to think about this for two minutes from your own experience. If you went to a shop with a complaint, which response would you prefer to hear: 'Oh, I doubt if we can do much about that' or, 'Don't worry, I'm sure we can sort this out.' Even if, the problem does not get resolved to your satisfaction, the experience will still leave you with a better feeling if you have dealt with someone who is positive and helpful – as well as friendly.

Style of communication

If you are serious about trying to be positive, this is reflected in your communications – both verbal and written. You will talk enthusiastically and with a smile. You will highlight the benefits of something automatically.

Positive people don't talk something 'down' and neither are they condescending. Although they may be disappointed at times, because they are optimists they will rarely get angry or frustrated enough for this to show.

You can find out more about communicating with customers in a positive and purposeful manner later in this element.

Body language

It is impossible to feel positive and good about yourself and to sit hunched up, slouch or stare into space! Positive people sit, stand and walk tall. They smile at people and have the confidence to look at them when they are talking. Because they want to understand the customer they often 'reflect' body language – by shaking their head or nodding to show they agree with the customer.

▲ Personal presentation and body language are very important at work. What sort of impression do you give?

Try a simple test. Next time you go into a large store, try to spot a member of staff who looks positive, one who looks bored and one who looks negative, depressed or plain unhelpful. Then think about why you gained that impression – and what their body language was telling you. There are no prizes for deciding which one you would prefer to be served by!

The importance of presenting a positive image of the company

You have learned much about being positive yourself – but equally important is that customers should think positively about your organisation. Imagine you are visiting an employment agency which advertises jobs for administrators. When you walk in the receptionist looks pleasant and smiles but her desk is literally covered in papers and there are two unwashed coffee cups. On the floor are several carrier bags full of the shopping she did at lunchtime. Her coat is flung over a chair.

You ask if you can see someone about the administrative jobs advertised in the paper last night. But the receptionist says she didn't know about those and can't help you at the moment because the colleague who would talk to you is still out at lunch. You ask what time she will return. 'Oh, I've no idea', she replies, 'She's a law unto herself, that one.'

What would your overall impression be of this organisation – and how likely would you be to return? Remember, the receptionist herself hasn't been unpleasant, but you have still gained an unfavourable image of the organisation.

On the other hand, if the receptionist had been positive, knowledgeable and loyal to her colleague – and the atmosphere friendly and efficient – then you would have gained a positive image and told your friends about your experience.

The main points to remember to make sure that you promote a positive image all the time are summarised in the table that follows.

▶ Always look smart and cheerful and be approachable and friendly. Smile at people and stop what you are doing so that you can concentrate on what they are saying.

▶ Try to keep the 'smile in your voice' when you are on the telephone.

▶ See customers as an opportunity, not an interruption, no matter how busy you are.

▶ Focus on your customer and his or her wants and needs – not your own.

▶ Never criticise your organisation or your colleagues to a customer, even if there is a genuine problem. Sales people are taught that even 'rubbishing' the competition gives a negative impression and puts off customers.

▶ If you have to keep a customer waiting, apologise, explain why, and then get help.

▶ Answer the telephone promptly. If occasionally this is impossible then when you do answer, start by apologising for keeping the person waiting.

▶ Make sure you know the answers to basic questions you might be asked so that you respond promptly and accurately.

▶ If you don't know the answer to something, find out.

▶ If you can't help a customer, find someone who can.

▶ Be on time whenever you have agreed to meet or speak to someone.

▶ Never break your promises or let a customer down.

The importance of providing effective customer service

Effective customer service is possible only if *everyone* in the organisation cares about customers and realises their importance. This is often called being 'customer-focused'. In this type of business:

▶ the customer always comes first

▶ customer needs are identified quickly

▶ customer expectations are exceeded

▶ customers are consistently delighted with the service they receive.

Providing effective customer service produces benefits for the organisation and its staff.

The organisation benefits because:

▶ You help to increase customer satisfaction and loyalty. Loyal customers may stay with a company for many years.

▶ You help them to gain and retain customers – because satisfied customers tell their friends and relatives. This is cheaper than advertising for new customers!

▶ Talking to customers gives you the opportunity to promote your company and its products or service. Listening to them gives you the chance to find out valuable information which can help the business.

▶ You improve the image and reputation of the business as word gets around.

▶ You help the company to stay in business, increase its profits (which may finance a pay rise!) and even expand, especially if it is seen to be better than its competitors.

The benefits to you include:

▶ Greater enjoyment because you know you are doing a good job.

▶ A reduction in the number of problems and complaints you have to deal with.

▶ Greater job security – companies with many satisfied customers are unlikely to go out of business.

▶ Better promotion prospects – not just because you are seen to do a good job but also because successful companies often expand.

PEOPLE IN BUSINESS

According to the research report *The Stressful Queue*, customers in the UK spent a total of 92 days out of the past four years waiting in over 2,000 queues. They also spend approximately 40 hours a year 'holding' on the telephone. Not surprisingly, they are getting fed up.

This research found that 'queue rage' is becoming more common and is also affected by the time of day, the weather and the season. If you add in the problems of screaming children, queue 'jumpers' and the lack of information about the predicted wait then queuing becomes even more stressful. David Stewart-David, who carried out the research, found that queue anxiety can cause us to wildly overestimate the time we have had to wait. About three to four minutes is the maximum tolerance level to buy a train ticket. Couples are more likely to abandon a queue than single people, because they start to argue. The only exception is older people, perhaps because they have more time to wait.

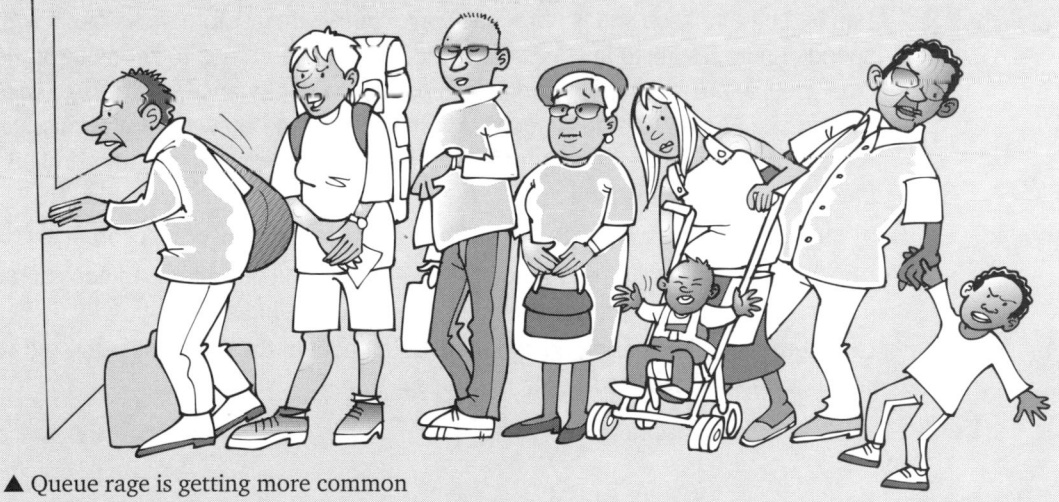

▲ Queue rage is getting more common

On the telephone, by the time six out of ten callers actually get through to speak to someone they are annoyed. They are even more infuriated if they have sat through several digitised messages saying, 'Please hold on, your call is important to us' when all they want is to speak to a real human being.

Researchers also predict our patience levels are constantly reducing because we are less used to waiting than previous generations. Today we expect fast food, fast IT connections and fast service – all the time.

1. Zoe, who works in Sales, receives a telephone call from Kathy Moore querying an invoice she recently received. She thinks she has been overcharged. Zoe checks the price of the item on her computer and finds that this is the same as she quoted Kathy Moore three weeks ago. She tells Kathy Moore that she will investigate and call her back as soon as possible. Zoe then phones Tim, who works in Finance. Tim says he will have to find out what has happened and call her back later.

   a) In the scenario above, who is the external customer?

   b) Who is Tim's internal customer?

   c) What is your opinion of Zoe's customer service?

   d) What could be the consequence if Tim forgot to call Zoe?

   e) What could be the consequence if Tim gave Zoe the wrong information when he did call?

2. Sara is having a bad day. Last night she had a fearful row with her boyfriend and they split up – yet again. She is also broke, and there are ten days to go before she gets paid. Her hair is a mess and she couldn't find anything clean or uncreased to wear this morning – so she put on the only pair of jeans which weren't in a heap on the floor. She arrives at work late, feeling miserable and fed up and finds several visitors already waiting in reception.

   a) What impression do you think Sara's customers will have when they see her arrive – both of her and her company?

   b) Suggest what you think Sara's attitude and manner will be when she deals with the first visitor.

   c) If you were Sara's friend, and walked into the office at this point, what would you do and what would you suggest to help to remedy the situation?

3. Dan is a bit of a snob and is apt to pick and choose the customers he deals with. He spends hours talking to anyone young and attractive and tries to keep out of the way if older people are waiting. He also judges people on appearance. Yesterday a middle-aged man in quite scruffy clothes appeared in the office and Dan was very dismissive and unhelpful. He has now found out that this was a senior director who had called in on his day off to collect some papers.

   a) Suggest at least two dangers of judging customers purely on appearance.

   b) Explain why all customers should be given the same attention and consideration regardless of whether they are internal or external, old or young.

   c) What type of impression do you think Dan made on the senior director and what effect might this have in the future?

▼ FOLLOW COMPANY PROCEDURES FOR COMMUNICATING WITH CUSTOMERS

Most companies have procedures which state how staff should communicate with customers. These are useful because they ensure that all staff respond in the same way and they also reduce the number of times staff need to ask someone what to do or what to say.

In some organisations, such as call centres, staff may even have a script they have to follow over the telephone, with a standard greeting and a standard ending. This type of communication was described on page 106.

In other companies, you may be allowed more flexibility, but there are still likely to be common procedures to ensure that all staff will:

▶ give customers prompt attention

▶ address them properly

▶ deal with complaints in the correct way

▶ keep company information confidential.

These procedures will apply whether staff are dealing with customers face-to-face or on the telephone.

Providing prompt attention

Many organisations have customer service standards. These may give target response times, for example:

▶ all telephone calls must be answered within six rings

▶ all letters must be acknowledged within three working days

▶ all visitors to reception must be acknowledged immediately on arrival. No visitor with an appointment to see a specific member of staff must be asked to wait for more than ten minutes.

The aim of these targets, of course, is to minimise delays for customers and to prevent some of the 'queuing' problems you read about on page 133. On a normal day, the targets should be quite achievable. Difficulties can occur on other days when you might be extremely busy, short-staffed and trying to do about six jobs at the same time. If three people are waiting to speak to you, the telephone is ringing and a senior manager wants to talk to you and is looking impatient – what do you do?

There are no totally fixed rules for this – for example, it would depend upon whether the senior manager is obviously in a frantic hurry and is signalling that only two seconds of your time is needed or whether he or she indicates that waiting isn't a problem. Generally, however, you will cope better in this sort of crisis if you:

▶ don't panic! This never helped anyone to work quicker or more effectively

▶ think external before internal in relation to customer priority

- think telephone before face-to-face (simply because the person on the other end of the line can't see you have a problem whereas your visitor can). Say 'I'm sorry but do you mind if I answer the telephone?' to a customer who is in front of you then keep the call short. If it is going to be lengthy, arrange to call back

- acknowledge customers who are waiting by looking at them and smiling, rather than pretending they don't exist! This gives them confidence that they will be dealt with soon

- start the conversation by apologising for the delay if someone has had to wait. A simple 'I'm sorry to have kept you waiting' is enough.

Styles of address

With all your customers you are always better to be more formal. You will never offend anyone by calling them 'Sir' or 'Madam'; but you could easily do so if you try to become too personal. Although this may seem very formal, you will find that many companies specify that you do this when you are dealing with external customers whom you don't know – regardless of their age.

If you know a customer's name then use it, for example, 'Hello (or Good morning), Mr Stevens.' Over time, if you get to know someone well, then they may ask you to use their first name but you should wait to be told.

Many organisations have a 'corporate style' that they train their staff to use along with certain words and phrases. For example, staff may be told to answer the telephone by giving a specific greeting, identifying themselves by the first name and then asking how they can help: 'Hello, Compass Software, Lee speaking, how can I help you?' They may also be told to close the conversation in a standard way, e.g. 'Goodbye. Thank you for calling Compass Software.' Some people like this approach and others do not – but if you are told to do this then you must follow your instructions. Giving your name is important because this makes the contact more personal – but remember that this also identifies you later if the caller had a problem with the call!

If there is no specific style to follow, then use your common sense. Other tips include the following:

- Remembering that 'Good morning' (or afternoon) is more formal than 'Hello', which itself is more formal than 'Hi'.

- Using someone's name during a conversation is always a good idea. First, it makes the person feel more important and second, it helps you to remember their name!

- Saying 'Goodbye, thank you for calling' is appropriate for an external call, saying just 'goodbye' is better for a senior, internal caller and you may just say 'bye' to end a call with colleague of your own age.

Health workers in the north west were wrapped over the knuckles for using northern terms of endearment to patients and visitors. An ambulance crew was in trouble for calling a man 'mate' and a ward sister had similar problems when a woman she called 'cock' lodged a formal complaint. Staff have also been warned to avoid using other terms, such as 'love' or 'duck' and ambulance crews have been instructed by managers to call patients 'sir' or 'madam' in future.

Some members of staff disagree with the decision. They argue that using friendly terms can be a good thing, particularly if someone is ill or in a panic. The managers, however, are worried about press reports and don't want to trigger any further complaints, so they are insisting that staff stick to the new rule.

You might want to consider what similar terms are regularly used in your region and what their effect might be in a business situation.

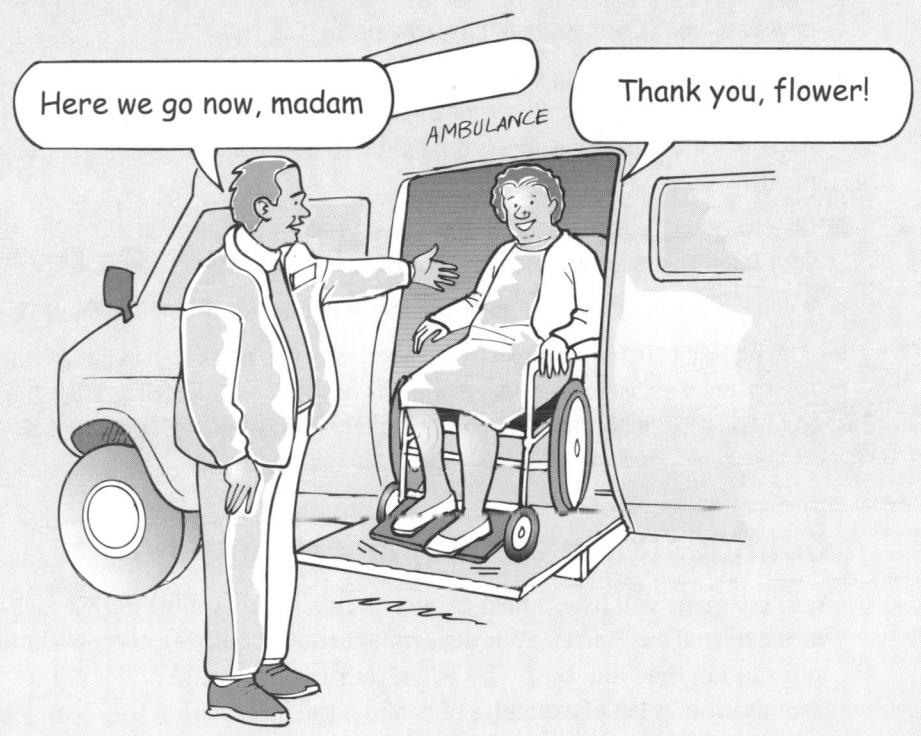

▲ Some health workers have to be very formal in their use of language but the public can still use friendly terms if they want to

Dealing with complaints

There are two aspects to dealing with complaints. One is the way you handle the complaint itself. This is dealt with on page 155. The other is the way you handle the person – and that links to your communication skills, your body language and the fact that the company will want you to pacify the customer and meet his or her needs. Many companies now issue guidelines or procedures on how to handle a customer with a complaint, although these may differ slightly depending upon whether the complainant is internal or external, and on the seriousness of the matter.

The main rules are shown in the following table.

Guidelines for handling a person making a complaint

▶ Never think you know what someone wants until they have spoken – and never interrupt someone who is making a complaint.

▶ Stay calm – take a few deep breaths if necessary.

▶ Don't take the complaint personally. Stay positive and think of it as a problem which you can help to solve.

▶ Look interested and concerned – so that your body language signals that you are sympathetic and want to help.

▶ Listen carefully – and make notes if the matter is complicated.

▶ Never contradict the customer, e.g. by saying he or she 'must be mistaken' or 'is confused' as this will make the situation worse.

▶ Don't make any judgements – you can't tell who is right and wrong at this stage – and *never* say your company is at fault (see pages 158 and 159).

▶ Use questioning skills to find out what the customer wants you to do. Some customers may not want you to do anything – they just want to tell you how they feel! In this case, if you have indicated the complaint has been taken seriously and will be passed on, this is usually enough.

▶ Check with your team leader or supervisor before you commit either your organisation or your team to any action that isn't within your own area of responsibility.

▶ If you can agree to do something yourself, without exceeding the limits of your job, do it!

▶ If an external customer is extremely angry and you feel you can't cope, then ask a more experienced colleague for help. Company procedures will always state that you do not have to tolerate insults or threats in any situation.

Confidentiality of company information

Your company will have a host of information it either must not or does not want to share with external customers. Your department (or your office) may also hold certain information that your boss – for whatever reason – would prefer not to share across the organisation. A list of examples of confidential information was given on page 93. For that reason, confidentiality can apply to both your external and internal customers, but is more likely to be critical with the former.

Some organisations have very strict rules about confidentiality which restrict communications between staff and external contacts such as their direct competitors. Flouting these rules is taken very seriously and can even lead to dismissal (see page 301).

Others have strict procedures in relation to vetting customers themselves. An example is when customers use telephone banking. Before they can even speak to someone they have to enter a code into their telephone and may have to pass extra security checks once they are in contact. If you work for an organisation where security of customer information is paramount, then you must follow the procedures that are in place. If you struggle with a particular customer, then ask your supervisor for assistance.

For most administrators, however, the main thing is to guard against inadvertently saying something that should be kept confidential. This can happen if you are trying to keep a customer happy by answering questions or giving a long, involved explanation (when probably a short one would do). It is also important to make sure that you do not breach the Data Protection Act, which protects individuals whose personal data is held by organisations (see page 140).

If you are not given any specific procedures but told to use your common sense, then use the guidelines in the table below to preserve confidentiality.

Guidelines for keeping information confidential

▶ If a customer (internal or external) asks to provide copies of documents then check that you can do this before you agree.

▶ If you work in a public area, keep 'sensitive' documents in a folder and position your computer screen so that it can't be read by visitors.

▶ If you are preparing a confidential document in your office, and visitors or internal customers are around, then a useful tip is to start a second document and 'switch windows' if someone approaches your desk (you can do this very quickly by pressing Alt+Tab). If you leave your desk, save your document and exit the program.

▶ Be careful of the information you disclose over the telephone. A 'prospective' (but unknown) customer may really be a competitor trying to find out more about your existing customers and your charges!

▶ Never talk negatively about your colleagues, department or your company – even by way of explanation. Sympathising with an external customer over a delay but sharing the information that 'It was even worse last week when our packers were on strike' is not going to instil confidence in your organisation and is giving away unnecessary internal information.

▶ Be wary of any information relating to other customers, internal problems, business plans or staff who work in the organisation and keep any explanations brief and totally related to the topic under discussion.

▶ If you are asked a question and are not sure whether you can disclose the information then simply say you do not know the answer but will find out. This saves a debate as to why you won't tell and gives you the opportunity to check what to do.

▶ Never get drawn into 'gossiping' with any customer, about anything, no matter how well you think you know them!

PEOPLE IN BUSINESS

Clear guidance on confidentiality is usually welcomed by staff, particularly those who work for organisations which deal with personal or commercially sensitive information. Some business customers can insist on confidentiality agreements being signed by their supplier, which means that all external discussion on the work being carried out for them is forbidden.

One organisation where you would think staff would be very mindful of confidentiality is the Inland Revenue, which deals with personal tax affairs. However, in an internal memo discovered by *Computer Weekly* in January 2003 it became clear that managers were concerned about unauthorised access to files and disclosure of sensitive information. In some cases staff were selling the information they had found when they were 'celebrity browsing' to find out how much famous people spent and earned. In other cases, they were finding out information about family or friends out of curiosity or using the information maliciously; for example, finding out how much an ex-spouse earned and then informing the Child Support Agency.

Under the Data Protection Act, breaching customer confidence by selling or buying personal data in this way is a serious offence, with an unlimited fine. The Inland Revenue is now bringing in a new policy on security which will include severe punishments for any of the 60,000 staff who break the rules.

OVER TO YOU!

1 For the next few days, check how long you are kept waiting in different places, both in person and on the telephone. You should also watch for the various techniques used by organisations to cope with problems, such as a sudden rush of customers. As an example, a supermarket will often open up more checkouts. (If you work part-time, you may be able to add to this from your own experience.)

Then make a list of 5 organisations and score the service you received, in terms of both promptness and attitude of staff, out of 5, where 5 is excellent and 1 is poor. Compare your lists with other members of your group to identify the best and the worst places in your area for speedy response times – with reasons.

2 Select any of the following reasons for complaining and role play the situation with a partner who is acting as an administrator for the organisation. Then reverse roles. As the customer, practise your assertiveness skills (see page 119). This means explaining clearly and not becoming aggressive. As the administrator, practise using communication skills that show you are helpful and positive – even if you can't actually solve the problem.

a) As a student, you have twice been sent to the wrong room for an evening class you are starting. You have been given a third room number and told that this is correct but you are annoyed about the disorganisation which has now made you late.

b) You ordered a present for a friend which should have arrived two weeks ago by mail order. You rang last week and was assured that it was in the post. On Monday you rang again and received the same answer. Today your neighbour delivered it to your door – it has the wrong name, wrong house number and the town is wrong. Only the postcode is right. You decide to ring to complain because you know you gave the information correctly and think it is only because of the skill of the Royal Mail and a kind neighbour that you received it at all.

c) You rang a travel agent to check if they had a brochure you wanted. They said they had. At lunchtime you trail through wind and rain to collect it but, by mistake, their only copy was given to someone else this morning.

d) You left a bracelet for repair at a local jewellers. You were assured it would be back by Friday – and you want to wear it on Saturday. When you go to collect it there appears to be a problem and the bracelet now won't be ready for another week.

3 Michelle has started work as administrator for a director at a company which designs websites for business customers. The company deals with a considerable amount of privileged information about its clients which must never be disclosed to anyone. From the following situations and requests, decide which information Michelle can disclose and which she can't. Then suggest what she should do in the cases where the information is sensitive.

a) An external customer wants the mobile phone number of the Michelle's manager because he has lost the business card on which it was printed.

b) An external customer says that she thinks the quote for their site to be redesigned is too high. She knows your firm recently updated another firm's site and asks how much they were charged.

c) An internal customer asks her if she knows whether the Directors decided whether or not to give an annual bonus at their last meeting.

d) An internal customer asks her if her boss will be available to meet an important customer next Wednesday.

e) A prospective customer asks if it is true the company won a recent award for website design.

f) An external customer asks if it is true that the company has been cutting back on staff recently.

▼ INTERACT EFFECTIVELY WITH CUSTOMERS

If you interact with someone then you reciprocate. In plain English, your communications are two-way – they talk and you listen, you then respond according to what you heard, and so on. You don't interact if you do all the talking or if you don't respond appropriately. Interaction is also difficult if you can't understand what someone is saying or if they never stop talking!

Interaction is important because otherwise the conversation is totally one-sided. Effective interaction takes place when you not only respond, but you say the right things, in the right way, at the right time and then check your customer has understood exactly what you meant.

The importance of communication

It is important to communicate with people to keep them informed about what is happening. However, there is a difference between simply understanding that communications are important and understanding how the whole process works – so that you use it to your advantage.

All communications take place between two people – the 'sender' (who has the information) and the 'receiver' – and goes through several stages, which are shown in the diagram below. If you interact properly, then the final stage (feedback) will result in you sending a new message, based on the response you received.

Communication takes place only if each stage is successful and this requires several skills, as you will see below.

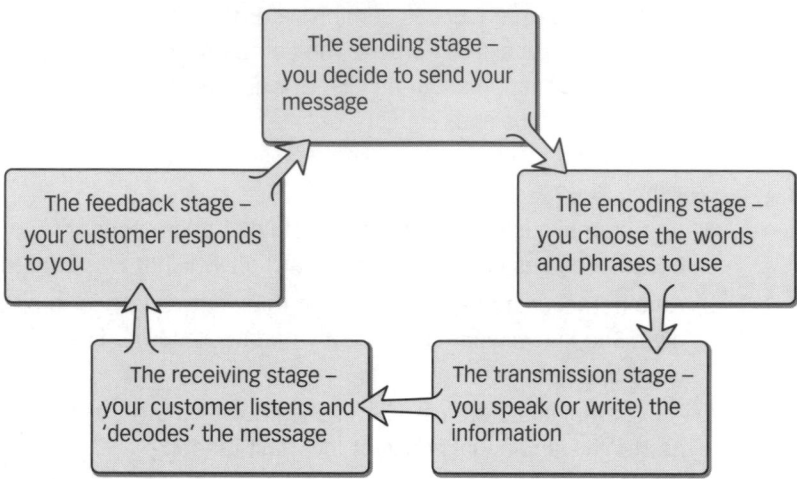

▲ The communication cycle

Appropriate verbal and non-verbal communication skills

On page 101, you read about verbal communication skills and how body language signals people's true feelings. Now you can see how these skills impact upon the communications cycle.

Stage 1 – The sending stage

You cannot send a message to a customer if:

▶ you don't know what you are talking about

▶ you haven't planned what you are going to say

▶ you are vague or imprecise

▶ you are trying to do two things at once.

Stage 2 – The encoding stage

A customer will not understand your information if:

▶ you use words or terms they do not understand

▶ your message is confused, vague or incomplete.

Stage 3 – The transmission stage

Your customer won't receive your message if:

▶ your message is distorted or interrupted (such as being cut off when you are on the telephone)

▶ there is too much external 'noise' or other distractions.

Stage 4 – The receiving stage

Your customers won't understand your message if:

▶ they cannot understand what you are saying

▶ your tone, attitude or body language distracts them

▶ they are too annoyed or angry to listen

▶ they are trying to do something else at the same time.

Stage 5 – The feedback stage

You need feedback to check that your message has been received and understood correctly. However, things will go wrong if:

▶ you don't listen properly

▶ you don't respond appropriately

▶ you don't give someone the chance to give you feedback.

Therefore you need to develop the skills listed below.

▶ The ability to think through what you are going to say – and its likely impact – before you speak.

▶ The knack of choosing the right words and phrases for the situation and the receiver.

▶ The ability to be precise and to get to the point, without sounding abrupt or curt.

▶ Confidence – so that you don't distract people by your own nervousness or apprehension.

▶ Listening skills – so that you don't have to be told something two or three times (see below).

▶ Reflective body language to show you empathise with the customer (see page 144 and below).

▶ Patience – to help if you are having problems.

▶ The ability to read and interpret your customer's body language – and react accordingly.

▶ Questioning skills – so that you can help to 'prompt' someone who is having difficulties themselves. These are the subject of the next section.

In 2002/3, the bank HSBC launched an advertising campaign which identified body language and how it differed between cultures and countries. It covered gestures which are acceptable in one country but not in another. The aim of the campaign was to tell customers that HSBC operated effectively on an international basis.

Although you may not have to deal with international customers yourself, it is useful to know that these differences exist. The 'thumbs up' gesture, for example, has different interpretations in various countries. However, some gestures are more universal, such as nodding the head for 'yes' and shaking the head for 'no', but probably the only truly international gestures are smiling and frowning. Showing the palms of your hand indicates honesty – covering your mouth with your hand when you speak can indicate the opposite. A shrug indicates a lack of understanding and a smile indicates a welcome. A sneer needs no translation, anywhere!

People who are interested in something often tilt their heads or stroke their chins as they consider what they are hearing. People who are uninterested lower their head or may try to 'block' a message by folding their arms. Someone who is fed up or aggressive may put their hands on their hips or point a finger – a gesture which is considered rude virtually everywhere.

People who are in harmony often 'reflect' each other's body language. As one person crosses their legs or leans on their arm, the other does the same thing. Watch for this the next time you are talking to a close friend and check how often you do it!

▲ Close friends can reflect each other's body language without realising it

The importance of questioning and listening skills

Even if you become an expert communicator, you will still meet people who struggle to communicate in response. Remember that interaction means two-way, so in this situation you have to develop skills to prompt a response.

Questioning skills

You may need to question a customer to obtain the information you need – but this shouldn't be an interrogation! Neither should you 'jump in' with questions too quickly, when you haven't given the customer enough time to respond. If the matter is personal or the person is nervous or anxious, then you need to be gentle in your approach, even if you have to be persistent. This may be the case if you can't understand the other person very well and need to clarify (check) that you have received their message accurately.

You will probably find it helpful to follow the guidelines in the table below.

The art of questioning

▶ Set the scene, if you need to gather specific information, by explaining you will have to ask a few questions and that this will help you to give a better service. This warns the customer what to expect.

▶ Ask one question at a time, otherwise you will confuse people.

▶ Ask questions in a logical order.

▶ Avoid inappropriate personal questions (for example, if a customer tells you they can't make an appointment for next week then don't say 'Why not?')

▶ Ask any essential personal questions in a private area and with tact (for example, instead of saying 'how old are you?' ask 'Could you give me your date of birth please?' – and be prepared to explain why you need it).

▶ Use pauses in the conversation and moderate your tone of voice so that you don't turn into an inquisitor by accident.

▶ Ask 'open' questions. The key words of 'who', 'what', 'when', 'how', 'why' and 'when' will usually cover all the different types of information you may need.

▶ Ask an appropriate 'follow-up' question if you don't get a full answer the first time or you are uncertain whether you understood the information correctly.

▶ Smile, don't frown (or look shocked), when you receive answers! You are there to obtain information, not to judge anyone.

▶ Write down the answers when you are collecting information. You will annoy people if they have to repeat themselves because you were trying to commit everything to memory and failed.

▶ Be diplomatic if you have to respond to a difficult question yourself. You can always try the politician's trick of not giving a direct answer – or answering a question with another question. For example, the internal customer who arrives just when you and your team are taking your first break all day and comments 'Do you lot never have any work to do?' doesn't deserve a direct answer. Simply smile sweetly and respond 'Oh, hello Ken – what can we do for you?'

▲ Asking questions shouldn't be an interrogation

Listening skills

It is pointless to ask questions if you don't listen to the replies and then respond appropriately. Most people are far better talkers than listeners. You can see this in action if you watch a group of friends exchanging news rapidly – and all interrupting one another in their excitement!

You can test your own listening skills quite easily by trying to recall a recent conversation. If you can remember more about what you said than what you heard, then you need to improve your listening skills. **Active listening** occurs when you concentrate more on the other person than yourself. If you are really good, then you can improve your observational powers to summarise how they felt as well as what they said – but this takes practice! When you deal with customers on the telephone, of course, you can't assess their body language so your listening skills become even more important.

To develop your listening skills, follow the guidelines in the table below.

The art of listening

▶ Recognise when your listening ability starts to fluctuate – such as when you are bored or uninterested in what someone is saying. Other 'trigger points' are when you are distracted, in a hurry, annoyed, uncomfortable or when you have just thought of something *you* want to say.

▶ If you feel your mind is wandering, deliberately 'switch on again'.

▶ Never interrupt. Wait until your customer has finished speaking. All conversations have 'natural pauses' somewhere!

▶ Focus on the person who is speaking, not yourself.

▶ Try to assess someone's attitude and manner from their body language and tone of voice if they are in front of you. If you are on the telephone, listen for non-verbal signals – such as a sigh, a laugh or even a long silence.

▶ Don't jump to conclusions as this makes you stop listening. Keep an open mind throughout the conversation. The next piece of information you hear might be the most important!

▶ Always repeat the information back to check that you have understood everything correctly.

Potential communication problems – and how to solve them

Communication problems can occur at any stage of the communications cycle (see page 142). They may be caused by you or by your customer who, you may remember, is the receiver in this situation.

At the sending stage

You will create problems if you:

- do not know enough to help the customer – especially if you then 'guess' the answer
- are overly nervous or over-awed by the customer
- struggle to express yourself properly
- are trying to do several things at once – including dealing with a customer.

You will solve these problems if you remember the following:

- Make sure you have all the facts before you start and be honest enough to admit when you don't know something. Then find out!
- Take a deep breath, relax, smile and try to focus on the other person and not yourself. Remember that you can only do your best.
- Practise your verbal communication skills and improve your vocabulary.
- Stop what you are doing when you have to deal with a customer.

At the encoding stage

You will create problems if you:

- do not know how to say what you mean
- don't speak clearly
- cannot communicate in the same language as your receiver.

You will solve these problems if you:

- think about what you are going to say before you say it
- speak clearly and concisely (see page 152)
- use words and phrases that they will understand.

At the transmitting stage

Your customer needs to hear you clearly to receive the message. You may find you have problems if:

- the area is noisy
- the customer is distracted
- the customer has a hearing impairment
- you have a bad telephone connection.

You can solve these problems by:

- ▶ moving to a quieter place

- ▶ choosing the best time and place – particularly for an internal customer who may be busy doing other work

- ▶ enunciating each word clearly if someone is trying to lip-read. *Never* shout at someone in this situation.

- ▶ disconnecting if you can't hear someone over the telephone – or they can't hear you – and ringing them back.

At the receiving stage

You will experience problems if:

- ▶ your customer cannot understand you

- ▶ your customer's strong feelings are getting in the way

- ▶ your customer is bored, distracted, nervous or angry.

You can solve these by:

- ▶ rephrasing your message if the customer doesn't understand you, rather than just repeating yourself

- ▶ making sure your tone, attitude and body language are appropriate

- ▶ obtaining help if you are dealing with a foreign customer with whom you are really struggling to communicate

- ▶ never interrupting a customer who is annoyed (see page 138)

- ▶ learning to read your customer's body language

- ▶ never expecting customers to listen to important information when they are concentrating on something else – such as signing a cheque or completing a form.

At the feedback stage

You will have problems if you:

- ▶ don't listen properly

- ▶ don't react appropriately to the information you receive.

Solve these by:

- ▶ improving your listening skills and then adapting your approach accordingly throughout the conversation.

Other types of problems, specifically linked to serious problems and complaints, are dealt with on page 155.

1. The best way to learn about body language is to become a people watcher. Airports, railway stations and cafés are ideal – anywhere, in fact, where you will find large numbers of people. See if you can spot people who are bored, impatient, excited, in a rush – and identify the signs that you see. Then compare your observations with others in your group. You may find it helpful to borrow a good book on body language (with lots of illustrations) from your college library, as this will give you some useful clues what to look for.

2. Identify what has gone wrong in each of the following communications. Then suggest how the problem can be solved.

   a) Carla works for an office supplies company. When she asks a customer over the telephone if he would prefer A4 or DL envelopes there is a long silence.

   b) Martin was trying to finish an urgent job when his boss asked him for a customer file. Now he can't remember which one was needed.

   c) Rawinda's boss asked her to ring the firm's help desk to say his computer was faulty. When she is asked to describe the problem she doesn't know what to say.

   d) Fiona is trying to make a good impression on a good-looking young male customer whilst she is helping him to fill in an application form. Only after he has left does she realise that she hasn't asked for some critical information that is required.

   e) Kelly is listening to a customer who is annoyed about a late delivery. She can't understand why he gets angry when she is insisting it was the fault of their supplier.

3. Test your questioning and listening skills by working with a partner on the following exercise. You have ten minutes to find the answers to the following questions:

   a) His or her favourite foods.

   b) The best holiday or day out he or she has ever experienced – and why.

   c) The qualities he or she looks for in a close friend – and why.

   d) What he or she would most like to be doing in three years' time – and why.

▼ USE APPROPRIATE TONE AND MANNER

You have already seen that tone and manner are important. However, whereas these should reflect a positive attitude at all times, there are occasions when you need to adjust the tone, manner and the language you use. This would be necessary if you were dealing with a particularly difficult customer or if you were giving very bad news, as you will see below. In addition, always remember the following.

▶ Being too friendly with a customer – or being over-familiar – is off-putting and many people will resent it. You will avoid this if you keep your conversations strictly business-like and don't venture into personal areas of discussion or use personal endearments.

▲ Over-familiarity can be alarming for customers

▶ Customers may not understand many of the terms used in your organisation or in your type of work. Therefore you should explain clearly any abbreviations or jargon which you have to use.

In other respects, consistency is important, as you will see below.

Being helpful at all times

It is easy to be helpful when you are in a good mood, when the customer is pleasant and when the situation is straightforward. It is far less so if you are depressed or overworked, the customer is being difficult and/or you can't understand what is required.

If you have problems staying positive in this situation, try putting yourself in the shoes of the customer. Concentrate on the customer's needs rather than your own and remember that few people are deliberately difficult unless they are having a problem! Your job is to help to solve that problem. If you can't, then ask someone else to help you.

Finally, a useful discipline on a really bad day is to remember that if you alienate all your customers and they disappear, your employer is unlikely to remain in business for very long and therefore you are likely to be looking for another job. This normally focuses your mind on being helpful, no matter how you really feel!

Being polite, calm and confident

It is obviously essential to be polite but this does mean choosing your words and tone with care. You will also appear to be impolite if you are abrupt or curt during a conversation – so do allow enough time in order to deal with people properly.

Another useful tip to remember is that people accept good news far more easily than bad. Therefore, if you have to give someone some unwelcome information your words and tone are doubly important. You can often soften your message by being sympathetic, apologising and then offering a positive suggestion.

If a customer is agitated or annoyed then it is easy to become ruffled yourself, especially if you do not know the answer to many questions that you are asked. You can avoid many problems if you focus on staying in control of the situation, and practise some of the assertiveness skills you read about earlier.

Control is easier if you are confident – and confidence often comes only with experience. There may be situations at the start where you are nervous and unsure, but it can help to watch more experienced colleagues and copy their approach. Be patient with yourself if you make a mistake or find yourself having difficulties. Simply do the best you can and ask for help when you need it. If you learn from the experience and are prepared to work at improving your skills then your confidence will increase quite naturally with every positive encounter you have with a customer.

Finally, a word of warning. Although a few customers may find a lack of confidence to be frustrating, far more customers will be alienated by over-confidence. Someone who acts as if they know it all and treats customers dismissively is far more dangerous than someone who is obviously learning the ropes and trying to be helpful. So no matter how experienced or confident you become, remember that a little humility is often very attractive.

1 Marsha has to tell a customer that they no longer stock a product he wants. Identify the best approach she should take and give a reason for your choice.

a) 'I'm sorry, we no longer stock that.'

b) 'There's no demand for that any more.'

c) 'I'm sorry, we don't stock that now, but I think you can still get them from Bates Brothers. Would you like their number?'

d) 'We aren't stocking that at the moment, but I'll let you know if the situation changes.'

2 Each of the following people is losing control over a situation. Identify the 'trigger point' which has caused it and then suggest, as a group, what the person could do about it.

a) Joanne greets a customer who has come to see her boss and asks him to wait a moment. When she tries her boss's telephone there is no reply and when she goes to his office there is no sign of him. Meanwhile the customer is becoming more impatient and Joanne is getting panicky.

b) Marianne is a senior executive in the company and can sometimes be difficult to deal with. Last time Jon dealt with her he didn't know enough to help her and felt he looked foolish. He is now dreading having to deal with her again.

c) Tara has to tell a customer that the price she quoted him yesterday is incorrect. Because of price increases it is now 6% higher and Tara looked at an outdated price list. She is not looking forward to giving him this information and asks an older colleague to do it for her. Her colleague refuses, saying Tara has to learn how to deal with these situations.

d) Nadia is frantically busy when she is interrupted by a customer who seems to want to tell her his life story. Nadia has lots to do and can feel herself becoming more irritated with him by the second.

3 Try to identify the 'trigger points' which make you feel you are losing control and the reaction that then follows. This could be anything from annoyance to butterflies! Then work out your own strategy for dealing with situations that have that effect. If you struggle to do this, have a word in private with your tutor.

PEOPLE IN BUSINESS

There are many types of business that use terms and jargon which are unfamiliar to most people. In fact, if you mention that you are doing an OCR award then many people may not know what you mean! In education, health, accountancy and the law – to name but a few – literally dozens of abbreviations and specialist terms are used every day which may be totally incomprehensible to many people.

In the legal profession, about a quarter of the complaints against solicitors concern communications and the use of terms that their clients don't understand. In order to help, the Law Society – which is the professional body for solicitors in England and Wales – has introduced a charter which calls for solicitors to communicate in plain English with their clients and to keep them informed.

The Law Society has also produced a number of customer guides to help people who have to deal with a solicitor for the first time. These are in addition to the Client's Charter, which specifies what customers can expect when they appoint a solicitor. The leaflets and charter are available in several languages and can be obtained from a solicitor or by following the links at www.heinemann.co.uk/hotlinks.

▼ CONVEY INFORMATION CLEARLY AND ACCURATELY

In order to communicate effectively you must bear in mind the need for accuracy and clarity when you communicate, remember that some types of information are confidential and know what your limitations are.

The importance of accuracy and clarity

There are several reasons why your communications should always be clear, accurate and concise – as well as timely and complete.

▷ **accurate** and **up-to-date** information prevents speculation, rumours and worry

▷ **clear** information reduces the danger of doubt or misunderstandings

▷ **concise** information means you don't waste people's time with unnecessary details

▷ **timely** information reduces problems and saves other people time and unnecessary effort

▷ **complete** information means that people don't have to come back to you to fill in the gaps.

In addition, making sure people receive the information they need, in the right way, shows you are concerned about them and want to help.

You will improve your accuracy and clarity by

▷ checking your facts and never guessing information

▷ noting down the details of a complex matter before you start to communicate

▷ checking facts you are given by repeating them back – such as details of times, places, telephone or catalogue numbers

▷ writing clearly – so that you can read your own notes

▷ checking the exact spelling of people's names and addresses

▷ being alert for feedback to make sure the receiver has understood you

▷ rephrasing what you are saying, or explaining yourself, if there is a communication problem:

Confidentiality and the limits of your own role

You have already learned about the importance of confidentiality on page 139. In any job you do, certain information will always be sensitive or confidential but another important aspect of passing on information is to know what your own limitations are (see also page 87). These will vary according to your job role. As you gain in experience and move up the career ladder you will have access to more confidential information – so you still have to find the right balance.

As a useful guide:

▷ Never speculate about the reaction or response of another member of staff to a situation.

▷ Never disclose internal discussions within the department to anyone outside it.

- Never discuss internal matters which are not directly relevant to the transaction with external customers.

- Never talk about one customer in front of another.

- Watch what you are saying over the telephone or to your colleagues when you are within earshot of a customer.

- If you are in any doubt at all about whether you should disclose information, always check first.

▼ RESOLVE DIFFICULTIES USING ORGANISATIONAL PROCEDURES

All organisations are aware that, no matter how well staff are trained, there will be some situations that create difficulties. These might occur because a customer has a special requirement or because there is a serious problem. In these instances, staff need clear guidance on what action to take. These are normally specified in company procedures.

You will learn more about procedures in Unit 4. These are simply a step-by-step guide for dealing with a situation. They are useful because all staff then do the same thing and know what action to take when a situation occurs. If they are unsure, they can simply refer to the procedures. For that reason, it is important that you are aware of any procedures that exist in any organisation which employs you – and that you follow them.

Procedures relating to customers' special requirements

Customers may have special requirements for many reasons, including:

- their own personal circumstances
- they have a physical impairment or disability
- they do not speak English very well
- they have particular requirements linked to their culture or religious beliefs
- they have an individual or unusual request.

Today, most organisations will actively promote equal opportunities to all their staff and visitors. They will provide special food options, such as vegan meals, halal or kosher meat, interpreters, wheelchair access, Braille buttons in lifts and so on. All these facilities help, but you also need to be aware of specific requirements and the options available to you – and where to obtain help and advice if you need it. These may be documented in specific procedures in the organisation.

For example, in your college, there will be procedures for dealing with students who have particular difficulties or disabilities, particularly in relation to key aspects of their study such as assessments or examinations. In all organisations, there will be specific procedures for dealing with people with disabilities in an emergency evacuation. In commercial organisations, there may be guidelines for staff who regularly deal with foreign visitors, including how to obtain an interpreter, the appropriate meals to serve and how to observe other important cultural differences.

In addition to finding out the procedures that exist in your organisation, you also need to gain the confidence to deal with people with a special requirement in a positive manner. The table on page 154 should help you.

Special requirements of customers

Special requirement	Likely result(s)	Tips to help
Personal circumstances	Increased stress resulting in irritability or impatience	Prioritise urgent requests Keep customer informed of progress Be sensitive to mood changes Stay calm!
Physical impairment or disability	Access requirements Assistance in emergency Assistance with special requirements	Know facilities in your building (e.g. disabled toilets) Be sensitive – most people treasure their independence Be additionally courteous, open doors, offer to read/complete a form, etc. Concentrate on the person, not the disability Allow additional time
Foreign nationals who do not speak English well	Difficulty reading forms and signs Difficulty understanding verbal information	Speak relatively slowly Use simple English words Use short sentences Listen carefully Repeat back what you hear Use sign language and gestures to help
Cultural or religious beliefs	Different expectations/needs Individual holidays Different clothing Different interpretation of body language Different food requirements	Learn more about the cultural beliefs of those you deal with regularly Be sensitive to different needs Be wary of the body language you use If in doubt what to do, ask a more experienced colleague for guidance
Individual or unusual request	Lack of official guidance on what to do/say	Stay positive Note down request in detail Never assume it 'can't be done' Ask a positive-minded senior colleague for guidance

Procedures relating to difficult situations

You may find yourself in difficulties for several reasons. You may have to handle a serious customer complaint, answer an unusual query or simply have a troublesome customer who doesn't react in the normal way.

Today 40% of business travellers are women – who have specific needs and requirements which are often different from those of male business executives. This fact has now been recognised by many large hotel groups after a series of studies and advisory panels of female travellers in which 80% of women travellers identified security as being their major concern. They also highlighted good health and fitness facilities, a room service menu with lighter and healthier meals – few women like eating on their own in a hotel restaurant or entering a hotel bar alone – and appropriate amenities in their rooms, such as skirt hangers and padded hangers, irons, ironing boards, good lighting and a full-length mirror.

As a result, the London Hilton Park Lane has refurbished the 30 rooms on its 22nd floor to become an all-women zone and offers a private check-in to make sure that names and room numbers remain private. The guests are served only by female staff and the rooms include women's magazines, powerful hairdryers, well-lit mirrors and a range of female toiletries. Special lift access controls entry onto the floor for enhanced security. The Hilton considers this improves on the standard precautions of spy-holes in doors, double locks and chain mechanisms.

This also means, of course, that staff must follow specific procedures to protect guests' privacy, with room numbers written down rather than spoken and strict controls over room allocation. Many women feel the change is long overdue as, within the travel industry, female business travellers often report that they are treated less courteously than men by airline and hotel staff. Good training and appropriate procedures should help put an end to this in the future.

Procedures for customer complaints

You have already seen how to handle customers with a complaint on page 137. In addition, virtually all organisations have procedures in place to deal with customer complaints. The aim of these is to ensure that:

▷ customers making a complaint receive prompt service

▷ all complaints are handled fairly and in the same way

▷ all complaints are treated confidentially

▷ all complaints are investigated properly by the right person.

The procedures may instruct staff how to complete a specific complaint form or to tell customers how to make a complaint. They are also likely to state the manager who must be notified if there is a serious complaint.

Complaints procedures will also give you guidance on the limitation of your own role. For example, although most retail staff may be allowed to exchange faulty goods they may have to ask for a receipt or other proof of purchase, and may not be allowed to agree to a 'special deal' or cash refund without proof of purchase unless they have the specific authorisation of the manager.

Normally the procedure for dealing with internal customer complaints is different from external customers. This is because all external customers have certain legal rights and it is important that these are recognised. Your internal customers may be able to complain, but are not normally able to take your company to court for letting them down.

▶ **Internal complaints** If you receive a complaint from an internal customer it is sensible to:

- write down the details and the nature of the complaint
- take personal action to put matters right, especially if you have caused the problem in the first place
- if the matter is minor but relates to one of your colleagues, pass on the message to that person to put matters right
- if the matter is more serious, see your team leader or supervisor in private and pass on the information. Do not discuss the matter with anyone else.

▶ **External complaints** These complaints can be divided into minor matters and serious issues. Most organisations encourage their staff to deal with minor matters as they occur and to use their initiative to remedy the problem, in accordance with the standard procedures. More serious matters should always be referred to someone in authority to prevent the situation becoming any worse. In many organisations *all* complaints have to be recorded.

An example of staff guidelines relating to external customer complaint procedures is shown below.

Example of staff guidelines relating to customer complaint procedures

A complaint is any criticism or adverse comment about our products or service. To ensure that we give all our customers the best possible service and deal with complaints fairly and promptly, all staff should follow the procedures below when receiving a customer complaint.

1 Customers may complain face-to-face, on the telephone, by letter, fax or email. Customers making a serious complaint should be asked to make this in writing or to complete an official complaint form. This ensures that all the relevant information is obtained.

2 For minor complaints, the aim must be to resolve the situation within 5 working days, to the customer's satisfaction. If this target cannot be met, the complaint must be referred to the Customer Services manager.

3 All serious complaints must be referred immediately to the Customer Services manager.

4 For serious complaints, a written acknowledgement must be sent to the customer, by the Customer Services manager, within 5 working days.

5 The Customer Services manager will be responsible for investigating any complaint with the appropriate departmental manager and staff.

6 Customers must be kept fully informed of the progress of any ongoing investigations into their complaint.

7 All investigations should be given priority with the aim of sending a full explanation to the customer within 15 working days.

8 All customers must be informed that if they are unhappy with the response they receive, they can write to the Chief Executive of the company.

9 Staff are encouraged to use their initiative in solving minor problems. All staff can replace or refund any damaged items against a receipt or other proof of purchase, e.g. a sales transaction recorded on the computer database. Unwanted items can be returned within one month of purchase.

10 All complaints must be recorded fully in the complaints log in the main Administration Office for monitoring purposes.

Procedures for answering queries

On your first day in a new job, every query can seem like a nightmare because you don't know the answer to anything. Over time, you begin to recognise standard queries and to build up a collection of information to help you answer these. This is why, on most reception desks, you will find a wide range of information available so that visitor queries can be handled speedily and efficiently. Most administrators keep this sort of information on their desk or in a file nearby, to help them cope with queries over the telephone or in person.

It helps if you have a good memory! Then you can remember the answers to questions you have heard before. It also helps you to answer basic questions from internal customers relating to work in progress within your department.

As you saw on pages 153 and 154, some customers may have more difficult or 'special' queries which you can't handle in the normal way. The golden rules are never to give a negative response without trying to find the answer and *never* guess! You may find specific procedures in place to help you. These are likely to tell you what to do and who can help you – and also give you guidance on what *not* to say or promise! An example is given below.

Procedures for dealing with customer enquiries

1 All staff should strive to answer basic customer enquiries relating to their own work area promptly and accurately. In any cases of doubt, the enquiry should be referred to an experienced member of staff or to the departmental manager.

2 All customers can ask for, and be given, information relating to the range of services we provide; the address of this office and the registered office, the name of the Chief Executive and other Directors, the mobile numbers of sales staff. For this reason, it may be helpful to direct customers to our website, which contains this information and other relevant details – including our customer complaints procedure.

3 No customers must be given any information relating to other clients or customers of this organisation.

4 Any enquiries relating to fee rates and discount terms must be referred to the Sales Manager or to another senior manager in the organisation.

5 Any enquiries relating to work schedules and work completion must be referred to the Operations Manager.

6 Any enquiries relating to advertising, publicity or charitable donations must be referred to the Marketing Manager.

7 Any enquiries relating to invoicing or payment of accounts must be referred to the Financial Controller.

8 Any enquiries relating to the supply of goods or services to this organisation must be referred to the Purchasing Manager.

9 No staff should answer press enquiries on behalf of the organisation. These must be referred immediately to the Chief Executive's office.

Problem customers

Some customers may be deliberately awkward; others may be difficult to handle for other reasons, for instance because they are very shy or won't stop talking!

You are unlikely to find procedures in place to help you deal with a chatterbox – although the information in the table below might help. Many organisations do, however, have procedures to help staff to deal with particularly awkward or aggressive customers. Staff who work in vulnerable jobs, such as Benefit Offices, are often protected by glass screens and have panic buttons nearby. The same protection is provided to staff who deal with large amounts of cash, such as bank tellers or petrol station attendants, together with specific guidance on how to behave if they are involved in a threatening situation, such as an armed raid. More recently, airline staff have received special training on what to do if passengers become violent or aggressive, for example as a result of too much alcohol.

The procedures will always focus on the protection of staff and will usually follow specific guidance from the Health and Safety Executive (HSE). This is because violence at work is covered by health and safety legislation (see Unit 3). You can find out more about the type of precautions employers by following the links at www.heinemann.co.uk/hotlinks.

Dealing with difficult customers

Difficult customers	Tips to help
The chatterbox	Be pleasant, note down their request Excuse yourself and say you must get back to work Use body language to help – turn back to your work and keep your head down!
Nervous, anxious or very shy	Take your time Speak gently and calmly Check they have understood you
Angry or aggressive	Never interrupt Be patient, reasonable and helpful If they are making a serious complaint, follow the guidelines on page 138 Get help if they don't calm down or if you feel threatened
Those who have made a mistake (e.g. arriving at the wrong time, complaining unjustifiably)	Identify exactly what has happened before you make any comments Don't put the customer in the wrong, e.g. 'You have made a mistake' Apologise for any inconvenience – it doesn't cost you anything! Try to put right any associated problems if you can
VIPs	Be aware that very important customers are probably the lifeblood of your organisation Treat their concerns seriously and do your best to assist – or summon help quickly

Expressing regret without admitting liability

All organisations will expect staff to express regret if a customer has a complaint or is experiencing a difficulty. This is sensible. Indeed, some organisations have found that keeping customers well informed, being courteous and providing pleasant surroundings has had more effect on customer patience and tolerance than any number of glass screens and security measures.

When you express regret – or apologise to a customer – you are not making a personal admission of guilt. You are acknowledging how the customer feels and saying sorry on behalf of the organisation for those feelings. This is still valid even if the customer is later proved to be wrong, but at the time thought that they were correct.

If you admit liability, however, you are actually confirming that you – or your employer – is in the wrong. There are two reasons why you should never do this. First, you don't know enough to admit liability unless you know all the facts of the case. A customer will tell you only his or her side of the story. This is why complaints are often investigated. There may be more to the tale than you first thought. Secondly, if you admit liability the customer may be able to use this in evidence if the matter went to court, and this could affect the final court judgment.

Therefore, no matter what your personal opinions may be, *always* express regret, but *never* admit your company is liable. Just note down the facts and say you will pass them on immediately to the appropriate person.

OVER TO YOU!

1 If you, or other members of your group, work on a part-time basis, identify and compare the procedures that are in place in your organisation to deal with customer complaints and problems. You can add to this discussion by talking about problem customers you have encountered and how you coped with them.

   If none of your group has a part-time job, then find out the procedures that exist in your college to deal with student complaints and how these affect the staff who have to handle them.

2 You work in a local insurance office. Explain exactly how you would deal with each of the following situations.

   a) A customer slips on your premises and hurts her ankle. She complains because the tiled floor is wet – which it is.

   b) A customer calls to enquire whether you can offer him the same terms as an on-line insurance company if he gives you all his business.

   c) A customer telephones to say he can't understand the terms of his insurance policy. You check the file but realise the information is very complex.

   d) The manager of another department rings to complain that you gave him incorrect information yesterday, which caused him considerable inconvenience. You are almost certain you gave him the correct details and he has made the mistake.

   e) A customer who obviously can't see very well approaches you and asks you for a claim form.

   f) A customer telephones to complain that the form you promised to send her three days ago hasn't arrived yet.

   g) A customer calls in to argue about non-settlement of an insurance claim. She says her neighbour made a similar claim two weeks ago and hers was settled. She wants to know why she has been treated differently.

3 Work in pairs for the following task. On your own, select any two of the scenarios below and decide two types of complaint or problem situation that could occur for the administrator who works there. One complaint or problem should be minor and the other quite serious.

Then role-play the complaint or problem with your partner, who should play the part of the administrator. For three of your role-plays you should be a 'reasonable' customer – on the fourth you can either have a particular need or be slightly more awkward or persistent! At the end of each role-play, decide how well the customer was dealt with and whether communications could be improved. Then reverse roles.

a) A theme park administrator who deals with bookings over the telephone and orders catering supplies.

b) A receptionist in a veterinary practice.

c) An administrator working at your local football club, processing ticket sales and season ticket requests.

d) An administrator working in a car hire company, processing bookings.

e) An administrator for a national firm of house builders which is currently involved in a new development in your town. This is currently running three months behind schedule.

f) An administrator in the central offices of a large shopping mall.

g) An administrator in a garage which both sells and services cars.

h) An administrator who works for your regional bus company and deals with timetables and schedules.

4 Your friend has started working for a small, local agency which rents out many private properties in the area. People often call in to pay their rent, sometimes in cash. She is concerned that she is often alone in the office and would be vulnerable if anyone demanded money. She also has to deal with angry customers at times, complaining about overdue repairs to their properties.

Working as a group, access the information on violence at work to be found by following the links from www.heinemann.co.uk/hotlinks and agree a set of procedures she could ask her employer to introduce which would help to protect her.

▼ RECORD INFORMATION ACCURATELY

Most organisations keep careful records relating to customer information and enquiries, as well as other types of feedback. They also have specific procedures for recording and following up complaints. You will be expected to participate in this process and to make sure that you keep full and accurate records – either on paper or electronically – in relation to all your own customer dealings.

It helps, however, if you have some idea of the type of information you will be expected to record and *why* it is required. This means you can see the purpose of the activity, and not view it as a time-wasting or unnecessary exercise.

Keeping accurate records of customer information, enquiries and feedback

Modern technology has revolutionised the amount and type of customer information that can be held by organisations and the way it is used. Some stores, such as Tesco, Boots and Marks and Spencer, operate a loyalty scheme. This provides valuable information on regular shoppers and their buying habits. When sales fall, the companies can send out special vouchers to tempt customers to return and buy again. They can target the vouchers to the products individual customers prefer to buy.

Large companies hold their customer data on a computer database. Your details will probably be held on your college's database. This will show not only your name, age and address but all the courses you have studied there and your results. This will help to inform staff if you make a new enquiry to the College at some time in the future and help them to advise you more appropriately.

A commercial organisation will normally bring up on screen an existing customer's record whenever they make a new enquiry. Not only can the member of staff view the previous items sold, he or she can also check particular preferences and the payment history of the customer. This prevents new orders being sent to someone who still owes a lot of money.

Enquiries from prospective customers may also be logged, particularly for goods which the organisation doesn't normally stock or for services which aren't usually provided. These may be reviewed or evaluated to see if stock lists need changing or updating or if additional services should be offered.

Feedback usually includes suggestions, comments and compliments received from customers. Many companies actively encourage feedback, either through suggestion boxes in a store or reception area or via their website. If you receive feedback direct, then you should record this appropriately. Compliments are always especially welcome and tell all staff when they are appreciated by customers, which is always good to know. Suggestions are evaluated to check if they are sensible and could be introduced without costing too much. Sometimes a customer may make a comment which would improve the facilities generally for everyone, but this can't be acted upon if the administrator who received the comment doesn't bother to write it down or pass it on!

The last suggestion said Josh should get his hair cut!

SUGGESTIONS BOX

▲ Feedback from customers can come in different forms

Recording key information

If you are entering information on a database, then the design of the form and the field titles will tell you what to enter. You will usually find that certain fields must be completed before you can save the customer record. These usually include:

▶ customer name (in full) and title

▶ address and postcode

▶ telephone number

▶ customer reference number (if new). On a database, this is often allocated automatically

▶ current order details.

If you are logging an enquiry where you couldn't help the customer, then you will need to note down exactly what was requested, and when.

If you are logging a suggestion or comment, make sure you take down the details and have a contact number. Your supervisor might want to obtain further details from the customer or thank them personally for their contribution.

Procedures for recording and following up complaints

Most organisations 'log' or record complaints. They do this for several reasons.

▶ To check that all complaints have been handled properly and promptly.

▶ To find out about common areas of complaint, which indicates action must be taken in this area to improve customer service.

▶ To avoid major disasters and to take action immediately at senior level, if required. An example would be a food store which received complaints about the sale of out-of-date products.

▶ When a complaint relates to returned goods, then the sales records have to be adjusted *and* the problem may need to be referred back to the supplier – particularly if the product is faulty or unsafe.

▶ To ensure a full record is kept, in case a similar situation or problem arises in the future.

▶ To keep a check on the number of complaints received overall and the trend. Although most companies prefer customers to complain rather than to keep a problem to themselves (and tell all their friends), if complaints are increasing then the managers of the company will obviously be concerned and want to take action.

You may therefore find that the procedures for recording complaints cover the following steps:

1 Recording the original complaint as soon as it is received, together with the date.

2 Recording the action taken, the date and the name of the person who took it.

3 In some cases, a follow-up call to the customer to check there are no further problems and the customer is satisfied with the service he or she received.

You may also be expected to monitor the complaints log, particularly if there is a timescale by which complaints must be acknowledged and answered in full, as you saw in the procedures on page 156. Monitoring the log means checking that no complaints are outstanding and, if there are, notifying your supervisor. If the log is kept on computer, this task is much easier, as you can quickly search for any complaints which have not yet been resolved.

PEOPLE IN BUSINESS

Under the terms of the Data Protection Act companies are restricted in the type of information they can keep on customers and what they do with it. This applies to all information recorded or processed by computer, as well as information held as a record within a filing system.

All the information that is collected must be obtained fairly and lawfully, normally with the consent of the individual. Only appropriate data must be held and this must be accurate and kept up-to-date. It must also be stored safely to prevent unauthorised access or damage. If it is 'sensitive' data, such as that relating to religious or political beliefs, racial origin or criminal convictions, then the explicit consent of the person is required.

All customers have the right to access data held about them and to stop organisations using it for marketing activities. There is usually an optional 'tick box' on most forms that are designed to collect data, to allow the person to refuse to allow it to be passed on to another organisation. If inaccurate data is held, a customer can insist that the entry is corrected or erased.

Only a few organisations are exempt from this Act. These include the police, tax authorities, health authorities and providers, those involved in education and social work, the government (if the data is held for purposes of national security), domestic users and those who hold data for the purposes of research, history or statistical use.

OVER TO YOU!

1 Suggest the action each of these organisations could take in response to the following information.
   a) An estate agent's records show that many people are enquiring about buying property in a certain area.
   b) The staff in an accountant's office say that many customers are regularly asking for information on updated tax and VAT rates.
   c) A heating contractor receives very positive feedback on a new type of boiler he has recently installed for the first time.
   d) A computer software supplier receives complaints that their website is slow and there is no facility online for answering queries.
   e) A travel agency receives information that a competitor is offering special discounts for a limited period.
   f) Several students at a college say that they were given incorrect information on fees when they made an enquiry.
   g) Several customers of a book club complain about delivery problems or damaged goods. The orders were processed on time and the company uses an external delivery company.

2 Shelley is working on the front desk when she hears the following comments. In each case, suggest what she should do both *immediately* – to solve the problem – and then later, to try to prevent a recurrence.

a) Several customers are complaining about having to wait a long time. They also say the chairs are uncomfortable and there's nothing to read in reception.

b) A manager from another department picks up some photocopying and complains about the quality, which he says is dreadful at the moment.

c) Two customers arrive complaining about getting lost around the building because there were no signs to show them where to go.

d) A customer cannot understand a form she has to complete. Shelley knows that everyone seems to have a problem with this particular form.

3 Some problems cannot be solved by staff, no matter how willing they are! Identify the problems which a good administrator should be able to suggest could be solved, from the list below, and those which would have to be handled more tactfully. Then say what you would say or do in each case.

a) A customer complains that there is nowhere to park nearby.

b) A customer complains that she has just spent 10 minutes trying to get through on the telephone.

c) A customer argues that the prices of some goods are much higher than those she has seen at a competitor's website.

d) A customer suggests the organisation should operate a delivery service.

e) A customer complains about the amount of litter outside on the pavement.

▼ ENSURE CUSTOMER REQUIREMENTS CAN BE MET

Customer satisfaction (or delight) is the main aim of most organisations. Many companies actually advertise that they aim to exceed their customer expectations on a regular basis! This can be achieved only if:

▶ the goods or service meet the needs of the customer

▶ the goods or service are exactly as agreed (or better)

▶ the goods are delivered by the required date

▶ the goods or service are *at least* of the required standard

▶ the customer is kept fully informed of any unexpected developments in a polite and courteous way

▶ any problems are dealt with promptly and in full.

You will meet these criteria only if you make every effort you can, at each stage of the process, to keep the customer happy.

Summarising the situation

During a conversation with a customer it is easy to lose track of the main focus of the discussion – particularly if various aspects are discussed and some are debated and others agreed. For that reason it is important to:

- summarise the situation as you understand it – and check the customer agrees with you
- check that the customer is absolutely clear what has been decided
- check that the customer understands any further action which has to be taken by them – and exactly what they must do
- check that the customer understands any further action which will be taken by you – and when this will be done.

The aim is to minimise the possibility of problems later because of a misunderstanding. Summarising the situation enables you to double-check that you and the customer are both in complete agreement about the current situation.

Keeping accurate records

For the initial needs to be met, a correct record has to be kept of the original request. If one detail is wrong, then a problem is simply waiting to happen. This means:

- writing down the request, carefully and clearly
- checking that nothing important is missing
- checking that both you and the customer understand what you have written (by reading it back to them and, preferably, asking them to sign it)
- never promising something you can't fulfil
- checking that every single detail is 100% accurate.

Further action

If you have promised to carry out further action then you must do so – to the right standard and *at least* by the agreed date. It is a good strategy to 'delight' your customer by exceeding the standards and the original time limit whenever you can!

Unfortunately sometimes a problem may occur which is outside your control, leading to a delay so that your original agreement cannot be met. You will then need to contact the customer and give them this information. It can often help if you put yourself in the customer's shoes at this point, and think about how you would feel in this situation. When you make the call:

- explain who you are and why you are contacting them
- be honest about the situation (you can still be tactful and discreet)
- apologise for the inconvenience if you are having to say that your original promise now cannot be fulfilled.
- tell the customer what will now happen and when. Don't make any promise now unless you absolutely know that it can be met
- make a record of what has been agreed
- read this back to the customer.

Some organisations like their staff to make final calls to a customer to check that they are happy afterwards. Whether you are calling an internal customer to find out if the information you provided is fine or asking an external customer if they now have all they need, your call will usually be appreciated.

If you receive positive feedback then you can note this as a compliment. If you receive good feedback with one or two suggestions, then this should give you ideas for the future. If you receive a complaint then you need to review what went wrong and why – and identify the extent to which your own actions may have contributed. Although you may not be perfect every time, learning from your mistakes is one of the best ways of moving forward.

PEOPLE IN BUSINESS

Many businesses use a variety of methods to keep in touch with their customers, both to obtain feedback and to measure customer satisfaction.

In many hotels and restaurants, both staff and managers will regularly ask guests if everything is to their satisfaction. In retail stores, managers and senior staff will observe customers and take action if they see someone is exasperated or annoyed. Most travel organisations, hotels and mail order companies send out questionnaires to their customers to obtain feedback on their experience and the service provided, and may offer prizes to encourage a high response rate.

Others prefer to use modern technology, such as using pop-up questionnaires on a website to check customer satisfaction or to ask customers to suggest improvements. Others use email, which may ask for individual comments after a transaction has been completed.

Richer Sounds, the national hi-fi retailer, gives each customer a feedback questionnaire along with their till receipt. All completed questionnaires are entered into a prize draw each month and staff are awarded bonuses related to customer feedback on their individual service. This company, in common with several others, also uses mystery shoppers. These are independent researchers who either telephone or visit a store and assess the staff on their performance. At Dixons, the managing director used to do this personally, and report his findings to senior managers afterwards. This had the obvious effect of making all staff very wary of the response they gave to customers!

Richer Sounds' staff also make 'customer happy calls' to check customers are satisfied with their purchases once they have got them home and aren't experiencing any unexpected problems. Staff are trained to emphasise that these calls are *not* to be treated as a 'sales opportunity' but are to assure customers that they aren't forgotten the moment they walk out of the door. Given the success of the business, this is obviously a policy that pays dividends in terms of customer loyalty.

▲ Mystery shoppers are used by some stores to get feedback on their performance

1. You have recently started work in the section of your organisation that makes travel arrangements for employees and you are shown how to find out train times on the Internet. As a group, decide the details you would need to obtain from your internal customers before you could correctly find out the information they require.

2. Suggest the possible consequences, and what you would do, in each of the following situations.

   a) On a request for internal photocopying, you write down 300 instead of 30 copies required.

   b) On your second day in a new job, when you are responding to a customer complaint, you forget to check the procedures. Only after the customer has gone do you realise you should have completed a complaints form – which requires more information than you managed to obtain.

   c) You promised a customer that a maintenance engineer would be with her last week. Because of heavy snow, his visit had to be postponed but she was quite reasonable when you rang. The visit was rescheduled for today but now you've just received a note that his van has broken down and he will be off the road until tomorrow.

   d) You tell a customer that she can't make an appointment to see a member of staff for two weeks because he is away on holiday. After you have completed the call, you realise you've muddled up your dates and he actually returns to work next week.

3. You work as an administrator at a large firm of decorators. Your boss, John Woods, is often out of the office and relies upon you and the rest of your team to deal efficiently and courteously with customers who contact the company in his absence.

   Role play each of the following situations with a colleague in such a way that you will always do your best to meet customer requirements. Make notes in each case, using your own initiative about the questions you should ask and the information you should record. Then reverse roles. Finally, pass your notes to your tutor, who will act the part of John Woods and assess your performance.

   a) You receive a telephone enquiry from the manager of a large insurance company that is moving to the area. He wants to know if John is interested in quoting for redecorating the offices they have just bought. He also wants to know if you can guarantee that the work will be completed by the end of the month.

   b) You phone Joyce Adams of Bright Homes on John's behalf. He can start work for them a week on Monday but only if he knows the customer paint preferences for plots 18, 20 and 24 immediately. If you obtain these over the phone, you must get confirmation in writing in case there are any disputes later.

   c) You make a 'customer happy call' to Theresa MacDonald, whose house John's team finished decorating last week. John is worried because one of his new trainees left some brushes there and didn't remove all the rubbish properly.

   d) You receive a call from Jan Phillips. She claims that she sprained her ankle when she fell over some paint pots left out by one of your workman. She wants her bill to be reduced to compensate for the accident.

Working in business organisations

Introduction

Business organisations can seem mysterious when you haven't worked in one. You may be aware that some are large and some are very small, that some produce goods and others provide a service, but beyond that you may have little appreciation of the aims of its owners or managers. It may be difficult to understand some of the terms used, such as 'capital', 'strategy' and 'objectives'.

Although individual organisations may differ in several respects, many of their aims and business ideas are often the same. Recognising these will help you to appreciate what your employer's business is all about. Similarly, although organisations may differ in terms of their organisational structure and job titles, knowing the main reasons for the way the business is organised – and how administrators support key job roles – helps you to understand how everything fits together to meet the aims of the business.

▶ There are different types of business organisation

This unit covers all these areas, as well as all the key aspects of working practices that relate to all offices and administrative jobs. It also looks at the issues which affect working conditions, including legislation such as health and safety and the rights and responsibilities of both employers and employees.

The aim of this unit is to give you a greater understanding of the business world as a whole and the activities that take place within business organisations. This enables you to be more effective in your own job because you will not only be able to focus better upon your own work, and realise why you should be doing certain tasks, but you will also realise what everyone else around you is doing and why managers make many of the decisions that they do.

Wherever you work as an administrator, you will find the information in this unit invaluable to your overall business knowledge and your future personal and career development.

Unit summary

This unit is divided into four sections.

▶ **Describe and compare business organisations**. This section covers the different types of business organisations and their distinguishing features, the reasons why organisations develop and how they do this, as well as the aims and objectives of organisations.

▶ **Explain how business organisations are structured**. This covers the main functional areas of organisations and how departments are organised to meet the organisation's objectives. You will find out about the roles of people at different levels in the organisation and the way in which administrators contribute towards the work of the company.

▶ **Identify and explain effective working practices**. This focuses on planning and organising work, as well as the importance of retaining flexibility. It examines the factors that can affect efficiency and how you can aim to improve your own performance at work.

▶ **Identify and explain issues affecting working conditions**. This section covers the factors that affect working conditions, including environmental considerations, health and safety issues and the legal responsibilities of employers and employees.

Assessment

Your assessment for this unit will consist of a written examination of two and a half hours. You also have an additional 10 minutes to read the paper before you start writing.

There will be four questions on the examination paper, one for each main section of the paper. Each question will have a number of sub-sections and you will be expected to answer all of these.

Some of the questions in the 'Over to You' sections of this chapter are practical activities to help you to understand more about various topics. Others are similar to the type of questions you will find on the examination paper. Answering these will give you practice in how to think and respond to achieve good marks.

▼ DESCRIBE AND COMPARE BUSINESS ORGANISATIONS

It is a truism that most organisations are different and yet they are the same. Organisations are often different in terms of their size, ownership and internal structure but they usually have the same type of reasons for their existence. Wherever you work you will find that two essential ingredients are very important – money and customers. Money is important because all organisations need to either make a profit or balance their books to survive. Customers are important because without them many organisations wouldn't exist. Unhappy customers can cause problems for any business – from your local hospital to a major superstore.

In this first section you will learn about the main types of business organisations, their distinguishing features (so you can tell which is which), their advantages and disadvantages and the reasons for these differences. You can then have a better understanding of the factors which differentiate businesses which operate on a small scale, on just a local basis, and those which operate nationally or even internationally and are often household names.

All organisations in Britain either belong to the private or the public sector of business.

▶ The **private sector** includes all those organisations that are privately owned. These are owned by private individuals and operated with the aim of making a profit or surplus.

▶ The **public sector** comprises those organisations that are owned by the state and run for the benefit of the general public. The public sector employs millions of people in Britain and is operated to provide services which are required by everyone, regardless of income.

The private sector

There are five main types of organisation in the private sector. These are as follows.

▶ **Sole traders**   These are businesses owned by one person. This person may employ other people to help, but there is only one owner. Examples include many local businesses, such as greengrocers, small cafés or takeaways, taxi firms, newsagents and sandwich bars.

▶ **Partnerships**   These are businesses owned by two or more people. There is normally a limit on the number of partners which are allowed. Many professional organisations are run by partners, such as solicitors, accountants, dentists and doctors.

▶ **Limited companies**   There are two types of limited companies.

  – **Private companies** are often family enterprises. They are instantly recognisable because of the abbreviation 'Ltd' after the name. The owners are also the directors of the business and they each own a 'share' of the business. The larger the share each person holds, the more control they have over the way the business is run.

  – **Public companies** are normally larger. In this case the company has the abbreviation 'plc' after the name. The owners are large institutions or private individuals who have bought shares in the business on the Stock Exchange. The business is run by salaried directors who may, or may not, own shares themselves. If the shareholders are unhappy with the way the business is run, they can sell their shares.

▶ **Charities**   Charities are in business for the purposes of helping other people and promoting special causes. All charities in Britain with an annual income of over £1,000 have to be registered. Many types of organisation can register as a charity – not just the famous names you read in the press and on television, such as the NSPCC or RSPCA. Many are small local charities or charities which focus on issues such as health or education. The main difference between organisations that are allowed to have charitable status and other business organisations is that all surplus money (profit) is used for social benefits, rather than repaid to investors.

To understand each of these organisations properly, it is important to look at them in more detail.

Sole traders

The smallest type of business organisation in Britain is a sole trader. Your local florist, grocer, plumber and all the market traders you see are likely to be sole traders. Carolyn Parker is an example of a sole trader. She trained as a hairdresser but always wanted to have her own salon. She used her savings to rent a shop, buy the items needed to equip it, pay for advertising and buy the basic stocks she needed. The profits she makes will be her reward for starting the business. However, she is responsible for paying all the business expenses and must also pay national insurance and income tax on her profits to the Inland Revenue.

If Carolyn is unsuccessful and makes a loss, then the business will close. If she owes money, then she is personally responsible for paying her debts. She could have to sell her personal possessions to do this and even be made bankrupt. This is because all sole traders have *unlimited liability* for all their debts.

As a sole trader, Carolyn is self-employed and makes all the decisions as to how the business is run. She must also keep accounts which show how much profit or loss she has made over each year. Despite all the extra work, Carolyn prefers being a sole trader to working for someone else. This is one of the main reasons why many people decide to set up their own business. They decide that the benefits are greater than the disadvantages. These are both listed in the table below.

Key features of sole traders

The good
▶ It is easy to set up the business, especially if the sole trader is using his or her own name.
▶ The sole trader is independent and is his or her own boss.
▶ Quick decisions are possible as there is no one else to consult.
▶ The owner can keep all the profit after paying any tax due.
▶ Opening hours and days worked can be flexible to suit the needs of the business.
▶ Other staff can be employed to help at busy times.
▶ A personal service to customers can be provided because the owner will get to know them as individuals.
▶ Bad (unpaid) debts can be avoided because customers are known to the owner and most purchases are paid for immediately.

- ▶ Paperwork is straightforward unless the business is registered for value added tax (VAT) when special accounts must be kept.
- ▶ The financial affairs and accounts are private and known only to the owner and the Inland Revenue.

The bad

- ▶ Long working hours may be necessary for the business to be successful.
- ▶ The owner earns no money if the business is closed through holidays or sickness.
- ▶ Success depends on the skills of the owner, who may have little business experience or knowledge of accounts, paying staff or managing staff.
- ▶ It can be difficult to raise the capital (money) to pay for expansion.
- ▶ The business ceases to exist on the owner's death.
- ▶ It may be difficult for a small business to compete against larger competitors (such as small grocers against supermarkets).

And the even worse

The owner has *unlimited liability* for all the debts. This means the owner is personally responsible and may have to sell personal belongings to raise money. He or she can be made bankrupt if there is not enough money to pay all the debts.

Partnerships

Many people like the idea of starting their own business but do not want to do this on their own. They prefer the idea of working with a partner. In Britain, the minimum number of people required to start a partnership is two and the maximum is normally 20. Many partnerships are run by professional people, such as doctors, dentists, solicitors and accountants, who are not allowed by their professional body to set up a limited company.

Jez and Mike decided to set up in partnership after working in IT. Jez was a skilled computer programmer and Mike concentrated on graphic design. Together they thought they could offer a service to small businesses designing websites. They have pooled their savings to rent the premises and buy the equipment they need and have taken advice from a solicitor who counselled them that, because they will both be legally liable for the actions of each other, it would be sensible to draw up a **Deed of Partnership**. This is a legal document which sets out the details of their agreement, including the salary of each partner, the share of the profits each will receive and the procedure to follow if there is a dispute. This is good sense, as it may save any arguments later, especially if the partnership is ended.

Jez is an excellent salesman and will be good at making new contacts and obtaining business. Mike is attending a business course to help him understand how to do the accounts and the paperwork. Both are aware that they will have joint responsibility for the success of the business and will gain several benefits from operating as a partnership. They are also aware of the drawbacks. Both of these are summarised in the table below.

Key features of partnerships

The good

▶ It is easier to raise capital as all the partners contribute.

▶ Additional partners can be brought in as the business expands, up to a maximum of 20.

▶ Problems or worries can be shared and discussed.

▶ Between them, the partners have more skills and ideas. The business can benefit from their joint expertise.

▶ Responsibility and working hours can be shared.

▶ The business affairs and financial accounts are still private.

▶ A Deed of Partnership can be signed to prevent disagreements if the partnership ends.

The bad

▶ The partners may not agree about major business decisions.

▶ The profits must be shared.

▶ All the partners must be consulted before a major decision is made.

▶ The actions of one partner are binding on all the others.

▶ The death or retirement of a partner means that his or her share must be taken out of the business. Because this can cause financial problems for the business, it is usual to take out a life assurance policy to cover this amount.

And the even worse

The partners normally still have *unlimited liability* for all the debts and all may be made bankrupt if the business fails and they cannot pay the money owing.

ORGANISATIONS IN BUSINESS

Many famous businesses started out as partnerships. Charles Rolls and Henry Royce got together to start Rolls-Royce, famous for its cars and aeroplane engines. Richard Branson, chairman of the Virgin Group, first started his enterprise with Nik Powell, a childhood friend. Bill Gates, the founder of Microsoft, originally had a partner, too, called Paul Allen.

Often these partnerships don't last, either because the partners disagree over something important or because one wants to develop the business further or in a particular direction and the other does not. Henry Ford's first business, the Detroit Automobile Company, failed within its first two years because of partnership arguments.

The entertainment world is not without costly partnership splits either. One of the most famous was between Elton John and his business partner/manager John Reid. Their dispute cost Elton John £8 million in legal fees. More recently, the American rapper P Diddy, ended the 50–50 partnership between his own record label, Bad Boy Entertainment, and Arista Records, which had existed since 1996. Although the split was said to be amicable, the cost of buying back his label to develop it in his own way was estimated at between $20 and $30 million.

Private limited companies

Many private companies are formed from partnerships or even by sole traders. They are far more suitable if the stock is expensive, several staff are employed and there could be a danger of unpaid debts. This is because the owners of a limited company are protected by limited liability. Instead of having to sell private possessions to pay any debts, as a sole trader or partnership must do, the owners can lose only the amount they have invested in the business – and no more.

Leanne started her business as a sole trader. She had completed a catering course and wanted to work for herself, arranging business lunches for financial firms in the City of London. Then she met her husband, who became her business manager, ran the office and handled all the paperwork. The business was very successful – so much so that Leanne employed more staff and then bought her own kitchen premises and equipped it with modern catering equipment. Her accountant advised her to convert the business into a limited company with herself and her husband as the owner/directors. They both decided to take 50% of the shares in the business, so they would own it between them.

The main difference is that Leanne and her husband now became employees of the company, which pays their wages. This is because a limited company is *separate* from its owners. All the assets – such as property, equipment and vehicles – are owned by the company. The company can be sold to someone else and would still exist after the death of the owners until it was officially 'wound up'. Corporation tax is now paid on the company's profits, although Leanne and her husband will still have to pay income tax on their salaries.

There are several benefits to running a limited company, but also a few disadvantages, as you can see in the table below.

Key features of private limited companies

The good

▶ The business can remain small with just family members as shareholders. Under European law, one person can set up a private company on his or her own.

▶ All the shareholders have limited liability and can never lose more than the amount they have invested.

▶ The financial affairs and accounts are still private between the owners, the accountants and the Inland Revenue.

▶ No fixed amount is required to start a limited company. The owners may invest only £100 or £200 at the start.

▶ The owners have direct control over the business.

▶ Shares in the business cannot be sold or transferred to anyone else without the agreement of the existing shareholders and cannot be sold to the general public.

▶ Banks and other financial institutions are more willing to lend money to limited companies, both to start up and for expansion. This makes expansion easier.

▶ Additional capital can be raised by selling shares to family members, friends and employees.

The bad

▶ Limited companies have to comply with more regulations than sole traders or partnerships. They must register with the Registrar of Companies and large companies must have their accounts audited (checked) by an accountant.

▶ The owners have to decide on the structure of the company and how it will be run and complete official documents to 'form' the company. This usually costs about £200.

▶ The company must comply with the requirements of various Companies Acts.

▶ The business must have a distinctive name which is not the same as an existing company, if this could cause confusion to customers and suppliers.

And the even worse

Shareholders have the same number of votes as they hold shares. This gives more power to those shareholders with the most shares who may be able to outvote the others.

Public limited companies

This is the largest type of privately owned business organisation and includes many of the famous names you regularly hear about, such as Marks & Spencer, Halifax, Vodaphone and Boots. The shares in a public limited company are traded on the Stock Exchange and can be bought by the general public and large organisational investors. The directors run the company, and are paid a salary, and can choose whether to own shares or not. The shareholders, who own the shares, have nothing to do with the running of the business on a day-to-day basis but will expect to receive a dividend twice a year as a reward for their investment.

Not all companies can choose to become a plc. They need to have a good financial track record and to have at least £50,000 in paid-up share capital before they can 'float' the company on the Stock Exchange. This is the term used when a public limited company is launched.

There are several advantages to doing this, although it doesn't work out for every business – as you will see when you read about JJB Sports on page 190.

Key features of public limited companies

The good

▶ The amount of capital available for expansion is greatly increased as there may be thousands of shareholders.

▶ Additional finance can be raised in various ways. The company can borrow money from a range of financial institutions, issue additional shares or ask for special loans.

▶ A public company can still remain quite a small business. The minimum is two directors and two shareholders.

▶ If the company is successful then the value of the shares increases. This increases the overall value of the business.

The bad

▶ A public company is registered with the Registrar of Companies and has to comply with many regulations.

▶ The financial affairs of the company are public knowledge and often quoted in the press.

▶ Shareholders expect a dividend as a reward for their investment and will also want their shares to increase in value. If the shares fall they may sell, which will lower the price even more.

▶ Share prices can be affected by external events outside the company's control, such as the Iraq war.

▶ The original owners lose much of their control over the company, which can cause problems for many founders.

And the even worse

The aims of the directors and the aims of the shareholders are often different. The directors will want to retain some profits (called reserves) to pay for developments, modernisation and future expansion so that the company has a good long-term future. The shareholders will want quick results that increase the share value and to receive a good dividend twice a year, which limits the amount that can be kept back as reserves.

Charities

In 2003, the Charity Commission register listed 166,000 charities and this number is increasing by about 1,800 a year. Although most are very small, others are very large indeed. In 2002, the annual income of each of the top 421 charities was over £10 million and the total income for all charities was over £26 billion. They employed more than 300,000 full-time paid staff and had a small army of unpaid volunteers, equivalent to another 1.4 million staff.

Some charities receive special grants or fees from the government and also special relief from tax and business rates. Because of this they must abide by a number of regulations, and are overseen by the Charity Commission. They have to demonstrate that they are operating in the public benefit and are limited in the activities they can carry out, linked to their **charitable purpose**, such as to prevent and relieve poverty, promote human rights or provide care, support and protection to the aged or to children.

Charities are overseen by trustees who have to operate in accordance with the Trustee Act 2000. The trustees are responsible for ensuring that the money raised by the charity is managed carefully, as if it was their own. Being a trustee is a voluntary position. The trustee must not receive a salary, although some expenses, such as travel, can be repaid.

Some charities choose to have limited status – like a limited company. In this case they apply to be a company 'limited by guarantee'. The majority, however, do not do this.

Today, large charities are run on a professional and business-like basis. They are divided into departments and employ professional fund-raisers and administrators. They spend money on advertising and promoting the charity but, unlike other types of business, they operate on a **'not-for-profit'** basis. They aim to make a **surplus** every year, after necessary expenses, which is used to support and promote their own particular cause.

All charities and voluntary organisations have to be properly governed and keep accurate records. If a charity went bankrupt because of incompetence, or if the funds were used for non-charitable purposes, the trustees may find that they are both legally and financially liable.

The following table summarises the key features of charities.

Key features of charities

The good

▶ Charities operate for a specific purpose which must be clearly stated when they register.
▶ Charities can raise money by attracting sponsorship, carrying out street and door-to-door collections, running charity shops and sending out catalogues, organising appeals, holding special events and asking private individuals to make regular donations.
▶ Elderly people can donate money in their wills without this being subject to Inheritance Tax – no matter how much they leave.
▶ All charities with an annual income of over £10,000 must be registered with the Charity Commission
▶ Charities have to publish their accounts and are accountable to the Charity Commission for the way they operate.
▶ The charity's trustees are responsible for ensuring the charity meets its legal obligations.
▶ Large charities are run as sophisticated businesses with the largest ones employing thousands of professional staff.
▶ Charities can reclaim the tax on donations from taxpayers through the Gift Aid scheme and from payroll giving schemes.

The bad

▶ Trustees are legally liable if the charity breaks the law.
▶ When donations fall generally, charities have to compete against each other for funds – some people think there are too many charities.
▶ Telethons, such as Comic Relief and Children in Need reduce the money available for small charities.
▶ Collecting money in tins and boxes means the charity loses out on the reclaimed tax – yet people don't like being committed to regular donations.
▶ Charities should keep a percentage of their money as reserves in case of a poor year. Deciding how much is difficult. Too much in reserves reduces the money spent on the charitable activity, too little can be risky.
▶ Charities often use direct mail shots to try to raise funds, which can irritate some householders who receive many requests.

And the even worse

Charities are not immune from other business pressures and problems. In 2003 the Charity Commission reported that low share prices and poor methods of accounting had left nearly one-third of charities with too little money set aside in reserves.

SPECIAL NOTE

At present, charities must operate in accordance with the Charities Acts 1992 and 1993, but the government is currently reviewing charities and there is likely to be a new Charities Act in 2004. The number of acceptable 'purposes' is likely to increase and the Charity Commission may be renamed as the Charity Regulation Authority. You can find out more at www.heinemann.co.uk/hotlinks.

ORGANISATIONS IN BUSINESS

Charities have hard decisions to make when they have a problem, just like other business organisations. In 2002, the Guide Dogs for the Blind Association announced that it was having to close 15 training centres and make staff cutbacks because of financial problems. Not only had the charity overspent by £16 million in the previous year, but the general fall in share prices had reduced the value of its reserves by £20 million.

This was nothing new for the charity, which receives all its income through donations and fund-raising activities. Guide Dogs needs nearly £45 million a year to continue its work of training and providing guide dog services to visually impaired people and yet, since 1992, had been spending more on its service than it receives in income. In addition to its main activities, the charity also funds research into canine health and human eye conditions. As well as running its remaining centres, breeding and caring for dogs it also needs to pay the salaries of the 1,200 people it employs. The association estimates that it will need to raise an extra £5 million a year by 2004 to cope with demand for its services.

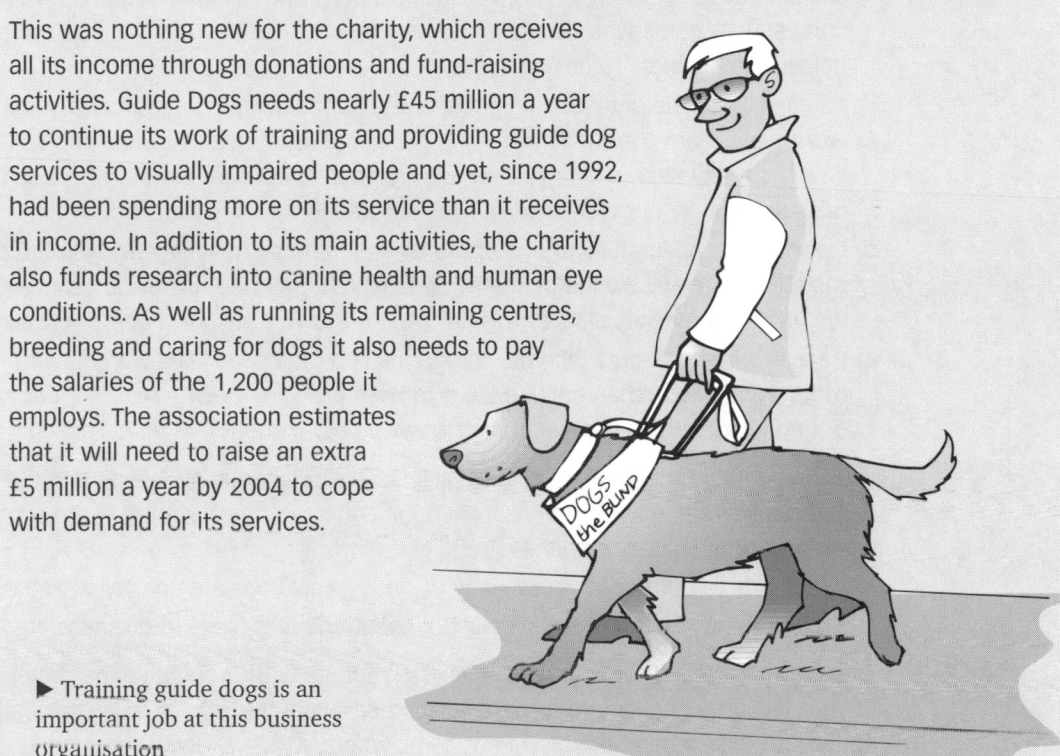

▶ Training guide dogs is an important job at this business organisation

OVER TO YOU!

1 Answer each of the following questions as quickly as you can. Which type(s) of business organisation:

a) has only one owner?

b) has between 2 and 20 owners?

c) is owned privately by shareholders?

d) is owned by shareholders who may be members of the public or large institutional investors?

e) is controlled by trustees?

f) is controlled by the owners who are also the directors?

g) is controlled, on a day-to-day basis, by salaried directors who may not be shareholders?

h) aim to make a profit for the owners or shareholders?

i) aim to make a surplus and distribute this according to their main purpose?

j) have unlimited liability for the owners?

k) have limited liability for the owners?

2 Identify the type of business organisation which employs each of the following speakers. Then state why you chose this answer.

a) I work for a large company which publishes nearly 250 local and regional newspapers. Originally it was a family business and the family still owns about 30% of the shares, even though we floated on the Stock Exchange in 1988.

b) I work for three accountants. Tom and Steve started the business but were joined by Greg about ten years ago. Greg is our tax expert. Tom concentrates mainly on large company accounts whereas Steve advises our smaller clients. Their combined skills have helped the business to be a success.

c) I originally started out working in marketing but decided I wanted to do something more worthwhile. I am currently involved in planning our homeless campaign this Christmas, which is a key focus of the year for us. We have to account carefully for every penny we raise and spend, but we get terrific job satisfaction when we do well.

d) I work in the head office of one of the largest regional travel agencies in the country. All the shares are still owned by the same family that started it over 50 years ago, but today we have 12 branches all over this area and our own transport fleet for customers.

e) Dave is a friend of ours who fits car alarms and radios. He likes working for himself and rents a small workshop outside town to keep his costs down. Dave's great with cars, but no good with paperwork, which is why I help him out and do his accounts.

3 Your friend Katya has worked for a small local car hire company – Superhire Ltd – for the past three years and has recently applied for, and been offered, a job in the administration office of a large children's charity.

a) Identify three *differences* in the way these organisations are controlled and operated.

b) Explain three *similarities* which exist between the two types of business organisation.

4 Find out more about the Charity Commission and its work. You can either enter the name of your favourite charity into a search engine or follow the links at www.heinemann.co.uk/hotlinks to the Charity Commission website, where you can search for charities by name. Most charities publish their latest accounts on their website so you can see how they raise money and if they are doing well.

The public sector

The public sector includes all organisations which are owned by the state and operated on behalf of the general public. The state, of course, is basically the same as the government, so that all government departments and organisations funded by the government, such as Job Centres, the National Health Service, most schools and colleges and the army are also classed as the public sector.

To answer questions on the examination paper, you need to understand two main types of public sector organisations – public corporations and local authorities. You also need to be able to identify the main differences between organisations in the private sector and those in the public sector.

Public corporations

Public corporations are businesses that are owned by the state. Today there are fewer public corporations than in the past because some companies which used to be owned by the state have been 'privatised' or moved back to the private sector, such as British Gas and British Telecom – which now operate as public limited companies. This is because the government must help public corporations in financial difficulty – and this money mainly comes from taxpayers. This is the main reason why the goverment prefers to own as few businesses as possible today.

The argument for the government owning any company is because it is felt to be in the public interest. The government oversees the way the organisation operates by appointing a Minister to be responsible for the overall policy of the organisation and reporting on its activities to Parliament. This is usually the relevant Secretary of State so, for example, the Secretary of State for Trade and Industry will report on developments on postal services (see page 183).

On a day-to-day basis, each business is run by salaried executives. There is a chairman and a board who are responsible for running it, along normal business lines. It used to be the case that public corporations were not expected to make a profit but allowed to 'break-even'. In this case it is expected to balance its books, year on year. If it makes a loss, the state will have to help it by awarding it grants or subsidies which cost the taxpayer money. This is one reason why the state owns very few business organisations these days and generally expects each business today to operate profitably, like organisations in the private sector. It is also felt that businesses are more efficient if they have to compete openly with other companies and do not have special privileges or the protection of the government.

Today there are only a few public corporations. These are:

▶ **The Bank of England**. This manages the government's finances and part of the economy, such as interest rates. The government would not want its money managed by a private (or even foreign) organisation.

▶ **The BBC**. This has to show programmes 'in the public interest' which have a cultural, educational and (impartial) newsworthy content. It is, of course, also allowed to show other programmes but the overall content is monitored. It is funded through a licence fee, paid by everyone who has a television, and doesn't have to raise money by advertising or subscriptions, like ITV or Sky.

▶ **British Nuclear Fuels** (which the government plans to privatise). It has long been considered important for the state to own the major processor of nuclear fuels for security reasons.

▶ **The Royal Mail Group** (which runs both post offices and the Royal Mail service). This is actually a company in which the government owns the majority of the shares. It aims to provide a mail service where the price of a letter is the same no matter where it is posted or sent to within the British Isles, which it couldn't do if it had to focus just on commercial considerations.

ORGANISATIONS IN BUSINESS

Network Rail is a special case. This is the organisation that replaced (and now owns) Railtrack. It is a 'not-for-profit company limited by guarantee'. This means it is in the private sector (it is a company) but as it doesn't have to make a profit, some would argue that it is really in the public sector as the government has to come to its assistance if it makes a loss! Railtrack was criticised for investing too little in the railways to ensure passenger safety because it had to pay a dividend to its shareholders. Network Rail is therefore run on a different basis, although it is still having financial problems and originally had to be supported by a £21 billion package guaranteed by the government. You can find out more by following the links at www.heinemann.co.uk/hotlinks.

Local authorities

Local authorities provide services for the local community, although the need for certain services often varies, for example between a rural community and an inner city area. If you worked for your local county hall, town hall or district council, then you would be employed in the public sector.

In most areas of the country, **county councils** offer services across a large area and **district councils** run specific services for smaller communities. For example, social services and education would be overseen by the county council but the district council would undertake refuse collection. In 1993, some authorities gained **unitary status**. These authorities can now act independently and are not responsible to the county council for the services, they provide.

Local authorities need money to provide their services. They obtain this from:

▶ the government, which pays each council a revenue support grant every year

▶ householders, who pay council tax based on the size and value of their house

▶ businesses, who pay business rates on their business premises

▶ loans, when they need extra money for a project

▶ council house rents

▶ the sale of services in the area, such as leisure centre charges.

They spend their money on providing a number of services, as shown in the diagram below. These are undertaken by the public sector because it is felt that they should be available to everyone, regardless of income. It shouldn't matter whether you are rich or poor, you should still be able to receive an education, be protected by the police or fire service, and have your rubbish collected.

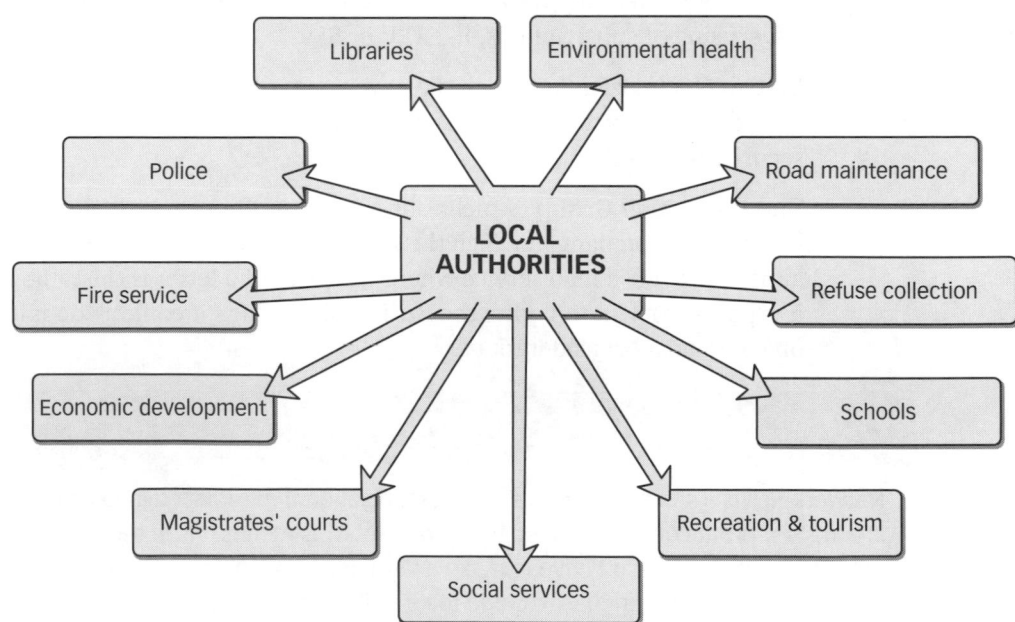

Because they use public money, local authorities are accountable to parliament for the money they spend and the services they provide and also to the people in their area. Each year, a council must publish its budget and send a copy to every council tax payer. Their

activities are also often covered in the press – particularly the local press, which will be very critical of poor decisions or high spending.

Council policy is decided by council representatives (councillors) who are elected by local people. Most represent a political party so that the authority may have an overall Labour or Conservative majority. The mayor is a long-serving councillor who represents the council at official functions.

Local policy is decided during council meetings of various committees, such as for transport, education and planning. The day-to-day running of council operations is carried out by paid employees, often called local government officers.

If a council is unpopular, then many councillors, who are elected by local people, may find themselves not elected at the next round of local elections. This can change the type of decisions that are made by a council. However, the salaried employees do not lose their jobs. These are the Chief Executive of the council and all the officials who will continue to do the day-to-day work of organising and administering all the services provided to the community.

ORGANISATIONS IN BUSINESS

The Royal Mail service has had a bumpy ride over the last few years. Not only has it lost money – its operating losses between April 2001 and November 2002 were £460 million – but it was forced to come to terms with greater competition in the mail market. Although the majority of mail deliveries in Britain are still made by the Royal Mail service, the government now allows some private operators to compete by delivering letters on a restricted basis.

The government owns the majority of shares in the business, but it has to operate like companies in the private sector, and not spend more than it receives in income. Alan Leighton, the chairman, therefore announced plans to reduce its current costs by cutting up to 30,000 jobs between 2002 and 2005 and closing more than 3,000 small post offices. It has scrapped its second delivery service and, in April 2003, increased the price of stamps by 1p, increasing revenues by up to £15 million a month.

To help to motivate Royal Mail employees, each is now being paid a dividend of up to £800 if the business makes a £400 million profit in 2004/5. By then it must be operating more efficiently to survive, especially if the government sticks to its plans to allow full competition for mail services by 2007. Royal Mail is still arguing that these plans are unfair as competitors will want to deliver only bulk business mail in city and urban areas, which costs mere pence to deliver, as opposed to private correspondence to rural areas all over the country which is far more costly. You can find out more by following the links at www.heinemann.co.uk/hotlinks.

▲ Rural postal deliveries cost more than those in urban areas

The private and public sector – key differences

As you have seen, there are several differences between organisations in the private and public sector, in terms of their ownership, who controls them, why they exist and their main objectives and the liabilities of those involved with them. To help you identify these quickly, the main ones are shown in the table below.

Private and public sector organisations – key differences

	Private sector	Public sector
Ownership	Private individuals – shareholders in the case of limited companies	The state
Control	Sole trader – the owner Partnership – the partners Private company – owners who are also directors/ shareholders Public company – directors on day-to-day basis Charities – trustees + executives	Public corporation – Ministers report to Parliament; business run by Chairman and board Local authority – elected councillors decide policy; run by local government officials
Objectives	Mainly to make a profit Charities make a surplus and distribute this according to the purpose of organisation	To provide a service considered to be in the national or public interest and available to all, irrespective of private wealth. Should balance income and expenditure
Liability	Sole trader/partnership – owners personally liable. Companies – liability for debts limited but directors responsible for abiding by Companies Acts. Charities – trustees liable for funds and must abide by Trustee Act and Charities Acts.	Public corporation – chairman/directors have legal responsibilities but ultimately the state. Local authority – councillors and executives have legal liability for funds and management.

OVER TO YOU!

1. All local authorities publish their budget for the year, together with details of the services they offer. You can obtain a copy for your area from your local council or find out more about them on their website. Ask your tutor if you are unsure of the name of your local authority and enter the name into a search engine, such as www.google.co.uk to access the website. Then see how much you can find out about the area in which you live and how it is run and controlled.

2 Fatima has just obtained a job in the social services department of her local authority, after working for Taylor and Reid Ltd, a family business which sells and maintains burglar alarm systems.

   a) Explain how the ownership and control of the two types of organisation are different.

   b) Explain how the main objective of each type of organisation varies.

   c) Explain why services such as social services, refuse collection and education are undertaken by the public sector, rather than by private sector companies.

3 The Bank of England, the BBC and the Royal Mail are all examples of public corporations.

   a) Identify three differences between a public corporation and a public limited company. Use the chart on page 184 to help you identify these.

   b) Suggest *one* reason why there are so few public corporations in Britain today.

▼ EXPLAIN HOW BUSINESS ORGANISATIONS DEVELOP

A few business owners start a small enterprise and have no desire to grow much larger. They do not want to run a chain of shops or operate a business empire. They simply want to earn enough to have a good living, pay their own bills and have some leisure time as well.

Generally, however, most businesses change over time. Some grow rapidly and then collapse – or encounter serious problems. Others grow more steadily and carefully, stage by stage. Others, through shrewd management, good luck or a combination of these, start small and end up as household names which continue to flourish over many years.

However, all businesses must regularly review the way they operate to remain competitive and up-to-date. No business can afford to stand still. As obvious examples, most businesses today have a website, whereas these were virtually unknown ten years ago and almost all businesses now accept a range of payment methods, including credit and debit cards, yet twenty years ago most people paid in cash or by cheque.

In this section you will find out why different types of organisations need to develop and how they do this. You will also see how these developments have affected them both internally, in the terms of the way they operate and externally, in terms of the impact of their development on customers and competitors.

Reasons for development

Many businesses start small and then continually expand. This is how some famous business people, such as Richard Branson, become the head of very large enterprises. Others, such as your local newsagent, may prefer to continue to operate on a much smaller scale. The degree to which a business develops will generally depend on the ambitions of the owner and the opportunities for growth and expansion in that industry.

If a business plans to develop, several aspects need to be considered. These include the existing business ownership – and whether it will still be appropriate, the way in which the business will operate in the future, the different ways in which it can grow and develop and the effect of the development on the business as a whole.

The first questions to ask therefore concern the following areas:

▶ **Capital** How will the development be financed? This requires capital – but where will this money come from?

▶ **Liability** If the organisation is small, then unlimited liability may not be a problem. If the size of operations is going to increase, then this type of liability is unlikely to be sensible.

▶ **Specialisation** As the business expands, should it continue to do what it does already – and is good at – but on a larger scale? This is called specialisation.

▶ **Diversification** Alternatively, should the business look for additional business opportunities or even change what it does altogether? This is known as diversification.

The cost of the development

If a business wants to develop its operations it will need capital to pay the costs involved. The way in which it can obtain capital will vary, depending upon the type and size of organisation.

▶ Banks and other financial institutions are more inclined to lend to limited companies than to sole traders or partnerships

▶ Well-established limited companies, with a good track record, will find additional capital easier to obtain

▶ Many companies don't like to borrow too much. In this case they can issue additional shares. Remember, however, that only public limited companies can raise large sums of money this way by selling shares on the Stock Exchange.

▶ Some small companies, with excellent chances of growing rapidly, can obtain finance through a venture capital company. These are specialists who, in exchange for lending capital, take shares in the firm and therefore benefit if the business does well.

▶ Another way of financing a development is through **reserves**. Reserves comprise 'saved' profit from previous years. This method preserves the independence of the business, but slows down development as there is a limit to the amount of reserves which can be amassed, year on year.

Bear in mind that the business will still be focused on achieving good profits and will want to keep the costs of any new development to a minimum.

In some cases, the need for capital can lead to a review of the ownership and the liabilities of the owner.

Business ownership and liability

Sole traders and most partners are personally liable for all the debts of the organisation. This does not matter too much if the business is operated on a small scale, but can be very risky if the organisation grows and more money is involved, such as for expensive stock or because many business customers are allowed credit when they buy goods and services. Credit means buying now and paying later, so there is a greater risk of bad (unpaid) debts.

In addition, as a sole trader or a partnership, the business and the owner are the same thing. Therefore, if you were injured on the premises, you would sue the owner. A company is different. It has a separate legal identity. So if you hurt yourself in Next, you would sue the company – not the manager of the shop or even the chief executive of the organisation. For this reason, many owners of large businesses prefer to operate as a company so that they cannot be held personally liable in this type of situation.

▲ If you are injured on a company's premises you would sue the company, not the shop's manager

Generally, it is unlikely that any business would want to expand and develop and retain sole trader or partnership status. The exception, as you saw on page 173, are professionals who are not allowed to do this, such as doctors and solicitors.

Specialisation or diversification?

A large pharmacy and cosmetics business wants to continue to expand but is under pressure for business by its competitors. It has a good name and many loyal customers, but its profits are starting to decline. The managers want to see the business grow and develop but are split into two camps.

▶ Those who think they should continue to do what they know – and if necessary curb developments until they get this right.

▶ Those who think they should offer additional or different goods or services (such as eye tests, nail bars and 'men only' stores).

This was the position in which Boots the Chemist found itself a few years ago. You can read what happened in the next 'Organisations in Business' feature on page 188.

Sticking to what you know – and developing expertise in this area – is known as **specialisation**. It means that the organisation concentrates on its **core business**, which is usually the main activity from which it makes its money. Motorola makes telecommunications equipment but had managed its own IT and computing operations. It then decided to get rid of these by asking a specialist company to do this for them. This was because it felt that it didn't have the expertise to do these tasks properly and they were distracting everyone from the main purpose of the enterprise. Motorola therefore decided to specialise at what it was good at.

The opposite approach is **diversification**. This means deliberately extending the range of goods or services to meet new challenges. Sometimes this is done because the existing area of operations is seen as too narrow and therefore risky. In others, it is because new opportunities are identified. Sometimes the business continues to operate in the original way and *extends* its services or operations. An example is Express Dairies – whose rounds staff no longer deliver just milk but books, CDs, contact lenses and magazines to householders. Under a seven-year licence, they can now also deliver up to 46 million postal items a year and the company is looking at increasing its distribution network.

In other cases the business may change direction altogether. Modern farming provides excellent examples of diversification. Because of problems managing and making a profit from running traditional farms, both the government and the Countryside Alliance have promoted a policy of diversification for farmers. Some have been very successful, such as farmers who have set up touring caravan parks on their land, those who have diversified into offering quadbiking and paintballing and those who have converted their barns into self-catering holiday cottages. In a more novel diversification, Sally and John Robinson, of Byland Abbey farm started selling bras over the Internet to supplement their cattle business. Their new enterprise currently sells more than £500,000 of goods a year – and earns considerably more than the farm.

ORGANISATIONS IN BUSINESS

Many large organisations diversify their operations. Boots began to experiment with ways to make the chain more interesting and different. It introduced its Wellbeing services (such as reflexology, aromatherapy, dentistry, chiropody and optician service) in 12 stores, opened Pure Beauty stores, and started Boots for Men stores. Not all of these ideas proved successful.

The Boots for Men stores closed in July 2001 and, in 2003, Boots said it was closing down most of its Wellbeing services and closing the Pure Beauty stores. Its aim of persuading customers to pay for massages and manicures in its stores was labelled an expensive mistake. Only dentistry, chiropody, opticians and laser eye surgery clinics will remain.

Boots had even tried to expand internationally with plans to open 1,000 Boots branches in 10 countries, but acknowledged that this, too, was a mistake and said it would pull out of the Netherlands and Italy. It will now concentrate more on its core business as a national retailer.

Diversification isn't always a mistake. Marks and Spencer not only sells food, clothes, furniture and homeware products but also diversified into financial services some years ago – offering loans and investments and managing its own credit card facility. Tesco not only sells food, clothes and financial products in its stores and online but has diversified into selling DVDs, plasma televisions and mobile phones. In early 2003, it announced plans to offer an online travel service and to provide a new retail telecom service. Choosing the right direction and keeping costs down are usually the most critical factors for diversifying successfully.

Ways of moving forwards – or backwards

Many businesses grow slowly by ploughing back profits into the business, year on year, to finance expansion. Others borrow money from financial institutions to expand or develop. There are other ways of becoming larger, more quickly.

▶ **A merger** is one way of doing this. The business joins with another and is now much larger and more powerful than it was before. For example, in 2001 the Halifax and the Bank of Scotland merged to become HBOS, and the Royal Bank of Scotland (a different organisation) merged with Nat West. Mergers are carried out because both organisations benefit. They are larger, because their overall customer base is much bigger, and they can also reduce costs by combining premises and reducing staff.

▶ **A takeover** is another alternative. In this case one company buys control of another by buying its shares. It may buy a competitor, so that it can have a larger share of the market; it may buy a business which has expertise that it doesn't possess in-house or it may buy a business in another area or region so that it can expand quickly. An example was the car dealer Lookers, which had over 60 dealerships in England and wanted to move into the Scottish market. Instead of opening its own dealerships in the area, it bought the Scottish car retailer Taggarts for £5.6 million. It benefited because Taggarts was already well established in Scotland and this meant Lookers didn't have to start from scratch in developing their business north of the border.

Sometimes, of course, organisations want to revise an earlier development plan. One way of doing this is through a **demerger**. In this situation, the company separates the business so that one part is 'hived off' and set up as a separate organisation. In 2001, BT demerged its mobile phone business, MM02 and set it up as a new company because it wanted to separate its mobile phone operations from its main business. In July 2002, Kingfisher demerged its electrical goods stores, which include Comet, into a new business called Kasa Electricals, and retained its DIY business, which includes the UK market leader, B&Q.

The impact of development on organisations

Organisations do not plan to develop without good reason. They will usually aim to develop to:

▶ increase their customers, sales and profits

▶ reduce their operating costs per item sold so that they can sell at a more competitive price

▶ offer a wider range of services or products

▶ operate over a wider area.

As you have seen, sometimes they are very successful, at other times this may not be the case. Normally, slower developments have less impact on an organisation than rapid change, and successful developments obviously have greater benefits.

All developments and changes, however, have some impact on the operations of the company.

▶ **Aims, objectives and strategy**. You will read about these on page 192. All of these may be affected by ongoing developments.

▶ **Changes to jobs and job security**. Expansion and successful development will increase the number of jobs on offer and improve job security for existing staff. Conversely, contraction will do the opposite. Boots forecast up to 700 job losses in March 2003, when it announced the changes outlined on page 188. A merger can also result in job losses because of duplication of skills and jobs. Diversification will increase the range of jobs on offer and the skills required. Tesco, for example, will need travel staff to operate its online travel service. There may be better opportunities for some staff to specialise and more promotion opportunities.

▶ **Company reorganisation**. A change in size may mean that the company needs to be reorganised, to take account of these changes. Lookers, mentioned on page 189, will need to include its new Scottish dealerships in its overall company structure.

▶ **Different methods of working and different administrative procedures**. The methods which suit a small business aren't always appropriate as the business grows. In the case of a merger, both companies will have their own ways of working – and their own forms and procedures. These need to be reviewed so that the company works effectively as a whole unit. In addition, larger businesses are more difficult to manage and run, which can be something of a challenge for managers used to operating a small company. They may need greater administrative assistance and expertise.

▶ **Different working conditions or place of work**. As a company grows and develops, there is likely to be more specialised equipment, a greater range of staff benefits and services and working hours may change, particularly if the business is open longer hours. Staff may also be offered the opportunity to work in different locations.

▶ **Selling to new markets**. A company which expands by selling different products or selling to different countries will need specialists in these areas, such as new production managers or regional managers. It will also need to adjust its administration systems to take account of these new sales.

▶ **Greater public scrutiny**. Businesses which convert to a public limited companies will be open to greater public scrutiny from the press and City of London analysts. If these analysts do not agree with decisions made by the directors, then there will be adverse publicity and the share price may fall quite steeply. This can lead to some owners deciding to *buy back* their company – as you will see below.

ORGANISATIONS IN BUSINESS

Many public limited companies start from quite small beginnings. A good example is the JJB Sports chain. Dave Whelan, the founder, started the chain in 1971 by purchasing a small shop in Wigan, called JJ Bradburn Sports, for £12,000. By 1994, he owned 123 shops and, to finance further expansion, he floated the company – now called JJB Sports – on the Stock Exchange. Today there are 444 stores around the country.

In early 2003, however, Dave Whelan and his family – who between them own 39% of the shares – were thinking of buying back their company. JJB shares had fallen by two-thirds between 2002 and 2003 after a dip in profits following the World Cup and also because many City investors disapproved of the purchase of the discount chain TJ Hughes, which the company acquired in April 2002. Some think that the problem is that sports clothing has lost its appeal to the young, although trainers are still popular.

Buying back the company means that it changes its ownership from a public limited company back to a private company. This would return direct control to the owners. The company would also save money by not having to pay dividends to shareholders, which currently costs about £18 million a year. However, to do this, Dave Whelan would have to raise enough money to buy out all the remaining shareholders at a price they find acceptable. Current estimates say this would cost him about £290 million.

JJB is not the first retailer to move away from the Stock Exchange. British Home Stores, Allders and Jaeger have all been returned to private ownership and in 2003 Hamleys and Selfridges announced similar plans. Their main concern was low share prices over the past few years through factors outside any company's direct control, such as falls in consumer spending after the terrorist attack in the US on 11 September 2001 and when the Central tube line was out of action in London.

OVER TO YOU!

1. Jenny opened her first shop four years ago, after training as a florist. A year later another shop in a nearby town became vacant, so Jenny bought it. Now she wants to expand further but needs more capital. She also feels she needs more help with the day-to-day running of the business. Jenny could take on her friend Sue, as a partner. Sue is a good florist and also has excellent business skills. Alternatively, Jenny could stay on her own. At the moment, she can't decide what to do.

   a) Jenny is a sole trader at present. Identify 4 advantages and 4 disadvantages of this type of ownership.

   b) Suggest 3 benefits and 3 disadvantages of taking on Sue as a partner.

   c) If Jenny stayed on her own, she could convert the business into a private limited company. Suggest 2 reasons why she might want to do this.

2. In the table below, the terms and the corresponding definitions have been mixed up. Rewrite the table, so that the terms and definitions are correctly matched.

Business terms and definitions

Diversification	One company buys control of another.
Merger	The company concentrates on its main business activity, which it knows and is good at.
Specialisation	The company varies the products made or services because it thinks there are opportunities in these new areas.
Demerger	Two companies join together to become larger, more powerful and to reduce their costs.
Takeover	A large organisation decides to split up its operations.

3 Read each of the following accounts of a business development which was announced or took place since 2002. Then, as a group, identify *why* the development took place and suggest 2 likely impacts on the organisation.

a) Cadbury Schweppes purchased Adams confectionery for £2.7 billion to make the company the world's joint leader in the confectionery market. Adams is the world's second largest chewing gum business and also produces bubble gum, cough sweets and breath fresheners.

b) Express Dairies, which supplies most of the UK's milk and cream, announced a planned merger with Arla, the manufacturer of Lurpak and Anchor butter. The new company will be called Arla Foods. The organisations argue they will be in a stronger position, given their complementary operations. Costs will also be reduced as head office functions will be combined and there will be some factory closures.

c) Tesco paid £377 million to buy 1,200 T&S stores – a convenience store chain. Many of the stores will be converted into Tesco Express small stores. Tesco knows the convenience sector is fast growing but had problems expanding into this area because planning permission was so difficult to get.

d) eBay, the online auction firm, announced it had bought the online payment system, PayPal, for £1 billion. eBay was already using PayPal as an external service provider but prefers to own and control all its own operations – from listing items online to receiving payments.

e) Dell, the computer company, announced that it wants to keep moving forward and continue to diversify. The company is famous for making and selling PCs and, although it sold printers, PDAs and point-of-sale terminals it did not make them itself. Now Dell has announced that it will make its own items and no longer intends to buy-in these items from established firms such as Palm or HP.

▼ THE IMPORTANCE OF CLEAR AIMS AND OBJECTIVES

All organisations need to have aims and objectives. An **aim** is a goal the business wants to achieve. Organisations in the private sector must make a profit to survive – so this is normally high on their list of aims. In the public sector, revenue comes from government grants and funding. Although public sector organisations may not have to make a profit, there are strict controls over how they spend their money.

In this section you will find out about **mission statements**, which set out the purpose of an organisation as well as its main aims. You will also learn about the difference between aims and objectives, how businesses make plans to try to achieve their goals and how the type of goals they have can affect the way the company operates in terms of its policy and culture.

Mission statements

The main purpose of a business is often stated in a mission statement, which often also describes how the organisation intends to achieve this. If you look at a mission statement you can usually divide it into three sections. These are:

▶ the **fundamental purpose** of the organisation, i.e. why it is in business

▶ what **activities** it is doing to achieve its purpose

▶ what **values and beliefs** are held by the organisation.

Some mission statements are quite short, whereas others can be much longer. For example, Sainsbury's plc has quite a short statement: 'Our mission is to be the consumer's first choice for food, delivering products of outstanding quality and great service at a competitive cost through working faster, simpler and together'. In contrast, the Greenpeace mission statement is much longer but starts as follows: 'Greenpeace is an independent, non-profit global campaigning organisation that uses non-violent, creative confrontation to expose global environmental problems and their causes. We research these solutions and alternatives to help provide a path for a green and peaceful future. Greenpeace's goal is to ensure the ability of the earth to nurture life in all its diversity.' Follow the links at www.heinemann.co.uk/hotlinks to read the mission statement in full.

Why have a mission statement?

Although there are some organisations which don't have mission statements – Richard Branson's Virgin group is an example – this is unusual. Today most businesses prefer to have one for the following reasons:

▶ The statement defines what the business is all about and this gives a focus or 'steer' for the organisation as a whole.

▶ It gives an insight into the organisation to the world at large.

▶ It differentiates the organisation from its competitors, who may be undertaking very similar activities.

▶ It helps the business to set objectives which are relevant and which lead to the achievement of the main aim or purpose.

▶ It helps to explain and define management decisions, which should be made with the main purpose and aims in mind. Without a mission statement it may be more difficult to think about possibilities and opportunities as broadly, or too easy for managers to focus on inappropriate ways forward which would not benefit the business overall.

▶ It helps to improve communication within the company.

Writing a mission statement

Mission statements may be devised by a senior person in the organisation and then agreed and amended by a group, or it can be the result of suggestions made by staff, who have all considered the main purpose of the business, its activities and its values and beliefs.

According to the experts, a good mission statement should be positive, visionary and motivating. It also needs to be clear and well written, otherwise people won't understand it. If it passes these tests and truly reflects the fundamental operation of the business then there are several benefits.

- It communicates a clear message to the outside world.

- It can help to inspire and motivate the staff who work there, who can take pride in the organisation and what it aims to achieve.

- It will help the organisation to set appropriate and clear objectives (see below), which will help it to achieve its purpose.

- If the objectives are clear and appropriate, they are far more likely to be achieved.

- If the objectives are clear and defined, preferably in measurable terms, then progress towards them can be monitored.

- It sends a message to all the **stakeholders** involved in the business about its intentions. Stakeholders are all the people who do, or may do, business with the organisation in the future or who have an active interest in its operations, such as employees, customers and suppliers.

- It gives specific guidance on behaviour by individual managers as well as staff, who know what the values are held by the organisation.

- It gives clear information about the customer needs it intends to satisfy and the way in which it intends to meet these needs.

Corporate objectives

Some mission statements also include objectives. These identify the practical steps that are taken by the whole organisation to achieve the main aim or purpose. It may be helpful to note that the word 'corporate' means 'the whole company'. This can be used in business to differentiate between this type of objectives and departmental objectives, which only refer to one part of the business.

All organisations set objectives, but not all of them include these in their mission statement. This is because the objectives may be very specific and set as measurable targets which are of main interest to the managers and staff who have to meet them.

Measurable targets always include numbers and timescales, so that progress towards their achievement can be measured; for example:

- to open six more stores within the next twelve months

- to increase sales by 10% over the next two years

- to reduce costs by 5% over the next year.

In each of these cases it is possible to check, quite easily, whether the objective has been met.

SMART objectives

Many experts think that all objectives should be **SMART**, i.e.:

- **Specific** – each objective relates to one particular goal

- **Measurable** – each can be measured to check success

- **Agreed** – this means that those who have the job of achieving them are in agreement with the target they have been given

▶ **Realistic** – otherwise they are unlikely to be achievable

▶ **Time-constrained** – then success or failure over a certain time period can be checked.

On occasion you may read objectives linked to a mission statement which aren't measurable or time-constrained. This doesn't mean to say that they are not specific, agreed or realistic, but that the objectives are continuous, over time, or that for the purpose of external communications the organisation has omitted specific numbers or timescales.

An example of a mission statement which includes objectives is that published for Cancer Research UK. They talk about their vision – this is the same as their mission statement.

Vision and objectives of Cancer Research UK

The vision of Cancer Research UK is to conquer cancer through world-class research. Through research into the causes, prevention, treatment and cure of cancer, the aim is to control the disease within two generations.

Cancer Research UK is working to achieve the following objectives:

1 To carry out world-class research into cancer.

2 To develop better treatments for cancer patients.

3 To improve the quality of life of cancer patients.

4 To reduce the number of people getting cancer.

5 To improve training and support of cancer research workers.

6 To provide authoritative information and advocacy on cancer.

To achieve these aims, Cancer Research UK will seek to:

7 consistently raise sufficient income to support our scientific ambitions.

8 raise awareness of Cancer Research UK and its mission.

9 recruit and retain high-quality staff across the organisation.

10 create the highest-quality infrastructure and support services.

(Taken from *Mission Statement of Cancer Research UK*, March 2003)

Strategic plans

Strategic plans are **long-term** plans related to the whole business. They relate to where the business wants to be in the future, as opposed to where it is now. This is how the business moves its 'mission' forwards, year on year.

Basically, the managers of the organisation need to decide upon:

▷ the goals of the company

▷ the resources they will require (i.e. time, money, staff, equipment, etc.) to achieve these goals

▷ the outcomes by which success will be measured.

Strategic plans are usually decided every year, but cover the next four or five years. Each year, progress is checked against last year's plan and a new one devised. This enables changes which have, or will, affect the organisation to be considered and plans revised against these.

One useful and common method is to carry out a PEST analysis, where the external factors which may affect the business are divided into four different headings:

▷ **Political factors** – such as changes to laws and regulations which could affect the business, such as increases in the Minimum Wage rate or changes to Health and Safety legislation.

▷ **Economic factors** – such as levels of unemployment, interest rates (which affect the cost of borrowing money), levels of customer spending, competitors and their plans.

▷ **Social factors** – such as working hours, more parents working, longer working hours, increased retirement ages, trends that change customer demand such as increased number of vegetarians, organic food, etc.

▷ **Technological factors** – such as developments with PCs, mobile phones, text and picture messaging, plasma screens, the Internet, etc.

As an example, a retailer may have the future goal of expanding nationally but will have to consider changes to employment legislation (see pages 299–306), the cost of borrowing the money for expansion, current levels of customer spending, competition in particular areas of the country, the type of goods to stock and the way in which goods can now be sold over the Internet. All these factors will then influence the strategic plans of the business.

Company policy and culture

The mission of the company and the objectives it sets both determine and influence the policy and the culture of the organisation.

▷ The **policy** of the organisation relates to the principles and ethics which the company believes in, which then affect what it does and how it does it. The Co-operative Bank, for example, has strict principles and this affects its policies about investment. It will not, for instance, invest money in companies which it considers do harm, such as the tobacco industry or in countries which do not respect human rights. Therefore the policy affects the type of business which is carried out, and with whom.

▷ The **culture** of the organisation relates to its style of behaviour, the 'atmosphere' in a company and the standards it prefers. Some organisations are very formal, with many rules and procedures. Others are more informal, yet the work still gets done. Generally, you can expect an organisation which uses public money or is publicly accountable (for example in the public sector or a public limited company) to have a more formal culture than one which is privately owned. This is because it has to be more careful about how it operates. The same applies to businesses which are expected to have very high standards by their professional bodies, such as doctors, solicitors and accountants. This is because one word of scandal could ruin them so they have to be very careful about how they operate.

This does not mean that other businesses don't have high standards – but they may have more flexibility in setting their objectives and how they achieve them. This can reflect a more informal culture in which individual enterprise, flexibility and even 'fun' is promoted – as you will see below.

ORGANISATIONS IN BUSINESS

Richer Sounds is a national hi-fi retailer. It was mentioned on page 110 because it was voted the top British-owned company to work for in 2003 by its employees and on page 116 because of its customer policies. The mission statement of Richer Sounds is quite straightforward, and identifies the three main focuses of the business – on customers, employees and profit (which links to job security for its employees).

Richer Sounds Mission Statement

1 To provide second-to-none service and value for money for our customers.

2 To provide ourselves with secure well-paid jobs working in a stimulating and equal opportunities environment.

3 To be profitable to ensure our long-term growth and survival.

Its objectives, however, give a better insight into its culture. Every year it sets 10 objectives, and every year these include two constant items:

▶ To keep the business fun

▶ Always to review what we do and make it better.

The 'fun' item is included because the managers honestly believe that working at Richer Sounds should be great for staff – and they measure this in their annual Colleague Attitude Survey. But they also believe that everyone should be committed to trying to continually improve the business – and they reward colleagues for positive suggestions and for excellent work. This is a good example of how you can gain an impression of the type of culture of an organisation, and its policies, from the objectives that are set.

OVER TO YOU!

1 The mission statement for Cambridge University is very short: 'The mission of the University of Cambridge is to contribute to society through the pursuit of education, learning and research at the highest international levels of excellence.'

Most educational institutions have a mission statement. Obtain a copy of the one for your college and compare it with the one above. Identify the ways in which it is the same – and how it differs. As a group, discuss the reason for these differences.

2 Ben and Jerry's is a well-known American ice-cream maker – with some wacky ideas and even wackier flavours – yet its mission statement is far more serious. Its mission is in three parts:

Product – To make, distribute and sell the finest-quality all-natural ice cream and related products in a wide variety of innovative flavours made from Vermont dairy products.

Economic – To operate the company on a sound financial basis of profitable growth, increasing value for our shareholders and creating career opportunities and financial rewards for our employees.

Social – To operate the company in a way that actively recognises the central role that business plays in the structure of society by initiating innovative ways to improve the quality of life of a broad community – local, national and international.

It also states that it holds a deep respect for individuals inside and outside the company and for the communities of which they are a part.

a) As a group, decide what this mission statement tells you about the purpose of the organisation and the activities it carries out.

b) What do you think are the values and beliefs of Ben and Jerry's?

c) Suggest two ways in which you think these values will affect the policies and culture of the organisation.

d) How would you feel, as a new employee, if you read a mission statement like this? Compare your ideas with other members of your group.

3 Max and Jason recently completed a horticultural course and have started in business as a partnership, redesigning and landscaping gardens. They are firm believers in working in an environmentally friendly way. They will not, for instance, use pesticides or advocate designs which would adversely affect the natural habitat of the area. Max thinks they should write a mission statement, but Jason is uncertain. He says that as they have only a small business, it isn't worthwhile.

a) Suggest four reasons why a mission statement would benefit their business.

b) What main factors about the business should the partners consider when they draft their mission statement?

c) Identify four advantages of having a clear, positive mission statement.

4 Kim wanted to work in publishing when she left college. She was offered her first job working at the *Big Issue*, which produces the street magazine produced on behalf of homeless people. Now she has just left and started work at a large educational book publishing company. During her first week she is involved in a discussion about the strategic plans of the company and their corporate objectives.

a) Why is it important that the company has a strategic plan?

b) Suggest three factors the company will consider each year when it makes its plans.

c) What is the main purpose of having corporate objectives?

d) As a group, suggest three ways in which the policy and culture of the *Big Issue* will have been different from Kim's new employer. To help, you can find out more about the aims and policies of the *Big Issue* and compare these to a large publisher such as Heinemann by following the links at www.heinemann.co.uk/hotlinks.

▼ EXPLAIN HOW BUSINESS ORGANISATIONS ARE STRUCTURED

Every business, no matter how small, must be organised or structured so that people know which tasks are their personal responsibility. This prevents misunderstandings and overlaps and some jobs getting left because no one knows who should do them.

As a business develops, dividing up the work properly between people becomes even more important, especially if staff work in different offices or even different locations. At some point it becomes necessary for a proper structure to be worked out. The most common method is to group people together according to their area of work – so that all sales people work together, all finance people and so on. However, this isn't the only method used.

Within all businesses, too, people work at different levels. In a small business there may be one boss and several staff, so that there are only two levels. In a large business you might find considerably more levels – from the managing director at the top, to members of the general workforce at the bottom. Each person, however, will have a specific role and these will vary, depending upon the level at which that person operates. You may already realise that a managing director is usually paid more than his or her subordinates, but in this section you will find out why!

At all levels of management, however, administrative support is required both at departmental level and centrally, for example, by the managing director and his or her team. Administrators play a key role in supporting the work of the company, so the final part of this section concentrates on the type of tasks they carry out and the importance of their effectiveness as a member of a team and department.

▼ FUNCTIONAL AREAS AND THEIR ACTIVITIES

In all organisations, certain tasks need to be carried out and these are often grouped together under different functions. For example:

▷ Some staff are involved with finance and money, such as making sure that payments made by customers are banked and that the invoices received by the business are paid.

▷ Others are involved with selling goods or services and making sure that prospective and actual customers know about new products or developments.

▷ Some are involved in buying the supplies required by the organisation, such as raw materials to make goods or stock to resell and general supplies such as equipment and stationery.

In a large organisation, the staff involved in each function often work together in the same part of the building. This is sensible, because they will normally need to communicate and liaise regularly about the work that they do. In this case, there are usually different departments, each with a title to reflect its function, such as Finance Department, Sales Department or Purchasing Department.

When you start work, you will find that the number of departments, and their titles, will vary from one organisation to another depending upon its overall size and the business it carries out. An organisation which provides a service, such as bank or insurance company, doesn't need a production department. These types of business wouldn't need a distribution department either, but for a large retail chain this would be essential. Many organisations have a human resources department, but some still call these their 'personnel' department and some call IT services 'computer services'. It is therefore important to use the information that follows as a guide to the overall range of functional areas and activities that are carried out and then remember to adjust this to suit the specific needs of any organisation with which you are involved.

Finance and accounting

Many business owners think this is the most important function of all. This is because finance is the lifeblood of the organisation. Unless the income received is greater than the costs and expenses that must be paid, the business will not make a profit. Equally, unless income is received regularly, so that the firm can pay its own bills and the salaries of its staff on time, there will be serious problems. It is the task of finance staff to record all receipts and payments and to monitor these on an ongoing basis for the managers. Today, virtually all financial transactions and accounts are produced by computer, which makes analysing the figures and producing future forecasts much easier. Finally, all companies have to produce annual accounts by law, called **statutory accounts**. These include their balance sheet and their profit and loss account.

Finance – main activities

▶ Producing invoices, checking payments are received and chasing up overdue payments

▶ Recording all money received (income)

▶ Checking invoices received and paying these

▶ Preparing the payroll and paying staff salaries

▶ Checking departmental budgets to ensure managers are not overspending and issuing budget reports

▶ Producing regular financial reports for managers

▶ Producing cashflow forecasts which show the expected income over the next few months and the expenses due – to enable managers to check there will always be sufficient to pay the bills

▶ Advising the managing director and the board on sources of additional finance. This would be the task of a senior member of staff

▶ Producing the statutory accounts every year.

Human resources

The human resources function is concerned with all the individuals who work in the organisation, and their welfare, as well as all prospective employees. It will also liaise with relevant external organisations, such as the Job Centre or any trades unions to which the workforce belongs. Human resources has a major role to play in making sure that the organisation employs suitable staff and that the needs of all the employees are met, so that they work in a safe environment, their legal rights are observed and they have appropriate opportunities to train and develop. This benefits everyone, given that staff who are happy in their jobs generally work harder, stay with the firm longer and are more committed to the success of the business.

Human resources – main activities

▶ Advertising job vacancies at the Job Centre, in newspapers or magazines or at an employment agency – whichever is the most appropriate for the job.

▶ Notifying internal staff of promotion opportunities.

▶ Receiving and recording all job applications, arranging interviews for suitable candidates and notifying candidates of the result of their interviews.

▶ Arranging training for staff – from induction training for new employees to internal and external training courses for existing employees.

▶ Ensuring that all staff receive a contract of employment and other essential information, such as details of the company's grievance and disciplinary procedures.

▶ Advising managers on employment law and the legal rights and responsibilities of the company and its employees.

▶ Keeping records of any grievances and any disciplinary actions and their outcome.

▶ Overseeing and monitoring the working conditions of staff.

▶ Ensuring the company complies with health and safety requirements and keeping accident records. (In some organisations, a separate Safety Officer may be appointed to do this.)

▶ Liaising with any staff associations or trades unions which represent the workforce.

▶ Recording sick leave and reasons for sickness.

▶ Carrying out company welfare policies. These may include long-service awards, help for families during times of serious illness, company loan scheme, etc.

▶ Providing employees with appropriate information which affects them, such as the company pension scheme, security policies and procedures, holiday entitlement, staff benefit schemes, etc.

▲ Job interviews are often carried out
by human resources staff

Production

The production function concentrates on the manufacture or assembly of goods and is therefore a crucial function in any manufacturing business. Production staff are responsible for ensuring that the goods are produced on time and are of the right quality. Quality requirements, of course, can vary. In some businesses they are highly critical. A filing cabinet may be 1 mm too wide, but this is unlikely to be noticed. The same doesn't apply to a silicon chip or a DVD!

In some organisations, production staff will also be responsible for obtaining and checking the quality of all the raw materials used. In others, this is the responsibility of the purchasing function (see page 204). However, production staff are likely to oversee the storage of any raw materials and to ensure that there are always sufficient quantities available for current production needs. Within production, maintenance staff will be employed to ensure that all the equipment and machinery is kept in good condition and any faults are rectified quickly. This is very important as a major hold-up can have serious repercussions on production schedules and overall profitability.

Production – main activities

▶ Planning production schedules to maximise machine capacity and staff levels.

▶ Storing and checking the stocks of raw materials.

▶ Producing or assembling the finished product.

▶ Checking the quality of the product both during, and at the end of, the production process.

▶ Checking that production is going to schedule and taking action if there are any delays or problems.

▶ Packing and storing the finished products, ready for distribution.

▶ Scheduling routine machine maintenance.

▶ Carrying out repairs to machinery and equipment as required.

Research and development

The title of this function is usually shortened to R & D and, in many organisations, R & D also includes product design. Staff working in R & D are concerned with new product developments as well as improvements to existing products or product lines.

New products may be developed because of technological or scientific advances or because someone has a good idea – like James Dyson and his bag-less cleaner. Improvements to existing products are often ongoing as a result of market research or customer feedback. In recent years, this has resulted in developments such as transparent jug kettles, ring-pull cans and microwavable packs.

R & D – main activities

The aim of R & D is to work with designers to develop a usable product that can be manufactured at a reasonable cost and sold at a competitive price, but the specific activities that are undertaken usually vary, depending upon the industry.

▶ In the pharmaceutical industry, scientists are employed to develop new medicines and drugs.

▶ In the food industry, technologists work with chefs to prepare new products such as ready meals (and low-calorie versions) and new sauces or flavourings.

▶ Electronic companies concentrate on new technology products, such as plasma screens and WAP phones.

▶ In some industries, R & D specialists improve production methods by the use of new technology such as robots and computerised quality control.

▶ In other industries, R & D concentrate on both the performance of the product and on its design. At Ford, for example, engineers will focus on improving performance and safety whilst reducing emissions. Designers will concentrate on the shape and look of the car – both externally and internally.

ORGANISATIONS IN BUSINESS

Some organisations started life as a good idea or based on research by the originator. James Dyson and his cleaner is one example. Another is Google – now the most popular search engine on the Internet.

Google was born in 1996 as a research project by two American university students, Larry Page and Sergey Brin, when they were in their early 20s. They used Brin's student room to develop their idea and then decided their prospects were so good they could put their studies on hold for a while. They raised $1 million to set up their own offices and almost immediately were handling 10,000 enquiries a day – Google now handles more than 150 million each day! The company is still privately owned – with no plans to change – and the owners employ around 300 people.

As a British example, if you travel by train then you may be interested to know that a small private UK company called Laserthor is in the process of developing a device to help rail companies get rid of leaves on the line. The system fits onto the underside of trains and sends out a laser that destroys leaves without damaging the track. If the company is successful, this will be an R & D development which will put an end to many standard British jokes about the leaves on train lines every autumn!

▲ Could this be the end of leaves on the line as an excuse for late trains?

Purchasing

All organisations need to buy goods. Manufacturing companies need raw materials, retailers need stocks to resell and every business needs equipment and consumables – from fax machines to sticking plasters.

Large companies usually have a separate purchasing function where specialist staff buy everything needed by the business. This is often cheaper because they can buy in bulk to obtain better discounts. Purchasing staff will also be responsible for taking out contracts with regular suppliers, making sure that the terms of the contract are met, especially in relation to delivery and cost, and that the quality of supplies is satisfactory.

Buying is often a skilled job, especially in the retail trade, as too much unsold stock reduces overall profitability. In the fashion trade, it takes a skilled eye to select the best lines for the next season. Finally, buyers have to evaluate the different sources of supply. Some organisations are very strict about issues such as reliability, quality, speed of delivery, possible shortages and – depending upon the item being purchased – these factors may be more important than price.

Purchasing – main activities

▶ Ordering stock and other items from authorised suppliers.

▶ Solving problems when there are delay or supply problems. This may mean chasing up the supplier or finding an alternative source of supply.

▶ Evaluating alternative sources of supply in relation to price, reliability, quality, terms of delivery, etc.

▶ Liaising with managers and stock controllers over levels of supplies and reordering as well as coping with changes in demand.

▶ Monitoring alternative supplies or sources of supply which could result in a cost saving or other benefits.

▶ Checking the quality of items delivered and referring problems back to the supplier.

▶ Maintaining good relations with key suppliers.

▶ (In a retail business) deciding and advising on the best lines to stock for the next season, bearing in mind current sales levels and future trends.

▲ Sales help to clear unwanted stock

Sales and marketing

Sales and marketing are responsible for promoting and selling the goods that are made or the service that is offered. Because the number of items sold has a direct relationship with the profit made, the activities carried out by this functional area are very important indeed.

Some people become confused between sales and marketing and think they are the same thing. Basically, sales is responsible for advising customers on the best goods (or service) for their needs, keeping sales records and actually selling to customers. Marketing staff are more involved with identifying future customer needs through carrying out market research or undertaking promotional activities to tell customers about the products and services that are available. In some organisations, many marketing activities are contracted out to specialist agencies who carry out market research or plan advertising campaigns or promotions.

Many organisations both promote and sell their goods and services online. Because of the relevance of their website to these activities, the overall design and content is usually, today, the responsibility of marketing rather than IT services (see page 209).

Sales and Marketing – main activities

▶ Obtaining feedback from prospective and current customers through carrying out market research. The aim is to obtain customer views on potential *and* existing products and/or services.

▶ Analysing customer feedback and using this to inform future business plans and developments.

▶ Producing advertisements (for newspapers, magazines, television, radio, hoardings, etc.) and direct mail shots to be sent to customers' homes.

▶ Devising sales promotions, such as in-store promotions, special offers and competitions.

▶ Organising publicity campaigns, such as through press releases about business activities and developments and sponsorship.

▶ Producing and distributing publicity materials, such as catalogues or brochures and sending these to customers.

▶ Contacting or dealing with customers either by telephone or face-to-face to sell the product or service.

▶ Negotiating discounts for bulk sales to special customers.

▶ Providing technical advice to customers.

▶ Answering customer queries and enquiries.

▶ Ensuring that the business website reflects the image of the company, that the content is up-to-date and that customer enquiries via the website are handled promptly.

Distribution

The distribution function is responsible for ensuring that all the goods produced or stocked by an organisation are delivered to the right place on time and in the right condition. In the case of a mail order or manufacturing company, the goods must be delivered direct to the customer. In the case of a large retailer, stocks will be held in giant regional warehouses and these must be transported to stores around the area, often in special vehicles, such as those which carry chilled or frozen items.

This may seem a simple job, until you consider that distribution has to be cost effective. In other words, it mustn't cost more than it needs to! To achieve this, most distribution staff try to obey some simple rules:

▶ the route of any vehicle must be planned carefully, preferably so that it goes in one direction to keep fuel costs down and save time.

▶ where goods are both delivered and collected, vehicles should preferably never return empty.

Because of the problems planning this, many businesses subcontract distribution to specialists. One such company is Eddie Stobart, whose large distinctive vehicles are often spotted on the motorways of Britain.

Distribution – main activities

▶ Ensuring that goods ready for despatch are properly stored.

▶ Ensuring that goods for despatch are properly packed and secure.

▶ Ensuring that the loads on the vehicles are secure and safe.

▶ Checking that perishable items are distributed in good time and in the proper conditions.

▶ Checking that deliveries made match orders in terms of quantity and type of goods – or notifying sales if there is any discrepancy.

▶ Checking that deliveries are being sent to the right customer and to the correct address.

▶ Scheduling the routes of vehicles.

▶ Notifying sales staff of delivery schedules so that customers (or stores) can be informed.

▶ Dealing with distribution problems, e.g. through bad weather or vehicle breakdown.

Administration

Traditionally, administration was often a separate function or department. Today you are more likely to find administrators working in every department throughout the organisation. This provides additional flexibility and enables administrative staff to be more actively involved with departmental work and to operate as a member of the departmental team.

Whether administration is separate or not, the activities carried out through this function are many and various and you will cover these in more depth on page 227 and 228. For that reason, a summary of administrative activities is given below, rather than a full list.

Administration – main activities

▶ Dealing with internal and external mail.

▶ Preparing documents – including letters, reports, meetings documents and spreadsheets.

▶ Transmitting and sending documents – both electronically and by post.

▶ Storing and retrieving documents – both electronically and in paper-based filing systems.

▶ Copying and distributing documents as required.

▶ Dealing with visitors and callers – both face-to-face and by telephone.

▶ Making arrangements – for travel, internal events and meetings.

▶ Keeping departmental and company records up-to-date.

Customer services

Whereas attracting new customers is the responsibility of Sales and Marketing, making sure that customers receive the best service possible at all times is the task of Customer services. In some organisations, *all* staff are responsible for providing customer service whereas in others this is a separate function. This does not mean, of course, that other staff can be casual about customer satisfaction. It simply means that a group of staff are specially trained to assist customers.

Customer services – main activities

▶ Answering customer enquiries about products and services; particularly those which involve more specialist advice and technical information than may be provided by general sales staff.

▶ Solving customer problems – from late deliveries to damaged goods.

▶ Providing after-sales service, including dealing with returned goods, replacing damaged goods, arranging for repairs to be carried out or arranging for a spare part to be obtained.

- Dealing with customer complaints. This involves understanding basic consumer law so that the customer's rights are known and upheld.

- Keeping records of customer complaints and analysing these with the aim of resolving problem areas.

- Recording and analysing feedback from customers to inform future plans. Whereas marketing are mainly concerned with customer views about specific aspects of the product or service, monitoring the satisfaction of existing customers is the role of customer services. This can mean issuing questionnaires or operating a customer panel.

- Using customer feedback to improve customer service such as the clarity of information and instructions, the range of acceptable payment methods or the number of customer care telephone lines/speed of response.

ORGANISATIONS IN BUSINESS

More and more businesses are now using technology to improve their customer service. This is absolutely essential for organisations that trade online. Customers don't expect to order online and then have to telephone or visit the company if something goes wrong. Good customer service usually includes sending an automatic email confirmation to electronic orders.

In addition, many websites contain a specific customer service area where frequently asked questions (FAQs) are answered. This helps customers, as they don't need to contact the company with a routine enquiry. It also reduces the number of calls to the organisation.

Email is useful as customers can send specific queries that are not answered on a FAQs page. Ideally the website will provide a link. The customer simply clicks on this to write the email. Needless to say, it is important that email enquiries are then answered promptly. The easiest method is to set up an automated system that acknowledges the email and says when a specific response will be sent. On other sites you may find a 'contact us' option or a PhoneMe button, which the user clicks on to make free telephone contact.

If you want to investigate sites that operate customer service sections online (such as tracking orders and/or FAQs pages), follow the links from www.heinemann.co.uk/hotlinks.

IT services

If you imagine, for one moment, the disruption caused to an organisation (or individual users) if the computer system fails, you can understand the key role that is carried out by the IT services department. Today virtually all large organisations operate a computer network. This will be the case in your college. All the computers are linked together so that emails can be sent between users and information can be shared – from customer records to health and safety procedures.

In a retail organisation the system is even more complex as most transactions are recorded electronically at the point of sale. You see this happen if you visit a large superstore. Your purchase is swiped through the system, the price is charged automatically, if you are a regular customer then this is also recorded or your name and address may be entered then; if you pay by card, the funds are also transferred electronically from your bank (or credit card company) to the store. Automatically, the store's stock lists, sales records and customer records are updated and the data is summarised, every day, for managers. Now imagine the problems if this system crashed or a virus was downloaded or someone hacked into the system!

IT services – main activities

▶ Buying and installing new computers and linking these to the network.

▶ Recommending the purchase of new computers and/or software to keep up-to-date with technological developments and matching these to the needs of the business.

▶ Installing software on networked computer systems.

▶ Operating a help desk to advise users experiencing computer problems.

▶ Undertaking repairs to the computer system as required.

▶ Advising on (and/or purchase and issue) stocks of computer supplies including cabling, equipment such as scanners and zip drives as well as consumables such as printer cartridges and floppy disks.

▶ Connecting additional or new equipment to the system.

▶ Devising and monitoring a security system which allows access only to authorised users and protects the system against viruses and hackers.

▶ Operating a full back-up system for critical data so that this can be recovered quickly in the case of an emergency.

OVER TO YOU!

1 Purita is a bottled water company. It pipes spring water from a nearby source to a large tank room where the water is stored. The water is then fed automatically to the bottling lines and into recyclable plastic bottles which are also made by production operatives at Purita. The bottles are covered in shrink-wrapped plastic and stored in a large warehouse which is large enough to hold two weeks' production. Purita drivers deliver the drinks to supermarkets and other outlets. The company is fanatical about cleanliness. Maintenance staff are responsible for the cleanliness of the tanks and pipes and every day samples of the water are examined for quality by staff in the laboratories.

a) Identify three departments you will find at Purita from the description of its activities above.

b) Identify three other departments you would be likely to find within the company.

c) For any four departments of your choice, identify three activities which will be undertaken by the staff there.

2 Subiya has been working as a junior administrator in the Purchasing Department of a large carpet manufacturing company. There are two internal promotion opportunities available, for an assistant administrator in Finance or an assistant administrator in Human Resources.

a) Suggest three activities Subiya's colleagues currently carry out in Purchasing.

b) Suggest three activities Subiya will carry out as a junior administrator in the department.

c) Subiya cannot make up her mind which job she would prefer. Bearing in mind the difference between the activities that are undertaken in Finance and Human Resources, what factors do you think she should consider before she makes her decision?

3 Kelly has recently applied for the job of help desk administrator in the IT Services department at her company. She thinks her previous experience in customer services might help her.

a) Describe four activities Kelly will have undertaken in customer services.

b) Identify three activities that Kelly's new colleagues in IT Services will undertake.

c) Do you think Kelly is correct that her experience in customer service will come in useful? Give a reason for your answer.

d) In which area will Kelly have to improve her knowledge and skills – and why?

▼ ORGANISING THE ACTIVITIES TO SUIT THE ORGANISATION'S OBJECTIVES

You should now be familiar with organisations that divide up their work into functional areas and understand how these are likely to be structured. However, businesses will do this only if it fits the way they operate, the type of activities they carry out and if this type of structure would help them to meet their objectives. If it does not, the structure will be a little different.

No matter how a business is organised, however, it is absolutely vital that all the departments or groups that exist communicate and interact regularly. Otherwise each will work in isolation and it is doubtful whether the organisation's objectives will ever be achieved.

In this section you can find out about the alternative methods of structuring an organisation as well as the importance of regular interaction between departments and groups.

Different organisation structures

There are six different variations you need to understand. Remember that each will depend upon the type of organisation, its size, the work it does, the area it covers and the objectives it is trying to achieve.

By area of work

An organisation which is structured into functional areas is divided by areas of work, such as finance, production and purchasing. However, other types of business may do this and yet have different names for their departments or groups, because they often undertake specialist functions which have a particular name. This separation is used because there are features common to each type of work. Examples include:

▶ newspapers – which may divide up its areas of work into news, features and advertising.

- book publishers – which usually have an editorial department, a design department and a production department.

- charities – which undertake activities such as fundraising, as you will see in the 'Organisations in Business' feature about Amnesty International, opposite.

- film production companies, which have divisions for pre-production staff (casting, finance, locations), production work and post-production work (advertising and distribution).

▲ The three stages of film production

By product or service

In this case, the organisation offers a variety of products or services and splits up its workforce into those which concentrate on different ones; for example:

- large publishing companies – which produce newspapers (one division), magazines (another division) and books (a third division)

- legal firms – which divide their operations into areas of law, such as employment, property, litigation, probate, etc.

- local authorities – which have departments named after the services offered, such as Housing, Social Services and Planning

- pharmaceutical companies – which produce drugs, toiletries and hospital supplies

- colleges – which are divided into departments linked to the courses they offer, such as Art and Design, Building and Construction, Information Technology and Business Administration.

By different markets or customer

Many organisations supply to different types of customer. The most obvious differences are private individuals/business customers and retailers/wholesalers, but in other organisations there are customers with very different needs. Examples include the following.

- Banks, which have separate divisions for private accounts and business (corporate) customers. They may separate these even further, into small business customers and large corporate customers.

- Computer firms and telecommunications companies that supply to private individuals and business customers. This is because their needs will be very different.

- Breweries that not only brew beer and/or lager, but also run chains of pubs or inns. They will supply their product to trade customers only but will be involved in retail operations through their food and drink outlets.

- Furniture and clothing manufacturers that sell the majority of their products to the trade but which also operate factory shops or mail order divisions and sell direct to the public.

- Hospitals – which have separate departments such as pathology, psychiatry, radiography and physiotherapy for patients with different types of needs.

ORGANISATIONS IN BUSINESS

Amnesty International is a worldwide movement of people campaigning for human rights, with around two million members all over the world. Its supporters come from many different backgrounds and hold different political and religious beliefs. The work of AI is directed by an International Secretariat based in London with a staff of nearly 400 researchers, campaigners and legal and other experts.

Amnesty International UK, with a head office in London, has more than 195,000 members, and hundreds of affiliated groups and organisations across the United Kingdom. There are about 120 paid staff and 70 volunteers working in four departments under a director.

▶ The Campaigns department plans and develops AI's campaigns, lobbies politicians, keeps the media informed about current events and concerns, and educates people about human rights.

▶ The Marketing department raises funds to pay for AI's work, raises AI's public profile and holds high profile events, and keeps the membership informed through its magazine and other materials.

▶ The Human Resources department recruits and looks after staff and volunteers.

▶ The Finance department includes both Finance and IT.

You can find out more about Amnesty International by following the links at www.heinemann/hotlinks.

By geographical location

This is a popular option for organisations which operate on a national or international basis. It means that each regional division can be overseen by its own manager who is familiar with the area, the customers and, in the case, of international organisations, the language and culture. Examples include:

▶ larger retail organisations, such as Tesco or Marks & Spencer, which have stores all over the country. These are often grouped into regional areas and overseen by regional managers

▶ international companies, such as Ford Motors, which has its headquarters in the USA but also has a European division. Most large banks, too, have international divisions

▶ large international delivery companies, such as DHL and Fedex, which have collection and distribution points all over the world.

By project groups/matrix structure

Project groups are a popular choice amongst small hi-tech companies and consultancies. The business 'bids' for different contracts to do work for outside organisations. As each contract is won, a project group is put in charge of this particular work. When this task is completed the team is disbanded and/or members are reassigned to a new task.

Each project group, however, needs the support of other members of staff (or departments) who provide the key operations, such as finance, marketing and human resources. This leads to a matrix structure, illustrated below:

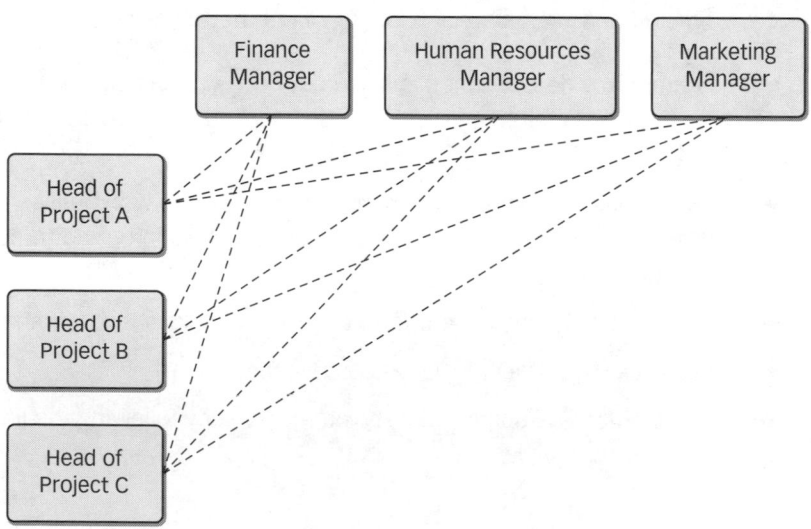

▲ A matrix structure

Fundamentally, a matrix structure is therefore a combination of functional departments and other sections or teams that undertake special projects or work in different areas.

Examples of organisations that use this structure include:

▶ large construction companies, such as Balfour Beatty, which bid for contracts to build bridges, motorways and office blocks worldwide

▶ large defence companies, such as BAE Systems, which bids for contracts to build aeroplanes from the Typhoon to the European Airbus

▶ small media companies, such as Moonfish in Manchester, which bid for contracts to develop websites and undertake online marketing campaigns.

By centralised/decentralised services

Centralisation and decentralisation can relate to the organisation itself and how it makes decisions, to the functions carried out within the business or to services within the organisation.

In a **centralised** organisation, virtually all the major decisions are made at head office or at a central headquarters. At head office, too, may be the key functions, such as Finance, Marketing and Purchasing. This kind of structure is commonly found in retail firms. The manager and staff of an individual branch receive information and instructions from head office on virtually everything – from the lines they must keep in stock to the way their window display must look. All difficult or unusual problems must be referred to head office.

The advantage with this approach is that all branches then operate in the same way. The disadvantage is that they may be inflexible and unable to respond quickly to a situation or take into account local needs and differences. Often the managers and staff may feel that they have little influence over the way the business operates and their views are not seen as important.

Because of these problems, many organisations prefer to operate in a more **decentralised** way, by giving more responsibility and freedom to individual managers and staff. They may allow branch managers to hire their own staff and take important decisions related to customer service. This is the choice of many larger retailers and superstores, who prefer to train their managers to such a level that they can run most of the day-to-day operations in the store using their own initiative. Certain functions are still likely to be undertaken at head office by key functional areas, such as marketing campaigns and the production of publicity materials, IT support, purchasing decisions in relation to future stocks and finance, because the organisation will want these coordinated throughout the organisation and undertaken by expert staff.

Services within an organisation can also be **centralised** or **decentralised**. Centralisation has benefits – it is usually cheaper, more expensive equipment can be purchased and expert staff can be employed. Examples of centralised services often include:

▶ **Reprographics and printing**. At your college much of the photocopying and printing may be carried out centrally. This enables the college to afford expensive colour photocopiers and to employ specialist staff. It is cheaper than trying to provide large photocopiers throughout the organisation or to use outside firms.

▶ **Filing and retrieval**. This is common in businesses which need to store large numbers of important files, such as building societies or banks, which may keep many thousands of mortgage records and house deeds. These have to be stored securely. In some cases, special automated and robotic systems are installed so that the documents are safe from damage through flood or fire and are retrievable by specialist staff at the touch of a button. The files can be accessed or borrowed only by authorised personnel.

► **Mail**. An organisation, such as a large mail order company, which receives thousands of orders through the post and despatches a similar number of parcels each day will have a centralised mailroom. So, too, will a company that regularly sends out thousands of direct mail shots. This enables it to purchase expensive automated equipment and employ staff who become expert at the job.

Centralisation is not always the answer, however, and there are several disadvantages. The work can be repetitive, the systems can be inflexible (especially in a crisis) and there are often more procedures to follow for users – such as filling in forms to obtain a file or arrange for photocopying to be done.

For that reason, in many organisations, some services are likely to be **decentralised**. In this case you will find each department undertaking their own work. Typically, these are likely to include:

► **Sending faxes**. These days, fax machines are so cheap that you may find one in virtually every department in the company.

► **Routine photocopying**. This means that the majority of jobs can be done quickly and easily on a standard copier. Modern copiers also allow documents to be downloaded direct from a computer, which makes things even easier!

► **Administration**. Enhanced communications through networked computer systems has meant that administrators can access information and send emails, very quickly, to colleagues in other parts of the organisation. For that reason, administration is normally now a decentralised service.

Interaction between departments and groups

Constant interaction and communication is vital between all departments and groups in a business, no matter how it is structured. This can be by email, by memo or in face-to-face meetings. The whole organisation will move forward and achieve its objectives only if people cooperate with one another. This means each person keeps the others informed about what is happening and developments which may affect them.

▲ Cooperation and communication are essential in all organisations

Some examples can make this clearer.

- Prospective students make an enquiry about a full-time course at college. They often do this through a central department, such as Student Services. This department then has to communicate each student's intentions and their personal details to the right department, before an interview can be arranged or for the tutor to confirm that a student can start on the course. Individual tutors constantly interact about the content of a course, the progress of students and to organise assessments.

- A customer telephones the wrong department, or branch, about a problem. It is much more efficient if the person who receives the call informs the correct department about the problem so that someone can contact the customer quickly. This is better than just giving the customer a different number to ring. If customers have to ring a call centre, constant interactions are required between the staff who receive the calls and those who can provide specialist help or advice.

- A sales administrator is leaving. The sales manager wants a replacement so he contacts Human Resources and agrees with them the requirements of the job and the content of the advertisement. They receive the applications and negotiate with him the best times and days on which the interviews should be held. Human Resources is a function which needs to interact constantly with other departments over their staffing and training needs.

- A web development project group finds a new way of solving a problem related to the design of a site, because of the skills of a new expert programmer who has joined their team. They tell the other groups about this, to help to save them time, too. For this reason, many team leaders meet on a regular basis to exchange information and expertise.

- The manager of a regional store discovers that they are selling one major product line at a far higher price than their competitors. She raises this with head office who investigate the problem and agree the price can be reduced to match the competition. This means that, over the next few months, the company sells far more than it would have done otherwise. Most large firms have systems to encourage constant interaction between head office and branches – in both directions – so that information can be shared and discussed.

- The IT staff decide that security of the computer network would be improved if they redesign the log-in procedure. Before they do this they talk to the managers of all the departments, who talk to their own staff, to make sure that everyone knows and so that those with useful ideas can contribute to the process. Most organisations operate a consultation process before they introduce major changes to involve and inform the staff who will be affected.

1 Match up the following organisations and their *type* of organisational structure correctly. In each case, state why you think this type of structure has been chosen. Your options are:

a) area of work

b) product or service

c) different market or customers

d) geographical location

e) project group/matrix

f) centralised organisation

  i)   A large building company that has a house building division and a commercial property division.

  ii) An international bank, which has regional offices in London, Amsterdam, New York, Hong Kong and Sydney.

  iii) A food company, which has dairy foods, drinks, confectionery and snack foods divisions.

  iv) A national greetings card retailer that operates from a head office in London and allows its branch managers little freedom to make their own decisions.

  v)   An advertising agency where creative teams work together to devise and produce advertising campaigns for clients but are supported by the key functional areas of the business.

  vi) A police headquarters which has staff in its communications section, CID and forensics as well as the uniformed branch.

2 Suggest three advantages and three disadvantages of centralising a service such as filing or photocopying.

3 Suggest two consequences of each of the following lapses in communication and interaction between departments or groups:

a) At a sales and production meeting, the sales staff don't mention that they are currently promising some customers that their orders can be completed two weeks early.

b) A customer service representative receives several complaints about the new ordering system, which was recently introduced by the IT staff and is running very slowly. Rather than pass this on to the IT manager, she waits until the Regional Manager is in his office and tells him instead.

c) The IT staff plan to upgrade a program on the network which will mean that the network will be unusable tomorrow afternoon, but don't tell anyone.

d) For financial reasons, it is agreed to reduce the amount spent on advertising but the following week's management meeting is cancelled so no one tells the Human Resources or the Marketing staff.

e) Head office changes the date of a training course for staff but does not check with the branches if the new date is suitable.

4 As a group, suggest two reasons why each of the following departments or groups may need to communicate and interact with each other.

a) Human resources and production.

b) Purchasing and marketing.

c) One project group with another.

d) A head office to a branch office.

e) A branch office to head office.

▼ THE ROLES OF PEOPLE AT DIFFERENT LEVELS OF THE ORGANISATION

In a very small business, there may be just one manager but in most organisations there are far more. You will often find there are several levels of management, all with different roles and responsibilities. Some aspects of the management role are common to all managers, but others change depending upon the level of the job.

Organisations which have many levels are known as **hierarchies**. They are likely to be quite large organisations – your local authority or hospital may have as many as six or seven levels – and so might your college if you counted down each level of staff from the Principal at the top.

In this section you will learn about the main roles of the people you will find in a hierarchy, especially the managers at different levels. Once you understand what constitutes a management role there is another bonus. You will quickly learn how to recognise if people are given the title 'manager' when they are not really managers at all. Sometimes this is done by businesses to increase the morale or the status of some staff – who may perhaps really prefer a pay rise instead!

Finally, when you are at work you may hear the term **line manager**. It is helpful to know that this is not a job title. It simply describes the person immediately above someone else. So your line manager is your own boss, to whom you are responsible. If you look at an organisation chart, which shows all the managers, then you should see a vertical line connecting that person to you or to the staff in your department – hence the term 'line' manager.

The roles and responsibilities of managers

There are many different job titles for managers, as you will see in this section, and many different ways in which they may be grouped together in a hierarchy. Regardless of this, it is possible to put them into a general list or 'rank' order to see how their roles differ.

The top of the tree

All organisations have someone at the very top. The traditional title in commercial organisations is Managing Director. A common alternative title is Chief Executive.

The role of this person is to decide and agree with the directors the strategy and main aims of the organisation, and then ensure that these plans are implemented throughout the business. The title 'managing director' comes from the joint role of managing the company and being a member of the board of directors.

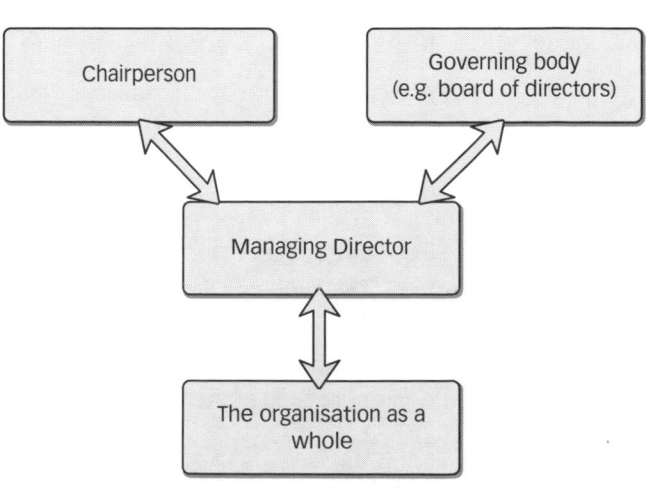

▲ The MD is a key link person in an organisation

Managing Director – main responsibilities

▶ Acting as the main link upwards, between the board of directors and any governing body (such as in a school or college) or with the Chairman of the company, who chairs the board of directors and is often the 'public face' of the organisation.

▶ Acting as the main link downwards, between the board of directors and the organisation as a whole.

▶ Ensuring that the strategic plan and corporate objectives are agreed to promote the company's main interests and are in line with its values.

▶ Ensuring that the strategic plan and corporate objectives are continually kept in mind by the whole organisation.

▶ Supervising changes over long-range planning and strategy.

▶ Checking the achievement of strategic plans and corporate objectives.

▶ Monitoring the financial contribution of all departments, divisions or branches and spearheading remedial action if there are problems.

▶ Maintaining an effective organisation structure. This may mean making changes to the overall structure at times.

▶ Networking with other MDs and senior managers in related organisations, i.e. having informal links with people with similar interests.

▶ Motivating the staff in the organisation to work hard and do their best.

The board of directors

Most large organisations have some type of governing body. Schools or colleges have boards of governors. In business, the title is board of directors.

Board of Directors – main responsibilities

▶ Deciding on the overall 'mission' of the business.

▶ Agreeing the long-term policies and the overall (corporate) strategy of the business.

▶ Agreeing the corporate plans and strategic objectives.

▶ Ensuring that financial resources are sufficient for the plans to be met.

▶ Monitoring the overall financial stability of the business and authorising major items of expenditure.

▶ Making key financial decisions, including deciding on how profits should be distributed. This includes agreeing the level of reserves and dividend payments to shareholders.

▶ Ensuring the company operates within the law. This includes publishing statutory accounts and a collective responsibility for the health and safety of all employees and visitors to the organisation.

▶ Managing different areas of the business to ensure that the activities of staff achieve corporate objectives.

▶ Monitoring overall results and external influences on the business (such as the actions of competitors) and adjusting plans and priorities where necessary.

Levels of management

The simplest way to start is to divide all managers into one of three levels:

▶ **Senior managers** – including anyone with the word 'director' in the title. Other titles used for senior managers include divisional manager, regional manager or department head.

▶ **Middle managers** – these may have the job titles such as deputy manager or branch manager. There is a senior manager immediately above them.

▶ **Supervisory managers** – who are the first level of management above the staff. Their job titles include supervisor, section leader or team leader.

One major difference between these levels is that the more senior the level, the longer the timescale over which they have to plan, as you can see in the table below.

Management levels and responsibilities

Senior managers	Set long-term plans covering the whole organisation – timescale up to 5 years
Middle managers	Involved in planning for own area or department – timescale 1–3 years
Supervisors and team leaders	Involved in achieving current plans (up to 1 year) and day-to-day operations

Senior managers are often also directors, with a seat on the board – but not always. In a very large company, or one that operates on a global basis, you may find senior managers who are not; for example an American-owned company with an American board, but an operation in Britain. In this case, the manager responsible for the British operations would be a senior manager, but would not be a director. This may also be the case for a company which has many different divisions. Apart from anything else, there may simply be too many divisions for each manager to be a director!

Generally, however, you can expect all senior managers to be responsible for a major area of the business. For this reason, you can also include the **heads of large departments** in this category.

Senior managers – main responsibilities

▶ Organising their own area to achieve the corporate objectives of the business.

▶ Monitoring the performance of their area and taking corrective action if there are problems.

▶ Operating within the budget they have been allocated.

▶ Helping to decide plans for the future relating to their own area and the best ways of achieving these.

▶ Cooperating with other senior managers over strategic issues and problems.

▶ Overseeing and monitoring operations within their area and liaising with their own managers and staff.

Middle managers have this title because they are literally in the middle, between senior managers or directors who are above them, and supervisors who are below them. They have a key supportive role upwards and downwards in helping to translate the strategic plans and objectives into the operations which must be undertaken to achieve them.

Middle managers – main responsibilities

▶ Supporting their own senior manager in running a key area of the business.

▶ Overseeing the operations to ensure that targets and objectives are met.

▶ Liaising with supervisors and staff over the scheduling and allocation of work.

▶ Balancing the needs of staff with ensuring that jobs are completed on time and to the right standard.

▶ Coordinating the work of different sections for which they are responsible.

▶ Being a key communication channel between their own manager and those below them.

▶ Helping to solve day-to-day problems on behalf of their own manager.

▶ Taking responsibility for any specific projects allocated to them by their manager.

Supervisory managers are at the first level of management and have direct contact with staff on a daily basis. They all usually need technical experience to be able to help solve day-to-day problems and to be able to give advice to their staff.

The main difference in terms of job titles is that a supervisor or assistant manager is responsible for an area of work – such as a payroll supervisor or the assistant manager of a shop. A team leader, however, is responsible for a group of people. The group may be together permanently (e.g. a sales team) or only temporarily (e.g. a project team).

Supervisory managers – main responsibilities

▶ Carrying out the instructions of their own line manager.

▶ Ensuring that their section or team runs smoothly and operates safely.

▶ Planning and controlling day-to-day operations to make sure targets are met and standards are achieved.

▶ Allocating resources (i.e. staff and materials) in their own area or within the team to meet requirements.

▶ Resolving operational problems promptly.

▶ Managing and motivating their own staff or team.

▶ Keeping their line manager informed of problems and developments and advising on future issues.

Knowing who is important in a business is very useful if you work there. At least you then know who you must impress if you want to move onwards and upwards! But titles can be confusing, especially if you work in the public sector, for a specialist organisation or for a foreign organisation, such as one with American executives and job titles.

You probably already know that in your college the chief person is the Principal and the title Vice Principal is often given to his/her deputy. American organisations – and some British – give their top people titles such as President or Vice President. Local authorities and some companies prefer the title Chief Executive or Chief Executive Officer to Managing Director. The Chairman of a company is also very important, but less likely to be involved on a day-to-day basis.

Some government-related organisations, such as the BBC, use the title Director General and the term Principal Officer may be used instead of Senior Manager. The government itself, of course, is headed by the Prime Minister and Cabinet Ministers have a similar role to company directors.

In a specialist company, you will find different terms again. The term Managing Editor is often used in publishing and a scientific company may use the title Scientific Officer. In marketing and advertising you will often hear the term 'account manager'. This type of manager is, however, somewhat different. They manage the accounts of certain clients but are not, in the formal sense of the word 'managers'.

Hierarchies in business

An organisation which has only two or three levels is said to have a **flat structure**. This is the case for many small businesses. An example would be a local travel agent with a branch manager and several travel advisers.

This is illustrated graphically as here.

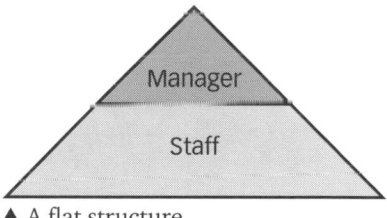

▲ A flat structure

If you looked at the head office of a national travel agency, however, you would see a rather different picture. You may see several levels of management – with the assistant branch managers at the bottom. In this case you would be looking at a **hierarchical structure**.

A hierarchical structure can be shown as a pyramid shape, simply because there is usually only one person at the top and far more at each lower level. At each level, the individuals will have different titles but these will vary depending upon the number of levels and the type of organisation. Some large organisations may have as many as 7 or 8 levels in the hierarchy. An example of two organisations with a hierarchical structure is shown in the diagram on page 224, showing different job titles.

You should note that any combination of levels or job titles is possible, in any organisation. It will depend upon how the organisation is structured and the preferences of the person at the very top!

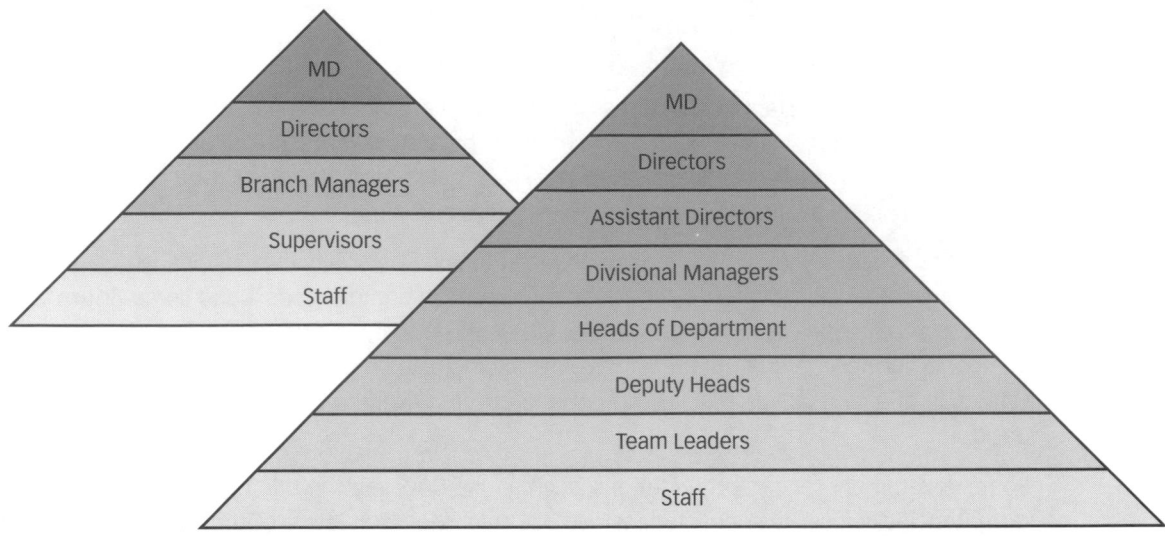

▲ Job titles in a hierarchical structure

Why have a hierarchy?

As an organisation grows and develops, and more people are employed, then it becomes impossible for one manager to control everyone for whom he or she is responsible. In management terms, this is called **span of control**. If the 'span' becomes too wide, then the manager cannot cope. Before this happens, it is usual to employ other managers (or promote some of the best staff) to take on a management role.

▲ This manager's span of control is too big for him to cope

The organisation may now have increased from two levels to three. Over time, the same problem is likely to recur, as even more staff are recruited. At this point another level of managers may be introduced, and so on.

Other changes also take place. Because there is a larger number of staff, the organisation cannot be run on an informal basis any longer. In a very small business, individual staff may just ask their manager if they want a day off or to leave early or even for a pay rise. They can easily check with a colleague what to do if a problem arises. This is not as easy in a large organisation. There have to be rules to make sure everyone is treated fairly, for example everyone has the same holiday entitlement and is paid at an appropriate rate for their job. There need to be procedures so that everyone operates in the same way.

For individual staff, the jobs that they do start to become more specialised. In a small business, you may be jack-of-all-trades – and do everything from sending out invoices to receiving visitors or buying stationery. In a large firm, the finance department will look after the invoices, visitors will be greeted on reception and stationery may be bought by purchasing staff.

The main features of a hierarchy are therefore as follows:

▶ The organisation will have a tall structure with several levels.

▶ There will be more than one level of manager, sometimes several.

▶ Managers will have a relatively narrow span of control, i.e. they will not be responsible, individually, for large numbers of staff.

▶ The jobs done by individual staff will be more specialised.

▶ Staff will be allocated to a specific area – this may be one functional area or one division or department.

▶ The business operates on a more formal basis. For example, there will be a standard job application and interview process and there may be guidelines on dress and the layout of business documents.

▶ There will be more rules and regulations to ensure everyone is treated fairly and legal responsibilities are met, for example on overtime and hours of work, on holidays and personal days off, on pay awards and relating to disciplinary and grievance procedures (see page 300 and 301).

▶ There are more systems and procedures to ensure that everyone works in the same way. These will include formal health and safety procedures, customer service standards and so on.

OVER TO YOU!

1 Susie is pleased because, after several years of working in administration, she has just been promoted to the role of office supervisor. She will be responsible for five administrators and will report to the departmental head.

a) Describe four responsibilities Susie will have in her new job.

b) Describe four responsibilities of her head of department.

2 An insurance company employs a customer service team of six, who are overseen by their supervisor, who reports to the sales manager. On Friday, the group are being visited by the group sales director and the MD and are keen to make a good impression.

a) Explain four responsibilities of the Managing Director of the company.

b) Identify four responsibilities of the group sales director.

c) The sales manager operates at 'middle management' level.

   i) What does this term mean?

   ii) Identify three responsibilities of a middle manager.

3 Billy is nervous because, after several years of working as a member of a team, he has the opportunity to become team leader. Explain four ways in which Billy's job will change as a result.

4 Kieran works for a small firm of accountants. There is a senior partner, three department heads and the staff. Kieran has now applied for a job in the finance department of a large firm and will report to the accounts supervisor. This person reports to the head of accounts, whose boss is the finance manager – whose own boss is the finance director.

a) How many 'levels' are there at the firm of accountants?

b) What type of structure exists at his new company?

c) Explain three differences Kieran is likely to find in the way the firms operate, because of this difference in structure.

▼ THE IMPORTANCE OF EFFECTIVE ADMINISTRATION

Administrators work to support managers at all levels in the organisation and often operate at different levels themselves. The most senior administrators are likely to:

▶ support the MD and the directors. In this case they are often known as PAs – short for personal assistants

▶ be responsible for key aspects of work within a department, such as the departmental budget and the allocation of administrative work

▶ manage their own teams of administrators, and report direct to the head of a department.

Administrative staff may work in a central department, in functional departments, in regional offices or be attached to specific teams. They may start at a relatively junior level and, as they gain in experience, move up the ladder.

Many opportunities are available because of the importance of administration to the organisation. Managers are busy people, with many responsibilities. They need the support of effective administrators to help them to do their own jobs and to run their section, department or company successfully.

In this section you will see how the range of tasks undertaken by administrators has a critical role in supporting the aims of the company both at department and team level.

The range of administrative tasks in a company

One of the reasons why many people want to become administrators is because the work is varied and interesting. There is a combination of routine tasks and new or different jobs – which can be either a worry or a challenge, depending upon your point of view!

Even within an organisation, if you change jobs or are promoted, you will find yourself with some tasks which are similar and others which are completely different, because you are working in a different department or have more responsibility.

Routine administrative tasks

The following tasks are carried out by most administrators, no matter where they work.

▶ Dealing with telephone callers, answering enquiries, taking and passing on messages.

▶ Preparing documents, such as letters and reports, using word processing, spreadsheets and presentation packages.

▶ Collecting and distributing incoming mail, preparing and despatching outgoing mail.

▶ Storing documents accurately in paper-based files and retrieving documents and files as required.

▶ Preparing and transmitting electronic documents, such as emails and faxes.

▶ Photocopying and collating documents and distributing these as required.

If they are carried out effectively, they each support the work of the company in several ways, as you can see in the table below.

Tasks carried out by administrators support the work of the company

Task	Support for the company
Answering enquiries and taking messages	Improves customer relations and responsiveness
Preparing documents	High-quality, prompt response and following house-style gives good impression of company and maintains image to customers and other stakeholders
Collecting/distribution mail correctly	Enables managers and staff to make daily decisions based on latest information
Preparing/dispatching outgoing mail	Ensures prompt response to customers and other stakeholders
Filing and retrieving documents	Enables all staff to access paper records quickly and easily
Preparing and transmitting electronic documents	Enables fast responses to be made in important situations without jeopardising quality or courtesy
Photocopying documents	Enables staff to receive prompt information on issues which affect them

Additional tasks

The following tasks may be carried out because they are required by a particular department, or because an administrator has specific responsibility for an area:

▶ Greeting and dealing with external visitors and callers to the organisation.

▶ Keeping computer records, such as a customer or stock database, up-to-date.

▶ Keeping departmental planners and diaries up-to-date.

▶ Finding and researching information as required.

▶ Arranging meetings, including preparing meetings documents, booking and preparing the room and arranging for refreshments.

▶ Making travel arrangements and hotel reservations.

▶ Assisting with the arrangements of special events, such as sales conferences or visits by VIPs.

▶ Purchasing (or liaising with the Purchasing Department) over supplies of stationery and keeping stock records.

▶ Preparing the paperwork related to departmental interviews and greeting interviewees.

▶ Recording minor departmental expenses and arranging repayment for staff through the petty cash system.

▶ Keeping staff records up-to-date by logging sickness absence, holiday leave and attendance at training events.

▶ Organising internal training events by helping to prepare materials, notifying those who will attend, booking the room and refreshments.

▶ Keeping specific departmental records and undertaking other departmental duties, such as responding to internal queries.

This is not an exhaustive list! It will depend upon where you work, who you work for and their own job role.

▲ Arranging meetings can be another important duty for an administrator

Each week, *The Times* newspaper includes a special section for administrators and PAs called 'Crème'. A similar section appears each Monday in *The Guardian* entitled *Office Hours*.

The Times usually features the work of different administrators and their jobs. Articles have included being a PA and providing administrative support to managers from a horse breeder to the MD of a music company. Another article focused on television administration, working for the BBC or Granada. In this area you would need interpersonal skills, office experience and excellent IT skills.

Follow the links to the Crème website from www.heinemann.co.uk/hotlinks. For a different approach, you can also read *The Guardian* section online. In both cases you will find lots of information about the role of administrators in businesses today and links to other useful pages.

The contribution of effective administration

All managers are focused on their own jobs and responsibilities. A manager cannot concentrate on achieving targets and moving his or her area forward unless the important, fundamental tasks are routinely undertaken to a high standard. This means that administrators must do their job effectively. An administrator who forgets to pass on an important message, loses a vital document or upsets an important customer is a liability and will create more problems.

The contribution of an effective administrator is invaluable. Not only are tasks undertaken promptly, so that deadlines are consistently met, but the work is always of a high standard. It never needs checking and the manager can rely upon the quality to be excellent, regardless of whether it is a page of information for a team briefing or a presentation document to an important customer.

In addition, in most teams and departments, the administrator is the key link person between the manager and the rest of the staff by knowing:

▶ the manager's movements and plans for the next few days (or weeks)

▶ the best action to take (i.e. what the manager would want to happen) if a problem occurs in the manager's absence

▶ what information must be passed to other people and when

▶ what information must *not* be passed on – and why

▶ which tasks are the most critical, and must be done promptly

▶ how to answer problems and queries that arise unexpectedly.

1. You have already seen how effective administration supports the work of the company in the table on page 227. This table related to general tasks which are carried out by virtually all administrators.

   Working in a group of three or four, devise your own table, this time based on the additional or departmental tasks of administrators shown on page 228. Select five tasks, of your own choice, and in each case decide how they support the work of the department or team.

   Then compare your selection and your ideas with those of other groups.

2. Mark has recently been made team leader of a project group and is arguing that he needs administrative support to complete the project on time.
   a) Suggest four reasons why Mark thinks this support is important.
   b) Identify three tasks his administrator will carry out.
   c) Describe two ways in which the appointment of the administrator is likely to benefit the team on the days Mark is away on business.

3. a) Melanie is Tom's administrator but is known to be a bit of a disaster. Suggest two consequences of each of the following mistakes she has made this week.
   i)   On Monday she muddled up the contents of two envelopes and sent the reps' reports to a customer, instead of the invoice the customer was expecting.
   ii) On Tuesday, she confused Luton and London when she was typing out the departure airport for Tom's visit to a client in Brussels next week.
   iii) On Wednesday, Tom arrived at a meeting with the MD to find the photocopies of his report had two pages missing, one upside down and three in the wrong order.
   iv) On Thursday, Melanie accidentally deleted an urgent report she was typing and had to start all over again and finish it in a rush.
   v)   On Friday, she forgot to tell Tom's team that all their expense claims must be in by next Wednesday for payment that month.
   b) Suggest three reasons why administrative tasks must be carried out effectively to support the work of the organisation as a whole.

▼ IDENTIFY AND EXPLAIN EFFECTIVE WORKING PRACTICES

In the previous section, you have seen that administrators must work effectively if they are to support the work of their company, their manager, their department and/or their team. This may seem obvious, but the reality is less simple. Very few administrators aim to be ineffective or poor at their jobs, yet this can happen if they haven't been properly trained or are lazy or careless.

It helps, therefore, if you understand what you have to do to work effectively. This doesn't mean that you will never make mistakes, but they are likely to be far fewer and have less disastrous consequences.

In this section you will learn how planning and organising your work, amongst other things, will improve your personal efficiency. You will also find out why it is important to be flexible and how to achieve this, even when you think you are swamped with work. Finally – and probably most important – you will look at the ways in which you can develop your personal performance, long after you have finished this book. This will enable you to continually improve and develop throughout your career.

▼ THE IMPORTANCE OF PLANNING WORK EFFECTIVELY

Good planning is essential in all organisations. The problems which occur otherwise are shown in the story in the press about a disabled man who had waited twelve months for council workmen to paint a special parking space outside his house. To his horror, the very day after the job was done the road was resurfaced and his newly painted bay disappeared under the tarmac. To make matters worse, he was then told it had all been a mistake and the resurfacing should never have included his road.

▲ The negative effects of poor planning can be infuriating

An example of poor planning in an office would be to prepare a long report and find out only after you've distributed 50 copies that there's something wrong with it or that some important information has been missed out. You then have the problem of retrieving all the existing reports and destroying them, as well as correcting the original and copying and distributing it. This does nothing for your professional image with everyone who received the wrong version and also takes up a considerable amount of your time. It is also a waste of resources.

In contrast, if you plan properly this type of problem is less likely to occur. The aim of planning is to think in advance, consider all the possibilities and aim for a 'right first time' outcome.

The benefits of this include the following.

▷ A clear mind (and less stress) because you can focus on the overall job you have to do with fewer distractions.

▷ Fewer unexpected problems which may hold you up or create difficulties for you or for other people.

▷ A more accurate estimate of how long a job will take – so that you can allocate sufficient time for it.

▷ The ability to monitor your own progress better, because you know all the tasks you have to complete to finish the job.

▷ Better use of your time – because you can work quickly and effectively and will make fewer mistakes.

▷ Far less danger of holding other people up through unforeseen problems.

▷ Far less danger of having to admit to everyone you've done something wrong.

▷ A successful outcome first time round – because you will know exactly what you are trying to achieve and know when you have achieved it.

▷ The ability to complete any job more quickly and more easily.

▷ Increased confidence in your own ability to do complex tasks.

Key stages in the planning process

What does good planning entail? If you were organising a major event – from a house move or wedding to the holiday of a lifetime – you would need to go through several stages to ensure that nothing was forgotten and everything was completed at the right time.

1 **Draw up a draft schedule or checklist**   List absolutely everything that has to be done in a schedule or checklist. In a planning meeting, this can be done by several people to draw up a master list or master plan. At this stage it is useful, too, to think about the resources you will need and to check their availability.

2 **Prioritise the list**   Put the list into the correct sequence or priority order. Some tasks will need to be done at the outset, others may be less important. Some might be dependent upon the efforts of, or information from, other people.

3 **Decide upon deadlines**   Identify the target date for the completion of each task – or the deadline for partial completion of large tasks. This is particularly important if you are working on the overall task with several other people.

4 **Reality check**   Check that the schedule makes sense and the whole task can be achieved by the final deadline. This will be possible only if you include in your planning some allowances for contingencies, interruptions and the other commitments you have to fulfil. You should also bear in mind aspects such as confidentiality, which might make a difference.

5 **Start work**   Work steadily down the list and tick off the items as you complete them, so that nothing is forgotten. Making notes as you go is often helpful, as you will see on page 237.

6 Monitor progress Review and report back on your progress to other people who need this information or who are dependent upon the final outcome.

Each of these stages is described in more detail in the sections that follow.

Drawing up the schedule – and the importance of clarifying the purpose

Good planners ask themselves several questions even before they start to draw up a schedule. The key words to note are easy if you remember the Rudyard Kipling poem:

> I keep six honest serving men
> (They taught me all I knew);
> Their names are **What** and **Why** and **When**
> And **How** and **Where** and **Who**?

▲ These key words are essential to good planning

In other words:

▶ **What** is the overall task that has to be done? What is the required outcome?

▶ **Why** does it need to be done, i.e. why is it needed and what is its purpose? This gives you valuable information in relation to quality, amount of information or detail required and indicates the type of resources you are expected to use and the level of confidentiality. Knowing the purpose often saves you having to ask many questions later!

▶ **When** must it be completed by? Are there any parts of the overall task that must be done by a specific date? Do you have to report back on progress at specific intervals?

- **How** should it be done? This relates to the way you will do the job and the resources you will require, such as the help of other people, certain items of equipment and materials.

  - **people** include all those upon whom you are dependent for additional information, help or expertise. Identifying the correct person in each case and checking their availability is essential.

  - **equipment** includes items such as computers, fax machines, photocopiers, shredders, calculators and scissors. Basic items you own yourself aren't a problem, but larger items may be, particularly if these are shared among several people.

  - **materials** includes paper, pens, filing folders, presentation wallets and envelopes. Remember that paper comes in many different types and sizes – and so do envelopes. Whereas most routine items are available, special ones may need to be ordered, and large quantities may have to be reserved or obtained in advance.

- **Where** should it be done? This may also relate to the availability of resources and where they are sited or, in the case of an event, where it will take place.

- **Who** is involved? This includes the person who wants the task and all those who will be involved in helping you or depending upon you for information.

It can be useful to summarise this information in writing, so that you don't forget anything important, in a similar way to the form shown below.

Outline Planning Sheet

Full description of task: Update welcome pack for new employees

Reason required: Current pack out of date. To include information on new staff benefits and to include new company video.

Task given by: Jan Marlow, Human Resources Manager

Final deadline date: 24 June

Level of confidentiality: Medium – for internal use only.

Activities List

Activity	Deadline date(s) agreed	
	Partial completion	Full completion
Book photographer		2 May
Obtain photographs		12 May
Arrange printing of new folders	14 May (book)	16 June
Order copies of company video	14 May (book)	16 June
Update information pages	24 May (drafts)	18 June (final)
Copy finalised pages		21 June
Assemble 50 packs		22 June

Resources List

People: Ken Davis (photographer), Mark Kent (printer), Phil Bartlett (video), Jan Marlow (to finalise draft pages)

Equipment: PC, photocopier, stapler, thermal binder

Materials: Blue folders with company logo, white paper for inserts, blue dividers.

Additional Notes

Photographer to cover reception area, canteen area and training unit.
Folder design and video cover design will be agreed by Jan Marlow on 12 May.
Finished packs to be taken to Human Resources Office.

Report progress at HR meeting on 16 May

Prioritising the list

The importance of prioritising, and how to separate tasks into different categories, according to their urgency and importance was covered on pages 90–91. You may find it helpful to review these pages now.

Good planners carrying out a complex task often prepare a daily priority list, bearing in mind the key difference between urgency and importance.

▶ **Urgency** relates to how quickly a task must be done, i.e. tasks which must be completed by a specific deadline. The task becomes more and more urgent the nearer you are to the deadline.

▶ **Importance** relates to those jobs for which you have personal responsibility as well as those where there will be serious consequences if they are not done. You are normally judged by how well and how reliably you complete important jobs.

Fundamentally, when you are making out a planning schedule, you need to take into account one or two other aspects as well when you are deciding how to allocate your activities.

▶ Urgent and important should be listed first. These include:

– tasks which are crucial to the overall job

– tasks where there could be delays or problems because they involve other people or will need time to sort out

– tasks which other people need you to complete quickly before they can start work.

▶ Your next jobs are all the remaining urgent tasks which should be done as soon as possible.

▶ The next jobs are important but not urgent. Include in this group backing up any work you are doing on a computer!

▶ You now have time for non urgent tasks which are not vitally important. These could include tidying up your files and making out a fresh checklist every so often. These will help you to be more organised but, in a crisis, a failure to do them wouldn't threaten the whole project.

Finally, remember that the partial completion of one task, the receipt of information from someone else or a short delay may mean you have to add new tasks to your list or change the schedule around a little. Keeping an eagle eye on the tasks you still have to do, and reprioritising these on a regular basis, is absolutely essential.

Deciding upon deadlines – and taking account of other people

The deadline for the overall tasks, and some of the jobs you have to complete, may be non-negotiable because the work is required by someone important or is required for a certain event to be held on a particular day.

In other cases, you may have more scope in deciding and agreeing deadlines. This is useful, particularly if you need the cooperation of other people to complete certain aspects of your work. General guidelines are as follows.

▶ The requirements of senior executives and your boss are top priority. So, too, are any commitments related to important customers and clients.

▶ Your own supervisor may be relying upon you to undertake certain tasks but be able to give you more information or advice about which deadlines are critical and which are negotiable. You should, however, bear in mind your supervisor's other commitments and responsibilities. If your supervisor's own reputation is dependent upon certain tasks being completed by a certain date, he or she will expect to be kept informed of progress (see below) and consulted *immediately* if there are any unexpected problems. Even if the job is going well, if you need to liaise with your supervisor over aspects of the task, do allow enough time. Don't expect your supervisor to be willing (or able) to drop everything to do something for you at a moment's notice.

▶ Your colleagues will also have their own work to do – and their own priority list. It is neither reasonable nor fair to expect them to reshuffle this just to suit you. Whilst they may be willing to do so in an emergency, they will expect emergencies to be rare events! If you are constantly running to them at the last minute, before too long you will no doubt receive a chilly reception. For this reason, discuss aspects of the job on which you will need information or assistance from them in advance and *mutually* agree a time and date on which you can sort this out. Then calculate a realistic deadline around this information.

Reality check – and the level of confidentiality

Your reality check is a quick review when you look at:

▶ the tasks you have to do

▶ the deadlines you have agreed

▶ the overall timescale

▶ any other aspects which you need to consider.

Under 'any other aspects' include your other commitments and responsibilities. It would be silly, for example, to schedule a complex task in a week where you have already booked two days' holiday or if that is the same week you need to complete *another* long and complex task.

▲ A reality check includes being sure about your deadlines and the time available

Wise planners also often schedule in an extra day or so (if they can) for unexpected problems and delays, particularly if they are reliant on information or help from several other people. This gives you some breathing space if something goes wrong.

It also helps to schedule a little more time if you are involved in anything which is particularly confidential. Confidentiality has already been covered in this book in Unit 2 on pages 93, 138, 139 and 152. In relation to planning, you need to think about the level of confidentiality and whether this is high, medium or low.

If the confidentiality level is high, then it is likely that:

▶ you can pass on information or discuss certain matters only with your boss or supervisor in private.

▶ you can do certain tasks only when you are on your own.

▶ the information you need is restricted and you will either need special permission to obtain it, will only be able to see it in a certain location or borrow it for a specified time.

A medium level of confidentiality may mean that you have to be sensible and not take the work into any public areas (as in the task on the planning sheet on page 234).

All these factors are likely to affect your scheduling and your overall deadline.

Starting work

At this point you should have planned as much as you can and be ready to tackle the first activities you must complete. It helps if you are tidy and well organised and keep all the work related to the task neatly together in one or more clearly labelled folders.

If developments occur which you need to note down then you can either do these on a checklist or 'to do' list (see page 238) or write Post-it notes to yourself and stick them on the appropriate folders. The most important point is to *write everything down* and not try to rely on your memory!

Monitoring progress – reviewing progress and reporting back

At specific stages you need to check how well you are doing and whether you are still on target to complete every task by, or ahead of, its deadline. If you do this regularly – even daily with a very important and urgent job – then you can remedy problems before they become serious, simply by changing your priorities and reorganising your schedule or list. You can do this by

▶ having a checklist and ticking off the work you have completed

▶ completing tracking documents (see page 381) that show each step in a procedure

▶ reviewing your progress regularly against the time available

▶ doing random checks on the work completed and the quality of your work.

You may be expected to report back at specific intervals or your boss may be the type who expects you to report back only if there is a problem you can't solve yourself. And some bosses will tell you not to bring them a problem, only a solution! In this case, they don't just want to know what has gone wrong, but what you suggest should happen to put things right again.

If you have specific occasions on which you have to report back on progress, most bosses will normally expect more than an 'It's OK, thanks' response. You should prepare to report back by giving a brief summary of what you have done and achieved, the tasks yet to be completed and a short evaluation as to whether you are on schedule or not. If you are having any problems, say what you have done to try to sort things out – or suggest what can be done. Bear in mind that it isn't wise to blame one of your colleagues for a problem. Stick to discussing the issue and be charitable. 'Unfortunately we had a day's delay because Karen had to finish another important job' is far better than a pained expression, a sigh and the comment, 'Well, Karen didn't get round to it until Thursday.'

Finally, if an emergency or disaster strikes which threatens the overall deadline, don't wait until the next scheduled reporting session to let your boss know. The quicker the information is received, the more easily the problem can be solved.

Planning aids

Administrators who regularly undertake quite complex jobs over a long period can use a variety of planning aids to help them.

▶ A **diary** can range from a large, page-a-day type to a smaller version with up to a week on view on each two pages. You need the size that will enable you to write clear information on the tasks to do under each date if this is your major planning aid.

▶ **Wall charts** and **planners** are pinned on the wall. Some are designed for special purposes whereas others are more general. A 'perpetual' planner has no fixed dates so can be used every year. On some types of planners you need to write the information with a 'wipe-off' pen, on others you stick on magnetic strips or labels. The danger with magnetic boards is having too many coloured symbols and shapes so that it takes you longer to set up the planner and then interpret the information than it does to do the task itself! Remember that a planner shouldn't be a work of art but it should be clear and easy to follow.

▶ **'To do' lists** can be written in a notepad, typed out and clipped to the front of a file or even scribbled on a jotter. The system itself is less important than the fact that you regularly look at your list, check off the items as you do them and, at the end of each day, carry forward any outstanding items.

▶ **A checklist** is a more formal version of a 'to-do' list. Whereas a 'to-do' list can cover all the jobs you have to do in a day (or week), a checklist normally relates to one major task. In this case all the activities that need to be done are listed, in priority or sequence order, and each is ticked off as it is completed.

▶ **Electronic planners** include electronic diaries and PDAs (personal digital assistants). There are three main benefits of using an electronic diary program. You can enter information under each day and edit it easily, you can quickly search for the name of a person or a commitment without searching through every page and you can ask the computer to remind you when you need to do something. Apart from the risk of computer failure, the other obvious problem is that you can't carry it around with you if the diary program is on your main PC. For that reason, some people prefer to use a PDA (see page 239).

ORGANISATIONS IN BUSINESS

One of the most frequently used electronic diary programs in business is Microsoft Outlook, because it is compatible with other Microsoft Office software, such as Word. Outlook can be used to maintain your diary, organise and manage lists of tasks you have to do and keep an address book of your contacts. You can use it as your main email software program and also use it to check the schedules of other people in your team – which makes it easier to arrange meetings when everyone is free. An alternative, stand-alone, inexpensive electronic diary package is Lotus Organiser 6.0, which looks similar to a paper diary on screen.

Administrators who prefer to use a PDA will find a wide range available from companies like Palm, Sony, Toshiba and Compaq at prices ranging from less than £100 to £600. The price obviously determines the features. Virtually all have a touch screen and most incorporate handwriting recognition. Most incorporate a 'to do' list, an address book, a calculator and a memo pad and are compatible with a PC so that information can be downloaded easily. The electronic diary provides the same types of reminders that you would find on any package, including a buzzer or alarm that can be set to remind you when you have to do something or be somewhere.

Additional features include 'bluetooth compatibility' which means that you don't need wires or cables to connect to your PC. On the more expensive versions you can store games, photographs and video files or even access and edit Word documents. Their value mainly depends upon whether you like gadgets, need to input important information regularly when you are away from your desk – and have the money available to buy one!

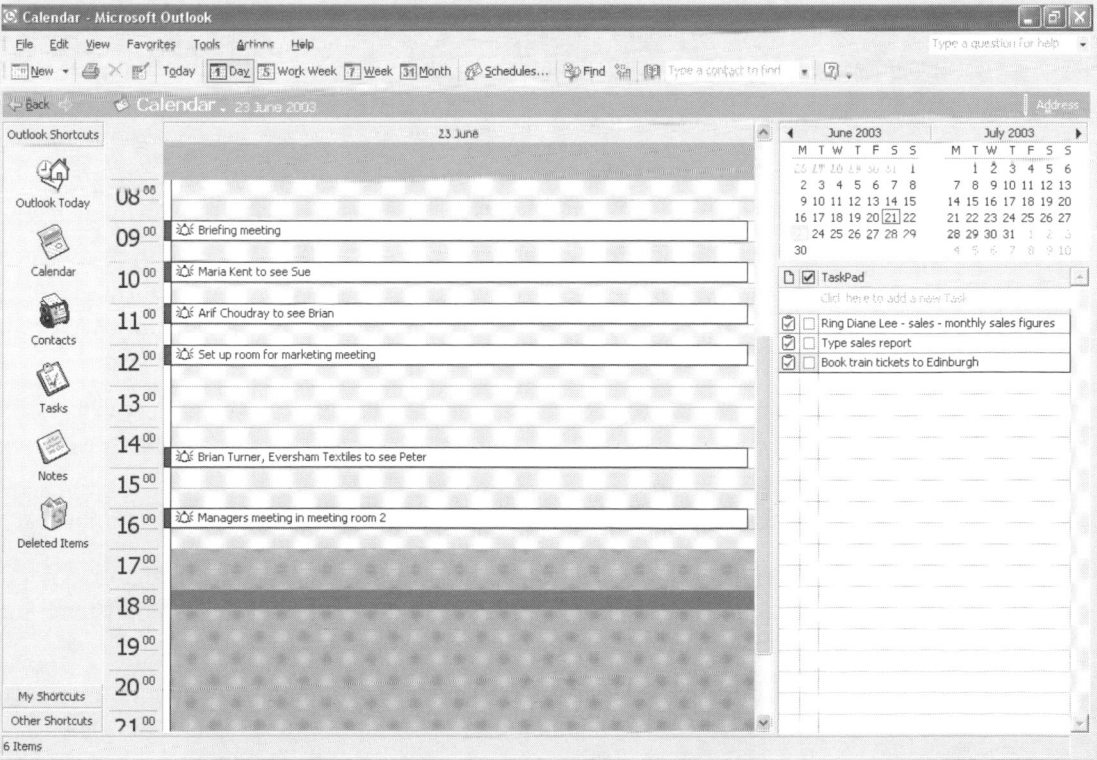

▲ An electronic diary program

1 a) Are you a natural planner or is most of life a complete surprise? And really, do you prefer it that way? Do the quiz below to find out whether you are a 'natural' at planning or will need to work at it!

Test your planning potential

Answer True or False to each of the following questions.

1 I know exactly what I am doing this weekend because I prefer to make arrangements in advance.

2 I like to think about the future and plan what I will do.

3 Before I go shopping, I always make out a list so I won't forget anything.

4 I jot down all important appointments in my diary or on a wall calendar.

5 I never forget a birthday and buy my cards in advance.

6 I am always punctual – or even early.

7 I take pride in handing in work on time.

8 I store important documents carefully so I can find them quickly.

9 I prefer to write things down than to try to rely on my memory.

10 I enjoy working out the best way to do a complex job.

Give yourself 2 points for each *True* and 0 points for each *False*. Then add up your score and check the result on page 307.

b) To help to convince yourself that planning works, identify five benefits of planning work.

2 Find out more about planners, electronic diaries and PDAs yourself by looking in any stationery catalogue or searching online. Simply use a good search engine, like www.google.co.uk and then enter the item (or type of software) about which you want to learn more. Then compare your results with other members of your group.

3 Dani's boss is wondering whether he can trust her with a new and complex task. He asks her to convince him by explaining five actions she will take to ensure she delivers it right first time – and on time.

You are Dani's friend. What do you think she should say?

4 Jon far prefers working on his computer to writing on paper and is thinking of throwing away his paper diary and using an electronic diary program on his PC instead. Identify three advantages and two disadvantages of doing this.

5 Your boss wants to involve you in helping to make a number of important arrangements relating to the visit of some important visitors from abroad next month. You will be helping to create folders which include samples of your products, photographs of the process and keying in text which will need to be translated into Portuguese.

a) Identify four key aspects you would need to check before you started work.

b) You have five tasks listed for day one: ordering the special stationery and folders that are required, asking production for the samples, starting keying in the introduction, booking the photographer and informing the translator. If you could complete only four of these, which would you choose – and why?

c) Explain why you would need to take into consideration the commitments of others involved, including the photographer and the translators, when you were doing your work.

d) Your boss is keen that the visit is kept 'under wraps' in case your competitors find out. Identify two ways in which you would ensure that this is the case.

e) At the first 'report back' meeting you have completed the first section to schedule but are still waiting for the photographs which are due tomorrow. There is a delay with the folders and you don't know when those will arrive. You have agreed to send the translation agency the printed pages as soon as those are completed and they require two weeks to do their work. Prepare a brief report to give to your boss which emphasises the key problem that must be solved.

▼ THE IMPORTANCE OF ORGANISING THE WORK AREA EFFECTIVELY

Some people are extremely well organised. Everything, from their shoes to their pens, is stored neatly and tidily and can be found easily. Others are the opposite and live in a state of chaos.

Most of us are between these two extremes. We may have good intentions but if we are very tired, busy or preoccupied (and sometimes, even if we're not!), then we may put off many of the jobs we don't really like – such as tidying up.

At home, you can often get away with this, unless you are terribly untidy and live alongside someone who is very organised. At work, it's rather different. People who work in chaos create problems both for themselves and for everyone else who has to work in the vicinity, and are rarely popular with their colleagues. If you tend to spread out your belongings, pile things up and forget to move them, or lose things on a regular basis, then now is the time to review your methods of working!

The several benefits are:

▶ you will work more efficiently

▶ you will waste less time

▶ you will be able to find things quickly and, even better, not lose anything

▶ the items you use regularly will stay in better condition

▶ you'll be less stressed and less likely to lose your temper

▶ you will be able to complete jobs more quickly and more easily.

Keeping your work area neat and tidy

Your work area isn't just your desk, but also any other area in which you are carrying out a specific job, such as in a photocopying room, a stock cupboard or next to the fax machine. Your desk should *always* have ample clear space on the top for you to put current documents or files on which you are working. A few rules will help you to keep this area as clear as possible and to work as efficiently as possible:

▶ Work on only one job at once. When you have finished the job, put away all the related papers and other items where they belong before you start the next task.

▶ If a new task arrives before you've finished the last one, put it in your 'in' tray (see page 243).

▶ If more post arrives during the day, put that in your 'in' tray, too, until you can deal with it.

▶ Make sure all your files and folders are clearly labelled.

▶ If new papers arrive which relate to a specific file or folder, then put them into it.

▶ File regularly, so that you don't end up with documents from your filing tray spilling everywhere. As an interim measure, you can pre-sort documents alphabetically and put them into a concertina file. This means individual papers are easier to find in a hurry, too.

▶ Keep stationery in folders in your drawers, to avoid it getting crumpled and creased.

▶ Tidy out your desk drawers every couple of months. Assess what is in there. Throw away any rubbish or thing that isn't required any more and see how many items could be better stored somewhere else. Try to keep clutter to a minimum.

▶ Be prepared to review your storage arrangements regularly, especially if the way you work changes or you take on a new job. If you start backing-up documents on CD, rather than floppy disk, then you may start with one or two CDs in your drawer. Over time you may end up with several more, so then you need a CD holder and a place to keep it – and you must decide what to do with the old pile of floppy disks once these are no longer required.

In communal working areas

The guidelines for working in an area which you share with other people are simply based on courtesy and consideration for others. Hopefully your colleagues will operate in the same way!

▶ Try to control the space you use and keep it to your allocated area. Don't spread your work and belongings about all over the place.

▶ Complete each part of a job before you start the next.

▶ Stack completed work neatly to one side.

▶ If you are interrupted, or have to leave the area and are in the middle of a task, put your work together in one place with a note on it identifying yourself as the 'owner' and saying when you will return to move them.

▶ When you have finished, clear up after yourself and put everything back in its proper place.

▲ Drastic measures should not be needed if everyone is neat and tidy

Organising materials and equipment

You will find it easier to be neat and tidy if you have a system for organising the materials and equipment you regularly use. In addition, you will find things more quickly, be less likely to lose your possessions, need to move around less to get what you need and find that your things last a lot longer.

Your desk area

You will keep the top of your desk clear if you group the equipment and materials you need together. Ideally you will have an L-shaped desk with your computer monitor and keyboard at one side. On the other side is your main working area on which you can store other items. A variety of desk aids are available to help you:

▶ **Filing or paper trays** will stack to hold separate groups of papers. Label each tray. If you have four trays, the best order is 'in', 'pending', 'filing', 'out'. Other people prefer only to have 'in' and 'out' trays on their desk and to put documents to be filed in a tray on the filing cabinet and 'pending' papers in a folder.

▶ **Desk tidies** are ideal for all the items which otherwise clutter up a drawer, e.g. paperclips, eraser, staple remover, pencil sharpener, elastic bands.

▶ **Pen tidies** can hold pens, pencils, highlighters, scissors and sticks of glue.

Other items you may want to keep on your desk may include a stapler, hole-punch and sticky tape dispenser. Points to remember:

▶ Group items on top of your desk logically. If you are right-handed put your telephone to the left and your pen holder to the right; vice versa if you are left-handed.

▶ Place everything you regularly use within easy reach – to save having to get up and down to get what you need.

- Keep your pencils sharpened, your stapler filled (and have a spare supply of staples in your drawer). Don't chew the ends off the pens you use!

- Keep everything you don't use frequently in a drawer. In your top drawer (normally lockable), keep your calculator, stamps, notebook and any confidential papers.

- Put rubber bands in an envelope in a drawer if you use a lot of them, so that they don't end up all over your desk.

- If you store drawing pins in your desk drawer, keep them in a box or tin with the lid on firmly.

- Store stationery items and file folders you use regularly lower down.

In communal working areas

In communal areas, the equipment provided will be shared by everyone – and some of the materials. For example, in a photocopying room there is likely to a supply of paper, a stapler, hole punch and guillotine or rotary trimmer, probably on a table near to the photocopier.

Golden rules here are:

- Think about what you need to use before you start – so that you minimise journeys to and from your desk.

- If you move small items of equipment around to help you to do the job better, or more quickly, remember to put it back again afterwards. Ideally the equipment should be grouped so that you are working in a sequence, either from left to right or vice versa.

- *Never* be tempted to take possession of something that is a shared resource, even if it is better than the one on your desk!

- *Never* move heavy items of equipment on your own or without specific permission.

- If you are doing a 'messy' job – such as collating by hand where your work may be spread out everywhere – try to choose a quiet time or do it in a separate area where you won't be in everyone's way.

- Bear in mind the health and safety of others. Don't move or place anything so that it would create a hazard, such as putting a box of paper behind the door.

- If you have borrowed anything from a colleague, return it promptly afterwards to its owner, without having to be reminded.

Minimising waste

First, a few facts and figures on office waste to get your attention!

Facts and figures on office waste

▶ Every year businesses throw away over one million tonnes of paper. That's about 190 trillion sheets.

▶ Each tonne of paper needs 17 trees to produce.

▶ Waste costs British businesses over £15 billion a year and 20% of this is paper-based.

▶ Offices use over 12.5 million tonnes of paper every year – and this figure is increasing by 20% a year.

▶ The average UK office worker uses over one tree's worth of paper every year (nearly 15,000 sheets of A4 paper or 30 packets)

▶ 60% of the average office worker's bin is waste paper.

▶ The vast majority of paper can be recycled, but the UK recycles only about 25% of its paper.

In addition:

▶ Britain throws away 2 million printer and toner cartridges every year – enough to stretch from London to Milan

▶ If each office worker in the UK used one fewer staple each year, 120 tonnes of steel would be saved.

▲ Carelessness causes a waste of valuable resources

If you had your own business and had to pay for every sheet of paper used then excess waste would no doubt annoy you. If you were keen on saving the environment you might immediately replace all the waste bins with recycling bins. This might ease your conscience, but wouldn't help your budget very much.

At work, it is amazing how many resources are wasted each year, through lack of thought, lack of planning or carelessness. There are two ways to try to control this:

▶ by identifying the activities which are most likely to lead to wasted resources

▶ by identifying the ways in which waste can be minimised.

Critical work activities

These include:

▶ **Photocopying** – if the copies are useless because the original is of poor quality or crooked, the size of paper or the ratio is incorrectly selected or too many copies are made.

▶ **Manual collating** – if pages are grouped or stapled incorrectly or completed work isn't stacked properly so that some sets become crumpled or unusable.

▶ **Printing** – if repeated drafts are taken, unnecessary print-outs made, documents aren't proof-read properly or the wrong setting is used in relation to the quality of the print-out it is a waste. (Using 'best' instead of 'draft' for internal documents is a waste of ink or toner.)

▶ **Tidying out files** – you can reuse good folders or remove polypockets to use again.

▶ **Any other task** – if you work sloppily and don't think about what you are doing, such as scribbling a note on the back of a brand new envelope because it's the nearest thing to you!

Ways to minimise waste

You can save your own time, the environment *and* reduce the amount of money your company spends on stationery if you routinely remember to do the following.

▶ Check documents carefully before you print or photocopy them.

▶ Learn to proof-read properly (preferably on screen) and never completely trust your spell-checker! (See Unit 1, page 14.)

▶ Take a test print or a test photocopy before starting a long print run and double-check that it's absolutely perfect.

▶ Make sure the photocopier glass is kept clean.

▶ Save paper by photocopying on both sides.

▶ Take only the exact number of copies or print-outs that you need.

▶ Store paper properly so that it is kept flat, in a cool place and away from direct heat, sunlight or damp. Keeping it in a box or folder will help to prevent it getting creased or torn.

▶ 'Fan' paper properly before putting it into a paper tray.

▶ Use the correct type of paper for the job you are doing.

- Check the setting (under 'properties') before you make computer print-outs and use 'draft' setting for internal documents or genuine draft copies to save ink.

- Print out pages from the Internet only in black and white (grey scale on your 'properties' setting) unless you need colour for a specific reason.

- On an ink jet printer, give copies a few seconds to dry before touching them, otherwise they smudge.

- Don't print out emails unnecessarily.

- Send an email attachment rather than sending out multiple print-outs.

- Send a draft document to someone electronically for checking, rather than a hard (paper) copy.

- Convert out-of-date printed paper into scrap pads.

- Shred waste paper and use it for packaging. Put any remaining 'clean' paper into a recycling bin.

- Put tops back on pens when you have used them, especially highlighters and marker pens, which dry out quickly.

- Replace the top *tightly* on correcting fluid immediately after use.

- Reuse envelopes for internal mail items.

- Reuse brown file folders by reversing them.

- Separate transparent folders and polypockets from old documents which are being thrown away so that they can be reused.

- Re-label and reuse A4 ring binders, lever arch and box files whenever they are still in good condition.

- Collect paper and toner cartridges for recycling.

ORGANISATIONS IN BUSINESS

There are many ways in which offices can be made more environmentally friendly. Waste paper can be recycled, as can toner and printer cartridges. Solar-powered calculators remove the need for batteries, stapleless staplers can hold together documents of four to eight pages without the need for staples and sticky tape can be bought that is biodegradable. Even bottles and cans from the vending machine or office kitchen can be recycled without too much trouble.

Some organisations specifically supply recycled stationery and environmentally friendly equipment, whilst other firms provide other environmentally friendly office services, such as insurers Naturesave who put part of their profits towards saving otters in Devon.

For links to organisations which offer help and advice to businesses follow the links at www.heinemann.co.uk/hotlinks.

1 A new junior member of staff has been allocated the desk next to yours. Within two days it's a tip, and four important papers have suddenly disappeared. You are certain they are somewhere underneath the pile of files and folders on her desk.

   Suggest six ways in which she can organise her work area more efficiently.

2 You are given the task of clearing out two filing drawers in the office.

   a) Suggest three ways you would tackle this job to make as little mess as possible and reduce inconvenience to other office users.

   b) Suggest three actions you would take to try to minimise waste and be as environmentally friendly as possible.

3 Tahira's main job is preparing documents on her computer. Nick's tasks include photocopying. They both work in a small company where the boss lost his temper recently about the amount of waste and threatened that no one will get a pay rise this year unless the cost of stationery is reduced rapidly.

   Suggest six actions *each* of them can take to help to reduce waste.

4 a) Identify four actions you would take to ensure that you have organised your personal materials and small items of equipment in the best way.

   b) Identify four benefits of doing this.

▼ THE IMPORTANCE OF WORKING FLEXIBLY

You may be an excellent planner and like everything to be neat and tidy, but then you can get irritated if anything interferes with this! Yet flexibility is essential if you are to do your job properly, enjoy it and stay sane.

Most people who work in business will tell you that crises occur in cycles and often out of the blue. For much of the time you may be quite busy but life is relatively peaceful. On other occasions, things become hectic. Dozens of jobs seem to need doing at once and plans and arrangements change constantly. At this point you can become very stressed and wilt under the pressure *or* you can try (hard!) to keep your sense of humour and take it as a challenge. In this case, you need to have a strategy to cope and the key word here is flexibility. This means you can change and adapt when you have to, without too much effort.

There are three main occasions when you have to demonstrate your flexibility:

▶ when you are planning, continually monitoring your own progress and adjusting plans when necessary

▶ when you have to cope with the unexpected

▶ when you are having problems.

Flexibility during planning and monitoring

When you plan, as you saw on page 232 and 233, you need to decide the action you must take and constantly check your progress. You also need to think about potential difficulties and what you should do to prevent or overcome these.

The problem is that all plans are 'today's best guess'. They are not carved in tablets of stone and may need to be changed. They *must* be changed if they are not working or if the situation changes. You cannot possibly foresee all the difficulties that may actually happen so, on some occasions, you have to react and respond to actual events. This is why *continuous* monitoring is so important. The key points are to:

▶ think about potential difficulties when you are planning, but don't expect to think of everything

▶ build sufficient time into your schedule so that small problems and distractions won't immediately threaten a critical deadline

▶ check and monitor progress frequently

▶ take action if something is going wrong.

▲ If the warning bells are sounding it is time to take action

Responding to contingencies and communicating changes

A contingency is something that could go wrong, as in the phrase 'contingency plans'; this means planning for the unexpected. But as you have just seen, you can't always foresee everything that could happen. For example:

▶ Someone who promised you important information is off sick and not expected back for two weeks. Your deadline is next Tuesday.

▶ An external supplier rings to say that the items they should supply are delayed because of circumstances outside their control.

▶ A customer is visiting two days earlier than originally expected which shortens the deadline.

▶ Someone has used all the folders you need and you can't get any more until next week.

▶ Your photocopier or your computer is out of action for a couple of days.

In all these cases you will be expected to think of a way around the problem. You will gain the respect of everyone, especially your boss, if you can suggest solutions yourself rather than immediately running for help.

Solving the problem

Start by thinking about the type of problem and the range of solutions available. Very few problems are unsolvable and someone has to find an answer – so it might as well be you!

▶ Solve problems about resources by thinking of alternatives. Who else can help you, what other suppliers are there, what other equipment or materials are available, where else can the job be completed?

▶ Solve problems relating to time by working harder or faster, dropping unnecessary jobs so the task is pared down to its essentials or asking for someone to help you.

▶ Solve problems outside your remit, or where you genuinely cannot suggest a solution, by talking to your supervisor as quickly as possible.

Communicating changes

When the best action to take has been agreed, or your boss has told you what to do, then you need to think about how any changes will affect other people. Some changes will have a huge effect on people (such as moving forward a deadline), others will have less effect (such as using different folders). The key point is that people know what is happening, so that they can adjust their own schedules or expectations accordingly. Therefore:

▶ Communicate *promptly* if a change will affect other people, for example, because they will have to work quicker or because you can't provide information they expected or because they now have to do their own job in a different way. The sooner they know, the better.

▶ Always communicate to everyone who *may* be affected. It is better to tell too many people than to miss someone out in this situation.

▶ Tell your supervisor or boss personally if you cannot meet his or her own specific requirements for some reason.

> Remember you will often be giving people a bit of a shock. Don't expect them to be thrilled if there is a major change that will create a problem for them. State the reason politely, so they understand what is happening and why, and don't hesitate to apologise if it helps. This isn't always because you are admitting you've made a mistake – though if it is your fault, don't push the blame elsewhere! You may be simply apologising that you are giving them bad news and they will be inconvenienced. If you thank someone for being understanding this often helps too.

Reporting difficulties with meeting deadlines or targets

Most people are quite reasonable about a change to a schedule or a way of working if they get sufficient notice and are allowed time to think about it. They appreciate that problems occur and ways of solving them need to be found. In most cases, this rescues a deadline or target and means it can still be met so the overall objective is still achieved.

If an *interim* target cannot be met, then this may not be a total disaster, providing you have set them in the first place. This is the benefit of setting deadlines within a schedule for partial completion of a task. Setting and monitoring interim targets gives you immediate warning whilst there is still time to rescue the situation.

If the *final* deadline is threatened then this can be very serious indeed, especially if the job is very important. If your boss has promised the MD that an important report for a client will be completed by Tuesday afternoon, and the MD intends to fly out to Central Europe with it on Wednesday, no one will be happy if you suddenly announce on Tuesday morning that you're running three days behind schedule. Your boss has the unenviable job of explaining this to the MD (which makes your boss look incompetent) and, if the situation can't be rescued, the MD is going to arrive in Central Europe with the task of explaining the problem to an important client whilst still trying to make a good impression!

It is therefore sensible to 'grade' your deadlines in relation to the 'worst thing that could happen' if they aren't met. As a general rule of thumb:

> Deadlines that relate to work promised for external customers and senior executives in your organisation are crucial. Notify your boss *immediately* you suspect there may be a problem so that action can be taken before it is too late.

> Deadlines that relate to other internal requests may appear to be less critical, but may be affecting a customer at some stage. Contact the person concerned, explain the problem and try to *negotiate* a new deadline. If you are told this is impossible, refer the problem to your supervisor so that you can get help.

> Deadlines that are obviously just internal, such as clearing out the stock cupboard by Friday, may not be critical (unless you are clearing it out because you are moving office rather than because it's a mess). If you are uncertain of the purpose of a job, double-check. Then talk to the person who asked you to do the job.

A final tip. If you are swamped with deadlines and can't meet them all because you are too busy, other people aren't being cooperative or you simply don't have the equipment or resources available, then you may feel quite ill and stressed as a result. This is because you feel out of control of the situation.

Rather than take three days off to recover – or decide to change job – there is a coping strategy you should try. List all your important jobs and their deadlines and then ask to talk to your boss in private. Explain your problem and ask your boss to help you to reschedule your jobs so that they are achievable. Often busy managers aren't totally aware of the workload of all of their staff and are quite willing to give practical advice and help when it is needed.

After you've worked through the list, ask for a follow-up meeting in another two days, to talk about your progress. Then get on with tackling the list in the recommended order. This benefits everyone. You feel less burdened with responsibility and your boss is involved and knows what is happening. There are no nasty unexpected shocks around the corner. Your honesty will be appreciated and you can learn more about prioritising from the way in which your boss tackles the list.

Finally, if you ever work in an organisation where you feel your boss is unapproachable, in this situation (or if your boss is unavailable) ask a senior, more experienced colleague to help you in this type of situation.

OVER TO YOU!

1 Your boss has to send off a large pack of information to a regional office. You have made out a checklist of everything that is needed and aim to tick things off as they arrive from various departments in your organisation. A courier has been booked to take the pack next Tuesday.

a) Suggest two reasons why you will need to monitor progress on this job very carefully.

b) Identify one potential difficulty that might occur that you could reasonably foresee.

c) Identify one difficulty that could occur that you would not normally foresee or schedule into your plans.

d) For **both** of the difficulties you identified in (b) and (c) above, state what action you would take to try to solve the problem.

2 Your boss, the training manager, has planned an induction session with new staff for Friday at 10 am. You are helping to prepare the materials required and set up the room. For each of the following situations below, state:

a) what action you would take in response

b) to whom you would communicate the change, if anyone.

   i) Your boss has asked you to prepare a spreadsheet which includes this year's sales figures up to last Friday. When you talk to Finance, they can provide the information only up to the end of last month.

   ii) Your boss wants to use a data projector to give a PowerPoint presentation. When you check the training room you find the one that is kept in there has been sent for repair.

   iii) Your boss informs you that he has to attend an urgent meeting in the MD's office at that time on Friday and says he now can't start the session until 10.30.

3 You have a problem with all the following deadlines or targets.

a) List the tasks, in the order of importance, identifying the one that you think is the most critical.

b) For each task, state what you would do and to whom you would report your difficulties.

   i) Completing the day's photocopying for staff in the department because the machine is out of order. The technician is due in the morning.

   ii) Ordering letter-headed paper. Your supervisor asked you to do this last week but you forgot. There are now only 100 sheets left in stock.

iii) Sending a fax to confirm your boss's hotel booking for tomorrow night – because the hotel fax has been engaged all afternoon.

iv) Recording expense claims for departmental staff. Unless these are with Finance by Friday they won't be paid this month.

4 a) Suggest two reasons why it is useful to set deadlines within a schedule for partial completion of a task.

b) Identify three reasons why it is important to communicate changes or problems in meeting targets promptly.

▼ THE FACTORS THAT IMPACT ON EFFICIENCY

Most bosses are – understandably – far more concerned to help a normally hardworking and efficient member of staff who is experiencing difficulties than they are to assist someone they think is a time-waster and who brings most of their problems on themselves.

Being efficient means that you focus on the jobs you are doing, do them to the best of your ability and without undue delays. It means you use your initiative to solve problems, take responsibility for your own actions and keep your boss informed about progress. If you do this consistently, people learn that they can trust you and rely upon you.

Listening to instructions and following them

Efficient people know what they are doing. They get the job 'right first time'. They don't miss out an important aspects of a job and neither do they do tasks they were never supposed to do. Quite simply, they focus on what needs to be done and do it.

If you see an efficient person being given instructions, you can expect to see a whole series of reactions which helps them to deal with the task speedily and accurately.

▶ They stop what they are doing.

▶ They *concentrate* on what the other person is saying.

▶ They immediately start to write down the key facts relating to the task.

▶ They ask questions if they are unsure about anything.

▶ They repeat back the task to make sure all the details are correct.

▶ They agree where and when they can check back with the person concerned if there is a problem or difficulty.

▶ They agree a realistic time for completion.

▶ If they have made scribbled notes, they may immediately rewrite these so they are clear and in a logical order.

▶ They include the task into their schedule so that they don't forget to do it.

▶ They prioritise the task according to its urgency and importance.

▶ Before they start the task, they reread their notes to refresh their memory.

▶ When they are doing the task, they constantly check their notes to make sure they are following their instructions.

If you compare this approach to someone who tries to listen to instructions whilst they are typing or on the telephone, doesn't bother to write them down and then forgets to include the task in their 'to do' list, you can quickly see why one person is very efficient and the other is not. Even the action of watching an efficient person take down instructions is reassuring to the person who is giving them. They feel that they have left the job 'in good hands' and are safe in the knowledge it will be done properly and in good time.

Using time efficiently

Time is one of our most precious resources. Once an hour or a day has gone, you can never have it back again. Despite this, many people talk about 'making time' for something or 'saving time' when in reality they can do neither. Many courses are held on 'managing time'. These concentrate on using time as wisely as possible, both at work and at home.

You can recognise someone who manages their time well instantly because they always seem to get through more work than other people and be able to fit more activities into their private lives. This is the bonus of time management. If you use your time more efficiently, you have more quality time for the things you enjoy.

There are two key aspects to using your own time efficiently. The first is to recognise your own bad habits in relation to time wasting. The second is to learn a few useful time management skills.

Bad habits and time wasting activities

▶ Chatting and gossiping to people. This wastes your time *and* theirs!

▶ Starting one task before you finished the last one because you are bored or fed up with it.

▶ Getting distracted by reading irrelevant documents or information when you are filing or using the Internet.

▶ Making a mess of a job so you have to start all over again.

▶ Putting off jobs you don't like, so they pile up and become overwhelming.

▶ Looking through jobs and taking ages to decide which one to start.

▶ Allowing (or even encouraging!) people to interrupt you constantly.

Time management skills

▶ Make a list and set yourself a target of the jobs you want to achieve that day. Reward yourself if you meet your target.

▶ Do important and urgent jobs at the start of the day.

▶ Do jobs you dread as soon as you can, to get them out of the way.

▶ Stick with a job until it is finished whenever you can.

▶ Be well organised and keep things in the right place, to save hunting for them.

▶ Group similar jobs together and do them in one batch, such as sending faxes, making photocopies or sending emails.

- Plan what you are doing before you start, to avoid silly errors and mistakes.

- Think before you go anywhere, so that you can plan the shortest route and don't forget anything. Let your head save your legs!

- If you need to be left in peace to finish an urgent or complex job then *tell* people – so that they know you don't want to be interrupted unless it's very important.

- If something takes longer than expected and this is your fault, identify what you did wrong and learn from it.

- Concentrate when you are working and check your work carefully, so that none of your jobs rebound on you because of your own mistakes.

- Treat other people's time as *their* valuable resource. Don't waste it by distracting them or keeping them waiting.

- Learn to deal with distractions – see below.

Distractions and how to deal with them

Distractions can take up your time or take your mind off the job you are doing and can upset anyone's plans or schemes to be a good time manager.

Some distractions are relatively easy to deal with. If the office geek tries to describe in detail how he improved the operating speed of his computer, you may find it quite easy to get rid of him. You can hardly do that with an important customer or your boss – and may be less tempted to do so if the distraction is your friend giving you a fascinating account of her exploits last night!

Distractions can come in all shapes and sizes. They include:

- unexpected callers and visitors

- the telephone ringing

- new emails

- interesting (but irrelevant) content on Internet sites when you are looking for information

- interesting documents that cross your desk

- other people's conversations and activities

- your own thoughts and personal plans

- other jobs you still have to do and keep worrying about

- anything that interests you more than the job you are doing!

You can put these into three groups: those concerned with you, those concerned with impersonal matters and those relating to other people.

Your personal distractions

If you have serious worries or problems relating to your private life then these can distract you quite severely. In this situation, you need to talk to your supervisor or manager in private. Many organisations provide additional help for employees in this situation by providing a counselling service. Find out the options open to you, but don't pretend there is nothing wrong. If the situation is serious, then you need support.

The situation is very different if you are distracted because you can't decide what to wear or where to go on Friday night! Most people learn to operate in two modes and concentrate on thinking 'work thoughts' during the hours they are paid. This takes self-discipline but is much easier if you enjoy your job and are busy. If you find yourself getting distracted because you are often bored, then you should perhaps consider a change of job.

Impersonal distractions

These can include interesting documents, articles in a magazine, attachments to emails and Internet sites: anything, in fact, which is not strictly relevant to the job you are doing!

We are all distracted by such things at times, but the frequency with which this happens and the length of time you remain distracted are important here. If you spend half the day reading things of interest, rather than of relevance, then you will waste a lot of time. If you struggle with this, try to limit yourself. Allow yourself five minutes breathing space, after which time force yourself to turn your attention back to the task in hand.

People

If you are very busy or have an important task to finish and the people around you, visitors or callers are the problem then you may feel that you have less control. There are, however, a few tactics you can use.

- ▶ Explain to your colleagues how busy you are, tell them your deadline and ask them to leave you in peace. Ask nicely, there's no need to be irritable, then put your head down and show you are serious by your body language.

- ▶ If someone ignores your pleas, and continues to interrupt, again use body language to help. Keep your body position where it was and only turn your head to face them. Keep your fingers on the keyboard or your pen in your hand. Answer briefly. Say you can't stop now but will speak to them later and get back to work again.

- ▶ If the distraction is your boss or an important visitor, then do much the same thing but this time remember to have a pleasant smile on your face, to be courteous and to say that you're really sorry but unfortunately you can't break off now. It's the same message, but put a little differently! If they insist on giving you information, write it down and put it to one side for later. (Obviously, if it's very urgent or important you'll have to break off, and practise your flexibility skills!)

- ▶ Ask casual internal callers to the office to come back later, to see someone else or arrange to ring them. Alternatively, ask if they can send you an email with their request.

- ▶ If the phone is constantly ringing or external visitors are arriving, ask if your colleagues can help. If someone will take your calls for the time being then reroute your extension to their phone. Another alternative is to put your phone onto voicemail, if you have that option.

- ▶ If you have a very important, urgent and complex task to finish, see if you can do this in a separate area where it is quieter and there are fewer interruptions. Check with your boss if you can put a 'please do not disturb' sign on the door.

ORGANISATIONS IN BUSINESS

The technical term for keeping yourself busy by doing something you prefer to do (which is really unnecessary), rather than something you should do, is a **displacement activity**. According to e-Grindstone, which publishes a top list of these every year, people who work from home are the most likely to indulge in them – given they can watch a spot of daytime television or even convince themselves they should wash up or sweep the floor before they start a difficult but tedious job.

We all indulge in displacement activities from time to time. A suggested top ten list for administrators is given below but you may like to add to them!

1 Walking to the vending machine to buy a drink.

2 Waiting for this morning's post to arrive on your desk.

3 Constantly checking your email in case something interesting arrives.

4 Working out whether you can afford a new outfit this month on your spreadsheet package.

5 Checking out the latest holiday offers on lastminute.com

6 Sending a text message to your best friend.

7 Checking the breaking news on bbc.co.uk

8 Hunting through job sites to see if there's anything interesting.

9 Totalling up on your calculator how many calories (or points) you've eaten today.

10 Checking the Internet to find ten illnesses you might have because you sneezed twice this morning.

▲ It is very easy to get distracted by non-essential activities, even when you have a lot of work to get on with

The importance of effective communication

Effective communication aids efficiency because people get the right message the first time round. They understand the words and the tone. There are no misunderstandings or unnecessary hurt feelings.

If you are an effective communicator then people will clearly understand you whether you are writing to them or speaking to them. This is because you will take care to ensure that:

▶ you speak or write clearly and don't use terms the recipient wouldn't understand

▶ you think about the recipient and their possible reaction, and the situation, before you start

▶ you are polite and courteous in relation to the words and phrases you use and your overall 'tone'

▶ you include only accurate information and don't make wild guesses or assumptions

▶ you keep your communications relatively short and to the point – so they are easy to read

▶ you don't miss out important information

▶ you use the best method of communication for the situation

▶ you check your written communications carefully before you send them

▶ you communicate promptly, in good time for the recipient to respond properly

▶ you listen carefully to verbal replies and respond appropriately to 'feedback' however you receive it.

The importance of identifying and following procedures

All organisations have procedures. These will cover such areas as greeting and dealing with visitors and callers, handling complaints, what to do in an emergency and how to report faults and serious problems. Procedures are simply a series of steps to follow in a certain situation.

Procedures exist so that everyone will do the same thing in the same way. Normally, they have taken some time to devise and are the result of experience. They should be the best way of doing something which fits in with everyone else in the organisation and their responsibilities.

Identifying procedures

Important procedures relating to safety and employee matters, such as how to log on to the computer system, will be given to you at induction. Procedures relating to your job role will be given to you within your department. This is because the type of procedures you need to know will be different, for example, if you work in customer service or work in finance.

In some organisations, a procedures manual is kept in every office, so that you can easily refer to it if a new or different situation occurs. However, this is more likely to be the case in larger organisations. If you work for a small firm, there may be fewer written procedures but you may still be expected to do things in a certain way. In this case, when in doubt, always ask a more experienced colleague for advice – or your boss.

Following procedures

When you have found the procedure, obviously you must follow it. Many people do not: either because they don't understand it or try to take shortcuts because they think parts of it are unnecessary. In most organisations there is a regular review of procedures at intervals, so if you feel strongly that something is a waste of time you should raise it with your supervisor before this type of review. In the meantime, it is not your job to judge the procedure, but to do it! There may be reasons for doing certain things that you are not aware of, but this doesn't mean they aren't good reasons.

There are several dangers if you insist on 'doing your own thing' and ignoring a laid down procedure.

▶ You are likely to have missed out certain important aspects of the task.

▶ You have probably not done the task in the most efficient way.

▶ You will probably have to backtrack over what you have done to fill in the gaps and this takes time.

▶ You will probably inconvenience several other people in the process.

▶ In some cases, you may be risking your own safety or that of others.

▶ If other people are involved in the procedure, they won't understand what is going on.

▶ In some cases, the consequences can be very serious, for example, if you seriously misled a customer who decided to take legal action, or if you inadvertently disclosed confidential information.

OVER TO YOU!

1. Bushra is busy filing when her manager interrupts and asks her to phone a restaurant and book a table for him to take some clients to lunch. Half an hour later she realises that she can't remember the name of the restaurant and he never said how many clients there were, nor the time he wanted to go. She rings to ask him and finds he has gone to a meeting and will be away for the rest of the morning.

   a) Identify four mistakes Bushra made when she received her instructions.

   b) Explain two ways in which listening to instructions and following them is related to efficiency

   c) As a group, suggest what Bushra could do now to try to rescue the situation.

2. a) How good a time manager are you? Do the quiz on the next page to find out. Although this is not a serious quiz, it is intended to give you some idea of how far you have to go to improve your skills in this area.

   b) As a result of your score, identify five ways in which you could improve your own skills, starting now!

Test your time management skills!

1 You wonder where the day went
   a) rarely
   b) sometimes
   c) all the time.

2 If you are faced with three boring or difficult jobs, you
   a) select the most urgent and get on with it
   b) do a bit of each to keep yourself interested
   c) put them off until tomorrow.

3 If you are having a quiet day, you
   a) clear out a cupboard or drawer that badly needs it
   b) take it easy
   c) go off and chat to anyone who'll listen.

4 If you are looking for information on the Internet, you
   a) find it, print it and then log off
   b) struggle not to get distracted if something interesting pops up on your screen
   c) use it as a good excuse to find out about holiday destinations or do a bit of shopping online.

5 You discuss 'soaps' at work
   a) rarely
   b) quite often during your coffee break
   c) every morning, so you can compare your views on what happened with everyone else.

6 You are printing out a long document. You
   a) clear your filing whilst you keep one eye on the printer
   b) watch the printer whilst you have a short break
   c) go off for a break.

7 You have to deliver three documents to three different buildings. You
   a) plan your route so that you don't need to retrace your steps
   b) start with the first one on the list
   c) make three separate journeys to break the day up.

8 You have a complex job to do that requires a lot of thought. You
   a) do it when you are fresh and at your best
   b) leave it until you think you might get some peace and quiet
   c) do it in stages, over a few days, as and when you feel up to it.

9 A friend of yours calls in with some interesting news when you are trying to finish an urgent job. You
   a) explain you'll call her later, when you've finished it
   b) break off for a short time
   c) greet her with enthusiasm and suggest you both go for a coffee together.

10 How often do you surprise people by the amount of work you've completed?

   a) Quite often

   b) Occasionally

   c) You actually amaze them if you finish anything in time.

Score 2 points for every (a), 1 for every (b) and 0 for every (c). Then check your score on page 308.

3 a) Suggest three different distractions that could occur in an office.

   b) For each of the examples you have suggested, identify how an efficient administrator would deal with them.

4 a) Identify three ways in which effective communications aid efficiency.

   b) Suggest two ways in which you could assess your own communications to check if they were effective.

5 a) Identify two reasons why procedures are used in business organisations.

   b) Suggest four dangers of not identifying and following procedures.

▼ IDENTIFY WAYS OF IMPROVING PERFORMANCE IN THE WORKPLACE

Most people like to improve and develop in their work. This means they can take on more interesting tasks, cope with greater responsibility and move on to higher-level (and better-paid) jobs. Today, most organisations expect their employees to take personal responsibility for their own development. They will offer help, advice and support but they know that a highly skilled and competent employee may choose to go and work somewhere else eventually. For that reason, although both the organisation and the employee benefits from improved performance initially, the one who is likely to benefit most in the long run is the employee. You will therefore be expected to have a considerable interest in how you improve over time and to be keen to do so.

This means you need to be positively involved in a number of activities related to your personal improvement. These types of activity are the focus of this section.

How to obtain feedback on your achievement at work

Feedback is the response you receive from other people in relation to your work and performance. Sometimes you will receive feedback whether you like it or not. If your manager sets up a specific date for reviewing your work, then this is a formal feedback session (see page 265.) If your supervisor beams at you and says, 'What an excellent idea. That's great!' or shakes her head in exasperation and says, 'What are you like?' you are again receiving feedback, this time in an informal way.

Many employees say they would rather have regular feedback – positive or negative – than none at all. It is annoying to work hard and yet have no idea whether your boss is pleased with you or not. The temptation in this situation is to work harder and harder and then, if still nothing is forthcoming, give up. However, there are several ways to make sure you obtain feedback.

▶ An obvious method is to assess your own work by the results. Important criteria here are quality and quantity. You can therefore judge a task as being successfully completed if:

  – it was 'right first time', so far as you know

  – it was used, without any amendments or corrections

  – you are given more of the same type of work as a result or more challenging tasks to complete

  – you met your targets and any important deadlines (or if there was a delay, it had nothing to do with you).

▶ You can watch for clues. If you see someone finishing work you started, this may be a clue that what you did isn't good enough, but the originator didn't dare give it back to you so asked someone else to do it! Alternatively, it may be a generous gesture because you were busy. Find out the reason before you jump to conclusions.

▶ You can listen to your colleagues and ask them for feedback. If you are working in a team, you can quickly check and assess if everyone is happy with your work. Remember to watch their body language (especially their eyes and facial expressions) as well as listening to their responses. If you are still unsure, try a direct question, 'I thought I would do it like this, what do you think?'

▶ Ask your supervisor or manager for feedback. You might request a formal session (see page 265) if you are particularly concerned that you haven't had any type of review whatsoever since you started. An easier way is to tactfully make it clear you'd appreciate regular feedback. 'I'd really find it helpful if you could tell me if you're happy with this' doesn't put anyone under pressure but makes the point.

▶ Finally, check if any complaints or compliments have been received that directly relate to your work or to your dealings with a customer. If your department keeps a complaints

ORGANISATIONS IN BUSINESS

You may have travelled down the motorway on several occasions and seen lorries with the sign on the back 'If you think this vehicle is being driven well, please phone' – followed by a freephone number. Organisations which use this are part of the voluntary 'Well Driven? Scheme' that operates around the country.

One-third of the comments received are positive – and are immediately passed to the companies who are encouraged to pass them on to the drivers. This gives the drivers a commendation for working safely which encourages them to continue that way. Complaints are also fed back and can result in disciplinary proceedings and formal warnings against drivers who operate dangerously or discourteously.

This scheme not only shows that organisations are trying to be responsible, and are committed to clean and well-maintained vehicles and well-trained drivers, but also helps to provide feedback to a group of workers who might otherwise have to rely just on hand gestures from other drivers – both positive and negative!

For further information, a link to the website of the Freight Transport Association can be found at www.heinemann.co.uk/hotlinks.

log then you can check this without asking anyone. Or, again, ask the question. 'Do you know if Kevin Watts came back to us about this?' This is an open question to find out what his reaction was and doesn't imply you are expecting praise or criticism. Hopefully, if compliments are received, your boss will have the wisdom and sensitivity to pass them on – promptly!

Setting targets and planning to improve performance

You have already seen the importance of targets and planning in relation to work activities. You, too, can set targets and plan, this time in relation to yourself.

▷ Targets are useful because they help you to achieve specific, short-term objectives.

▷ Plans are important because they help you to think about your long-term goals.

Ideally, the two should link together. It would be rather odd, for instance, if your target is to develop your writing skills but your long-term goal is to work with animals.

The benefits of setting targets and making plans are several.

▷ You decide your main direction, which saves you drifting around aimlessly. (Don't forget, you can change your plans, they don't have to be unalterable.)

▷ From this, you can decide the best way to achieve your main goals.

▷ You can decide the key areas you need to develop.

▷ You can set targets linked to these.

▷ As you achieve them, your personal satisfaction and self-confidence increases.

Remember, however, that deciding your overall plan and targets may be the easy part. Consistently achieving them is far more difficult, especially if some are harder than you expected. You will stand a far better chance if you follow the golden rules outlined below.

Golden rules for target setting and planning

Don't set impossible or silly targets or make unrealistic plans. Avoid this by checking that all your plans and targets are:

▶ **Specific** – state exactly what you want to achieve

▶ **Realistic** – think about where you are now and, for your targets, identify the next logical step that you can achieve in the next few months – a year at the most.

▶ **Achievable** – don't be too ambitious. It's a recipe for disaster.

▶ **Positive** – go for what you want to learn, improve and develop – not for something you want to drop or get rid of!

▶ **Precise** – set a clear date for achievement.

▶ **Restricted** – setting too many is simply overwhelming (and unachievable). You should have one overall plan and a maximum of 3 to 5 targets in a year.

▶ **Controlled by you** – don't set targets over which you have little influence, i.e. I will gain promotion within 12 months. You cannot control this if there are no suitable opportunities.

▶ **Your own** – don't make a plan because it suits someone else or set a target which doesn't really interest you. If it's there, it's because you – more than anyone else – want to achieve it.

▶ **Written down** – so that it doubles your commitment and gives you a working plan.

Identifying opportunities for training

Some people mistakenly believe that the only way they can be 'trained' is by going on an external course. This isn't the case. You can learn in many different situations, both at work and 'off-the-job'. It all depends upon what you want and need to learn and the opportunities available.

Training at work

Training at work can be formal and official or informal and unofficial. For example:

▷ You can watch and copy someone who is more experienced at doing a particular task. One step further is to ask them to demonstrate how they do something.

▲ Informal training can take place whenever it is needed, and can be very useful

▷ You can ask an experienced person to coach you. In this case, they will watch you, make comments and suggest how you can improve. This is similar to what happens when you are learning to drive a car.

▷ You can 'shadow' someone. In this case you are observing them to see how they cope with a job. This is excellent training if you want to see how someone solves problems or copes with many different complex tasks in a day.

▷ You can 'swap jobs' with someone. The official term is **job rotation**. In this case you are exchanging job roles with someone else for a short time. In a small office, where you might have to cover in other people's absence, this gives you an invaluable insight into the work they do.

▷ You can check the internal training courses on offer to employees. These can range from team working skills to time management and are often interesting, fun and informative.

▷ You can look at the opportunities available for e-learning – where you are trained by using interactive computer packages.

▷ You can offer to help out if someone is away, so that you can learn something new.

Training away from work

▶ You can find out about short courses in your area, such as those which will give you specific IT skills.

▶ You can obtain information on longer courses, which lead to nationally recognised qualifications. Many of these are available on a part-time basis. Do bear in mind that your employer might be willing to offer you time off during the day but doesn't have to, once you have progressed beyond level 2, i.e. this qualification! For that reason, if you are really ambitious, you may have to think about sacrificing one or two of your evenings each week.

▶ You can investigate evening classes for specific skills – such as some IT packages and foreign languages.

▶ You can consider self-study – in this case you are studying mainly (or entirely) on your own. Contacting Learn Direct is one option if you want to learn something which you can't find in your own area. In other cases, you could take matters into your own hands. Many people who have developed their IT skills have done so with a good book or manual and a lot of determination and perseverance!

ORGANISATIONS IN BUSINESS

Blended learning is a new term. It relates to learning by a variety of methods, normally where technology is used to enhance or assist more traditional ways. For example, if you attended a course on a once-a-month basis but had online access to your tutor in between, plus – perhaps – videos and CDs to use then you would be experiencing blended learning. Some training providers have programmes which link tutor-led sessions to web-based sessions.

Critics argue that blended learning is just a fancy name for something that has been going on a long time. Most good learning activities have included a variety of methods. Others see it as a modern approach where learning can be tailor-made to suit each individual.

There are benefits if you like this approach. Often it is more flexible and you have more personal choices. Against this, if you enjoy working with other people you may find it a bit lonely to do much of the work on your own. If you like personal attention and quickly give up if you can't solve a problem quickly, then blended or e-learning isn't likely to be for you. But if you like working on your own and get annoyed at working at the best speed for the group as a whole, then you could easily enjoy the challenge.

The importance of reviewing work with a manager

Most organisations have a formal process (or procedure) whereby employees systematically review their work with their line manager. This might be once or twice a year. Ideally it should only supplement regular informal feedback, not replace it.

The common name given to this is the **appraisal system**. It normally operates as follows.

▶ You will be given advance notification when your review, or appraisal, is due and a date and time will be agreed that suits both you and your line manager.

▶ You will be given documents that explain how the system works. Normally, employees have the option to choose a different person to do the review if, for any reason, they feel the review would be unfair if it was done by their line manager.

▶ You will be given a form to complete. Designs vary but basically you are expected to prepare for the meeting by identifying the areas and skills:

– where you think you are competent and have done well since your last review

– that you have specifically improved since your last review and which were noted on your last action plan

– where you think you might have some weaknesses

– that you are interested in developing in the future.

▶ The review is held in private, the aim being that you can talk frankly and in confidence. During this session you should be able to talk about what you enjoy and feel positive about and focus on your future aims, plans and personal development. It is the job of your manager to link these to the goals of the business and the tasks undertaken by the department in which you work.

▶ At the end of the review, you should be able to agree on an action plan which will include your personal development objectives, supported by your manager. Remember, however, that in six or twelve months you will be expected to discuss your progress at your next review meeting.

If reviews are well organised and done professionally then they are normally very positive for everyone. You get the chance to sit down and talk about yourself – your hopes, dreams, fears, worries, concerns, aims and ambitions – with your manager doing the listening. Your manager then gives you feedback which you can use to help to focus on the future. Together you agree a way forward. Ideally, you should leave a review full of renewed energy and enthusiasm for the future!

In real life, this may not always happen. A manager may have a few criticisms to make or may be unable to agree to every suggestion put forward for practical reasons – not least that some training programmes may be very expensive and not all activities will link to the aims of the business.

If you are on the receiving end of criticism, try not to overreact. If you feel it is unfair, ask for specific examples. If you feel it is totally unjust, ask for thinking time and for the review to be continued at a later date. It helps if you can distinguish between positive criticism (meant to help you) and negative, which is just destructive and unhelpful. If you honestly think your manager meant well and had some justification, then think carefully. He or she could just be right! The bottom line is that you know what impression you are giving, which is one of the main reasons for having a review in the first place.

▲ A review meeting should help you to focus on your personal and career development

The importance of self-assessment

Self-assessment means identifying your own strengths and weaknesses and the areas you need to develop. Few of us are very good at this but this doesn't mean we shouldn't persevere. Your ability to do this depends upon whether you are prepared to face reality or prefer to delude yourself that all is well. Conversely, some people despair they will ever be any good at anything – in which case self-assessment becomes some sort of torture. Needless to say, a balanced approach is the best way ahead!

Everyone has strengths and weaknesses. You are not perfect but neither are you useless. You shouldn't look down on other people as incompetent idiots but neither should you think everyone around you is cleverer than you or was born with certain skills or abilities that passed you by. The stages in self-assessment are as follows:

▶ Start by thinking about your strengths. Count each strength only if you can think of evidence to support your opinion, for example 'I am good at proof-reading because I rarely need to retype anything because of errors'.

▶ Now think about your weaknesses. These are areas where you know you have more problems, and again it helps to think of examples, for example, 'I am not good at numerical work because I struggle to understand a page of figures quickly'.

▶ Now decide the key areas you would like to develop – not just because the idea appeals but because they will help you to be more proficient at your job.

▶ If you have identified more than five or six areas, prioritise these, so you can concentrate on the most important first.

▶ Now take action. You can include specific skills you need to learn in your review plans or talk to your supervisor. In relation to your personality traits you have to attack these on your own! If you know that you like to sidestep responsibility, or hate to think more than two days in advance, learn to laugh at yourself when you find yourself demonstrating these traits. The key point is that you are recognising when you do it – which is the first step to modifying or changing your behaviour.

Self-assessment is important because it helps you to:

▶ learn more about yourself (in private!)

▶ identify your strengths (no matter what anyone else says)

▶ identify your weaknesses (no matter what your parents and best friends say!)

▶ build on your strengths

▶ moderate (or eliminate) your weaknesses

▶ develop more self-confidence.

ORGANISATIONS IN BUSINESS

Investors in People is a national quality Standard that sets a level of good practice for the training and development of people. In order to meet the Investors in People Standard, organisations need to show that they are committed to the development of that people in order to meet their business goals. Once recognised, organisations are allowed to use the Investor in People logo on their stationery and in their advertisements.

Recognised organisations must maintain their commitment to the Standard. They are regularly reviewed to ensure that they are still meeting all the requirements of the Investors in People standard; otherwise recognition can be revoked. During these reviews, both managers and staff are interviewed.

If you work for an organisation that is a recognised Investor in People then you know that it is committed to helping you to develop and has a clear continuing programme of training and development.

INVESTOR IN PEOPLE

OVER TO YOU!

1   Sara moved to the finance department three months ago but rarely receives any direct feedback from her boss. She feels she has learned a lot during this time but would appreciate knowing that everyone is happy with her work. Suggest four ways in which Sara can obtain feedback on her achievements so far.

2   a) Decide your own plan for the next two years by thinking about the type of job you would like to be doing by then and the skills and qualifications you will need. If you are unsure about these, then research this by looking at local job advertisements for the jobs you have in mind.

b) Now identify four targets – two for this year and two for next – which will help you achieve your goal.

c) Arrange to talk to your tutor, in private, to discuss your plans and targets and obtain feedback on whether these are realistic and appropriate in relation to your current course and abilities.

3. Buki works as a marketing administrator but would love to become more involved in website development, which is part of their departmental work. He knows that he would have to improve his IT skills first.
   a) Suggest three ways in which Buki could obtain training to improve his IT skills.
   b) Suggest two ways in which Buki could learn more about the company's website.

4. a) You are about to attend a first review with your manager. Suggest three ways in which you would be expected to prepare for this session.
   b) Identify four benefits of reviewing your work with your manager.

5. a) Explain what is meant by the term 'self-assessment'.
   b) Suggest three reasons why self-assessment is important.

▼ IDENTIFY AND EXPLAIN ISSUES AFFECTING WORKING CONDITIONS

Working conditions are important to everyone. They relate to the physical environment in which you work and the way you are treated at work. Most organisations are keen to provide good working conditions because this helps them to retain good staff. If people work in a bright, well-designed building with the right equipment for the job they are not only happier, but are able to do their work more efficiently – so the business as a whole benefits.

Where the health and safety of employees is concerned, it is a legal requirement to provide working conditions of a certain standard. Organisations must also abide by their legal responsibilities in relation to employment legislation, which is concerned with the terms under which people are employed and how they are treated at work.

Employees also have legal responsibilities in relation to health and safety and, in respect of employment law, towards their employer. Ignoring these – breaching them, in legal terms – can result in disciplinary action or even dismissal.

In this section you will learn how the environment you work in can affect efficiency and you will also find out about your own, and your employer's, legal responsibilities in relation to health and safety and employment law. This information is vital when you start work, so that you know the actions you must take – and those you must not – as well as the legal rights you have as an employee in a variety of situations.

▼ THE OFFICE ENVIRONMENT AND EFFICIENCY

We are all affected by our environment – especially when we are working. If you are at home, trying to concentrate, then you are far more likely to be successful if you have a separate desk, with everything you need nearby and a bit of peace and quiet. If you are trying to work on the kitchen table, with the phone ringing and everyone talking then any task you are doing will be more of a struggle.

The same applies in an office. An environmental psychologist in New York, Gary Evans, divided 40 female office workers into two groups. He put half of them in a quiet office and half into a noisy office and then monitored them for three hours. He found that those in the noisy office had higher stress levels and also made 40% fewer attempts to solve a difficult puzzle. There was a significant reduction in their overall performance.

This was just one aspect of an office that he changed. If you include other negative factors, like too little space to work, poor lighting and essential resources not close to hand, the situation becomes even worse. It is for these reasons that office design and layout is so closely linked to efficiency.

The importance of office layout

Offices may be open-plan or individual.

▶ An **open-plan office** is a large area in which several people work together, often in 'cells' or cubicles made of sound-proof screens. These give each worker privacy whilst reducing the noise. Many people prefer to work in an open plan office because they are near to others, so it is easier to exchange information in a team and they like being in a lively environment. If you are sociable by nature, you will probably prefer this.

▲ An open-plan office helps to create open communication

▶ **Smaller, individual offices** are a feature of many older buildings. In this case you may share an office with another person or even work on your own. Some people like the privacy, but others feel lonely and isolated.

Regardless of the overall environment, there are some basic considerations to be taken into account when offices are designed, so that people can work efficiently. These are the type of problems which architects and office designers face when new office blocks are built or when businesses decide to refurbish an old building to give it a new, modern look which will maximise the efficiency of staff.

The factors to consider include:

- the building or office itself and its features, such as windows, doors, lighting, ventilation, etc.
- the size of the area and number of staff or groups
- the type of work that will be undertaken and the work areas required
- the need for supervision
- the equipment that will be used
- the overall décor and furnishings.
- health and safety.

Each of these is considered separately below.

The building or office and its features

Unless a building or office is being built or refurbished from scratch, then there will be fixed windows and doors and these will affect the layout of the furniture and the position of staff.

- Every worker should have good 'natural' light – so desks, where possible, should be positioned near a window. Windows should be clean, safe to open and have adjustable blinds to minimise glare, particularly onto computer screens, and should be double-glazed to prevent draughts. Good artificial lighting is also essential. If the windows are small, the lights are likely to be on all day, and all offices need good lighting for winter days and evenings. Today there are many attractive options which are far better than the old-style fluorescent tubes which used to be a feature of many offices.

- Doors – both their number and position – will determine where furniture and equipment can be placed, because they contribute to the natural traffic routes of staff. These should be kept clear, with no furniture placed which could be hazardous. In a large open-plan office, the room may be designed to deliberately include specific traffic routes.

- Ventilation must be good so that there is an adequate supply of fresh air for everyone. In most offices, it is simply enough to be able to open the windows. In some offices air conditioning is fitted so that everyone is cool even on the hottest days.

- Heating must enable people to work at the right temperature. The minimum temperature determined by health and safety laws is 16°C (there is no maximum temperature). The heating should be adjustable. Desks shouldn't normally be placed directly next to radiators.

- Numerous power points are essential to minimise the use of adaptors, which can be dangerous. Electric equipment should be placed close to its power source to prevent wires and cables trailing across a room. Many modern offices have wire management, where the wires are concealed in the furniture and sockets are concealed in the floor. Desks can then be placed in open spaces, rather than just against the walls.

The size of the area and the number of workers or groups

Under health and safety legislation, each office worker should have a minimum of 11 cubic metres of space if they are permanently in the office. This is important to enable each person to have enough room to work comfortably. The amount of available space per worker is obviously reduced if the office is overflowing with furniture and equipment – so plans to install a new, large piece of equipment could be rejected if this reduced the amount of space to an unacceptable level.

If there is more than one group of workers, this is likely to decide the layout in most open-plan offices. Quite obviously, it is sensible for staff who need to communicate frequently to work close to each other.

The type of work and work areas required

Many large open-plan offices are deliberately designed to have separate areas, for different types of work. There may be:

▶ a reception area at the entrance, with a reception desk and visitors chairs, screened off from the rest of the office

▶ large working areas, with cubicles, which each contain a desk, telephone and computer equipment

▶ separate, screened-off meeting areas with special tables and chairs, or areas for discussion groups with low tables and sofas

▶ quiet or private areas, with acoustic screens, for those who need to work on a difficult task or hold a confidential discussion

▶ a separate area (or room) where large or noisy equipment is used with enough space for supplies to be kept and for people to work easily

▶ a rest area for staff, with low tables and chairs and a vending machine.

A relatively new trend is a 'hot desking' area where desks and telephones are provided for staff who frequently work away from the main site and do not need permanent facilities. These desks are shared amongst this group of workers rather than 'owned' by one person. This helps to maximise the space available for staff who are permanently in the office.

In a building with individual offices, there are normally specific rooms allocated for different work areas or sections.

Workflow is always considered at this point. Even in the smallest group of office staff, the work will normally 'flow' in a certain direction. This will determine where areas are positioned and where people are seated within an area. This reduces the amount of time for documents and information to be passed from one section – or person – to the next.

The need for supervision

Supervisors and team leaders need to be readily available if there is a problem. They also need to know what is happening and what staff are doing. Normally, therefore, you will find supervisors and their staff close together.

If the supervisor is working in the same area then the desks should be positioned so that supervisor and staff can see each other easily. The supervisor may also need privacy to meet people or talk to them without being overheard. In an open-plan office this is normally obtained through the positioning and height of different screens or the provision of separate discussion areas. In some individual offices, the supervisor works in an adjacent office with a glass partition between this office and the main working area.

▲ Supervisors must be available for their staff but will need privacy for some aspects of their work

The equipment being used

Most offices need a wide variety of equipment from computers and fax machines to large photocopiers and filing cabinets. The following factors need to be considered in relation to their position.

▶ **Accessibility**   All staff need rapid access to equipment and storage units they use frequently, so administrators normally have a keyboard and VDU on their desk and work close to filing cabinets they use regularly. They may have their own desktop printer or a larger printer may be shared among several people. In this case, it needs to be nearby so that print-outs can be obtained and checked easily. Fax machines should be placed so that people can immediately see when a new message arrives.

▶ **Noise**   Acoustic office screens reduce the noise from equipment quite considerably. Communal equipment, such as a printer, can be silenced by attaching an acoustic hood. Very large, noisy equipment is better sited in a room of its own to minimise noise and distraction.

▶ **Space**   Photocopiers have specific space requirements to ensure there is a free flow of air all around them. Space is also required around some items of equipment so that people can use them easily. There should be a table or flat surface near to a photocopier on which documents can be stacked, stapled or cut and equipment such as a rotary trimmer or heavy duty stapler available. Filing trays should be placed near filing cabinets and somewhere where folders can be opened for papers to be inserted. You therefore need to think about space not only in terms of the size of the equipment, but how it will be used.

▶ **Safety**   All electrical equipment needs to be near a power socket. Noise and space considerations also link to safety. No equipment should be placed where it would create a hazard.

The overall décor and furnishings

At one time, most offices were painted cream, all filing cabinets were grey and desks were brown! Today, any quick glance through an office furniture catalogue or visit to a modern office suite will show you how things have changed. Light and bright colours are chosen with a non-reflective finish, again to reduce glare.

Many offices today are decorated in corporate colours (the same colours used on the letter heading and company logo). You might find blue or green walls, red or navy carpets and office chairs in a variety of checks or patterns. In some large suites of offices, each area is 'colour coded' – so that you move from the blue area to the green to the red – and so on. Even the filing cabinets are coloured to match, which should reduce the chance of filing a document in the wrong one!

According to the experts, colour does us good. So, if you can't persuade your boss to change the wall colour or floor covering, then you could buy some brightly coloured pen pots, filing trays and paper clips, put some jazzy posters and pictures on the walls and replace the wilted spider plant with a brightly flowering geranium (and remember to water it!) to cheer everyone up.

Health and safety

Some of the major considerations relating to health and safety have been mentioned in the sections above, and you will learn more about health and safety in the next section. However, in relation to office design, the major considerations are summarised in the table below.

Office design, layout and health and safety

▶ All workers must have sufficient working space – a minimum of 11 cubic metres.
▶ The minimum temperature must be 61°F (16°C). There is no legal maximum.
▶ There must be sufficient light (preferably natural light) to avoid fatigue.
▶ There must be sufficient ventilation.
▶ Glass in windows and doors must be specially laminated or strengthened to make it safe or be protected against breakage or marked (e.g. by black crisscross wires) so its presence is obvious.

- ▶ Sliding doors must be fitted so that they cannot be dislodged and those which open upwards must have special fittings to make sure they cannot fall down on anyone. Those which open in either direction must be fitted with a viewing panel so that you can see someone approaching.
- ▶ All traffic routes, corridors and passageways must be kept clear.
- ▶ Floors should not be uneven or slippery and the type of floor covering should be appropriate.
- ▶ There must be sufficient power sockets so that adaptors are not required.
- ▶ Power sockets must be close to where equipment will be used so that there are no trailing wires or cables.
- ▶ There must be enough space for equipment to be used safely (e.g. for filing cabinet drawers to be opened).
- ▶ Desks and other working areas must be at the correct height or be easily adjustable.
- ▶ All fittings, such as storage shelves, must be at an appropriate height and be able to easily support the weight of items placed on them.
- ▶ All flooring must be securely fastened and non-slip.
- ▶ There must be handrails on stairways and stairs must be well lit.
- ▶ Chairs for IT users must be adjustable (see page 288) to suit the height of the workstation and user.
- ▶ Noisy equipment should be kept in a separate area or acoustic hoods should be used.

ORGANISATIONS IN BUSINESS

Office design and refurbishment is big business, with some companies spending large sums of money on their office makeovers. Those who do a fantastic job can enter the annual Digital Office Collection, run by *The Times* newspaper and Gestetner. In past years, submissions have been received from organisations with chill-out rooms, 'breakout' areas, touchdown rooms, horses galloping down walls and worktops modelled on aircraft wings.

Other companies pay extra to involve feng shui consultants to improve the 'chi' (energy) which flows through the business and, presumably, through the workers! Companies who have used feng shui to improve their business include Virgin Airways, Microsoft and the Midland Bank (HSBC) – to name but a few. This involves setting out the office so that 'chi' is maximised by the arrangement of furniture and equipment – the latter being placed in the 'wealth area' of the business.

Individual workers can also go on feng shui courses to learn how to set out their own desk or workstation – and reshuffle their pen holders, paper trays and PC to improve their motivation, efficiency, health and energy. At a cost of about £200 per person, it may be cheaper just to note the key points, which include having a solid wall behind your back, not a window, banning all cactus plants and keeping your desk free of clutter. In China, workers are even discouraged from having paper trays on their desks.

If you like the idea of feng shui, you can research this topic further in your library or on the Internet. You would, however, be advised to consult your boss before you arrive at work carrying a wind chime, an indoor fountain and a three-legged toad god to go next to your desk!

▲ If you are interested in feng shui at work you will need your manager's approval first!

OVER TO YOU!

1 Find out more about office design and layout by looking at some of the websites on line which show how some major design firms tackle this type of work. Follow the links from www.heinemann.co.uk/hotlinks to get some ideas.

2 Nazir and his staff are moving to a new office building. They will take up residence on the top floor, in a suite of offices. The layout is shown below.

a) As a group, from the layout shown, decide where you would place the following working areas. For each decision, give a reason for your choice.

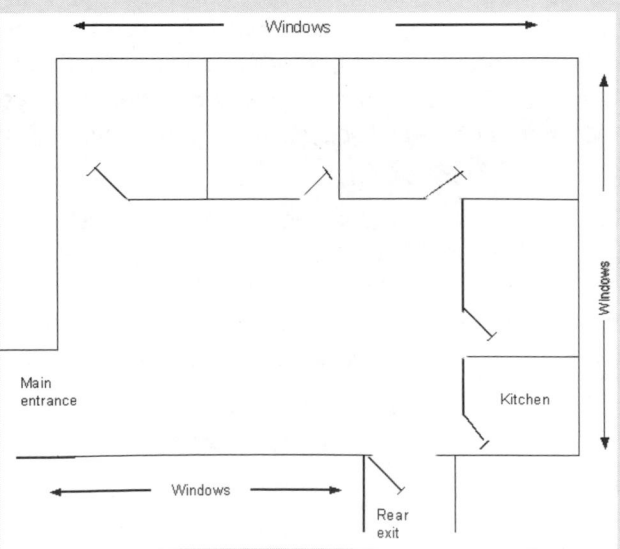

i)   Nazir's office

ii) The office of the senior administrator/supervisor

iii) Meeting room

iv) Photocopying room

b) Suggest four aspects of the building that Nazir will have taken into account before he decided to rent this office space. In each case, say why these aspects are important.

c) When the senior administrator first visits the building she needs to decide the layout of the main office, which will include the receptionist and three administrators. Identify, with reasons, three factors she must take into consideration when she plans the layout.

3   You work with two colleagues in the main office. You each have your own desk with a telephone and PC. There is a set of filing cabinets alongside one wall, a fax machine, a small photocopier and a communal printer.

You have all decided you would like to change everything around and brighten up the office a bit – even though your supervisor has told you there isn't much money in the budget for this.

a) Suggest three aspects you must take into consideration when you are planning the new layout.

b) Identify three factors which you must bear in mind before you move any equipment.

c) Suggest three ways you could brighten up the office without spending very much.

4   a) Identify six aspects of health and safety which must be considered when an office layout is being planned.

b) Suggest three hazards which could be present in an office where health and safety considerations had been ignored.

▼ HEALTH AND SAFETY ISSUES IN AN ADMINISTRATIVE ENVIRONMENT

If you are preparing to work in administration it's tempting to think that you don't have to bother too much with health and safety. After all, you might think that offices are quite safe places to work compared to construction sites, factories and oil rigs.

Whilst this is true, people still can get hurt in an office. Administrators have even been killed at work, although this is very rare. One office worker reached up to open a swivel window, lost his balance and fell to his death. On a more basic level, well over 1,000 office workers are injured every year at work and over a hundred are seriously hurt. What are all these people doing and, even more importantly, what do you have to do to ensure you are never one of these statistics?

Hazards and risks

A **hazard** is anything which could cause you harm or injury. This could be a heavy or sharp object or something as commonplace as the office door. A **risk** is the chance that you will be harmed or injured. There is obviously a greater risk of being seriously hurt if a heavy filing cabinet fell over on to you than if you trapped your finger in your desk drawer.

All employers have to evaluate risks by undertaking a formal **risk assessment** to decide whether each risk is high, medium or low and then check whether action needs to be taken to reduce the degree of risk so that fewer accidents will occur.

Potential hazards in an administration environment include:

▷ machinery and equipment that isn't properly maintained or not used safely

▷ hazardous substances which may be used carelessly or unsafely

▷ personal conduct and unsafe behaviour – which immediately increases the degree of risk

▷ untidiness and careless working – which does the same thing

▷ smoking, drinking and drugs.

You will find out how to work safely in these areas on page 281–284.

Health and safety legislation

Accidents and absence from work costs business an estimated £18 billion a year. Even a minor accident can cost up to £100, because a first aider needs to attend the scene and several people's work is disrupted. Accidents which result in absence from work cost far more. According to the Health and Safety Executive, up to 30 million working days are lost each year because of accidental injuries.

The aim of reducing both the costs and the distress of injury has resulted in several laws to help to protect employees and anyone else on the premises.

The Health and Safety at Work Act 1974

This Act is very important. Not only does it make both employers *and* employees responsible for health and safety, it is also an 'umbrella' Act under which other Regulations can be passed to ensure that health and safety laws are always up-to-date. The Act applies to all work premises, large or small, and to anyone who is there, such as employees, managers, visitors and external contractors (builders, plumbers) who are carrying out maintenance work. All these people also have personal responsibilities under the Act.

All employers must display the main terms of the Health and Safety at Work Act in a notice for their employees to read. Its key aspects are shown below.

The Health and Safety at Work Act 1974

All employers must:
▶ Ensure the health, safety and welfare at work of their employees 'as far as is reasonably practicable'. Specific aspects include:
  – safe entry and exit routes e.g. emergency exits not blocked
  – a safe working environment and adequate welfare facilities, e.g. ventilation, toilets and drinking water
  – well-maintained, safe equipment, e.g. safe wiring
  – safe storage and transport of articles and substances
  – provision of protective clothing
  – information on health and safety, instruction, training and supervision.

▶ Undertake the preparation and continual updating of a written statement on the health and safety policy of the company, where there are five or more employees. This must also be circulated to all employees.

▶ Allow for the appointment of safety representatives selected by a recognised trade union. Safety representatives must be allowed to investigate accidents or potential hazards, follow up employee complaints and have paid time off to carry out their duties.

All employees must:

▶ Take reasonable care of their own health and safety, e.g. by obeying rules.

▶ Take reasonable care for the health and safety of others who may be affected by their activities or actions.

▶ Cooperate with their employer or anyone acting on his or her behalf to meet health and safety requirements.

Other relevant Regulations for administrators

There are very many Regulations which cover specific aspects of health and safety. Some of these apply to all employees, others apply to all or most administrators.

A summary of these and their main aspects, is shown on page 280.

The importance of taking precautions

Organisations take many precautions to try to prevent accidents and many of these are a legal requirement. These safeguards can be defeated, however, if employees themselves don't take precautions when they are working. No one has the time to follow you around to make sure you always wear rubber gloves if you are handling a toxic substance which could cause a rash. Once you have been told to wear them, and the gloves have been provided, it is then your responsibility.

There are many other precautions you should take. Examples include:

▶ making sure no one can trip over your personal belongings

▶ mopping up any spills promptly

▶ never running down corridors, around corners and up and down stairs

▶ never trying to lift or carry an object which is too heavy for you to handle alone

▶ never carrying more files or folders than you can safely see over

▶ never moving equipment so that the wire is trailing

▶ never leaving a drawer of your desk or filing cabinet open unnecessarily

▶ handling breakages carefully, particularly broken glass

▶ following specific instructions you have been given

▶ never using equipment unless you know what to do

▶ having respect for even small items of equipment that could cause injury, from a paper knife to a stapler.

The list is almost endless!

Those that apply to all employees:

Workplace (Health, Safety and Welfare) Regulations – These cover four specific areas: a) the work environment (ventilation, temperature, lighting, space); b) safety (in respect of traffic routes, floors, windows, escalators, stairs, etc.); c) facilities (toilets, water, seating, rest areas); d) housekeeping (maintenance and cleanliness).

Fire Precautions Act and Regulations – All business premises must possess a fire certificate and have suitable fire precautions – such as fire-resistant doors, fire extinguishers, break-glass alarms and a fire alarm system.

Employers' Liability (Compulsory Insurance) Regulations – All employers must take out insurance so employees who are injured at work can claim compensation.

Health and Safety (First Aid) Regulations – All organisations must provide adequate and appropriate first aid equipment and facilities and trained first aiders. The number of first aiders must be appropriate to the risks in the workplace.

Health and Safety (Safety Sign and Signals) Regulations – Safety signs must be displayed to identify risks and hazards and written instructions on how to use fire-fighting equipment.

Reporting of Injuries, Diseases and Dangerous Occurrences Regulations (RIDDOR) – All organisations must notify the Health and Safety Executive (HSE) of any serious or fatal injuries and keep records of certain specific injuries, dangerous occurrences and diseases.

Those that apply to all or most administrators:

The Display Screen Equipment Regulations – All employers must assess the risks to staff using VDUs and workstations, pay for eye tests and spectacles/lenses if these are prescribed for VDU work and plan work activities to incorporate rest breaks. For further details, see page 287.

The Control of Substances Hazardous to Health Regulations (COSHH) – All hazardous substances (such as toxic cleaning fluids) must be clearly labelled and stored in a special environment and users provided with protective clothing.

The Electricity at Work Regulations – These govern the design, construction, use and maintenance of electrical systems.

The Noise at Work Regulations – These require employers to check noise hazards and reduce these where possible and provide ear protectors if necessary.

The Provision and Use of Work Equipment Regulations (PUWER) – These relate to the maintenance and safety of all work equipment. Employers must make regular checks and inspections and provide appropriate training and instructions for users.

The Manual Handling Operations Regulations – These govern the way items should be lifted and handled. Preferably an automated process must be used but if items are moved manually employees must be trained properly to minimise injury.

Personal Protective Equipment at Work Regulations – Protective clothing and equipment must be provided when risks cannot be eliminated. They must be free of charge, fit properly and be kept in good condition.

▲ It is important to take note of safety precautions at work

Identifying and following safe working practices

All organisations have codes of practice which relate to safe working practices (see page 290). In addition, there may be separate procedures for staff which state how to use particular items of equipment or certain materials or substances. These aim to control the working practices of individuals where there is likely to be any risk. However, there is unlikely to be a procedure to tell you how to make a cup of coffee or how to hand someone a pair of scissors!

On page 278, you read about the potential hazards to administrators. Below are the safe working practices to bear in mind for each of these areas.

Unsafe use of machinery and equipment

The equipment and machinery you use is likely to include a photocopier, computer, printer, fax machine, shredder, rotary trimmer or guillotine and stapler. None of these items is seriously hazardous, unless you work unsafely.

Safe working practices include:

▶ Using all equipment and machinery according to its purpose and the way you were trained.

▶ Never undertaking operations you should not attempt, such as poking around inside a photocopier or trying to dismantle your keyboard!

▶ Keeping liquids well away from *all* electrical equipment.

▶ Closing the lid when you are photocopying so that you are not blinded by the ultraviolet light. This won't cause permanent eye damage but doesn't do your eyes any good.

- Never using equipment or machinery which is broken, damaged or marked 'do not use.'

- Reporting any unusual smells to your supervisor promptly. Both photocopiers and laser printers can emit ozone fumes. Normally, these are within very safe limits, but a strong smell could indicate a fault.

- Switching off electrical equipment immediately if you smell burning or hear crackling, and reporting the matter. Put a 'do not use' notice on the equipment until it is declared safe.

- Reading the instruction manual before you attempt to clean any item of equipment – and following it!

- Never using any item of electrical equipment if the wire is damaged or the plug is loose.

- Switching off equipment when you are told to do so.

- Using appropriate safety equipment when it is provided, such as a safety step-stool.

Unsafe use of substances

Fortunately the number of hazardous substances in an office is few. But this can lead to complacency – you may think it doesn't matter how you handle common, everyday items, but this isn't the case. Safe working practices include:

- Handling toner with care. Toner is the black, powdered ink used in photocopiers and some printers. Most modern equipment uses sealed toner bottles or cartridges which are far safer. Toner must be stored in a cool, dry place away from direct sunlight and on a flat surface and used bottles or cartridges disposed of *exactly* as instructed. They must never be incinerated as the toner dust can ignite.

  If you have an older machine, where toner dust can get on to your hands or clothes, then use rubber gloves and – if there are any spillages – wash it off immediately with *cold* water (otherwise it sets).

- Correction fluid and some types of glue give off fumes, so they can be dangerous if you breathe them. If you have a sensitive skin, many can cause a rash. Therefore it is wise to keep the tops tightly fastened unless you are using them, make sure you don't lean over the bottles or breathe in the fumes and wash your hands promptly if you are very messy and end up with any substance all over you.

- Some strong cleaning fluids are even more unpleasant to use. Use rubber gloves and keep your face well away from an open bottle. Clean up any spillages quickly and make sure you don't inadvertently touch your face whilst you are working.

Personal conduct – unsafe behaviour

Interestingly, this category and the next are the highest causes of accidents in an office. You will see this if you look at the table below. It is hardly likely that anyone deliberately intends to walk into a moving or fixed object or to fall off a chair, but lots of people do – every year!

Main causes of accidents in an office – all resulting in more than 3 days' absence from work

Cause of injury	Major injuries	Less serious
Slipping or tripping (on a slippery surface losing footing or tripping over an obstruction)	50%	27%
Falling from a height (either downstairs, off a ladder or from a chair, racking or other item)	20%	11%
Being struck by a moving object (e.g. a door, something falling from a shelf or table or a falling object)	9%	13%
Handling, lifting or carrying an awkward or heavy object	7%	31%
Walking into a fixed object, e.g. a wall or desk	–	6%

Problems can usually be grouped into the following areas.

▶ Practical jokes which can get out of hand, such as throwing water around or setting off a fire extinguisher.

▶ Thoughtless actions, such as wearing a backpack without thinking about the people behind you or throwing something across an office (for evidence, see the number of people in the table hit by a moving object).

▶ Silly actions, like using a wet cloth to clean electrical equipment or cleaning a new piece of equipment without reading the instructions.

▶ Deliberately flouting safety instructions, such as ignoring a fire drill, wedging open a fire door or trying to lift something heavy on your own.

▶ Stupid actions, like standing on a swivel chair to open a window or walking backwards because you are talking to someone.

Untidiness or careless working

'Good housekeeping' is a phrase often used in relation to health and safety. Your employer must have procedures in place in relation to cleaning, maintenance and the safe storage of dangerous or flammable substances. Top priority is given to rectifying problems that could be hazardous, for example an electrical fault or a broken rail on a staircase. There will also be procedures in place to ensure action is taken if anything is damaged or broken – from a glass pane in a door to spilt liquid on the floor. This is why you see areas cordoned off in a supermarket if there has been a breakage, so that no one is injured as a result.

You need to follow this example in your own work area, for example by:

▶ cooperating with your employer over routine maintenance checks to equipment you use – even if this is inconvenient at the time

▶ reporting damage or faults, using the correct procedures

▶ picking up anything you drop (including paper, which can be treacherous on a carpeted floor) and wiping up instantly anything you spill

▶ never putting unwrapped broken glass or china in your waste bin.

- never leaving uneaten food on your desk or in a desk drawer

- closing drawers and cupboard doors after you have found what you need

- never piling up files or folders on a desk or – even more important – on a high shelf where they could fall off and injure someone

- never leaving boxes of stationery or other items on the floor, where someone could trip over them

- never leaving scissors, drawing pins or other sharp objects lying around and, even worse, covering them up with paper so they cannot be seen.

Smoking, drinking and drugs

Today most organisations have specific rules about smoking in the workplace because they have to provide smoke-free areas for their employees. They may also have a separate area set aside for smokers, but this is not a legal requirement.

Drinking alcohol or taking drugs is always discouraged at work and, in some organisations and for some employees, it is completely forbidden. This is the case where employees could risk or cause serious injury if they were even slightly intoxicated and not concentrating properly. Virgin Trains, for example, bans all employees from drinking alcohol up to 12 hours before they start work and conducts random drink and drug tests on all its employees – not just drivers but office workers too.

All organisations have explicit rules which cover this area and these form part of the contract of employment you will read about on page 294. For example, Marks and Spencer state in their handbook that the employee must be able to do their job unaffected by alcohol, drugs or other substances. Employees who ignore these rules will face disciplinary action and, in some cases, can be summarily dismissed (sacked). This would be the case, for example, if someone was drunk at work or took illegal drugs. If you are taking prescribed medicine which could affect your ability to concentrate then you are wise to inform your supervisor.

Dealing with low-risk matters

After an organisation has undertaken a **risk assessment** (see page 291), then all risks in a workplace should be 'low'. However, this does not mean that the level of risk will never change. If equipment develops a fault, if it is moved, if new ways of working are introduced or anything else occurs that could affect the situation, then the risk level can increase.

If this happens, then you may need to report the matter immediately (see next section) or simply put it right yourself by taking appropriate action. You are more likely to be able to do this if the risk relates just to yourself or your own working area. For example:

- the way your own desk or workstation is set out, especially if you use a computer (see page 287)

- the way you sit at your computer and the way your chair is adjusted (again, see page 287)

- the way you use equipment and materials on a day-to-day basis. For example, if you type whilst you are talking on the phone by wedging the phone in your neck this can cause serious neck problems. You should ask for a telephone headset if you need to do this regularly

- if there are breakages or spillages in your own area – or untidy habits which create hazards

- if you spot a hazard in your own area, such as a pile of files that could fall over, a trailing wire, a broken chair or a desk drawer left open

- if someone else is working unsafely – such as leaving obstructions in a traffic route or propelling themselves along the floor on the castors of their chair.

The need to report accidents and potential hazards to the appropriate person

All organisations have procedures for reporting accidents and potential hazards. These tell you exactly what to do if either of these situations occurs.

Reporting accidents

Organisations have a legal duty to record accidents and all those with more than ten workers must keep an accident book and not dispose of this until at least three years after the last entry. The procedure is likely to include: how to contact a first aider, where the medical room is, how to contact a doctor or send for an ambulance and when to complete an accident report.

As you will see on page 293, the information collected in accident reports is important because it can be used to help to reduce further, similar accidents. For these reasons, if you witness an accident – or are involved with one   it is important that you follow the procedures, which normally involve recording:

- the date, time and place of the accident

- the name and the job title of the injured person

- the details of the injury and any first aid that was given

- what happened immediately afterwards, for example whether the injured person went back to work, went home or was taken to hospital

- the name and signature of the person reporting the accident.

Reporting potential hazards

It will not usually be the role of a safety representative or safety officer to deal with reports about hazards that relate to minor maintenance issues. These will go to the person responsible for this area, such as the building supervisor, electrician or caretaker. Sometimes, however, you would be expected to inform your supervisor or manager first, out of courtesy.

Hazards you would be expected to report include:

- problems or faults with equipment you use

- maintenance problems, e.g. a loose carpet tile, a damaged plug or a broken blind

- building problems, e.g. a broken pane of glass, slippery steps because of ice, a jammed door

▶ consistent or serious unsafe working practices or disregard of safety instructions by another member of staff. In this case, of course, you should see your supervisor rather than anyone else.

The importance of emergency procedures

Organisational procedures will also cover other emergencies, such as an evacuation because of fire. These will include what to do about other people on the premises, such as visitors or outside contractors. This is why most organisations have a visitor book, so that they can tell how many people are on the premises. Many visitor badges also have instructions on the emergency procedures on the reverse, so that everyone knows what to do if the fire alarm sounds and where to assemble.

Although it is impossible to have procedures to cover every type of emergency, you are likely to find that various events have been grouped into this heading, such as bomb threats and gas or water leaks. The exact procedure may be slightly different in each case. For example, in the case of a fire alarm, bomb threat or gas leak, the entire building is likely to be evacuated. If it is a water leak, only a specific area may be cleared. If there is a bomb threat, you may be told to take your belongings with you, to reduce the number of items that must be searched. If the fire alarm sounds, then it is more important that you leave the building quickly.

The aim of having clear procedures is to ensure that everyone takes the correct action promptly and no one does anything which could endanger the lives of others – such as using a lift in an emergency evacuation. Practising what to do, such as in a fire drill, enables managers to check the procedures are working properly. Procedures also help officials, such as fire marshals, to deal with difficult situations. For example, all procedures will include a section on how to deal with anyone with a serious disability in an emergency, especially if they are on an upper floor and the lifts must not be used.

First aid

All employers have to carry out an assessment of their first aid needs. This means identifying the level of risk to their employees at that workplace and deciding what first aid equipment, personnel and facilities are required.

Under the Health and Safety (First Aid) Regulations (see page 280) there must, as a minimum, be a suitably stocked first aid box and an appointed person to take charge of first aid arrangements. All employees must be informed about these arrangements and know where the first aid box is kept and how to contact those who are responsible for first aid. This information is usually found in a notice in every office.

In a small firm, the person responsible need not be a trained first aider but may simply replenish the first aid box, take charge if someone is ill or injured and call an ambulance. To be a first aider, a person must have successfully completed an approved training course and hold a current first aid certificate.

The number of first aiders required depends several factors, including the number of employees and the degree of risk at the workplace. All these factors are considered during the assessment. Therefore, a large chemical factory would need far more than a shop. Offices are classed as 'low risk', which means that a minimum of one first aider is required if there are between 50 and 100 employees. Above this number, an additional first aider is needed for every 100 workers. Bear in mind that these are the *minimum* requirements – and many businesses may have more out of choice.

The items kept in the first aid box should again be appropriate to the degree of risk, so whereas a first aid box in a hotel kitchen would need burn dressings, in an office these may not be necessary. It is not normal to hold drugs – even paracetamol – in first aid boxes. This is because administering drugs can cause complications unless a patient's full medical history is known.

The provision of a first aid room will also be considered during the assessment. If a room is provided it will normally have a sink, with hot and cold running water, a couch with clean blankets and a pillow, a chair and a telephone. It will also be the place where first aid supplies are kept. This room must only be used for first aid and must be clearly signposted.

Health and safety and display screen equipment

On Monday, Michelle went to see her doctor. For the past few weeks she had been suffering from peculiar headaches and her shoulders and neck were stiff. She started worrying that she had caught a strange virus and might have something seriously wrong with her.

She was rather surprised when her GP focused on what she did at work. When she told him she was an administrator and used a computer he smiled knowingly. He then asked her several questions about the way she worked and, instead of a prescription, gave her a list of instructions to change her working habits. Within a week, Michelle was cured.

Michelle is not the first – and won't be the last – administrator to have this type of experience. Today, administrators routinely use computers at work and take them for granted. Computers may not look very dangerous. Yet many people suffer quite painful conditions simply because they take little account of how they are used and how they should be used. The problem is that a computer user is in a fixed position – head staring at the screen, hands on the keyboard, the rest of the body immobile. This position may be held for several hours, leading to problems which can include:

▶ musculoskeletal disorders such as repetitive strain injury (RSI) and upper-limb disorders (ULDs) to hands, wrists, arms, neck, shoulders or back. These are caused by repetitive movements – such as by keying in text or using a mouse and continual poor posture

▶ tired eyes or migraine if the screen is flickering or unclear.

Using a computer at work is covered by the Health and Safety at Work (Display Screen Equipment) Regulations 1992. The key aspects of these are summarised on page 288. The Regulations introduced minimum standards for the use of VDUs (visual display units) and the design of workstations. Your workstation includes your screen, keyboard, printer, chair and work surface – as well as the space around you, the lighting, temperature and noise levels. The Regulations state your employer's responsibilities in relation to all these areas. They don't, however, allow for users who don't take common sense precautions for themselves! Like Michelle, many computer users can often make simple adjustments themselves, which can make all the difference.

To start, users should carry out a short risk assessment on themselves by checking that:

▶ they are sitting up straight, with their lower back properly supported by their chair

▶ the area under the desk is clear, so there is plenty of room for their legs

- their feet are flat on the ground – if not, they should use a footstool.
- the height of the seat is correct so that their arms are horizontal when keyboarding
- they are not straining their neck to look at documents or work they are copying
- there is enough space for their equipment and documents
- they have tried different arrangements of keyboard, screen, mouse and documents to find the best one for them
- the screen is clean, at the correct angle and the brightness and contrast settings suit them
- there is sufficient lighting to see clearly but no reflections on the screen
- they have regular short breaks or changes of activity – and refocus their eyes regularly during a long job (perhaps by looking out of the window).

Health and Safety at Work (Display Screen Equipment) Regulations 1992

These require all employers to minimise the risks of VDU work by:
- ensuring that all workstations, related furniture, computer software and the working environment of VDU users meet the minimum requirements of the Regulations
- planning work so that all users have regular breaks or changes in activity
- noting the special needs of individual staff
- offering eye tests, on request, to employees who use a VDU for more than one hour a day and provide special spectacles if these are needed
- providing health and safety training and information
- ensuring that workstations meet minimum standards. These include
  - display screens which are clear and can be adjusted easily
  - adjustable keyboards with a matt surface and clear symbols
  - work surfaces which are large enough for the work and non-reflective
  - stable, adjustable work chairs which give good back support
  - satisfactory lighting with glare minimised and comfortable noise and heat levels
  - appropriate software and systems.

▶ Sitting properly is an essential health and safety precaution

ORGANISATIONS IN BUSINESS

Musculoskeletal disorders (MSDs) currently affect over a million people every year and the risk factors that cause them can be found in almost every workplace. It is estimated that over 12 million working days a year are lost because of MSDs and the cost to the economy is estimated to be over £1.25 billion a year.

As part of their drive to reduce these figures, the Health and Safety Executive (HSE) launched a Priority Programme in 2003 and updated many of its guidance notes on the use of display screen equipment to include advice on modern ways of working, such as using lap-top computers, a mouse, a trackball as well as working from home. In addition, the DSE Regulations were also updated.

One simple tip is to learn a few keyboard shortcuts. These reduce the need to use your mouse. The most helpful ones to learn are Control + B (bold), Control + S (save), Control + C (copy), Control + X (cut), Control + V (paste), Control + P (print).

Alternatively, you can investigate ergonomic keyboards, mice, tracker balls and other devices which have been designed to reduce strain. You can even buy software that reminds you to take regular breaks and gives you examples of exercises you should do when you are working. Useful sites where you can obtain more information can be found by following the links from www.heinemann.co.uk/hotlinks.

Some experts are critical about the potential benefits of ergonomic devices. They argue that they will never help if workers are constantly under pressure to produce work too quickly. They claim that the stress of having to work to tight deadlines with little help or support is the major cause of MSD. This is one of the reasons why the HSE is targeting business organisations with its new Priority Programme. To find out more, go to www.heinemann.co.uk/hotlinks.

OVER TO YOU!

1. As a group, identify five Health and Safety laws or regulations which must be taken into consideration by a company which designs or refurbishes offices. To help, use the chart on page 274–5, which identifies the health and safety factors related to office design and the information on Health and Safety laws and regulations on pages 278–280.

2. Petra has been asked to assess risks in her own area. For each of the following situations, decide:
   a) whether the risk of an accident occurring is high, medium or low
   b) which risks Petra can deal with herself and which she must report
   c) the action she should take in the case of the risks she can deal with herself.
      i)   On the first sunny morning of the year, Petra is horrified to see how filthy all the computer screens are.
      ii) A filing tray is on top of a cabinet near the door. Every time the door opens, sheets of paper float off the top and onto the floor.
      iii) There is a small sink in the corner with a temperamental water supply. Some days the water is scalding hot.
      iv) The hooks on the wall opposite the sink are used for hanging coats. One tall member of staff claims they are at a dangerous height but no one else is affected.

v) The plastic guard on the guillotine has been cracked for weeks but is still in place.

vi) The shredder was moved across the office last week, but there is no nearby power point so the wire is draped across a desk.

vii) The newest member of staff is an untidy worker. Somewhere under a pile of papers on her desk is the electric stapler.

viii) Staff often forget to turn off the laser printer at night because it's used by them all, so no one feels responsible.

ix) The trolley used for moving stationery has a broken wheel, so it's unusable.

x) The carpet just inside the door was damaged when some filing cabinets were moved. It's now slightly torn.

3 a) You witness an accident in your workplace. Identify five details that you would be expected to include on the accident report.

b) Explain three benefits for organisations of having procedures for dealing with accidents and fire evacuations.

c) Identify two other types of emergency situation where you would be expected to follow procedures.

4 All the administrators in your office use computers on a daily basis. Several of them are complaining about neck or back pains.

a) Describe six actions they can take themselves to minimise or prevent these problems.

b) Identify three actions their employer has to take because of the requirements of the Health and Safety (Display Screen Equipment) Regulations.

▼ EMPLOYERS' RESPONSIBILITIES UNDER HEALTH AND SAFETY LEGISLATION

Organisations cannot 'trust to luck' that they are complying with the law, but need to have policies and ways of operating to ensure they stay within it. This section summarises these and identifies the main actions that are taken by employers to ensure they meet their responsibilities.

Safety policies and procedures

To comply with the Health and Safety at Work Act, all businesses must draw up a **safety policy** if they employ five or more people. This policy should state the aims of the company in relation to the health and safety of employees. It should also include key members of staff and arrangements for carrying out the policy. This is likely to include training and instruction, company rules, emergency arrangements, the system for reporting accidents and the identification of risk areas. The policy must be revised regularly to make sure it stays up to date.

The organisation will then decide its own **codes of practice** which state the procedures all employees must follow if there is an emergency evacuation or if an accident occurs. It must ensure all accidents are recorded and accident records are kept according to the law (see page 285).

Risk assessment

Under the Management of Health and Safety at Work Regulations, all employers are required to carry out risk assessments on all types of work activities that may potentially cause harm or ill-health. This means looking carefully at what is going on in their workplace to check if they have sufficient precautions in place. They must:

- look for hazards
- in each case, decide who might be harmed and how
- check if the existing precautions are adequate or if more could be done
- write down the findings
- review the assessment regularly and revise it if necessary.

Additional, specific risk assessments must be carried out in the following areas:

- Under the Fire Precautions (Workplace) Regulations, all employers must carry out additional fire risk assessments by identifying potential sources of ignition which could start a fire, identify who would be harmed and then evaluate existing fire precautions and check if these could be improved.

- Under the Health and Safety (First Aid) Regulations, the employer must assess the risk level of the working environment when deciding upon the facilities, equipment and staff to provide first aid (see page 286).

- Under the Health and Safety (Young Persons) Regulations, special risk assessments must be carried out in respect of young or inexperienced workers. A separate set of regulations – the Health and Safety (Training for Employment) Regulations – also covers students or school pupils undertaking work experience in a company. Both of these groups are at increased risk and must receive proper training to minimise the risk.

- The risks to staff of using VDUs and workstations must be assessed under the Display Screen Equipment Regulations.

There will be procedures in place to make sure risk assessments are done regularly to comply with the law.

Preventative measures

Organisations are expected to put in place preventative measures as part of their risk assessments and to comply with health and safety laws and regulations. These include:

- putting up safety signs where these are required
- ensuring equipment is checked and maintained regularly
- providing protective clothing
- storing hazardous substances in special areas
- providing basic requirements under the Workplace (Health, Safety and Welfare) Regulations, i.e. an adequate number of clean, working toilets, drinking water, a clean workplace, adequate space, light, ventilation and temperature and so on.

▲ Safety signs must be used in accordance with health and safety legislation

Training

Health and safety law requires all employers to provide information, instruction and training for staff.

Information

The HSE advises employers to identify:

▶ who needs to receive this (e.g. employees, visitors, sub-contractors, temporary staff)

▶ what information must be provided

▶ when it should be provided (e.g. at induction, during the first visit, when a job changes). The information should always be provided before it is required – not after!

▶ how the information should be provided, whether during a talk or demonstration, on paper or on computer. However it is provided, it must be easy to understand

▶ ways of checking that people have understood it and are acting upon it.

Instruction and Training

The Management of Health and Safety at Work Regulations state that employers must provide health and safety training for people when they start work, when their work or responsibilities change if this exposes them to new or increased risks, periodically to refresh their skills and to take account of any new or changed risks. Training must be provided during working hours and no employee can be charged to attend.

Employers will have procedures to identify the following:

▶ Who needs to be trained. There may be special groups, such as young workers, who need extra training. All managers and supervisors must receive specific training to carry out risk assessments and control risks in their own areas.

▶ What training is required to comply with the law and to minimise accidents in that particular workplace. Training for new employees, for example, will normally be different than for existing employees and will include:

– recognising risks in the workplace

– taking precautions

- emergency and evacuation procedures
- employee responsibilities to comply with organisational rules and good practice
- how to use work equipment and personal protective equipment.

▶ How the training should be given and by whom.

▶ When the training should take place.

Safety committees, safety representatives and safety officers

In many organisations a **safety committee** operates. This is made up of representatives from management and employees. The committee checks that all legal requirements are being met and reports to management on any working conditions which breach safety regulations or company policy. If there is no safety committee, these duties may be undertaken by a **safety officer**.

Many businesses also have **safety representatives** who attend meetings of the safety committee. These representatives are appointed by recognised trade unions and elected by union members and not by the employer. They follow up complaints made by employees relating to health and safety, carry out inspections every three months and are involved with any consultations involving Health and Safety Executive (HSE) inspectors. They must also be consulted by the employer about any changes in the workplace that might affect the health and safety of the employees or any information or training the employer plans to provide for staff.

In many organisations, a **safety committee**, or a **safety officer** is responsible for regularly reviewing the company's accident record. **Safety representatives**, who attend meetings of a safety committee, are also involved in investigating accidents, together with the safety officer. They can recommend improvements and then check that recommended action has been taken. They also check completed accident report forms and accident records and monitor accident rates to ensure that these are not above the national average and that there is a regular improvement in standards.

OVER TO YOU!

1. Each of the following groups of people are considered to be more vulnerable in the workplace and special precautions need to be taken when risk assessments are being carried out. They are: staff with physical disabilities, visitors or members of the public, new or inexperienced staff, young workers and pregnant women.
   a) As a group, suggest two specific circumstances in which each of these groups could be particularly at risk.
   b) For each of the circumstances you have identified, suggest ways in which an employer could reduce this risk.

2. Subcontractors who are building an extension at a college are issued with specific instructions by the safety officer. They are informed that if they do not agree to abide by these they will not be allowed to work on the premises.
   a) Suggest two reasons why the college issues these instructions.
   b) As a group, suggest three precautions the college may insist are taken by the builders as part of their routine operations.

3 The following complaints have been received by a safety representative. Identify those on which the management must take action as part of their legal responsibilities.

   a) Although the waste bins are emptied every night, the cleaners don't clean VDU screens for staff.

   b) Some new staff have been employed for four weeks now but haven't yet received any health and safety training.

   c) Electricians check equipment every twelve months but this disrupts work in the office when they visit.

   d) Two windows have been jammed for six months now so the only ventilation is a tiny portable fan.

   e) The safety signs and instructions relating to the fire equipment are torn and unreadable.

   f) Although lorries frequently use the back yard area, there are no warning signs in place.

   g) The key to the hazardous substances cupboard is locked away and can't be obtained when the supervisor is at lunch.

   h) There aren't enough power sockets in the office, so adaptors are always used.

4 Identify five different responsibilities of employers under health and safety legislation.

▼ THE RIGHTS AND RESPONSIBILITIES OF EMPLOYERS AND EMPLOYEES AS SET OUT IN THE CONTRACT OF EMPLOYMENT

A contract of employment is a legal document which sets out the details of a person's employment. It defines the legal relationship between the employer and the employee. When both parties have signed it, it is then binding. This means that both employer and employee have to obey and observe its terms. If they do not, then they are in breach of the contract and there are legal repercussions. An employee who breaches the contract can be disciplined and may be dismissed. If an employer breaches the contract, then the law is on the side of the employee who may decide to take legal action.

Because your contract of employment, wherever you work, is so significant, it is important that you understand the items it is likely to contain and how these will affect you at work. This is particularly the case in relation to your own rights and responsibilities, and those of your employer, as these define the actions that either of you can take – and those which you must not. These are the main focus of this section.

The Contract of Employment

After you have been working for any organisation for more than one month then you have the legal right to receive details of your terms and conditions of employment in writing. This document must be sent to you within two months of the date when your employment started. It doesn't matter whether you are employed on a full-time basis or working only a few hours each week. You may receive a letter with these details or a more formal document, entitled Contract of Employment or Main Terms of Employment.

You will be instructed to read the document, sign one copy and return it as proof that you accept and agree to the conditions. It is therefore important to check that you understand it!

Key items in a contract of employment

Your letter, contract or statement of main terms must contain certain, specific items. Other items of information must also be provided but can be in a separate document or you must be told where you can find them.

Within the contract must be the following information:

- your job title
- your hours of work
- your place of work
- the main terms and conditions of your employment
- your pay and other benefits, such as sick pay and holiday pay
- the date on which your employment started
- the name of your employer
- your own name.

Additional information that can be given in a separate document is as follows:

- if the job is temporary, the date on which the job will end
- details of any trade union agreements which relate to you
- details of your employer's grievance and appeals procedure (see page 300).

Further information to which you must have access includes:

- details about sickness benefits and sickness entitlement if you are ill
- pension scheme details
- how much notice you must give if you want to leave the job
- details of your employer's disciplinary rules and procedures (see page 301).

An example of a Statement of the Main Terms of Employment is shown on page 296. It is called this because a full contract would contain all the above information. Instead, like many organisations, Alpha Supplies prefers to summarise the main terms and refer the employee to other documents for further details.

STATEMENT OF MAIN TERMS OF EMPLOYMENT

This statement, together with the Employee Handbook, forms part of your Contract of Employment and sets out the main terms of your employment with Alpha Supplies Ltd.

Name:	Rachel Pickup
Job Title:	Administrator
Place of work:	Alpha Supplies Ltd, Main Street, Newton, NT3 2PE
Date of commencement of employment:	24 November 200–
Salary:	£12,500 per annum plus employee bonus scheme
Date paid:	28th day of each month by BACS credit transfer.
Hours of work:	37.5 hours each week over 5 days, Monday to Friday.

Holidays: Annual holiday entitlement and holiday pay is calculated on the basis of 20 days for each full calendar year of employment plus 8 statutory public/bank holidays. The annual entitlement increases with length of service, details of which are provided separately. The holiday year runs from 1 April to 31 March and unused holiday entitlement may not be carried forward from one year to the next.

Holiday pay: Normal rate for all holidays including statutory public/bank holidays.

Sick pay entitlement: You will be entitled to paid absence due to sickness or injury under the company's sick pay scheme on the following basis:
Up to 8 weeks' service: Nil; After 8 weeks' service: Up to 2 weeks at full pay and 3 weeks at 50% pay in any 12-month period. You may also qualify for statutory sick pay.

Absence from work: Your supervisor's permission must always be obtained in advance for planned absence. In the case of an unexpected absence you must notify your supervisor by 10 am on the first day whenever possible. To qualify for statutory sick pay and payment from the company's sick pay scheme, you must complete a self-certificate when your absence lasts from 0.5 to 7 days, including Saturday or Sunday. A doctor's or hospital certificate must be produced for all absences exceeding 7 days.

Health and safety at work: All employees must comply with the company's health and safety policy and with all the rules laid down by the Health and Safety at Work Act and all other relevant regulations. A copy of the health and safety policy and the relevant requirements will be issued during your induction period.

Notice: This contract can be terminated by notice by either party as follows:
Notice by employer: Under 1 month's service – Nil. Over 1 month but less than 5 years' service – 1 month
5 years' service or more – 1 week for each completed year of service up to a maximum of 12 weeks
Notice by employee: Under 1 month's service – Nil. Over 1 month – 1 month

Disciplinary rules and disciplinary procedures: The disciplinary rules and procedures are fully explained in the Employee Handbook.

Grievances and grievance procedure: If you have a grievance relating to your employment, you have the right to express this in accordance with the company's grievance procedure. This procedure is described fully in the Employee Handbook.

Date of issue of this document: 20 November 200–

I acknowledge receipt of my Contract of Employment and the Employee Handbook and confirm that I have read and understand these documents. I understand that any amendments to this statement will be agreed with me and confirmed in writing within one month.

Signed .... (Employee)

Signed .... (Employer)

This contract is subject to the information submitted on your application form being correct. The company reserves the right to withdraw any offer of employment or to terminate your employment without notice if any information provided by you is found to be false or misleading.

Terms and conditions within a contract

Although a few employers may issue standard contracts to all their employees, it is more common for contracts to vary both between different workplaces and between different groups of employees. This is because the exact terms and conditions are unlikely to be the same. As long as the employer doesn't include anything which is against the law, this is quite permissible. For example:

▶ **The working hours** for different groups of employees may vary. Some may work shifts, others may be expected to work flexible hours. In this case, the specific starting and finishing hours may be omitted from the contract.

▶ **Holidays**. All employees have the legal right to a minimum of four weeks' paid holidays if they work full-time, but some employers may be more generous than this.

▶ **Sick pay**. There is no legal entitlement to sick pay but many employers will pay their employees for a maximum number of days at their normal rate of pay. The number of days will vary between organisations.

▶ **Notice**. There is a minimum amount of notice that you, or your employer, has to provide if the contract is terminated. Some employers extend this, particularly for senior staff. For example, a manager might have to give longer notice than a more junior employee.

▶ **Job requirements**. These will vary depending upon the type of job and workplace. If you work for an organisation which is very busy at a particular time of the year, your contract may state that you are not allowed to take holidays at this time except by special agreement with a senior manager. If you deal with members of the public, your contract may state that you have to observe company dress guidelines or wear a uniform.

▶ **Disciplinary rules and grievance procedures**. The rules and procedures between individual workplaces will vary so must be checked carefully (see pages 300–1).

▶ **Training**. Your contract may state the training events that you must attend as part of your job and which are provided free by your organisation.

▶ **Health and safety**. Your contract is likely to refer you to the company policies on health and safety. These must be followed by all employees.

▶ **Company rules and regulations**. Some of these may be set out in a separate document. They are likely to cover the procedures to follow if you are absent from work because of illness, the company non-smoking rules, the rules relating to using IT equipment and specific security regulations. Some organisations which are very strict about security may even include specific terms, such as the 'right to search' which gives them the ability to search employees if there is reasonable evidence of theft.

▶ **Codes of behaviour and other company policies**. Again these are likely to be in separate documents, such as an employee handbook. They relate to rules for employees, and also codes of practice within the company. For example, many organisations have codes of behaviour and policies in relation to equal opportunities (see page 302); maternity, paternity and parental leave policies; policies on breaks from work and emergency leave and welfare policies for staff (such as assistance if someone is ill for a long time). The company may also have a promotion policy but would never promise promotion in a contract in case this couldn't be guaranteed.

Employee and employer rights and responsibilities

Both employers and employees have certain legal rights, in respect of their contract of employment and in areas of employment governed by other legislation. A summary of these is shown below.

Legal rights of employers and employees

Employer rights

All employees will

▶ meet the terms of their contracts, i.e.
- work the hours stated
- turn up for work or comply with absence procedures
- do the work they are asked to do as part of their job
- comply with any other conditions stated in the contract

▶ follow health and safety regulations

▶ comply with other laws related to their work e.g. not drinking and driving.

Employee rights

All employers will

▶ pay employees according to their contract

▶ issue an itemised payslip showing gross and net pay and any deductions

▶ comply with all statutory employment laws and regulations

▶ provide a safe working environment

▶ provide appropriate training

▶ allow employees to join trade unions or staff associations

▶ allow them access to confidential records kept on them as employees

You may think that if you read your contract and related documents, sign it and abide by it then that is the end of the matter. This isn't quite true. This is because both you and your employer have two types of rights and responsibilities to each other.

▶ **Express rights and responsibilities** are those that are specifically listed in the contract.

▶ **Implied rights and responsibilities** are those which are supposed to be so obvious that they don't need to be listed. This is fine if you know what they are, but if you don't then you could easily risk doing something wrong.

The implied rights of your employer are that you:

▶ are reasonably competent and possess the skills you claimed you had at the interview

▶ are 'ready and willing' to do the work and will do what any 'reasonable' employee would do in a situation

▶ will take reasonable care of your employer's property (such as equipment and furniture)

▶ will work towards the objectives of the organisation

▶ are prepared to carry out reasonable instructions and requests

▶ will be honest

▶ will not disclose confidential information

▶ will behave responsibly towards other people at work

▶ will be prepared to change when the job changes, for example when new technology is introduced into the workplace.

Your implied rights as an employee are that your employer:

▶ will treat you reasonably

▶ will give you the opportunity to participate in and be consulted on company matters which would directly affect you

▶ will never ask you to do anything which is illegal.

OVER TO YOU!

1 a) Identify six examples of specific information (express terms) you will find in your contract of employment.

b) Suggest three additional items (implied terms) which are not included because they are considered to be so obvious.

2 a) Identify three rights you have as an employee when you start work.

b) Identify three rights of your employer, after you have signed your contract of employment.

3 Rachel Pickup is your friend. She has recently received the document illustrated on page 296. Read this carefully and then answer the following questions.

a) Rachel has been told she has to work flexible hours but thinks she will work only 9 am to 5 pm every day. Is Rachel correct or could her starting and finishing hours change each day?

b) Rachel is planning to get married next year and would like to 'keep back' some of her holidays and have an extra week for her honeymoon, with pay. Can she do this?

c) When Rachel starts work she discovers that a colleague, who has worked there for ten years, has four more days' holiday each year than she does. She doesn't think this is fair and wants to complain. Can she do this? Give a reason for your answer.

d) What must Rachel do if she wakes up one morning with 'flu?

e) Why do you think Rachel wouldn't qualify for sick pay from the first day she starts work?

f) Why do you think it is important that both the employer and the employee must give notice if the contract is being terminated?

▼ OTHER PROTECTION OFFERED BY EMPLOYMENT AND EQUAL OPPORTUNITIES LEGISLATION

All employees have two types of rights at work. They have contractual rights in their contract of employment and **statutory rights**. Statutory rights are the legal rights of everyone in the country. No employer can take these away or reduce them. Contractual rights can only give more rights, not fewer.

Nevertheless, you will not find your statutory employment rights detailed in your contract of employment because it is not your employer's job to tell you what they are. They include:

▶ your rights to be protected against being dismissed unfairly

▶ your rights to be treated fairly and not to be discriminated against

▶ your rights to receive equal pay, if you are doing equivalent work

▶ your statutory rights in relation to all other aspects of your employment which are covered by legislation.

There are too many employment laws to list all your statutory rights in this book. You will learn about more of them if you study at a higher level or at work, if you consult your trade union or staff representative. Only the main ones are outlined below. If you have a keen interest in this area, then you can use the 'Organisations in Business' feature on page 305 to investigate other areas yourself.

Protection against unfair dismissal

Most organisations have two types of procedures in place:

▶ **Grievance procedures** enable employees to complain about the way they are treated

▶ **Disciplinary procedures** enable employers to take action about the way employees behave.

These procedures help to give workers protection against being treated unfairly because:

▶ staff know what to do if they have a problem

▶ staff concerns and complaints are investigated fully by the appropriate manager and the outcomes are recorded

▶ staff can obtain help and advice from a staff representative or trade union official who can accompany them at any formal meeting

▶ all managers know the action they should take in a situation

▶ all staff are treated in the same way.

Grievance procedures

Most concerns and complaints made by staff are dealt with rapidly and informally. Occasionally, however, there may be a serious issue relating to the way an employee is treated which cannot be resolved this way. In this case, the employee may use the official grievance procedures. There are usually three stages:

1 The complaint is investigated within the department. The employee may be accompanied by another person, such as a colleague or trade union representative. The employee's manager has to give a response to the grievance, based on the initial investigations. This may be the end of the matter if the employee is satisfied.

2 The complaint is pursued outside the department. If the problem is not resolved then a more senior manager will consider the evidence and make a decision.

3 The complaint is pursued outside the organisation. Some companies allow for a further interview to be held with an outside third party who will make a recommendation. The Advisory, Conciliation and Arbitration Services (ACAS) is the main body which undertakes this type of work.

Disciplinary procedures

In this case, the employer has a complaint about the employee. There are normally three or four stages:

1 A verbal warning is given for a first or minor offence. It must be made clear to the employee that this is an official warning and not a friendly chat!

2 A written warning is issued for a serious offence or a repeated minor offence.

3 A final warning will be issued if the employee has previously received a written warning and repeats the offence or commits a further offence within a specific period. This warning can be issued straight away if the offence is serious.

4 The employee can be suspended, demoted, transferred or dismissed if the offence is very serious or continually repeated. A very serious offence is often called **gross misconduct**. The employee may be instantly dismissed (sacked). The reasons which are judged to be valid reasons for dismissal due to gross misconduct are usually included in the employee handbook. Examples are shown below.

Disciplinary procedures are in place to prevent anyone being sacked unfairly or anyone being unfairly treated without being able to take action. The procedures will also state the length of time the warning will stay on the employee's record, assuming there are no further offences.

There are laws which state when an employee may, or may not, be dismissed. If an employer ignores these then he or she could be guilty of breaching employment laws, and the employee could take the case to an employment tribunal.

Grounds for dismissal

These are likely to include:

▶ stealing or collaborating with others to obtain company property unlawfully
▶ being drunk or taking drugs
▶ possessing illegal substances at work
▶ fighting on the company premises
▶ wilful disregard of health and safety instructions
▶ deliberate disregard of company policies on Equal Opportunities and harassment
▶ smoking in unauthorised areas
▶ falsifying company records or accounts
▶ persistent unauthorised absenteeism
▶ abusing the computer system (e.g. by hacking into files, stealing a password or sending an offensive email)
▶ conduct outside work that would bring the company name into disrepute
▶ passing on confidential information to a competitor
▶ accepting bribes from a competitor or supplier
▶ deliberate disregard of management instructions
▶ any other substantial reason.

Legal reasons for dismissal

There are four types of dismissal:

▶ **Fair dismissal**. In this case an employee is sacked for a valid reason which is 'reasonable' in the circumstances. Examples include:

– The employee has breached the terms of the contract of employment/company rules, e.g. is a persistent bad time-keeper or has stolen goods.

– There is no work for that person to do. In this case the employee is **redundant**. If the employer has followed the agreed procedures to ensure this is fair, there is nothing the employee can do.

– The employee cannot do the work because he or she has lied about their qualifications or is continually incompetent despite receiving training.

– The employee has been convicted of illegal activities, e.g. a representative has lost his or her driving licence because of drink driving.

– There is some other major reason, such as the employee continually refusing to carry out reasonable requests.

▶ **Wrongful dismissal**. In this case the employer has ignored the minimum statutory notice period. This is allowable only if the employee has committed gross misconduct.

▶ **Unfair dismissal**. This occurs when an employee is dismissed for no good reason. Certain reasons are automatically considered unfair, such as being a trade union member, being pregnant or taking maternity leave, or insisting on statutory employment rights.

▶ **Constructive dismissal**. In this case an employer has made an employee's life so unbearable that he or she is forced to leave.

Anyone who has been dismissed unlawfully can take their case to an employment tribunal. This is an informal court which deals with employment disputes and can award compensation to an employee who is found to have been unfairly treated.

Equal Opportunities and the law on discrimination

Most organisations today have equal opportunities policies and include a statement in their job advertisements and employee handbooks which states that they do not discriminate against anyone 'on grounds of colour, race, nationality, ethnic or national origin, sex, being married or disability.' Although such a policy is not a legal requirement, there are several benefits to having one.

▶ The policy enables a company to state its commitment to equal opportunities and to operate a workplace free from discrimination.

▶ The policy helps to promote good workplace relations.

▶ All managers and staff know the standards they must uphold.

▶ The policy helps to protect the employer against claims of sex, race or disability, discrimination or bullying, harassment or victimisation in the workplace.

▶ An employment tribunal will look more favourably on an organisation which has such as policy – and keeps to it – than one which does not.

You should note that discrimination is not just unlawful when people apply for jobs. It is unlawful at any time, such as when training is being planned, if people are applying for promotion or if employees are being dismissed through redundancy.

There are three specific laws to protect against discrimination. The details are given in the table below. From 2006, discrimination on the grounds of age, religion or sexual orientation will also be unlawful.

Laws against discrimination

The Sex Discrimination Act 1975 (as amended)

This Act makes it illegal for anyone to be discriminated against on grounds of gender (or gender reassignment) – either directly or indirectly. In employment, this applies to recruitment and selection for jobs and promotion, training, the way you are treated in a job, dismissal and redundancy. Discrimination can occur in two ways:

▶ **Direct discrimination** is where one gender is obviously excluded, e.g. 'only men need apply'.

▶ **Indirect discrimination** is where a *condition* would make it more difficult for one sex to comply, e.g. 'only those over 6' 6" need apply'. Even if this is unintentional, the employer is still guilty of discrimination.

There are some exceptions, such as acting and live-in jobs, if the employer can show that a Genuine Occupational Qualification (GOQ) applies to that job.

The Race Relations Act 1976 (as amended by the Race Relations Act 2000)

This Act makes it unlawful for anyone to be discriminated against on grounds of colour, race, nationality or ethnic origin. Again both direct and indirect discrimination applies. An employer advertising 'only white people need apply' would be guilty of direct discrimination. One advertising 'only those who can speak English as their first language need apply' would be guilty of indirect discrimination.

Again there are certain special circumstances under which it may be justified, such as restaurants for authenticity, but these are relatively rare.

The Disability Discrimination Act 1995 (currently applies to businesses with over 15 employees. From 2004 it will apply to all businesses).

This Act is concerned with discrimination against people with disabilities in employment, when obtaining goods and services or buying/renting land or property. The disability may be physical, sensory or mental but must be relatively long term (i.e. last more than 12 months). Employers must not treat a disabled person less favourably than able-bodied persons whether in recruitment, training, promotion or dismissal unless it can be justified. Employers must also be prepared to make reasonable adjustments to the workplace to enable a disabled person to do the job. In this case, discrimination is not divided into 'direct' or 'indirect' but is 'less favourable treatment that cannot be justified'.

Anyone who suffers discrimination, either on grounds of sex, race or disability, can complain to an employment tribunal.

Organisations also have policies to protect employees against harassment and victimisation, because these issues are closely linked to discrimination.

▶ **Harassment** is unwelcome behaviour which upsets, offends or frightens someone. It is sexual harassment if the behaviour is linked to gender and racial harassment if it is linked to ethnic origin or culture. The law protects employees through the Protection of Harassment Act 1997. All organisations should therefore make sure that employees know how to report any instances of harassment or discrimination.

▶ **Victimisation** is when one person is singled out for unfair treatment by another person. This would include being threatened or bullied. Again, if this is linked to gender, race or disability, it is classed as discrimination.

▲ No employee has to put up with unfair treatment

The law and equal pay

For many years, it has been a government aim that men and women who do the same or equivalent work are paid the same wage. The **Equal Pay Act 1970** was introduced to make it unlawful to offer different pay and conditions just because one person is male and another is female. However, it is necessary to ensure that the jobs are 'equal' – especially when the duties of each person may be different.

▶ A woman is doing 'like work' to a man if she is employed in the same type of job. For example, if a woman and a man are both administrators and she mainly produces word-processed documents whilst he produces spreadsheets, they must both receive the same rate of pay.

▶ A woman must be paid the same as a man if the jobs have been rated as the same under a job grading study.

▶ If there has been no official job grading study, a woman can claim her job is of 'equal value' to a man's. In this case, an independent specialist may be appointed to decide on the value of each job. At the time of writing the trade union UNISON is currently claiming that all teaching assistants do work of 'equal value' in Lancashire to male technicians employed by the council and therefore should receive the same hourly rate. You may want to check the outcome at by following the links from www.heinemann. co.uk/hotlinks.

If men and women are paid at different rates, an employer can defend this on two grounds:

▷ There is an important difference between the two workers which has nothing to do with their gender. For example, the man might have worked for the company much longer or be better qualified.

▷ There is an important difference between the two jobs. For example, a man is expected to do heavy cleaning jobs and therefore cannot be compared to a woman who does light cleaning duties.

ORGANISATIONS IN BUSINESS

The Equal Opportunities Commission (EOC) is the official agency which was established in 1975 to help to eliminate sexual discrimination. It works to promote and monitor equal opportunities, provides advice and information, and helps to bring cases for employees who suffer from sex discrimination. Its equivalent bodies are the Commission for Racial Equality (CRE) and the Disability Rights Commission.

According to EOC research, despite the Equal Pay Act, women who work full time still only receive 81% of a man's hourly earnings. In some organisations the pay gap is as little as 5% but in others it is as much as 40%. In 2002, women actually slipped backwards, because men, overall, were awarded higher pay increases. Male white-collar (office) workers earn on average £610 per week whilst female white-collar workers earn an average of £405 per week.

To try to improve this situation, new employment laws were introduced in April 2003 which gave women the right to know how much their male colleagues are being paid to do the same job. A woman first needs to select someone who she think is being treated more favourably and doing an equivalent job in her organisation. She can then submit a questionnaire about his pay to her employer. A man can do the same thing, if he feels a woman is being treated more favourably than him but claims cannot be made about someone of the same sex.

You can find out more about the work of all the Commissions mentioned above by following the links at www.heinemann.co.uk/hotlinks.

Your other main statutory rights

There are a large number of employment laws that give you rights at work, most of which are outside the scope of this book. The key ones you should be aware of – for your own protection – are as follows:

▷ The right to be paid a salary at or above the minimum wage rate if you are over 18. You can find a link to the website that gives the current rate at www.heinemann.co.uk/hotlinks.

▷ The right not to be forced to work more than 48 hours a week, averaged over a 17-week period or to be asked to work more than 40 hours a week or do night work if you are aged 16–18.

▷ The right to choose whether or not to work on a Sunday.

▷ The right to receive maternity, paternity and parental leave in accordance with the law and the right to take time off in a family emergency.

▷ The right to receive redundancy pay if you are dismissed because there is no work for you to do.

▷ The right to apply to work flexibly if you have a child under 6 (or a disabled child under 18), providing you have been working for at least 26 weeks. The employer can refuse your request but only for certain specific reasons.

▷ The right to see computer records about you or paper files which contain your personal details. Your employer can make a small charge for providing this information.

▷ The right to be given reasonable time off to study or train for a qualification up to NVQ2 if you are 16 or 17 and working, or the right to complete training you have already begun if you are 18 when you first start work.

You can find out more details about your rights by following the links to the Employment Relations website at the Department of Trade and Industry from www.heinemann.co.uk/hotlinks.

OVER TO YOU!

1 As a group, decide the most appropriate action that should be taken in each of the following situations. You can choose between:

a) Stage 1 of the grievance procedure – interview with own manager
b) Stage 2 of the grievance procedure – interview with more senior manager
c) Stage 1 of the disciplinary procedure – verbal warning
d) Stage 2 of the disciplinary procedure – written warning
e) Stage 3 of the disciplinary procedure – final warning
f) Summary (instant) dismissal

   i) An administrator has already been warned verbally about repeatedly arriving late but has taken no notice.
   ii) An accounts clerk thinks he is unfairly being given more work to do than his colleagues and, to keep up-to-date, he is having to work late most evenings.
   iii) Two warehouse staff have a fight and one of them is hospitalised. Some valuable equipment is seriously damaged during the incident.
   iv) A new member of staff is always in a rush to leave at the end of the day and staff have now quietly mentioned that on any days the supervisor isn't around she sneaks off early. The supervisor decides to take action before things go too far.
   v) Two administrators think their supervisor is picking on them. They have already seen their manager but got nowhere. They think this is because he is intimidated by her too.
   vi) A member of the office staff is found smoking a cigarette in the stationery store, even though this is strictly forbidden. He has been warned about smoking in unauthorised areas before but, because he is an excellent worker, his supervisor decides to give him one last chance.

2 a) Identify four valid reasons why a member of staff could be instantly dismissed.
   b) Describe two reasons why a member of staff could be dismissed which would not be lawful.
   c) Identify three ways in which disciplinary and grievance procedures help to protect workers against unfair dismissal.

3 a) Identify four reasons why ethical companies choose to have an Equal Opportunities policy.
b) Describe the three main Acts which protect workers against discrimination.

4 Check your knowledge of employment rights by doing the quiz below. Then compare your answers with other members of your group before checking the answers on page 308.

Employment rights quiz

Each of the employees below is dismissed. In each case, decide whether the dismissal was fair or unfair.

1 A canteen worker refuses to wear a hat because she says she looks silly, even though her uniform is fully described in her contact of employment.

2 A part-time female worker complains that she should have been included on a training course run for her department and is sacked for being argumentative.

3 Tom has been having headaches recently which he blames on his computer. He thinks his eyesight is failing. He is sacked because his boss argues that using a computer is a critical part of his job.

4 A male administrator is sacked for downloading offensive material from the Internet during working hours.

5 An administrator is sacked for not having the IT qualifications she claimed to have at her interview. Despite extra training she still cannot cope with the work.

6 A member of staff is sacked for stealing computer supplies from the stock cupboard.

7 A cashier in a supermarket is sacked for refusing to work on a Sunday

8 A female administrator is sacked when her boss finds out she is pregnant. He says the firm is too small to cope with people being away on maternity leave.

9 A female Asian employee complains that a more senior member of staff has been harassing her and making racist comments which upset her. She is sacked for causing trouble.

10 A purchasing clerk is sacked for accepting money from a supplier in return for ensuring that the supplier's company received all his orders.

Key to quiz on page 240

16 – 20   This is a very high score and is admirable, providing you can cope with interruptions, problems and unforeseen delays without losing your cool because your plans have gone awry. Flexibility is also important (see page 248).

12 – 16   A good score. You are a good planner without being fixated on sticking to schedules. Just make sure any weaknesses don't let you down at a critical moment.

8 – 12   Acceptable in your private life perhaps, but you could have a few problems at work. Focus on the key areas to improve in a business environment.

0 – 8   A pretty disastrous score for an administrator! Even your friends and family must tear their hair out at times. At work, remember, you are being paid to think ahead – not to drive everyone mad.

Key to quiz on page 260

16 – 20   You are an excellent time manager but occasionally you focus on completing tasks above everything else. At times, you may need to think a little more about the people around you, too.

12 – 16   You are a good time manager but occasionally you may slip up in one or two areas. Try to focus on improving these.

8 – 12   You could improve quite considerably and gain many benefits. Try to identify 3 areas that could immediately make a difference.

4 – 8   You are not only wasting your own time regularly, but other people's as well. Unless you take urgent action, someone will point this out to you forcibly before too long.

0 – 4   At work, it appears that you think you are being paid to do anything except your job! Few employers will tolerate this for long.

Key to quiz on page 307

1 Fair

2 Unfair

3 Unfair

4 Fair

5 Fair

6 Fair

7 Unfair

8 Unfair

9 Unfair

10 Fair

Follow office procedures to complete tasks

Introduction

Sometimes people worry about the term 'procedures' and what they are. But in fact, you have been using procedures for years to do many things – from sending a text message to reheating a pizza!

In this unit you will learn what procedures are, why they are used and the benefits to the organisation and to you. You will learn about the type of procedures you will find in an office. Even more importantly, you will follow them yourself to carry out a range of tasks.

Procedures are written to help people to do a task in the easiest and safest way – but this does not mean that they are always perfect or never need updating. You will learn about the ways in which office staff can refer to procedures and what happens when procedures need improving.

This unit is essentially practical because you will have to demonstrate that you can follow procedures when you carry out certain office tasks. If you are someone who prefers to 'do' something rather than write about it, then you will not only enjoy this unit but also find that the information it contains will help you to do these tasks in the most effective way. You will then be able to use these skills at work – or adapt them – if the precise procedures you have to use there are slightly different.

▲ Procedures enable us to do things at home as well as in the office

▼ UNIT SUMMARY

This unit is divided into four sections.

▶ **Identify and describe a range of office-based activities requiring procedures**. This section shows you how to recognise and understand basic procedures, and the steps within them, which are used in relation to common office tasks. You will complete a special OCR Candidate Evidence Sheet entitled 'The Purpose of Procedures' with this evidence.

▶ **Explain the purpose of procedures**. This section covers examples of different types of procedures and their outcomes, and helps you to understand about the benefits of procedures to an organisation.

▶ **Follow procedures to carry out office tasks**. This is the main section of this unit and includes procedures relating to the storage and retrieval of information (both paper-based and electronic filing), the reproduction of information using a photocopier, sending and receiving information using a fax machine, controlling stock and processing incoming and outgoing post.

▶ **Review the ways in which procedures are implemented and their effectiveness**. The final section looks at the ways in which procedures are documented and supported and what happens when difficulties are identified and improvements are required. This will enable you to evaluate the effectiveness of procedures you use yourself to complete a certain task.

Assessment

Your assessment for this unit is in three parts.

1 You must be able to demonstrate that you can identify two different procedures involved in each of the following office-based activities and briefly explain what each is intended to achieve:

▶ the storage and retrieval of information (i.e. filing)

▶ the reproduction of information (i.e. using a photocopier)

▶ sending and receiving information (i.e. using a fax machine)

▶ controlling stock

▶ processing incoming and outgoing post.

You will complete a special OCR evidence sheet entitled 'The purpose of procedures' with this information.

2 You will prove you can follow procedures by doing 2 tasks in 2 types of activity from the following list.

▶ If you choose the **storage and retrieval of information**, then you will have to carry out filing tasks on two occasions and, on each one, correctly file and retrieve at least six different documents or files and retrieve at least six pieces of information. You will have to file at least one document in each of the following types of filing system: alphabetical, numerical system and chronological. You will have to create at least three new folders or files, achieve at least three documents or files and demonstrate you can work safely all the time.

▶ If you choose the **reproduction of information**, then on two occasions you will have to follow procedures to carry out photocopying tasks. On each occasion you must copy and assemble at least three documents correctly. You will also have to prove that you can photocopy single pages, multiple pages and make back-to-back copies, reduce and enlarge, and use different paper sizes. You will have to collate and fasten pages, replenish the paper supply when required, keep appropriate records and show you can keep waste to a minimum. Finally, you must show you can report problems as required and work safely at all times.

▶ If you choose **sending and receiving information**, then on three occasions you will have to follow procedures when you use a fax machine. On at least one occasion the document you send must be at least three pages and you will be asked to prepare cover sheets as required and check confirmation reports. On at least one occasion you will have to log and distribute five incoming fax messages. Finally, you must demonstrate that you can replace paper in the machine when this is required and report any problems that occur.

▶ If you choose **controlling stock**, then on at least two occasions you will have to follow procedures to issue stock against a minimum of three requisitions. You will have to show that you can maintain stock records, check stock levels and, on at least one occasion, replenish stock by completing a purchase requisition or order form. At least once, too, you will have to take delivery of supplies and store these appropriately and safely.

▶ If you choose **processing incoming and outgoing post**, then on at least two occasions you will follow procedures to receive and distribute at least ten items of incoming post, including some requiring special attention, and prepare at least six items of post for dispatch, including some special items. You must demonstrate you can determine the correct postage amount, use machines and equipment efficiently and work safely at all times.

Your work will be observed by your tutor, or another qualified person, who will tell you when you have done these tasks successfully.

3 For *each* activity you have undertaken you will write a review about the procedures you followed. You must be able to:

▶ Describe two ways in which the procedures are supported and promoted within the organisation.

▶ Identify any difficulty faced in following the procedures.

▶ Identify at least one possible improvement to the procedure that would increase its effectiveness.

▶ State your opinion of the overall effectiveness of the procedure based on your own experience of it.

You will write (or type) your review commentary on A4 paper. It is expected that you will probably use one A4 page for each of the two activities that you did.

▼ IDENTIFY AND DESCRIBE OFFICE-BASED ACTIVITIES REQUIRING PROCEDURES

A procedure is simply a series of steps to follow to accomplish a task.

▶ You follow a procedure every time you cross the road.

▶ You follow another procedure when you turn on your computer and 'log on' – especially at college where you have to log on to a network and enter your ID and password. If you don't follow this procedure correctly then you can't access the system.

▶ If you are an organised student you will follow yet another procedure when you enter a classroom. You will find somewhere to sit, put your bag on the desk, take out the materials you need and then (hopefully) put your bag on the floor, out of the way. You will also take your coat off so you look as if you are staying there for a while!

Some procedures are absolutely essential in all circumstances; others are less so. Logging on to the computer is in the first category. If you don't do it properly, you don't get in. Other procedures are highly recommended, such as when you cross a road. If you want to run through heavy traffic then you can but it isn't a very good idea.

If a procedure is essential or highly recommended then you are likely to be given it in writing or told how to do it over and over again. You were probably given a copy of your log-in procedures when you started at college. As a child you would have learned the Green Cross code or heard adults repeat it to you many times.

Your tutor would have been less likely to give you written procedures for entering a classroom! This is partly because you would be expected to remember these from school, partly because some of them are common sense and courtesy and also because, if you don't follow them exactly, it doesn't really matter – providing you don't disrupt anyone else.

Other examples of these differences – and how they relate to procedures you see carried out every day by people – are shown below.

Types of procedures

Procedure	Reason	Examples
'Must do' procedures	There are serious consequences (or complete failure) if they are not followed	Giving an injection Fire evacuation procedures Buying goods online Using a cash machine
Highly recommended procedures	The task is done more easily and efficiently	Using office equipment Processing outgoing mail Using a recipe
Suggested procedures	Useful but no one else seriously affected if not followed	Finding a book in a library Caring for a house plant

You will find the same applies to office-based procedures. Some must be followed every time, exactly as written; others are slightly more flexible; many are written down or told to you.

The steps in procedures

All procedures are given as a set of steps. These tell you the best order in which to do a task. In many cases they must be followed exactly in that order to obtain the desired result – such as logging on to a computer.

An excellent example of a book of written procedures is a recipe book. Each recipe gives you a series of steps to follow. If you get these in the wrong order then you could end up with something only half cooked or a culinary disaster. This is even more likely if you miss out a step altogether. If you are following a new recipe for the first time, it is sensible to read it through first, check you understand it, and then follow it line by line if you hope to end with something edible.

If you make a mistake with a recipe, it will not cause total chaos or inconvenience many other people. It is not the same in an office! If you skip part of a procedure here, then you can create havoc. It would be hard to convince your boss that it doesn't really matter that you've misfiled the only copy of a very important document or sent out several items of mail without any postage.

If you are trying to follow a new procedure for the first time it is therefore important that you read it first, check that you can understand it and then follow it – step by step. If you do a task only infrequently, it is sensible to refresh your memory by referring to the procedure again each time, before you start, until it is second nature.

Once you start to look for them, you will see procedures all over the place. They are on the back of many products you buy and on the front of all medicines under 'instructions for use', at the entrance to many buildings telling people where and how to obtain assistance or access and in every handbook or manual that accompanies a piece of equipment – from a DVD player to a washing machine. Sometimes procedures are written as a list of steps, and these may be shown as a flow chart (see page 315). If the procedures are complex there are often diagrams and drawings to explain what is meant.

OVER TO YOU!

1 As a group, decide whether each of the following activities will have:
   a) 'must do' procedures, with very serious consequences if they are not followed
   b) 'recommended' procedures, which enable you to complete a task efficiently and easily every time
   c) 'suggested' procedures – they help but are largely user preference.
      i)   refilling paper in your printer
      ii)   dealing with visitors at reception
      iii) dealing with a bomb threat received by telephone
      iv)   making a piece of toast
      v)   driving round a roundabout correctly
      vi)   sending a text message
      vii) grooming a dog
      viii) sending an email with an attachment
      ix)   setting a burglar alarm
      x)   washing a car

2 The steps issued by one organisation for replenishing a printer cartridge are given below, but they are muddled up. As a group:

a) suggest the correct order for these steps

b) identify any steps which you might not have known about if there had not been a procedure to follow.

    1 Close lid of printer.

    2 Replace with new cartridge and gently push top clip back into position.

    3 Open lid of printer.

    4 Check cartridge number is correct for printer before opening box.

    5 Wait until cartridge holders automatically move to centre of printer.

    6 Put used cartridge into recycling box.

    7 Release top clip of cartridge holder and remove used cartridge.

    8 Open cartridge box, remove wrapping and remove tape from bottom of new cartridge.

3 Identify the procedure you have to follow at college if the fire alarm sounds. Then suggest *why* each step has been included. It will help if you think about the consequences of not doing any of them!

4 a) As a group, decide the steps involved to replenish paper in a printer you use regularly.

b) Explain why this procedure may vary slightly if you use a different printer.

5 Some procedures are written as a list of steps, others are shown in a flow chart. The procedure for greeting visitors in an organisation is given below showing both styles.

a) Identify the main differences between these two styles.

b) Which do you prefer to use? Give a reason for your opinion. (*Note*: this is a personal decision and your views may not be the same as everyone else).

c) Identify three examples of procedures from the list given in question 1) above where you think it would be helpful to have illustrations or diagrams to help the user.

Procedures for greeting visitors

1 Greet visitor courteously.

2 Find out if visitor has appointment and, if so, the person he or she is seeing. If visitor has no appointment contact the Senior Administrator to see if the visitor can be seen. If not, offer alternative appointment.

3 Ask visitors who have appointment or who can be seen at that time to complete the visitors' book

4 Issue visitor pass and point out emergency evacuation procedures on reverse. Inform visitor that the pass must be handed back to reception upon departure. Ask visitor to wait in reception area.

5 Notify member of staff by telephone of visitor's arrival.

6 Remind member of staff if visitor is still waiting after ten minutes.

7 When visitor leaves, collect pass.

▲ Step by step procedures for greeting visitors

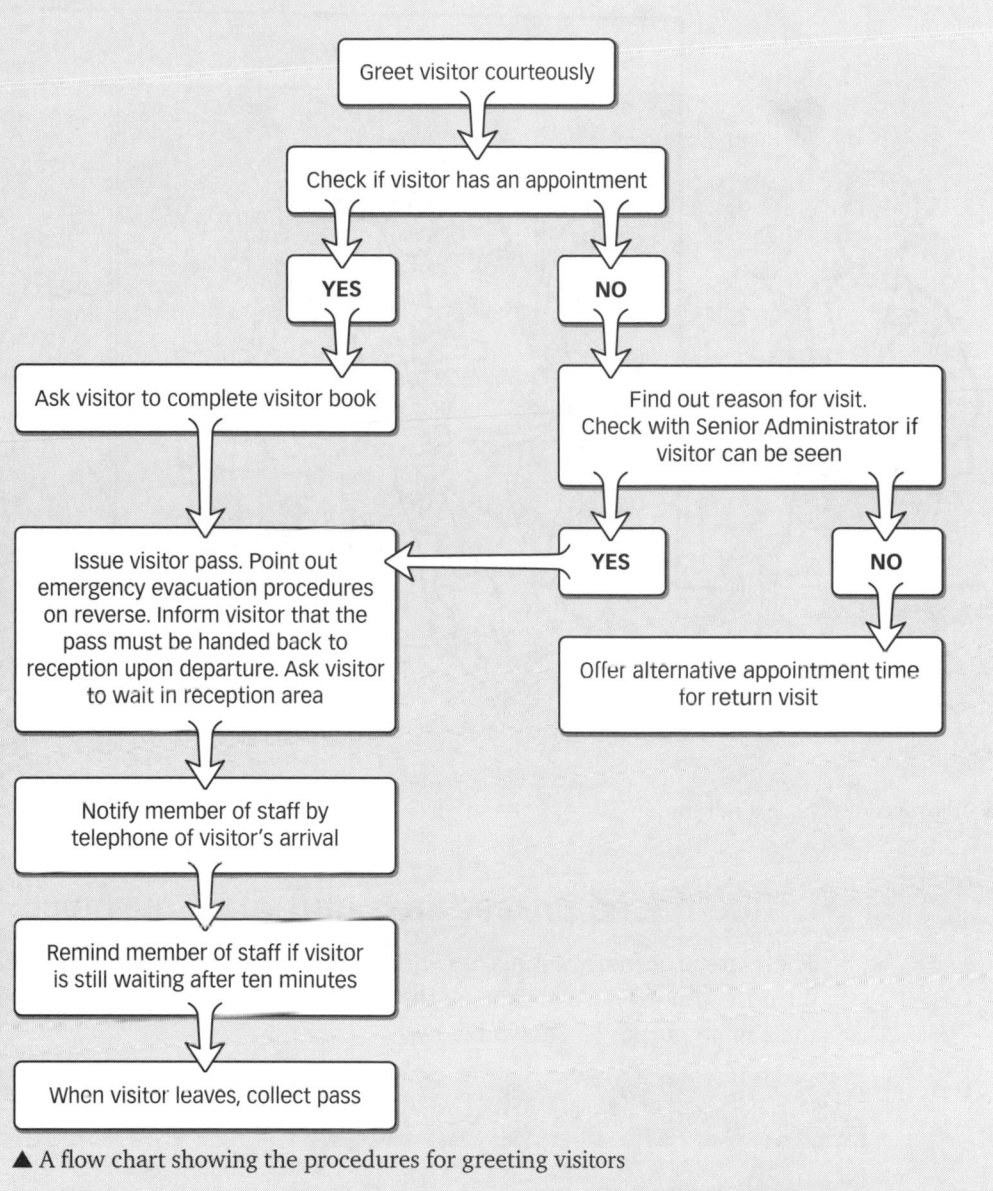

▲ A flow chart showing the procedures for greeting visitors

▼ EXPLAIN THE PURPOSE OF PROCEDURES

All procedures have a purpose. For example, the purpose of fire procedures is to ensure a building is evacuated as quickly as possible and everyone is safe and accounted for. The purpose of having a procedure for greeting visitors in reception is to ensure everyone is dealt with courteously and efficiently, and as quickly as possible, to give a good impression of the company.

In this section you will learn about the office-based procedures you will be using, their purpose and the benefits for the organisation of having these procedures.

▲ All procedures have a purpose

Office-based procedures and their purpose

There are procedures connected with many routine office activities and each of these has a purpose. An example of some of the main activities with which you will be involved and their main purpose is shown below.

The purpose of procedures for office-based activities

Type of activity/procedure	Purpose
Procedure for storing and retrieving information	To ensure that specific documents are stored correctly and can be retrieved easily
Procedure for reproducing information	To ensure that high-quality documents are produced with minimum wastage
Procedure for sending and receiving information by fax	To ensure that fax messages are sent quickly to the correct recipient and that received messages are distributed promptly
Procedure for stock maintenance	To ensure that stock is issued only against authorised requisitions and appropriate stock levels are kept
Procedure for processing incoming and outgoing post	To ensure that incoming post is distributed quickly to the correct recipients and that outgoing post is prepared correctly and dispatched promptly

In addition to an overall purpose for the main activity, there is also a reason why there are several different procedures involved when you undertake some of these tasks.

▶ **Storage and retrieval of information**. Information can be stored in filing cabinets (paper-based storage) or on computer (electronically). The overall purpose of having procedures in both cases is the same, but you will find that the specific steps to follow for different activities will vary. Quite obviously, you wouldn't retrieve information in the same way from a filing cabinet as you would from a computer.

You will find procedures linked to many aspects of filing and each of these has its own purpose, for example:

- a procedure for sorting and classifying documents; the purpose is so that all the documents are always stored in the correct place and order

- a procedure for creating new files; the purpose is so that existing files aren't duplicated by mistake

- a procedure for archiving material; the purpose is so that important or current documents aren't removed or thrown away by mistake.

▶ **Reproduction of information**. You can reproduce information by taking multiple printed copies or by using a photocopier. Again the overall purpose is the same, but some of the procedures you must follow will be different.

Again you can expect to find many procedures related to this activity, each with its own purpose, for example:

- refilling the copier with paper; the purpose is so that the correct paper is used and inserted properly into the copier to minimise paper jams

- reporting problems; the purpose is so that the correct person can deal with all problems promptly and correctly.

▶ **Sending and receiving information**. You can send and receive information by using a fax machine or by email. The purpose here is slightly different because you will use a fax machine to send and receive messages for other people, whereas you use email (normally) only to send and receive your own.

Procedures related to using a fax machine will include:

- using the equipment; the purpose is so that the fax message is sent accurately and speedily to the correct number

- distributing received faxes; the purpose is so that each one is given to the correct person as quickly as possible.

Controlling stock. This task involves several different activities, for which you can expect to find separate procedures, for example:

- recording stock issued; the purpose is so that a continual check can be kept upon current stock levels for each item

- storing new stock; the purpose is so that all stock is kept in good condition and used in rotation.

▶ **Processing incoming and outgoing post**. This involves dealing with the different types of incoming mail, preparing various types of items for dispatch and using a variety of equipment. Procedures will include:

- how to handle different types of incoming post; the purpose is to ensure that each type of item is dealt with speedily and correctly

- how to use postage scales; the purpose is so that the correct postage amount is calculated for every item of outgoing post.

The benefits to an organisation of having procedures

Many procedures relating to office-based tasks are contained in user manuals or handbooks, in other cases they are prepared by the organisation itself. This takes some time and effort but is considered worth doing because of the benefits.

▶ **Organisation**   Procedures enable many activities to be undertaken smoothly and automatically because everyone knows what to do and does it. As a simple example, imagine the accidents there would be on the roads if every driver could do his or her 'own thing' and the chaos and security problems there would be at airports if there were no formal check-in procedures. In any situation where several people are involved in different activities at the same time, procedures enable the activities to be carried out quickly and efficiently because everyone knows what they are doing.

▶ **Clarity of roles**   Procedures help to determine the correct person to deal with different matters. They tell you when you should contact someone else, for example, to report a problem or because a matter is outside your own area of responsibility. This is extremely helpful as it stops you doing anything you shouldn't and prevents two people duplicating each other's work or getting in each other's way.

▶ **Clarity of requirements**   Procedures spell out exactly what is required and what you must do. This is extremely helpful if you are doing something new or do something only occasionally. When you read the procedures about replacing a printer cartridge on page 314 you could see, at a glance, exactly what was required. This means that nothing is missed out or confused.

▶ **Quality assurance and meeting legal requirements**   Procedures help to assure quality. If the procedures are clear and well written they will lead to a successful outcome and high standards of work every time. There is therefore less need to check individual work or contributions for quality, which saves time. This is vital if poor-quality, inaccurate information or unfair treatment to individuals could have legal repercussions. You will therefore find 'must do' procedures in force in this situation – such as for employee grievance and disciplinary issues (see Unit 3, pages 300 and 310) and for dealing with customer complaints (see pages 156 and 162).

▶ **Safe working**   All employers have a legal responsibility to provide a safe working environment for their employees (see Unit 3, page 290). Procedures help to ensure this because they provide safe ways of undertaking activities. Again, where safety is paramount, you will find 'must do' procedures in force, as you have already seen in the case of fire evacuation procedures.

PROCEDURES IN BUSINESS

ISO 9000:2000 is one of a family of quality standards awarded to companies which can demonstrate they have consistent quality procedures relating to the production of goods. These include the way the business purchases raw materials, the way it stores them, how the products are manufactured or assembled as well as how they are inspected, packed and distributed. Some organisations will buy goods only from companies who have obtained this standard because they can then be totally sure that the quality of their supplies is always first rate.

Another set are the ISO 14000 quality standards. These cover environmental management and are awarded to companies which can prove they have appropriate procedures for dealing with environmental issues – including recycling.

In December 2001 the BSI Group announced that a further set of standards had been developed relating to computer-aided assessments. These are procedures for organisations which organise online assessments and include the steps to take to prevent cheating and to ensure that students who have special needs or who lack IT skills aren't disadvantaged. These may be of special interest if you ever do an online assessment as you will know that your exam will be equally fair for everyone.

OVER TO YOU!

1 As a group, decide the purpose of each of the following procedures.
   a) A procedure for recording borrowed files or documents.
   b) A procedure for taking multiple photocopies of a long document, which includes taking a test copy.
   c) A procedure for replenishing the paper in a fax machine.
   d) A procedure for checking new stock when it is delivered.
   e) A procedure for handling items of urgent post for dispatch.

2 Jessica has just taken over as senior administrator and decides to issue some new procedures to her staff. She is horrified by the number of untidy file folders because damaged documents have been included, documents have been punched incorrectly or inserted in the wrong place. She drafts out the following procedure:

1 Mend any torn documents with sticky tape before filing.

2 Remove any paper-clips from multi-page documents and staple the pages at the top left hand side.

3 *Either* use a hole punch with a ruler, set at the A4 position, *or* punch the document centrally by folding it in half, making a crease at the halfway point at the left-hand side and then aligning the crease against the arrow on the punch.

4 Use a heavy-duty punch for bulky documents.

5 Open the file folder, remove plastic tab and open prongs.

6 Insert all documents in date order, so that the most recent document is always on the top.

7 Secure the document with the plastic tab and close folder.

   a) Identify the purpose of this particular procedure.

   b) Explain three benefits to Jessica, her team and her organisation of introducing this procedure.

3 Many people have almost as many problems stapling documents correctly as Jessica's team had in punching documents correctly. If you staple a document so that the text is obscured, on any page, then the document is unusable unless the staples are removed and replaced. If you use a small, desk stapler for a bulky document then the staple will buckle and the end pages will become detached. You should use a heavy-duty stapler instead. Needless to say, the document pages must also be in the right order before you staple them at all and all the edges correctly aligned!

You are Jessica's assistant and she is just as concerned about the quality of stapling in the office as the quality of the file folders. She wants all documents to be stapled at the top left corner, about 1 cm from the top and side of the paper. She also wants staff to remember to keep their fingers out of the way and not to try to staple with the document and stapler in the air rather than on a desk! If they use the electric stapler they must remember to unplug it before trying to unjam it or refill it.

a) As a group, use this information to write a set of procedures for stapling a document correctly.

b) Identify the main purpose of these procedures.

c) Explain three benefits of preparing them.

▼ FOLLOW PROCEDURES TO CARRY OUT OFFICE TASKS

The procedures for all office tasks are written to enable many people to do these activities quickly, efficiently and safely and to deal with problems correctly. There is consistency because every member of a team will do the task in the same way.

Understanding these procedures means you can carry out many new tasks more quickly and organise your work before you start. Even if the procedures vary a little from one organisation or department to another you can make any required adjustments without any problem.

▼ FOLLOW PROCEDURES TO STORE AND RETRIEVE INFORMATION

All organisations need to store and retrieve a wide variety of documents on a daily basis. Many people undertake these activities, therefore there must be set procedures so that each person uses the system in the same way.

Paper-based filing procedures may relate to:

▶ good practice when filing, including the frequency with which documents are filed, accuracy and neatness

▶ the classification methods that are used. These relate to the order in which files are placed

▶ the creation of new files

▶ the storage of old files

▶ the retrieval of information from the files. This is especially important if people want to borrow documents or files

▶ confidential files and the documents within them

▶ the use of filing equipment and related systems

▶ how to work safely when filing.

Documents can also be stored electronically. You store a document this way every time you save an email or save a document on your hard or floppy disk. Some organisations go a step further. They store all their documents on computer, rather than in a filing cabinet. The documents are scanned into the system and then saved, using special software that indexes the documents so that they can quickly be retrieved. The ability of individual users to access documents can be varied, so that confidentiality can be protected. The amount of space that can be saved is incredible, given that ten CDs can hold the equivalent of 30 filing cabinets. In addition, filed documents can never be lost or become tattered and are always protected in the case of fire or any other type of disaster.

Obviously, in this case the type of procedures will be different and will relate to activities such as:

▶ checking documents before they are scanned, to make sure that they are complete and in the right order

▶ dealing with documents that cannot be scanned in the normal way, because they are handwritten or contain line drawings or illustrations

▶ entering the correct key indexing words, so that each document can be easily found

▶ entering additional protection, to restrict the viewing of confidential documents

▶ processing the original paper document, after it has been electronically stored. If they were all retained, it would defeat one of the main reasons for electronic filing, which is to save space.

PROCEDURES IN BUSINESS

If you work for the government in the future, then you will become involved in electronic filing because the government has a target of keeping all its records electronically by 2004. Because formal records are involved, rather than just documents, the rules which will govern the way the information is stored, retrieved and – eventually – destroyed will be very strict indeed.

A variety of procedures must be put in place to manage this system, so that all information is captured electronically. At present most people are in charge of their own emails, and can decide which to delete and when. They also store the documents they create on their own local disk drive or on the network, but decide themselves which title to give to some documents and when to delete them. Controlling all these aspects so that the whole system works effectively is a complex task.

Experts consider that eventually all business organisations will have to address this problem so that all information is stored and retrieved in the same way, because the current 'mix' of paper and electronic storage is unsatisfactory. Companies that want to move towards this can either buy the equipment they need or can use an agency to do the work. These scan and index documents for a monthly fee, and even store the originals. You can find out more about document management systems and electronic filing by following the links from www.heinemann.co.uk/hotlinks.

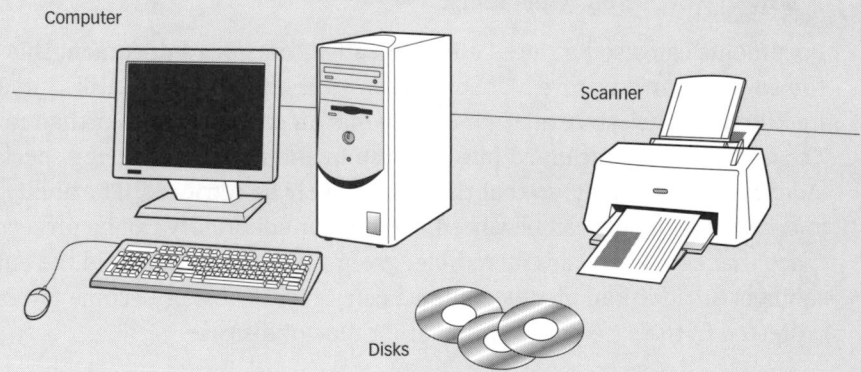

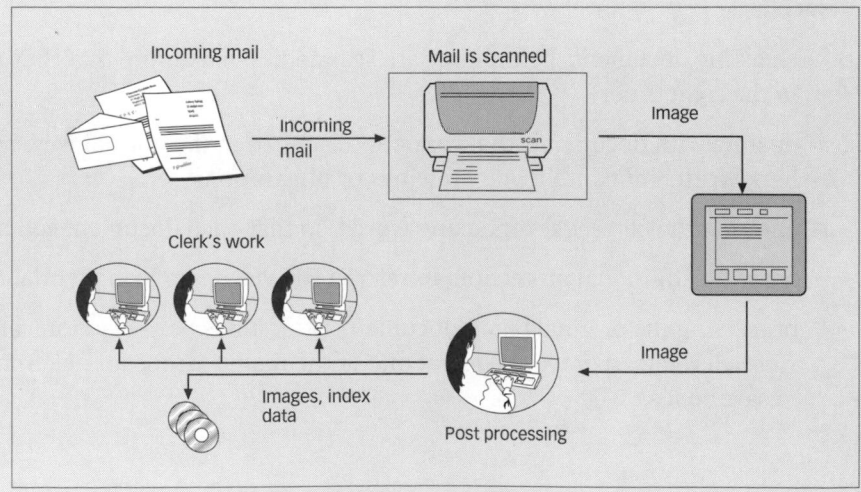

▲ Electronic filing is the way forward for many business organisations

Electronic filing is sometimes known as electronic document management systems (EDMS). These systems are expensive and, if you are undertaking your OCR assessment at college, it is far more likely that you will be involved in paper-based filing. For that reason, this is the main focus of this section. However, this will also help you to understand the type of processes that have been considered when electronic filing systems have been designed.

Good practice when using a paper-based filing system

Everyone who uses a filing system has certain basic responsibilities, even before they start to store or retrieve files. These ensure that all the file folders, and all the documents within them, are kept up-to-date, neat and tidy.

Good practice means doing things properly – from the moment a document arrives on your desk for filing. For that reason, you may find that the procedures relate to different stages in the filing process.

Stage 1 – storing documents for filing

Documents for filing should be kept in a large basket or paper tray, near to the filing cabinet. Some organisations ask staff to put a small 'release mark' (normally a small tick or cross) on documents to be filed, so that current papers are not filed by mistake.

Stage 2 – pre-sorting documents for filing

Ideally documents should be filed daily so that all the files are always up-to-date, but this may not be possible. Some files may have been borrowed by users, so cannot be updated immediately, or you may have other priorities which mean that the filing has to wait for a day or two. The danger then is that the files are out of date and the filing basket is piled high with paper. It is normally at that precise moment that someone needs a file urgently and you have to search through every piece of paper to get it up-to-date as fast as you can!

This situation is far less of a problem if you regularly pre-sort documents. If you use an alphabetical system (see page 325), then you sort all the papers into alphabetical order, grouping those for the same file together. You can then store these in an expanding or concertina file under the correct letter. If you have a numerical system, just put the file number on the top of each document and order them numerically.

The other advantage of pre-sorting is that when you are putting the papers in the files, you work methodically through the letters or numbers, rather than going all over the place and repeatedly going back to the same file.

Stage 3 – preparing documents for filing

You learned about this on page 320, when Jessica's staff were making a mess of it! All paper-clips should be removed from documents because they trap other papers behind them and replaced with staples. Torn papers should be repaired before they get worse. Documents should be punched squarely so that the folder looks tidy, not a higgledy-piggledy mess.

Stage 4 – filing the documents

Each folder should be located and removed from the cabinet. Take out only one folder at once in case you are interrupted and have to stop filing for a time, or else several folders will be missing from the system and no one will know where they are. Take out a folder gently, particularly if it's heavy or bulky, when you should slide your hand underneath to support it. Check you have the correct folder before you start putting documents into it and remember that the most recent document should always go at the top.

Replace the folder in *exactly* the right place and behind the correctly labelled tab. Special suspension pockets (see page 333) hold the folders in position. Ideally these are continuous, so that files can't fall between them. If they are not then you need to be doubly carefully or the folder could slide down to the floor of the cabinet drawer where no one will see it.

Stage 5 – coping with problems and checking the procedures

It can be extremely irritating to have twenty documents to file and find that you can store only five of them without encountering a problem. But it is never wise to simply dump the remaining fifteen papers back into the filing tray and ignore them, because they will still be there tomorrow – alongside the next day's papers and problems!

There will usually be separate procedures to tell you how to deal with problems such as:

▶ documents for which there is no file folder

▶ documents which could go in more than one folder

▶ missing files

▶ file folders which are too full to fit anything else into them

▶ drawers which have folders too tightly packed so you can't lift anything out without damaging it.

Some of these problems are covered in the summary of good practice procedures shown below, others you will learn how to solve as you progress through this section.

Using classification methods

All files are stored in a particular order. They may be stored alphabetically, numerically or chronologically. In each case there are certain procedures to make sure you are using the system properly.

Summary of good practice procedures for filing

DO

▶ File regularly (preferably daily) to avoid a backlog and staff referring to files which don't include the latest information.

▶ Pre-sort documents first and do this every day, so that recent documents can be found quickly.

▶ Prepare papers for filing – mend torn documents, remove paper-clips and replace with staples.

▶ Punch documents squarely.

▶ Lift out folders carefully, especially when they are heavy or bulky.

▶ Replace each folder carefully in the correct place.

DON'T

▶ Guess where something should be filed. If you are unsure, ask.

▶ Tug out a file folder by its tab – which will probably break off in your hand.

▶ Remove more than one folder at once from the system.

▶ Panic if you can't find a folder – check the borrowed files log.

▶ Put too many documents in an already bulky file. The normal procedure is to start a new file and label each folder with the dates, e.g. Jan–May 2004; May 2004–.

▶ Start a new file for every new name; instead check the procedures for starting a new file first.

▶ Overload a filing cabinet with too many file folders; instead check the procedures for archiving old files.

Alphabetical filing

In this case all the file folders are stored in alphabetical order. There are three variations you may find:

▶ **Alphabetical by name** is used when the **name** of the person or organisation is the most important factor, such as for customer files or personnel files. This is the same system you will find in the *Phone Book*, which is a good reference guide if you are ever worried about where a certain file should be placed.

▶ **Alphabetical by location** is used when the **place** is the most important factor. This is often called **geographical filing**. It is used by companies who have branch or sales offices around the country or customers all over the world.

▶ **Alphabetical by subject** is used when the **topic** is the most relevant item. Many managers and directors prefer this system because they can store documents under the key areas of work with which they are involved. A variation on this system is filing by product. This system is often used in purchasing offices. If a particular topic would cover many different items, then the files are often subdivided. For example, the heading 'IT equipment' could be sub-divided into computers, printers, scanners, etc. The Yellow Pages is an excellent example as entries are classified by subject.

Rules are required for all users of the system so that all files are kept in the right order and everyone knows where to look for a file. This may seem a simple matter but problems can easily occur. For example, if you are filing alphabetically by name:

▶ Would you put JPA Fabrics under 'J' or under 'F'?

▶ Which should go first, Six Steps Club or Seven Trees Hotel?

- Does 'The Playpen Nursery' go under 'T' or 'P'?
- Should you put St Anne's School under 'S' and, if so, does it go before or after Salford University?

You can imagine the chaos that would ensue if everyone simply guessed what to do! The table below shows you the rules to follow.

Rules for alphabetical filing

Rule to follow	Example of filing order
PEOPLE	
Surname first	Park Joanne
Short names before long	Park Joanne Parke Keith
If names are identical, follow first name(s) or initial	Parke Keith Parke Kevin
Nothing always comes before something	Jacobs P Jacobs Peter Jacobson Paul
Treat Mac and Mc as Mac and file before 'M'	MacDonald S McGowan L Marlow T
Ignore apostrophes	Oldfield J O'Ryan P Otterburn M
ORGANISATIONS	
Ignore the word 'The'	Top Shop, The
Change numbers into words	Five Star Travel Four Seasons Hotel
When names are identical, use street or town to decide order	Kenton Car Hire, Swindon Kenton Car Hire, Watford
Initials come before full names (ignore '&' or 'and')	JA Supplies J & A Footwear JTL Associates Jackson Engineering
Treat 'Saint' and 'St' as Saint	Sainsbury's J plc St Augustine's School Sale Motors
File public bodies under name, or town/city if the names are identical	Cheshire County Council Chorley Borough Council Connexions Service, Cheshire Connexions Service, Cumbria Customs & Excise, Her Majesty's

In all alphabetical systems, if there are too few documents under one name, location or topic to warrant a separate file, a **miscellaneous file** is often started. There may be just one large miscellaneous file (under 'M') or a separate one under each letter of the alphabet – usually at the front of that letter section. However, some organisations don't like miscellaneous files and claim that they just become a dumping ground for tricky to file papers and never get cleared out regularly. It's also true that few people look in this file when they are searching for something. This is where procedures are invaluable – you can check immediately the organisation's policy on keeping miscellaneous documents and find out where, if at all, they are stored.

Numerical filing

A numerical system is mainly used for larger systems which would quickly become congested under frequently used letters of the alphabet, because this would mean constantly reorganising the files. In this system each file is given a number, such as a customer number, an employee number or a supplier number.

There are two types of numerical systems:

▶ **Numerical by sequence**. In this system each new file is simply given the next available number. The exact procedures will tell you whether earlier numbers can be reused, if these become available when old files are removed. This is unlikely if the system is linked to a computer database, which automatically always moves forwards one number at a time.

▶ **Alpha-numerical**. In this system the files are numbered under the letters of the alphabet, e.g. A1, A2, etc. or there is a specific letter code before the number. For example, a company could have different codes for each department so S1, S2 = Sales documents; P1, P2 = Purchasing documents and PR1, PR2 = Production – and so on.

The advantage of numerical systems is that they can be very large indeed, so they are ideal in organisations such as hospitals, where thousands of patient files are stored. The disadvantage is that you cannot remember the number of each file, so you need a special index to find it. To help to speed up this process, many organisations which use numerical systems routinely quote the reference number on all their documents. This enables you to file a document quickly, without using the index, but can't help you if you are simply asked to find someone's file. In this case an alphabetical index is essential. An example of how an index links to numerical files is shown below. You will learn also more about these on page 335.

Numerical filing

Numerical file order		Alphabetical index order	
29071	Bradley, Lee	Bradley, Lee	29071
29072	Shaw, Marian	Heelis, Jamie	29074
29073	Sayed, Rehmani	Salifu, Samuel	29075
29074	Heelis, Jamie	Sayed, Rehmani	29073
29075	Salifu, Samuel	Shaw, Marian	29072

Chronological filing

This is a variation of numerical filing only this time the date is the number used to file the document. This system is routinely used by travel agents to file tickets (under date of travel) and by finance departments to file bank statements and petty cash vouchers.

It obviously helps if the date is written in the same format each time and this is often specified in the procedures to follow (for example, either 27.01.72 or 27/1/72 or even 27.01.1972).

OVER TO YOU!

1. Check your ability to file alphabetically by name by rearranging the list below into the order the files should be placed in a filing cabinet.

St Stephen's School	O'Connor J	Sam Tomkins
7 Seas Travel	S & J Plastics	Sound & Vision
OJB Suppliers	W K Thomas	Open Learning Inc
The Stationery Office	Oz Travel	The Trade Centre
Department for Transport	Samson & Watts	Sam's Taxis

2. Your organisation has branches all over England and the files for each one are kept geographically, firstly by county and then by town. For example, in East Sussex, the Brighton branch would be filed before the Eastbourne branch.

The counties and towns below are all muddled up. Put these into the exact order you would find them in a filing cabinet.

Staffordshire	Somerset	Shropshire	Suffolk
Stoke-on-Trent	Taunton	Shrewsbury	Southwold
Burton-on-Trent	Yeovil	Bridgnorth	Ipswich
Stafford	Bridgwater	Telford	Stowmarket

3. A senior administrator in a college keeps her files in subject order. She groups these under main headings but sometimes sub-divides these. She has asked you to type out a reference list so she can see at a glance the headings she uses. Prepare this list in strict alphabetical order.

Course list – part time	Advertising – courses
Examination results	Timetables
Supplies – stationery	Maintenance – building
Advertising – staff	Supplies – equipment
Training – IT	Contracts – staff
Supplies – IT	Enrolments
Maintenance – equipment	Training – other
Contracts – supplies	Course list – full time

4. Rearrange the following list twice to show, first, how the files would be ordered in the cabinet and, secondly, how the files would be listed on an alphabetical index.

Bartram C	73092	Bennett D	72039
Beardsley K	71037	Banks C M	71948
Beneduce S	72809	Bowman T	73991
Banks C	73109	Bellusci N	72358
Bibi Z	72820	Banda K	73987
Bargh S	71840	Barucha S	71003
Beardsmore K	72374	Bhojani N	71098

5 The administrator at college has listed some GCSE examinations in alphabetical order. She now wants these rearranged chronologically under the date when the first examination for each subject will be held. If more than one examination is scheduled for the same date, these should be in alphabetical order. Prepare the list that she requires.

Art and Design – 20 May	Geography – 8 June
Biology – 4 June	Gujarati – 12 June
Business Studies – 11 June	History – 9 June
Drama – 22 May	ICT – 18 May
Design and Technology – 5 June	Media Studies – 19 May
English – 10 June	Sociology – 9 June
French – 20 May	Spanish – 21 May

Problems classifying documents

Procedures for classifying documents will work properly only if users take care when they are filing. Sloppy mistakes can cause endless problems, for example:

▶ The name of two people or organisations can be very similar, e.g. J. Allen and J. Allan; Howarth and Parker or Haworth and Pickles. It is all too easy to select the wrong file in error!

▶ Numbers can easily be transposed. If you do this in error you could easily find yourself hunting for file 60398 rather than 60938. Even worse is copying the wrong file number on the top of a document to be filed and then putting it in the wrong folder.

▶ Documents can easily be placed in the wrong subject file if you don't check the master list and all the sub-divisions for a category carefully.

▶ In some cases, the document could easily appear to go in two or even three files. For example, if you are subject filing a document on an IT staff training day, should this go under 'IT', 'staff' or 'training' – or in all three? In this situation, you normally need to cross-reference the document. How to do this is explained below.

Cross-referencing

This procedure is used when a document can go in more than one place. Some organisations insist that, in this case, the document itself is copied and one copy put in every file. The problem with this is that the file folders become full very quickly and much of the copying may be unnecessary. For that reason, in other companies, you will be expected to **cross-reference** the document.

Cross-referencing means you put the document in the most likely place and put a reference note in all the other files. If you want to see how this is done, look in *Yellow Pages* again. If you look for an entry under the wrong subject title, it promptly tells you where to look for the entry you want.

Another time when cross-referencing is used is in an index system (see page 335). For example, a company may change its name so the file folder is renamed or a firm may expand and start up another branch or division and yet your supervisor wants all documents kept in the original file. In this case, to save people looking in the wrong place or going to the wrong file, it is sensible to put a reference in the index, for example:

> **Heinemann** – see under Harcourt Education, 6015

Creating files

There are normally specific procedures relating to the creation of files to avoid 'tiny' files which contain only one or two papers and to prevent duplication of existing files. It is all too easy to prepare a new file by mistake – especially if you are filing by subject. For example, your college could receive a letter from the Connexions service about careers. Unless you checked very carefully, you could start a new 'Connexions' file when you should put the document under Careers. For that reason, a master file list is often kept, which is checked before a new file is made out. In addition, you may have to obtain permission to start a brand new file.

An example of a procedure for creating a file is given below. Bear in mind that this may be different for many reasons, for example if the organisation doesn't have miscellaneous files (such as in a medical practice, where each patient must have an individual file) or if the file numbers are generated by computer.

Example procedure for creating a file

1 No new file must be started until there are at least six documents on a topic or organisation. Until that point, the documents must be stored in the appropriate miscellaneous file.

2 A new file must be created only by agreement with the senior administrator.

3 All new files must be listed on the master file list, according to the correct classification.

4 The new file folder must be completed clearly with the title of the file printed on the tab.

5 The visual tab in the cabinet must match, exactly, the title on the file folder.

6 All documents must be secured in the new file in the usual manner.

Archiving files

There is normally a routine procedure to review files which are old, haven't been used for some time or have come to the end of their natural life – for example, expenses which cover a particular financial year. The action to take often depends upon the contents, for example:

▶ Some files can be destroyed, such as files relating to an organisation which has ceased to exist.

▶ Some files can be destroyed, but only after a certain time period has elapsed. This is because there are specific rules or laws relating to their retention. For example, tax records must be kept for at least six years.

▶ Some files are archived and never destroyed. **Archiving** means putting into long-term storage. For example, all solicitors do this as they do not know when a legal case or claim may be resurrected, e.g. a divorce settlement with children involved where there may be a later dispute over access.

Because of the complexities involved, there is usually one person in charge of deciding which files can be disposed of and which must be archived. Opposite is an example of the procedures you may see, but you should be aware that these are likely to vary considerably, depending upon the type of organisation.

Example procedure for archiving a file

1 A file should be considered for disposal or archiving when one of the following applies:
   a) no papers have been added for two years or more
   b) the contents of the papers cover a period of more than five years
   c) the file has reached the end of a natural cycle, e.g. a member of staff has left the company.

2 All requests for disposal or archiving must be referred to the senior administrator.

3 When a file is closed, the date of closure must be written on the front of the file and entered onto the master file list.

4 The documents held in files for disposal must be shredded. Where possible the file folder should be reused and any transparent pockets or other storage items removed for reuse.

5 Files for archiving must be clearly labelled with an 'archive' label and placed in a secure storage box. The name of the file must be entered on the box label.

6 The archive storage box must be placed in the basement, or some other place for long-term storage, in accordance with the archiving classification procedure.

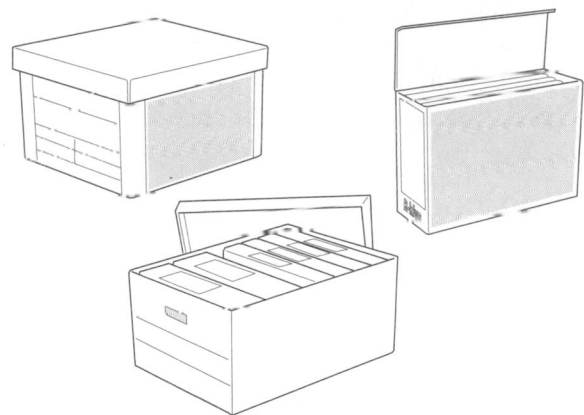

▲ Some files must be archived and never destroyed

Procedures for retrieving information from files

There are two main reasons why you will need to retrieve a file or a document it contains:

▶ You have to add a new document to the file.

▶ Someone needs to refer to a file to obtain information, which is why files are kept in the first place. Almost all organisations have specific procedures to control this process, otherwise a file could simply 'go missing' with no one having the slightest idea where to find it.

The procedures for adding a document to a file are straightforward and unlikely to be spelled out separately. Quite simply, you retrieve the file, insert the document correctly and return the file folder promptly to the system.

The procedures for lending a file or a document are likely to be far more specific but will vary according to the exact system used. In some organisations, no documents can be lent – only the complete file. In others the files are 'logged out' on a computer system which automatically generates reminders when the file must be returned. On other systems, all files must be returned within a specific time period. The following, therefore, is simply an example of the type of procedures you are likely to meet in this situation.

Example procedure for lending a file

1 Under normal circumstances, only complete files must be loaned. Individual documents must never be removed. If an individual document is required from a large file, this must be photocopied and the original returned to the file folder.

2 The borrowed file must be entered in the file log. All the following headings must be completed: name of file; date borrowed; borrower; date to be returned.

3 An 'out card' must be placed where the folder is normally kept. The date of expected return must be entered on this.

4 No files must be lent for an unspecified period. If the borrower will not state the date of expected return, refer the request to the senior administrator.

5 The file log must be checked daily and reminders sent to the borrowers of any outstanding files. If the borrower wishes to extend the loan period this can only be agreed after the file has been returned for updating, so that outstanding documents can be inserted.

Handling confidential information

Many files contain confidential information, such as:

▶ personal information on individuals, such as their age, address, medical history and details of personal relationships or problems

▶ financial information about individuals, such as how much they earn or how much money they owe

▶ financial information about your organisation or department

▶ future business plans of your organisation and decisions made at meetings

▶ information on customers, clients or contacts which would be invaluable to a competitor.

All organisations have strict procedures to cover highly confidential files and you may find you are not allowed access to these yourself. However, you may still handle documents which need to go into these. If you worked for a doctor, solicitor or accountant you would be dealing with highly sensitive information all day and would never be expected to discuss the contents of a file with anyone outside work.

Below is an example of the type of procedures you may find in operation in a business organisation where certain files contain highly sensitive information.

Example procedure for handling confidential files

1 All confidential files must be marked on the cover with a red sticker and the word 'confidential'.

2 These files must be stored in the red cabinets in each department and the cabinet must be kept locked at all times. The departmental manager and the senior administrator are the only key holders.

3 Access to these files is only by agreement with the senior administrator, who is personally responsible for keeping these files up-to-date, or the departmental manager.

4 No confidential files must be removed from the office without the express agreement of the departmental manager.

5 When confidential files are destroyed, the contents *must* be shredded and never placed in the waste or recycling bins without being shredded.

6 The senior administrator is responsible for archiving confidential files. These are kept in a secure area in the basement.

PROCEDURES IN BUSINESS

Surveys have shown that a large number of companies do not have adequate procedures for disposing of confidential information. In some cases sensitive documents are thrown away carelessly without thinking about the contents, despite the fact that the safe disposal of confidential information is now a legal requirement under the Data Protection Act.

Even in companies where all documents are shredded, there have been concerns that confidential documents are still stored on computer systems and back-up media. To help to solve this problem, the latest type of shredders have a heavy-duty motor which can shred floppy disks, CDs, DVDs, staples, paper-clips and credit cards – in addition to paper. Some are so powerful that whole files can be shredded in one go.

▲ Shredders must be used with caution

An alternative for companies who cannot afford to buy an expensive shredder is to use a shredding service.

If you do use a shredder, do so carefully! American shredder manufacturer Fellowes lists machines damaged by a variety of items dropped in by mistake, including scissors and paper knives. It also receives continuing reports of people leaning over them wearing a necktie or dangling jewellery – despite clear warning notices – and has warning tales of highly important original documents shredded by accident. Despite all these hazards, shredding is apparently a very therapeutic activity. If you're feeling stressed, it appears the best tonic is to go shredding for a while – and presumably focus on the person who got you into that state as you feed the paper through the cutters! To find out more go to www.heinemann.co.uk/hotlinks and follow the links to useful shredding websites.

Using filing systems and equipment

There is a large range of filing equipment and storage systems that may be used in an office.

Standard equipment

▶ **Vertical filing cabinets** are the most common type of filing equipment. They consist of a metal or wooden cabinet with a number of large drawers, four being the most usual. Inside the drawers there are usually suspension pockets which hang from side to side, often in a continuous row. Each pocket has a tab at the front giving the name of the file folder it contains.

Many cabinets are toughened to be resistant to fire and impact – so that if they were thrown down stairs or even out of a window in an emergency they wouldn't break open. All cabinets can be locked and today are fitted with a safety mechanism so that only one drawer can be opened at once – to prevent the cabinet tilting forward on the user.

▶ **Lateral filing cabinets** are large, open cupboards. Instead of shelves you will see rows of suspended pockets hanging from one side to the other, each with tabs on the side. The file folders are inserted sideways, usually to the right of the tab. A sliding door or blind is pulled down when the cabinet is not being used to protect the files from dust.

A variation is a multi-purpose lateral cabinet which has rows of pockets and some shelves designed to hold lever arch or box files (see page 335).

▶ **Horizontal filing cabinets** consist of a series of shallow drawers in a metal cabinet. The drawers may be very small – to hold A4 paper – or very large indeed, to hold architectural drawings up to A0 size. Because the drawers are shallow they are ideal for holding small quantities of special documents.

▶ **Rotary filing systems** are similar to the rotating display stands you see in many shops. They hold A4 lever arch or box files, or special folders, and spin round to give all-round access to the files.

Storage materials

A variety of materials are available for holding documents within a filing system:

▶ **File folders** are used to store most papers. They are available in a variety of colours and with optional fastenings. Some organisations colour-code their files, which makes it easier to identify different categories. In most organisations the papers are fastened into the folders but in others you may find that the papers are put in the folder but not secured.

- **Document wallets** (sometimes called **envelope wallets**) are used for transporting small quantities of documents or storing them on a temporary basis.

- **Ring binders** are used for storing small quantities of documents on a particular topic.

- **Lever arch files** are a larger version of ring binders, for greater quantities of documents on a certain topic.

- **Box files** are used to store documents which cannot, or must not, be hole-punched, such as important legal documents, presentation documents, catalogues and bound reports.

- **Index pages** or **dividers** are used to separate documents filed in ring binders or lever arch files.

Index systems

An index system is essential to guide users to files stored in numerical or alpha-numerical order. Index systems may also be used to keep small amounts of important information on particular topics, such as individual customers, suppliers or products, as you will see when you learn about controlling stock on page 360.

Today many indexes are created and maintained on computer, because the information can be entered and edited easily and specific entries can be found quickly by searching on specific criteria. If the system is large or electronic filing is in operation, then special software is used (see page 321). On a smaller system an index list can be created on a word processing package or more detailed records held on a database.

The more traditional systems include:

- **index cards** which are stored in a small cabinet with the key information written at the top. Guide cards help the user to quickly locate a card under a particular letter. The size of the cards means that additional reference information can be included on them.

- **Rotary index cards** are slotted on to a small drum in a metal or plastic box. The cards and the box are both small so can easily fit on a person's desk. These are ideal if only a small amount of information needs to be stored and is frequently referred to.

You use an alphabetical file index system by looking for the name and reading off the number alongside. This is the number under which you will find the file you want. *Never* remove the index card from the system – write down the number instead; otherwise you can easily put down the card and then forget to return it to the system.

Maintaining safe filing systems

As you have already seen, many types of filing equipment are designed to promote safety with 'anti-tilt' devices installed. It is also important that filing equipment is positioned so that it isn't a hazard – even when it is being used and a drawer is open. As a user of the system you also need to take certain precautions:

- always close a filing cabinet drawer when you are not actually using it

- always make sure the heaviest items are kept in the bottom drawer of a cabinet for stability – not two teaspoons and a jar of coffee!

- never carry too many file folders at once – so you can't see over the top

- always use a safety kick stool to reach items in a high cabinet.

PROCEDURES IN BUSINESS

One of the largest suppliers of storage systems in the UK, Kardex, has helped businesses as diverse as QVC (The Shopping Channel) and the Lancashire Constabulary to reorganise its methods of storage and filing procedures. Their DataStack unit can hold up to 250,000 documents and can be operated from a PC. Once the code number for the file is entered, the folder is automatically retrieved and presented to the user at working height. The system is estimated to save 50% of floor space over normal cabinets and special file tracking software enables the operator to monitor borrowed files and those due for archiving or disposal.

You can find out more about a wide range of modern storage systems at the Kardex website. The site not only gives you information about a wide range of systems but the images and graphics will help you to understand how the equipment operates – from lateral cabinets and their advantages to the more sophisticated systems. You can also find out how Kardex helps businesses that want to change to electronic filing if you go to www.heinemann.co.uk/hotlinks.

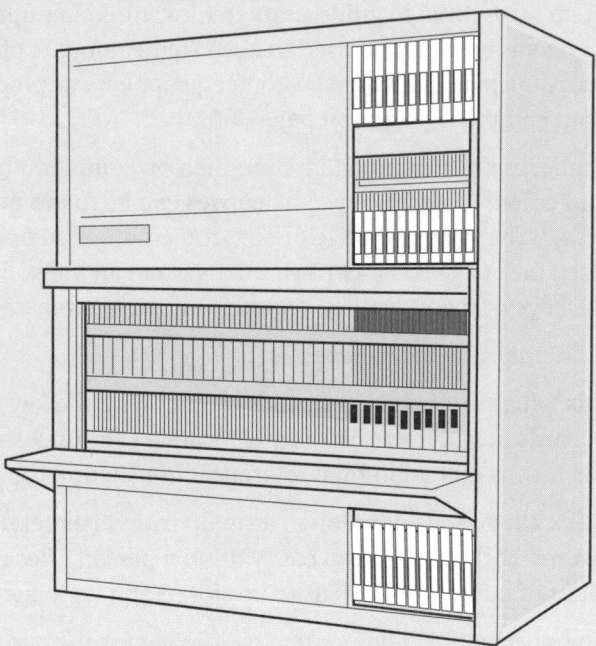

▲ A modern data storage system

OVER TO YOU!

1 Identify the filing systems you will be using for your assessment and then check that you know the answers to each of the following:

a) The procedure you must follow when you have to store a document in a file.

b) The procedure you must follow when you are retrieving information from a file.

c) The procedure to follow to open a new file or folder.

d) The procedure to follow to archive a file.

e) The procedure for cross-referencing, i.e. whether you should cross-reference documents which can go in more than one file or photocopy them.

2 Explain, in your own words, the purpose for each of the procedures you identified in **1** above.

3 Many problems are covered by procedures, but not all of them. This is because no one who writes procedures can possibly think of every difficulty that could occur. For that reason, on some occasions you need to refer to the procedures whilst on others you have to use your common sense.

Maria is filing documents when she encounters the following problems. In each case decide:

a) whether there is likely to be a procedure you should check to find out what to do, or whether you should use your own initiative

b) what the procedure – or your supervisor – would tell you to do in each case.

Check your answers with your tutor.

i) She has a bound report to file which must not be punched.

ii) She has made out a new folder but mis-spelt the name and there isn't enough room on the tab to correct it.

iii) She can't find a folder she knew she returned to the cabinet this morning.

iv) She has documents to file under both Smith and Patel but there are several files with these names.

v) She has a document to file in a confidential file to which she isn't allowed access.

vi) She has mistakenly punched a set of documents in the wrong place and they now look a mess in the folder.

vii) She is filing a document which she realises could go in one of three subject files.

viii) She can't find a document she filed in file number 67674 this morning, even though she can remember filing it.

ix) She has several papers waiting to go into three borrowed files which were all due to be returned two days ago.

x) When she lifts a bulky file out of the cabinet it splits open and all the papers fall on the floor.

▼ FOLLOW PROCEDURES TO REPRODUCE INFORMATION

You reproduce information when you take multiple copies on a printer. However, this method is no use if you need copies of a document you have received, rather than created. It is also relatively slow and expensive for large quantities. For these reasons, the most usual method of reproducing information in an office is to use a photocopier. This is the task you will have to do for your OCR assignment.

Photocopiers vary tremendously in terms of their size, speed and features. Some are small desktop models whilst others are very large, sophisticated machines which link to the computer system. For this reason, the procedures relating to their actual operation will vary considerably. 'Good practice' procedures, however, are almost always the same and are necessary to help to reduce wastage and keep costs to a minimum.

In this section you will find several example procedures. You must, however, check the exact operational procedures for your own photocopier before you start your assessment.

Photocopier facilities

The range of facilities available on a photocopier will depend upon its make and model. Today many photocopiers are digital. These can be linked to other types of digital equipment. This means that you can send a document straight from your computer to be copied or faxed to wherever you want. In a small office, you may find there is a digital multifunction copier which acts as a scanner and fax machine as well as the office copier. However, you still find many of the older type of analogue machines in operation – especially in a training office or public libraries. These have a more limited range of features and can operate only as a stand-alone copier.

The main type of facilities you are likely to find on a copier are shown in the table below. Find out those that are available on the photocopier you will use for your assessment. As a very minimum, you need to be able to copy back-to-back, reduce, enlarge and use paper of different sizes.

The main features of photocopiers

Feature	Explanation/variations
Black and white or colour as well	Digital copiers with a colour option are more expensive and printing in colour is slower, but many companies prefer the flexibility this gives them for important documents.
Copying speed	This can range from as slow as 15 pages a minute to over 100.
Paper trays and capacity	Can range from one small A4 paper tray to two paper trays (one large capacity, the other adjustable for A3 paper) and a bypass tray for labels or overhead projector transparencies.
Interrupt facility	Enables a long job to be temporarily stopped whilst an urgent job is done.
Duplexing (two-sided copying)	May not be available or can be an automatic feature with different options.
Reduce/Enlarge	Enables copy to be reduced or enlarged to fixed pre-set ratios. The best ratio is chosen automatically on some machines.
Zoom	Allows reproduction ratio to be set in 1% steps for more precise reduction/enlargement
Sample copy	Enables a test copy to be made automatically.
Image density and other adjustments	Adjusts exposure for light/dark text or dirty backgrounds (e.g. newspapers). On some machines you can also make adjustments for photographs, pale originals, etc. to improve clarity of copies.
Image rotation	Enables image to be rotated to adjust crooked image or to print on differently orientated paper (e.g. portrait to landscape)

Finishing unit	Options include automatic collating (see page 35), hole punching and stapling if required
Stack	This is the opposite of collate. It enables multiple pages to be inserted but each is copied and stacked separately.
User ID/counter	Enables usage to be logged per user.
Memory	Pages are scanned into memory before printing; routine jobs can be programmed into the machine and recalled as required.

Photocopier features are operated by means of a control panel. On modern machines these are touch sensitive. In particular, you need to make sure that you know where to locate the following:

▶ the Start key – to start copying

▶ the Clear/Stop key – to clear a wrong entry or to stop a job quickly

▶ the number keys – to enter the number of copies required

▶ the Sample copy key (if there is one)

▶ the adjustment keys for improving image density and clarity

▶ the special operations keys for reducing, enlarging, copying back-to-back.

Then check the machine itself so that you are clear about:

▶ The position of the document feeder – which feeds in originals. You need to know whether to put these print side down or up and – with a multi-page original – with the first page on the bottom or top.

▶ How to place originals on the exposure glass (for example, to photocopy a single page or a page from a book). Use the guide marks to help you.

▶ The position of the output tray(s) – where your copies arrive. Note that these may arrive in a different place depending upon whether they are single-sided or double; not collated or collated.

▶ The position of the paper tray where blank copy paper is held.

Checking copying is of an appropriate standard

It is a waste of time and paper if you cannot produce good-quality copies, especially if you are doing a long job and then have to start all over again. There are very many reasons why copies may be unusable. For example:

▶ the paper is the wrong size or colour

▶ the paper is crumpled, creased or torn

▶ the image isn't clear or is crooked on the page

▶ the background is fuzzy or grey so the image doesn't show up clearly

▶ part of the image is missing

▶ some of the pages are missing

- the image is too far to the left on a document which will be fastened down the left-hand side
- some pages have been copied back-to-back but others haven't
- on back-to-back copies, some images are upside down
- on back-to-back copies, the pages have been copied in the wrong order
- the pages have been fastened in the wrong order
- a reduced image is too small to read clearly
- too many copies have been made
- other explicit instructions have been ignored.

This may seem a long list, but it could be longer. There are many things that could go wrong when you are photocopying and the list above simply highlights the main reasons why copying isn't up to standard.

Procedures for good practice help users to overcome many of these problems by thinking and checking first – and then as they go. An example is given below.

Example good practice procedures for photocopying documents

1 Write down all instructions for copying carefully and check these with the person giving you the job. Check that you know:
   - the number of copies required
   - the size and colour of paper required for the copies
   - whether single-page or back-to-back copies are required
   - whether there are any special instructions to reduce or enlarge an image.
   - whether the copies must be collated and/or stapled.

2 Check the original carefully for quality. Clean up any dirty marks with special photocopier liquid paper. If the original is faint, on coloured paper or the background is dark then special adjustments will need to be made on the copier before you start. A test copy of one page should be made to check, and further adjustments made until the test copy is good quality. If you are still having problems, check the document glass is clean as dirty marks on this, or on the inside of the lid, will show up on your copies.

3 With a multi-page original, check the pages are in the correct order and all the right way up.

4 Key in any special requirements on the control panel and take one sample copy. Check that this is correct before taking any further copies.

5 Key in the exact number of copies required.

6 Check the copies constantly as they are being produced, so that you will notice any problems, such as creased paper (through a misfeed) or unstapled copies (because staplers have jammed in the machine). Separate any spoiled copies from the others. Stop copying immediately if there is a serious problem. When the problem has been rectified, recopy any spoiled pages to obtain the correct number of good-quality copies.

7 Tidy the area and return both the original document and the copies to the person who gave you the job.

Logging use of the photocopier

Most machines today do this automatically. Each user (or department) has a special code which must be keyed into the machine before it can be used. When this is entered, the machine logs the usage under that code number and can print out a report summarising the usage over a specific period for all the code numbers allocated. This enables managers to check whether any particular department or user is taking too many copies. This is important, not just because of the cost, but because different types of photocopiers are designed for specific types of use. If a low-volume copier is used too much, then it will probably break down more often and need replacing sooner than expected. If the equipment is rented, then the agreement may limit the number of copies a month under which a maintenance service will be provided.

On some older, basic machines, instead of a key code, you will only find a counter which records the number of copies. In this case you may be expected to write down the number you take in a separate log book, with headings as shown below.

An example of a photocopying log

Date	Name	Department	Start No	End No	Total no of copies
21/5	J Bates	Sales	20980	20985	5
21/5	W Bibi	Sales	20985	21140	155
22/5	L Hammond	Finance	21140	21170	30
22/5	B Vazin	Finance	21170	21242	72

The danger, of course, is that people forget to make an entry or don't bother to include any spoiled copies – which means that the final number doesn't tally with the start and end numbers. It is also a tedious job going through the log to analyse it for individual usage. This is why, today, most organisations have copiers which do this automatically – and which cannot be used unless the user keys in the correct code.

Refilling the copier with paper

You will need to refill the paper tray if the paper runs out or if you need to change the size of paper that is required for your copies. The exact procedure to follow will depend upon the type of machine and will be illustrated in the user handbook. If the paper runs out then printing will stop and a warning symbol will appear. You must then refill the paper tray to continue.

To do the task properly, it is sensible to make a few checks before you start.

▶ Find out which paper you must use. Some organisations buy multi-use paper which can be used in printers, copiers and fax machines. Others use different types of paper for these operations, because of the specifications of their particular equipment.

▶ Check the capacity of the main paper tray. This may take only a packet of paper at the most (500 sheets) or may hold as much as 3,500 sheets!

▶ Check how to access the paper tray. You may have to pull it out or open a lid or cover at the side or top. Whatever you do, don't pull or tug anything which appears to be fastened or held in a certain position.

▶ Check the position of any paper guides or 'fences' against which the paper must be aligned. If you have a wide paper tray, which takes two stacks side-by-side, check which side must be filled first.

▶ Although most manuals no longer say paper has to be fanned before it is placed in the tray, many people still prefer to do this to minimise paper jams. Check with your tutor if this is required.

▶ Don't put in any creased or crumpled paper. Remove any sheets that have been damaged and then 'square' the paper by holding it firmly at each side and giving it a few sharp taps on a firm surface. This makes sure all the sheets are aligned vertically and horizontally.

▶ Put the paper into the tray, making sure that the height of the stack doesn't exceed any limit marks indicated.

▶ Gently push the paper tray closed or close any lid or cover.

▶ Be patient! It sometimes takes a few seconds until the copier registers the new paper supply and is ready for use again.

▲ Make sure you follow your machine's guidelines when refilling the paper tray in the photocopier

Following procedures for the use of the equipment

On page 340, you saw the importance of noting down instructions for the task you have to do. You may also be given specific instructions relating to how to use the equipment. Many of these may relate to things you must and must not do, for example:

- Don't attempt any operations you haven't been shown how to do simply by guessing what to press on the control panel. It is highly likely that it won't work and someone else will have to spend some time sorting out the problem.

- *Never* open the machine to solve problems like clearing a paper jam unless you have been specifically shown how to do this. On some machines this is quite a complex operation and, if you don't know what you are doing, you could easily burn yourself on hot areas near the toner unit.

- Follow the procedures for reporting problems and warning lights on the control panel promptly to the person responsible. It helps if you understand the reasons for some of these so that you can describe them properly (see page 347).

- Only use the paper trays you are told you can use and change the paper or paper size only if you are asked to do so. If you change to coloured paper for a specific job, remember to change back to white paper before you leave the machine.

- If you are uncertain about an instruction or don't know what to do, always ask – never guess.

Using photocopying facilities

For your assessment you have to use a photocopier to produce single and multiple copies, make back-to-back copies, prove you can reduce and enlarge images and use different paper of different sizes. The normal procedures you would use for each of these operations are given below.

Example procedure for single copies or multiple copies of a single page

1 Check whether the original should be placed on the exposure glass or in the document feeder (this may be up to you).

2 If you are using the document feeder, check whether the original should be positioned print side down or up. The original is always placed face down on the glass.

3 If the original is on the exposure glass, close the lid.

4 Take a sample copy and check the quality. Make any adjustments required.

5 If further copies are required, key in the number on the key pad and press the Start key.

6 Remove all copies plus the original.

It is worth noting that if your machine has a separate Sample key, then you can normally key in the total and then use the sample key. This gives you a copy *without* deducting that one copy from your total number.

Example procedure for multi-page originals (not back-to-back)

1 Remove any paper-clips or staples and make sure all previously stapled copies are properly separated.

2 Check the original pages are in the correct order.

3 If the original pages are printed on only one side, place in document feeder. If originals are printed on both sides, then check if your machine can be programmed to reproduce both sides automatically. Otherwise you will have to make a master set of single-sided copies, by photocopying both sides yourself.

4 Set any collating, punching or stapling options that are required (see page 345).

5 Take a sample copy (or make a master set) and check quality. Make any adjustments required.

6 Key in number required and press Start.

7 Remove all copies plus original.

The procedure below assumes that your photocopier will do back-to-back copying automatically. If you have a very basic machine then this is more complicated, because you have to take a copy of the first page and then put that copy back into the paper tray (probably print side down, but check) and then copy the second document. This will then copy the second document onto the reverse side of the paper you first used. Because of this, back-to-back copying is not done very often on this type of machine.

Example procedure for back-to-back copying

1 Check the original is in the right order and all the pages are the right way up.

2 Check whether the original is copied on one side only or both and key this information into your copier.

3 Key in the fact that you want double-sided copies (if this is a separate operation to (2) above).

4 Set any collating, punching or stapling options that are required.

5 Take a sample copy and check the quality and make any adjustments required.

6 Enter the number required and press Start.

7 Remove all copies plus original.

A word of warning. If you are copying a large multi-page document back-to-back (particularly if you are also collating it) then on some machines your original pages will seem to disappear into the machine for quite a long time. This is because the copier has several tasks to do before your copies emerge – so be patient!

A good example of images which are often reduced or enlarged are articles from newspapers, or an extract from a book which is either larger or smaller than A4 paper. In addition, many organisations routinely enlarge information for customers with a visual impairment, so that it is easier to read. It is obviously more professional – and better for the reader – if any enlarged or reduced image is adjusted so that it is appropriate for the size of paper on which it is being printed.

The easiest way is to use one of the ratios for enlarging or reducing that has been preset into the copier. With some photocopiers, you can adjust this still further by using zoom – although the procedure below assumes that you haven't got this facility on your machine.

Remember that this is one operation where sample copies are essential until you know the results of selecting different ratios off by heart! This is important if you are enlarging because you may need to use a different size of paper or part of the image will be missing. To help, you can refer to the chart on below. Note that your copier may have several ratios between the figures shown here, but the chart should give you a good idea where to start!

Understanding enlargement/reduction ratios

Note that these are approximates, as it will depend upon whether you are using metric or inch ratios

Ratio selected	Approximate image size
200%	Four times as big (an A5 original would need A3 paper)
150%	Twice as big (an A5 original would need A4 paper, an A4 original would need A3 paper)
100%	Same size
75%	Half the size (you could fit two A5 images on A4 paper)
50%	A quarter the size (you could fit four A5 images on A4 paper)

Example procedure for reducing or enlarging an image and using paper of different sizes

1 Start by studying the image carefully in relation to the size of paper you have been told to use for your copies.

2 Check that the right size of paper is in the paper tray. If not, change it following the procedure given on page 341.

3 Place the original on the exposure glass, using the guide marks to identify the correct position, and close the lid.

4 Select the operation required (enlarge/reduce), then choose the ratio required.

5 Take a sample copy and check quality – especially whether the text is in the best position on the page and the right size. Make any adjustments. *Note*: moving the original to the left/right or up/down on the glass to adjust the position is very confusing. Expect to move it in the opposite direction to the one you would think!

6 If required, take further sample copy and check. Repeat until the best result is obtained.

7 Enter copies required and press Start.

8 Remove copies and original.

Collating and fastening copies

Collating pages means putting them into the right order so that you end up with complete sets of a multi-page document. You may be asked to fasten the copies. This is usually by stapling them, but sometimes bulky documents are bound together, using either a thermal binder that seals the pages together by heat and glue, or by adding a plastic binder. Some slide down the left edge, others can be fastened only by using a special machine. The main point to note, if you are fastening or binding a document down the left-hand side, is that you need a clear left margin of about 2.5 cm or you will obscure the text. You can set this on some photocopiers using the 'binding margin' facility.

Collating a document

Photocopiers which automatically collate documents often have a finishing unit at one side which includes a number of separate trays. The quantity of trays determines the number of collated copies that can be made at the same time. On other, smaller, machines you may still be able to collate but your printed sets may be ejected in a separate tray, each offset against the other so you can tell them apart. You can tell the machine to collate simply by selecting this option on the control panel.

If you have to collate by hand, then you need a large surface and a methodical approach. It is even better to have someone to help you if there are a lot of copies. Do each page separately. The procedure to follow now depends upon your own preference and the number of pages and sets you have to collate.

▶ You can put each copy of the first page face down and then add the next page to each set. Note that if you have to do a large number of sets then you may have to do this in batches. If you find that you have spare copies left over (or not enough for all the sets) then you've either gone wrong with your collating or your copying and will have to stop and check each set.

▶ You can start with the last page, and keep the text facing you as you add each page. This is often easier as it's immediately obvious if you've missed adding a page.

▶ You can space out all your page sets in front of you and take one from each set. This is more risky if you've a lot of pages. If you're making 30 sets of 3 pages, it's probably easier.

Whichever method you use, do a final check that all the sets are correct and all the pages are in the right order and then remember to offset your stack of finished sets so each is at 90 degrees to the next, to separate them easily.

Fastening a document

Ideally your photocopier will automatically staple for you. All you do is select the number and position of the staples from the range of options available on your machine. The most usual fastening for a short document is top left-hand side but a bulky document is more secure if it is fastened three times down the left side. An alternative is to fasten the document along the top.

If you are stapling by hand, use a heavy-duty stapler for bulky documents, so that the staples won't buckle and will fasten every page securely. Electric staplers are even better, but can be lethal if you don't watch what you are doing and catch your fingers. When you are stapling, be careful never to obscure the text on any page.

If you need to use a binding machine, then ask someone to give you a demonstration before you start. If you are using a plastic binder which slides over the pages then take care as some are very difficult to open and quite vicious. There is a knack to using these, so again it is helpful if someone shows you what to do.

Finally, if the document is to go into a ring binder it will need to be punched. This, too, is an option on some copiers today, although you will have to identify the number of holes you need and where you want them.

▲ Documents can be finished in a variety of ways, depending on their size and function

Following procedures for reporting problems

By now you should be able to solve many routine problems yourself, such as adjusting the settings if the original is too dark or light, refilling the paper and taking the obvious remedial action if the image is crooked or the copy is blank because you put in the original upside down!

Additional problems can also occur, some of which are beyond your control. The main reasons for these and the actions to take are given in the table overleaf.

Minimising waste

It will help to minimise waste if you *always*:

▷ Check you understand your instructions before you start.

▷ Only use the correct paper for the machine.

▷ Repair any torn originals and make adjustments for poor-quality images on originals at the start.

▷ Make sure the glass and the inside of the lid is always clean.

▷ Make sure the original is the right way up and in the correct position for copying.

▷ Check multi-page documents are in the right order with all the pages the right way up before you select back-to-back and/or collate.

▷ Double-check your settings carefully.

- Always take a sample copy.
- Print only the number of copies requested.
- Routinely make double-sided copies to save paper.
- Put any spoiled sheets of paper into a recycling container.

Procedures for dealing with problems

Problem	Suggested reason/action
The machine will not accept your keyed-in entries.	The machine is not switched on or is in 'sleep mode' and you need to enter your user code before you can start.
The machine asks you to wait.	Do as you are told! The machine may be warming up or registering a paper refill.
You don't know what you are supposed to be doing or how to do the job.	Ask a more experienced colleague or your supervisor for help.
No matter what you do, you can't obtain good-quality copies.	Check you are following the 'good practice' procedures correctly (see page 340). Then ask for help. The toner may be running low or the machine itself is dirty.
The machine will not allow you to select the option you want.	The reason will probably be given in the handbook. You may have tried to set an impossible operation (e.g. more stapled pages than the machine can cope with) or combination of operations. Check the procedure for the job in your handbook, then ask for help.
A symbol on the control panel denotes action is required.	Most symbols denote routine operations, such as paper low, toner low, routine maintenance check required. You can refill paper yourself but should notify the person in charge of the machine if another symbol appears.
The machine won't staple and/or punch.	The staples are jammed or the unit is empty; the punch waste box is full. These are normally simple operations, so you can ask someone to show you what to do.
The machine breaks down or stops printing.	The most common reason is a paper jam, which is shown on the control panel. You must ask a trained person to remedy this. If you have to leave the machine, put a notice on it to tell other people not to use it. If you are making multiple copies (or collating) when you are interrupted, you will need to check where you were when you resume to ensure you have nothing missing at the end.

Following safety procedures

Photocopiers are very safe to use providing that:

▶ they are positioned in accordance to the manufacturer's instructions and so that there is a good airflow around them

▶ they are connected properly and the cable and plug is in good condition

▶ liquids are kept well away from the machine. If any fluid is spilled into the copier, it must be turned off and disconnected from the power supply *immediately*

▶ small objects are kept away from the machine, such as paper-clips or staples which may fall inside. If there is a little tray for paper-clips, then use it!

▶ all covers and doors are kept shut when it is in operation

▶ used toner is always disposed of according to instructions and never incinerated. Spilled toner should be cleaned using cold water.

▶ only trained operators are allowed to undertake maintenance operations or remedy faults such as paper misfeeds.

▶ no one ever pokes around inside the machine, especially near parts which show the surface is very hot.

PROCEDURES IN BUSINESS

All ethical businesses have procedures in place to restrict what they copy. This is because photocopying from a book, magazine, newspaper or other 'original work' is illegal without a licence from the Copyright Licensing Agency or the Newspaper Licensing Agency. Your college, in common with other educational establishments, will be licensed to be able to give students photocopies of pages as handouts in class. If it had no licence, it would be breaking the law. A slightly different type of licence is needed for business organisations.

Copywatch is part of the Copyright Licensing Agency and is responsible for investigating reports of unlawful copying. In November 2002 its inspectors seized 500 photocopied sets of books from a shop in Nottingham where the owner was selling them. The business, Photocopier Maintenance and Servicing, had bribed local students to donate one photocopied copy of a book in return for free binding of their projects and, over time, had built up what amounted to a near library of business and medical books.

You may be relieved to know that as a student you are normally exempt from investigations by Copywatch. You are allowed to take a copy of an original document providing you are using it for research or private study without needing a licence.

You can find out more about copyright by following the links from www.heinemann.co.uk/hotlinks

1 Find out, and write down, the exact procedure you must follow on your machine to undertake each of the following activities:

a) produce single copies from a single or multi-page original

b) produce multiple copies

c) produce back-to-back copies

d) reduce and enlarge images and change the paper size if required

e) refill the paper tray when it is empty

f) collate and fasten pages.

2 Describe, in your own words, the purpose of each of the photocopying procedures you identified in **1** above.

3 Kristen is photocopying for the first time and you have been asked to help her.

a) Identify 5 ways in which you can help her to reduce waste.

b) Identify 3 safety precautions you would tell her about.

4 Many photocopying problems are covered by procedures, but not all of them. On some occasions you need to refer to the procedures whilst on others you might have to use your common sense.

Whilst you are using the photocopier the following problems occur. In each case decide:

a) whether there is likely to be a procedure you should check to find out what to do, or whether you should use your own initiative

b) what the procedure – or your supervisor – would tell you to do in each case.

Check your answers with your tutor.

i)   Your sample copy has dirty marks on it and the background is fuzzy.

ii)   Your sample copy is blank.

iii)   Your sample copy is crooked.

iv)   The paper tray is empty

v)   The paper jams in the machine.

vi)   An enlarged image is not aligned in the middle of the paper.

vii)   An enlarged image will not fit on your A4 paper.

viii) A reduced image is too small to read.

ix)   The machine stops for no apparent reason.

x)   The machine will not allow you to collate the number of sets you need.

▼ FOLLOW PROCEDURES TO SEND AND RECEIVE INFORMATION

You send and receive information every time you send an email on your computer and you must follow specific procedures to do this successfully. For your OCR assessment you have to use a different method and prove that you can correctly send and receive information using a fax machine.

Fax machines are generally very easy to use, but can vary tremendously – just like photocopiers. There are small, cheap desktop machines which use special (thermal) paper. At the other extreme are large plain paper machines which operate virtually automatically 24 hours a day, 7 days a week and link to the computer network. This means that messages can be prepared and sent from individual users and received messages are automatically forwarded to their computers. Needless to say, the procedures you will have to follow will therefore vary, depending upon the type and complexity of your machine.

The example procedures in this section assume that you are using a standard, mid-range fax machine for your assessment.

Fax machine features

Feature	Explanation/variations
Black and white and/or colour	Colour fax machines are available but most are black and white. Note it is sensible sending a colour fax only to someone who also has a colour machine!
Plain paper or thermal paper	Plain paper faxes are now common. These use the same type of paper that you find in printers/photocopiers. Thermal paper is supplied on a roll and copies fade over time if exposed to light.
Flat-bed or document feeder	Some large fax machines have a 'flat-bed' like a photocopier. Most, however, receive the original by feeding it into the machine.
Cover sheet	The option to produce a front page summarising the key details of the fax.
Verification or confirmation report	The option to receive a printed report after sending each fax to check transmission went smoothly.
Speed dialling/memory/auto-redial	Most faxes will store frequently used numbers in memory and a limited number can be dialled in one touch. Virtually all will try to reconnect if a number is engaged.
Fax memory	Enables originals to be scanned before sending and incoming faxes to be held in memory if the machine is busy or is out of paper or ink.
Automatic features	More expensive faxes offer options such as automatic fax forwarding to PCs, delayed fax sending until a later time (when phone rates are cheaper), automatic collection from another machine (called 'polling'), sending the same fax to many numbers automatically (called 'broadcast').

Understanding your fax machine

Before you start, it is useful if you understand the type of facilities and features found on a fax machine and what they do. A summary of these is shown in the table on page 351. All fax machines will operate as a simple copier but far more slowly than a photocopier. Apart from that the features will depend upon the size and cost of the machine. More expensive fax machines also transmit more quickly and hold more paper in the paper tray, and have more automatic functions. A multifunction fax machine will do other tasks as well, and may operate as the office printer, copier and scanner as well as the fax.

▲ Fax machines come in many shapes and sizes

Once you learn about the facilities available on the fax you are using, you need to locate the key items you will be using. These include the following:

▶ The **document hopper** which holds and supports the original document and the **document feeder** – which is the slot the original must enter to be faxed. At each side you will find **document guides** which are adjusted to match the width of the document.

If you are using a flat-bed fax, you may just place the original into the document feeder or on the top – just like on a photocopier.

▶ The **display panel** which shows you the status of the machine and the **control panel** which enables you to enter commands into the machine.

▶ The **document tray** where your original emerges and the **output tray** where incoming faxes or internal copies arrive.

▶ The **telephone handset** and **number keys** – in case you want to speak to someone before or after transmission or need to key a fax number into the machine.

The important keys to locate are:

▷ Stop – to terminate a transmission in an emergency

▷ Cancel – to delete numbers or commands you have entered by mistake.

▷ Enter – to confirm a command or setting.

▷ Start – to start transmitting or receiving a fax manually.

Complete facsimile cover sheets

A cover sheet is an option on most machines although the design varies. Without a cover sheet only a header is printed at the top of each page of the fax which simply gives the date, time, fax number, company name and page number in very tiny print. A cover page provides much more information and enables a short message or comment to be written as well. It is ideal if you are simply sending a copy of a document to someone as it saves you preparing a separate message yourself to explain what you are sending.

To send a cover page, you simply select this option before you transmit the document. An example is shown below. Some of the lines are entered automatically, others you have to enter yourself:

▷ The 'TO' line is entered automatically if you are using an abbreviated dialling system or your telephone memory. If you are dialling direct this line is often left blank.

▷ The 'FROM' line automatically enters the name of your company and fax number, because this information is stored in the machine and normally printed on the header of each fax.

▷ You must enter the total number of pages yourself and you will be prompted for this information.

▷ You will also be prompted to enter a comment or message – but make sure that you don't exceed the maximum number of words or characters allowed.

▷ On some machines you may be able to enter additional information, such as whether the fax is urgent or confidential.

Fax message

Date / Time:	02/04/2004 15:30
TO:	ECLIPSE SOFTWARE
FAX:	+44 3098 172887
FROM:	ACL TRAINING
FAX:	+44 200 289 2987
TEL:	+44 200 289 2088
TO FOLLOW:	02 PAGES
MESSAGE:	DETAILS OF E-MARKETING COURSES ATTACHED. PLEASE RING JOHN PICKUP TO BOOK PLACES.

▲ Example of a fax cover page

Following instructions for use of equipment

The way you will use the equipment will depend upon the specific instructions you are given. Your organisation may routinely send cover sheets or prefer to save paper by only sending them when they are essential. Fax messages may be sent on headed paper or a special form may be used. Whatever layout is customary in your organisation must be followed as well as standard conventions – such as numbering the pages properly (i.e. Page 1 of 3, Page 2 of 3, etc.).

When you are using the equipment you may be asked to:

▶ contact a firm which is a regular contact or someone completely new

▶ transmit a single or multi-page fax

▶ send a cover sheet – or not

▶ send a black and white or coloured original – or even a page from a book or extract from a magazine

▶ talk to someone either before or after transmission.

Each of these can involve you in slightly different activities. The other variation is whether you send the message automatically or manually.

▶ You send the message manually when you set the machine to manual, pick up the handset and, after keying in the number, you listen for the fax tone at the other end before you press Send or Start.

▶ You send a message automatically when you do not pick up the handset but use the keypad to tell the machine what to do. On most machines you now don't need to press Send or Start – but on some you do – so check!

Example procedure for a single-page fax to a regular contact

This is probably the easiest and most routine operation.

1 Check the document guides are correct for your original.

2 Insert the original document into the machine. Check which way to do this so that the print is the correct and right way (normally print side down, top of document first but make sure!).

3 The machine should now display 'ready' on the control panel.

4 Obtain the dialling tone (if necessary on your machine) and key in the abbreviated number code for your contact. Then press Start or Send (if the machine doesn't do this automatically).

5 Watch and wait! The machine will automatically contact the other fax and transmit the message, bleep you when transmission is complete and then return your original in the output tray.

6 Remember that if the receiving machine is engaged, the number will be automatically redialled after one minute, normally up to a maximum of six times.

7 When transmission has ended, remove the original and return it to the person who gave it to you.

1 Obtain the fax number from the message originator or by ringing the person or organisation and asking for the number or by checking the company's website.

2 Check original is in correct page order and count number of pages. Remove any staples or paper-clips. Number pages if required using correct format.

3 Set cover sheet option and key in required information for pages and message.

4 Set verification/confirmation report option.

5 Set document guides, fan pages of original (to stop them sticking together) and place in document feeder. Check whether the top page should be at the bottom or on the top of the set as this varies between machines.

6 Obtain a dial tone and key in fax number on the key pad. Check on display that number has been entered correctly. Press Start or Send (if necessary).

7 Wait until transmission has ended and original is returned in output tray. Verification report will now print out.

8 Check verification report confirms status 'OK' and return original and verification report to originator.

Dealing with unusual or poor-quality originals

These include originals which are not printed clearly on white paper with good margins, those which are on flimsy paper, are very valuable (so you daren't risk a misfeed in the fax machine) or are to be found in a book or bound report. Your options are as follows:

▶ Flimsy documents should be photocopied first, in case they are torn or damaged in the fax. Then transmit the copy.

▶ Fax originals must always have good margins all round or the text will be cut off. On some fax machines you can reduce the size of the image as you transmit the message but not on all of them. In this case, reduce it on a photocopier so that no text is lost and transmit the copy.

▶ An extract from a book or bound report must be copied on a flat-bed photocopier first (unless you have a flat-bed fax) because it can't be put into the machine.

▶ A document with a poor image or on coloured paper is unlikely to fax well unless you can make appropriate adjustments on your fax (see below). Again, therefore, photocopy it on white paper and make the necessary adjustments to the image density.

▶ If you can make adjustments on your fax, then you may be able to

  – increase the **resolution** if the print is tiny (you often need to select 'fine' or 'superfine'). The fax will then transmit more slowly in greater detail.

  – change the **grey scale** if you are sending a photograph or coloured print – but this is effective only if the receiving machine has the same capability.

  – adjust the **contrast** to lighten or darken the document. Choose light, if your document is light; and dark, if it is dark, to help to compensate.

Speaking to people before or after transmission

Because all fax machines have a telephone handset, you can speak to the person at the other end either before or after transmission – but not during it. Remember that this will be the fax machine operator who may not be your recipient and, because fax machines usually use a separate line, there will be no facility to transfer you to another extension.

It is generally simpler to speak to someone at the end of a message than at the beginning. In this case you simply press the 'call' option on your control panel whilst the message is transmitting. After transmission, when someone picks up the handset, your telephone will ring. Wait a few seconds before speaking. If you wish to speak to someone at the start, check your handbook, as this procedure can vary considerably from one machine to another.

You will know if the other person wants to speak to you because your phone will ring! Remember to be patient, once you have picked up the receiver, as you won't be able to start talking until the transmission has ended.

Logging and distributing incoming faxes

Faxes can be received throughout the day and night on a busy fax machine. All the messages need to be handled and distributed promptly on the basis that faxes are usually sent when a matter is urgent.

Logging incoming faxes is useful in case there is a query or the message (or person who distributed it) is missing. The log will show when it arrived and what was done with it.

Example of a fax log sheet

Date	Time	Message from	Distributed to
5 September	10.15	Jackson Fabrics, Dudley	Ken Bradley
5 September	11.00	Withington Plastics, Stroud	Sue Marsden

The main danger is fax messages being received and not noticed or – even worse – allowed to slither onto the floor and then thrown away as rubbish. This can happen with some basic machines that don't have a tray (or only a very small one), if the machine is badly positioned or in the next room. Assuming your machine is somewhere nearby, then you will hear it start and can then follow the correct procedure.

Example procedure for logging and distributing incoming faxes

1 Wait for message to finish transmitting, then remove all the pages from the tray.

2 Check all the pages are in the right order and the number matches that on the cover sheet.

3 Put the cover sheet on top and clip the pages together securely.

4 Enter the details into the fax log.

5 Deliver the message immediately to the named recipient. If this person is away then ask your supervisor who should deal with it.

Carrying out basic fax maintenance

Very little maintenance is required to keep fax machines running smoothly. Some are fairly obvious.

▶ All fax machines use paper, which needs refilling regularly. It may be stored in a small tray or a cassette – or in a paper tray similar to the ones you find in a photocopier.

▶ Fax machines also use other consumable items, such as ink and batteries. You will need to alert someone if you find copies are faint or any warning lights show on the control panel.

▶ Fax machines need to be kept clean – in particularly the air vents need to be clear of dust. Brush this away – never use water. They also need an air space around them – so don't push the air vents up against a wall.

The main task is replenishing the paper. The procedure will vary depending upon whether special paper is used or plain paper. Thermal paper is often provided on a roll, so you have to remove the old roll and replace it with a new one. You can tell when a roll is coming to an end because coloured watermarks appear on the paper.

The procedure below is an example for refilling a small plain paper fax, which uses a cassette. If you use a large fax machine with a standard paper tray then you are likely to find the procedures are similar to those for refilling a photocopier (see page 341).

Example procedure for refilling the paper

1 Check the amount of paper your fax machine will hold and the type you must use. Most machines take only A4 paper.

2 Slide out the paper cassette and/or open the lid or cover.

3 Unlock any fastening mechanism that holds the paper in place.

4 Fan the paper and then 'square' it by tapping the ends of the stack to make sure the edges are even.

5 Check which way up the paper must be inserted (normally face down). This is important because the 'right' (face) side is smoother. Most paper packets have this marked on to guide you.

6 Put the paper into the cassette or tray, making sure it is underneath any metal tabs at the sides or corners. Check the paper isn't stacked above the maximum level indicated.

7 Close any cover or lid on the cassette and slide it back into position. You may have to listen for a 'click' to tell you when it is in place.

Coping with the unexpected and reporting problems

When you are using a fax machine there is usually very little to go wrong. The machine itself will tell you if there is a problem. An alarm sounds if the paper needs refilling, if there is a paper jam or misfeed, or if there is a problem with transmission. The main points to note are as follows:

▶ If the fax machine won't work or respond to your commands, check that all the covers are closed and that it is plugged in and switched on. Remember that fax machines are usually left 'on' all the time, to receive faxes over night and at weekends.

▶ Use the cancel key if you make a mistake entering the number, and start again.

▶ Press the stop key if there is a misfeed with your original. Never try to tug out a document. Often pressing the stop key a few times will automatically release a document; otherwise lift the cover to see if you can remove it easily. If not, ask for help.

▶ If the print-out jams (e.g. a received fax) then the action to take often depends upon where the jam has occurred, so report the problem.

▶ Your fax will automatically redial a number that is engaged – although the number of attempts and the time between each varies. If you are still having problems then refer back to the originator of the fax. If you want to demonstrate your initiative, you could try ringing the recipient first to see if there is a problem with their machine.

▶ Display errors. There are a number of reasons why you might see a display error. Some of these are because of basic operator errors such as trying to key in too many digits. Others are more complex. Checking the handbook will tell you if you have done something silly, report the problem if you haven't.

▶ Communication errors can occur for many reasons, from lightning to poor telephone line connections. The reason is usually shown by a code on an error report which is automatically printed if the communication fails. You can check the meaning of these codes in the user manual.

If you find the problem occurred because of a problem obtaining the fax number, then check the number is correct and try to resend before reporting the problem.

If the problem occurred because of a breakdown in communications then you may be able to try again – it will depend upon the reason for the problem. If you do start again, resend the fax from the beginning. This is because, if the transmission failed part-way through, you will not know how many pages the recipient actually received. If the problem recurs, then you need to report it.

PROCEDURES IN BUSINESS

Fax procedures are likely to change in the future as fax machine designers add more and more options. As well as colour faxes, digital faxes which link to a computer network, multifunctional faxes that act as printers, scanners, office copiers and answering machines as well, more new features are being launched. One is the ability to block junk (unwanted) faxes. Another is the ability to send SMS messages to mobile phones using the numeric keypad. A recent development is voice recognition. Canon has recently launched a machine which uses UcanTalk software. After programming the fax so that it can recognise their voice, the user can simply speak the name of a contact for the fax to dial the number automatically and send the message.

These machines – and other new models – also have the ability to scan the original themselves and change the density to improve the image without any help from the user. Eventually the procedure for operating a fax machine may simply be to give it a document prepared on computer and then shout across the office to tell it to do the rest!

▲ Voice recognition technology means that fax machines are becoming increasingly sophisticated

OVER TO YOU!

1. Identify the correct procedure to undertake each of the following activities on your fax machine:

   a) Sending a one-page fax message automatically.

   b) Sending a multi-page fax message to a new contact.

   c) Logging and distributing an incoming fax.

   d) Refilling the paper in the fax machine.

2. For each of the above procedures, explain its purpose in your own words.

3. Many fax problems are covered by procedures, but not all of them. On some occasions you need to refer to the procedures whilst on others you might have to use your common sense.

   Whilst you are using the fax the following problems occur. In each case decide:

   a) whether there is likely to be a procedure you should check to find out what to do, or whether you should use your own initiative

   b) what the procedure – or your supervisor – would tell you to do in each case.

   Check your answers with your tutor.

i) You are logging an incoming fax when you realise it is unreadable because the quality is so poor.

ii) You are asked to fax two pages from your boss's passport to a travel firm. The passport is too thick to go into the fax and you don't know the fax number of the firm.

iii) You receive a fax marked 'Urgent' but the recipient is on holiday this week.

iv) You are trying to send an urgent fax to a regular contact but their machine is constantly engaged.

v) Your original document starts to crumple as it enters the machine.

vi) The phone rings as a message is coming through.

vii) Your confirmation report for a 6-page fax shows that the transmission broke down part way through.

viii) There is a warning light on the fax to say that the ink needs replenishing.

ix) As you are receiving a fax the alarm sounds to indicate the incoming message has jammed.

x) Your boss asks you if it is possible to fax a copy of an A3 poster which was produced by the marketing department.

▼ FOLLOWING PROCEDURES TO CONTROL STOCK

All offices use vast quantities of stationery and other consumable items every year, and these are expensive. Procedures are therefore needed so that several key operations relating to the consumable stocks held by an organisation will be controlled. Without any controls, people could just order and use anything they want, important items could run out and wastage would be high.

Some of the controls can be quite simple, such as making sure the stock is kept in a safe place – such as a lockable cupboard or store – stored properly to prevent damage and used in rotation to minimise deterioration. Other controls relate to the procedures for ordering and replenishing stock, issuing it to users and keeping stock records, which may be kept manually or on computer. In this section you will learn about the procedures for controlling many aspects of stock as well as how to update stock records.

▲ In a large stationery store, excellent stock control is essential

Understanding the stock control system

It is useful to understand how a stock control system works, so that you can see how the tasks you do contribute to its effectiveness.

At the start, a manager or supervisor must decide which items to keep in stock and how many. This is important because of the cost. Holding too much stock ties up company money that may be better used elsewhere. Holding too little stock is dangerous because frequently used items may run out. For these reasons, the following levels are agreed.

▶ The **maximum level** of each item is the most the company is prepared to hold in stock at any one time, bearing in mind usage and storage space.

▶ The **minimum level** of each item is the level at which stock must be re-ordered to allow for new deliveries to arrive.

▶ The **running balance** shows the level of stock at each date. When this balance is at, or near, the minimum level then new stock must be ordered but *only* to the point at which the maximum level will be held.

There will be a special procedure for ordering new stock, which will include having the order signed by an authorised person. When the replacement stock arrives, it must be unpacked and checked carefully so that any damaged items are returned for replacement and any missing items are noted and followed up, if necessary. It must then be stored correctly.

When staff need to obtain items they will have to complete a special form, called a **requisition**, which is counter-signed by their supervisor or manager. The stock is then issued and the stock records updated.

At regular intervals a **stock check** will take place. This is often called stock taking and involves counting the stock and checking the result against the stock records. Any discrepancies are reported and investigated as they may indicate pilferage. During this time, adjustments will also be made for any stock which has been accidentally damaged or deteriorated through age and which must be taken out of the system.

Maintaining stock records

There are two ways to keep stock records – manually and on computer.

Manual systems

Most manual systems include **stock record cards** which are stored in alphabetical order, often in a card index box. There is one card for each item held. Every time new stock is received or an item is issued then the new balance is calculated. If the balance shows the stock is approaching or below the minimum or re-order level then the item is included on the next order. The card is updated when the delivery has been unpacked and checked.

Some stock control systems include a system of 'flagging'. These may be coloured plastic clips that denote different things. For example:

▶ A red flag could indicate that an item is at, or near, its minimum level and must be included on the next order.

▶ A green flag could indicate that an order has been placed and is awaited. This helps to prevent the order being duplicated.

▶ A yellow flag could indicate a delivery is delayed, so that the supplier can be reminded after a few days.

An example of a manual stock record card is shown below. Check that you understand each entry. Bear in mind the following.

▶ The **Item** description should provide enough details so that goods can easily be re-ordered. If a particular named brand is preferred because it is considered good value, this may be included.

▶ The **Unit** is the quantity in which that item which is bought from the supplier. This may be the same as the quantities which are issued, but not always. For example, envelopes may be bought in boxes of 1,000 but issued in packs of 20, 50 or 100 to individual staff.

▶ The **Supplier** is the one approved to provide that product. You should never order elsewhere without the agreement of your manager.

▶ The **Cat. No.** is the item number as shown in the supplier's catalogue, so that this can be entered onto the order form.

▶ The **Department** column may be changed to record individual staff names in a small office or if stationery is held and issued to staff within a department.

▶ The records *must* be kept up-to-date and must be accurate, otherwise the next order may be made out wrongly or not at all!

▶ Manual cards must be written carefully so that they are clear and legible – print the entry if your handwriting is poor. Never cross out and overwrite figures or try to rub out an entry. Even correction fluid is frowned upon in some organisations because it could denote fraud. If you make a mistake, check the procedure to follow to make a correction.

Stock Record Card

Item: Acme 3.5" floppy disks   Unit: Box of 10   Maximum: 20 boxes

Supplier: Statline Ltd   Cat No: FD10892   Minimum: 5 boxes

Date	Received	Issued	Dept	Reg No	Balance
15 June					8 boxes
17 June		2 boxes	Sales	3012	6 boxes
18 June		2 boxes	Finance	3026	4 boxes
24 June	16 boxes				20 boxes
26 June		1 box	Production	3040	19 boxes

▲ A manual stock record card

Computerised stock control systems

Special computer programs are available and are often used in organisations where large amounts of stock are held. These have several benefits because they can print out special reports at the touch of a key, for example:

▶ **A stock valuation**, which shows all the stock held and how much it cost.

▶ **A re-order list**, which summarises all the stock at, or near, its re-order level.

- **A stock analysis** which shows how often stock is used. Stock which is rarely used may be dropped altogether.

- **A stock inventory** list. These are ideal if you are checking stock because the list prints all the items currently held and the quantity according to the system. When you are checking you simply count each item and put the physical count number alongside each entry.

- **An audit trail**. This shows every computer entry that has been made since the last audit trail was printed and is extremely valuable if there must be an investigation into a discrepancy.

In the same way that you had to be careful when adjusting mistakes on a manual system, you equally cannot simply change entries on a computer system. If you keyed in 50 cartridges received and then suddenly changed this to 30, it would obviously look suspicious. For that reason, you have to make adjustments to entries, which are then logged on the audit trail. The final entry must, of course, match the other paperwork in the system, such as order forms, requisitions and delivery notes (see pages 364 and 365).

An alternative method of using a computer for stock control, is to set up a database where each record relates to an individual stock item and design reports which will give you the information you need, such as a re-order list.

An even easier method is to use a spreadsheet package and to set up columns to link to the headings on a stock record card. The spreadsheet will then automatically add or subtract all items received and issued and calculate the balance for you. If your IT skills are very good, you can even set up the spreadsheet to identify which items need re-ordering automatically! The problem is that you will not be able to produce the same type of reports that can be obtained using a database or a stock control package.

Issuing stock against requisitions and maintaining stock levels

A requisition is an *internal* order, as opposed to an *external* order from a customer. You are likely to have to follow specific procedures for issuing stock, and these will depend upon the exact system in operation. For example:

- In some organisations, stock can be issued only on specific days or at certain times. In others, it is issued on demand.

- There is likely to be a maximum amount of stock you can issue to one user without special authorisation. Someone asking for 100 printer cartridges obviously can't use them all at once and – even if there is a special reason for needing these – it is likely to mean there are none available for anyone else for a few days.

- How to check the requisitions you are dealing with and what to do if there is a query or problem. In most organisations, requisitions must be counter-signed by a manager or supervisor but even then you may have a query if you can't read a quantity or don't have enough items in stock to complete the order.

Usually, you must update the stock records immediately after issuing the stock.

1 Stock must be issued only against a requisition which has been counter-signed by a manager. A list of managers allowed to do this is available separately for checking, if necessary.

2 Check the quantity requested. If fulfilling the order would present problems for other users because stock levels are low, contact the person concerned and state how many can be supplied and when the balance will be available.

3 Remove the requested item from the shelves and tick the requisition as 'completed' or indicate any balance to follow.

4 On the appropriate stock record, enter the date and the number of items issued.

5 Check if the running balance indicates this item needs re-ordering. If so, flag the item or enter it on the 'next order' list.

Completing a purchase requisition or order

This is the document which must be completed to order new stock. If you have a central purchasing department then you will complete an internal purchase requisition and send it to the purchasing staff to obtain the goods. If you work in a small office, you will make out an order and send it to your stationery supplier. You cannot usually choose which firm to send it to – all organisations usually have a list of approved suppliers because of price, delivery and reliability.

Purchase requisitions and orders vary in their design, although they usually include some key items which you need to understand. These are illustrated in the example opposite and include the following.

▷ On an order, details about the organisation so that the supplier knows where to deliver the goods or how make contact if there are any queries. On an internal requisition, this information isn't needed but there will be an instruction about where you must send the completed form and, often, how it will be dealt with.

▷ Sections which must be completed relating to the supplier. In many cases each supplier has a unique number. Every order and every requisition also has a unique number so that it can easily be identified. This may be pre-printed on the form you complete. The date must always be completed at the time the order is made out.

▷ Sections where you enter the items you are ordering. You must give a proper description (to match that on the stock record or in the supplier's catalogue) and include the item code. Remember the quantity must match the units in which the item is supplied. You cannot order 200 paper-clips if they are supplied only in boxes of 1,000! The unit price will be found in the catalogue. This may not be required if you are completing an internal requisition.

▷ Delivery and authorisation details. You may write a specific date under delivery or simply 'as soon as possible'. Then you need to have your order authorised by your manager. All organisations are very strict about which staff can sign external orders. You may, however, be allowed to sign an internal requisition yourself.

Frimley and Barlow

Oakleigh House
St John's Avenue
RIMMINGTON
RM1 6PP

Tel: 02893 477877

Fax: 02893 477232

VAT Reg No 598/4974/76

Email: Admin@fandb.co.uk

PURCHASE ORDER

To: Stateline Ltd
    21 Queen's Road
    RIMMINGTON
    RM2 3SM

Supplier No: 203
Official order no: 4039
Date: 17 June 200-

Please supply:

Quantity	Description	Item code	Unit price
14 boxes	Acme 3.5" floppy disks	FD10892	4.99
6	Screen cleaning wipes	SW48903	2.49
10	A4 ring binders — blue	RB69001	1.80
10	A4 ring binders — red	RB69002	1.80

Delivery: as soon as possible ....

Signed: .... *Jackie Foulds* .... Designation: ...... *Office Manager* ......

Suppliers should note that orders are valid only if signed by a designated executive
of the organisation

▲ A purchase order form

Taking delivery

Stock deliveries may arrive at a central point, especially in a large organisation where stationery is ordered by the purchasing department. Purchasing staff may also check the stock against the overall order before splitting it and distributing the items to the departments that ordered them. In this case you must check your own delivery of stock against your copy requisition, to make sure that you are receiving exactly the right quantity of the correct items.

If you have ordered goods direct from a supplier, then you will usually receive the goods yourself. In this case there will be a delivery note included which lists the contents. You may be asked to sign the delivery note. If you haven't the opportunity to check the items whilst the deliverer is present, mark the note 'received but not checked'.

The important point is that you must always check that the items you have received match those listed on the delivery note or copy requisition *and* your order form or original requisition. If they do not, this may be because:

▶ items are out of stock at the supplier (they are normally marked on the paperwork as 'to follow')

▶ items are no longer available (they may be crossed off on the order)

▶ items are missing (because the packer has made a mistake)

▶ too many items have been sent in error (note that it is not ethical to keep these as a perk!)

▶ the wrong items have been sent in error

▶ alternative items have been substituted deliberately, because the original ones weren't available. In this case it will be noted on the paperwork.

In addition, of course, some items may be damaged or may not work properly.

If there is a discrepancy because of a supplier's error then you must contact them immediately and explain. The same applies if goods are damaged or don't function properly. You can then arrange for them to be collected and replaced. The supplier cannot refuse to do this if the goods are faulty. If the supplier has substituted items and these are unsuitable, you can also reject these and return them unused.

You must notify your finance department if there are any missing or returned items, so that they are aware of the situation. If you have to complete a note listing any returns, then send them a copy to ensure that the returned goods are not paid for.

The problem starts if you find that an error is your fault because, for example, you wrote 1000 A4 ring binders instead of 100; or because you didn't see that ring binders are supplied in boxes of 10 and ordered 100, which resulted in 1,000 being delivered. In this situation, try not to panic! The supplier can insist you keep them but this is unlikely because most want to keep your business. You can appeal to your supervisor for help but you may gain more respect if you contact the supplier yourself first. Make your apologies and ask if they will take them back. If they refuse then you will have to admit your error, but the fact that you have tried to solve the problem yourself may help to soften your boss's reaction a little!

▲ Try not to panic if you have ordered more than you needed by mistake

Storing stock appropriately

Stock should be stored in a lockable cupboard. Sometimes this may simply be a metal cabinet but, if you are lucky, there will be a proper stockroom with slatted shelves reaching up to the ceiling. These enable the air to circulate freely and prevent damage or deterioration through damp. Ideally, the storage area will be away from direct heat or light – both of which can cause the deterioration of many stationery items.

It is not sufficient simply to stack everything that has arrived on the nearest shelf and lock the door again. To enable items to be found easily, used in rotation and stored correctly, there will be a separate place for different items and a reason for their location. For example, heavy items should always be stored low down and fast-moving items where they can be reached easily. Ideally, there will be clear labels on the shelves to show where items are kept.

An example of the procedures you will then be expected to follow is shown below – linked to the stock control system.

Example procedure for storing stock and updating the stock record

1. Handle all goods carefully and use a trolley for heavy boxes.

2. Follow the instructions on each box to make sure you open it the right way up and in the easiest way.

3. Unpack items carefully and don't remove wrapping paper unless it is necessary. Many items, such as paper, remain in good condition longer if they remain wrapped.

4. Always put new stock at the bottom (or back of a shelf) so that the oldest items are used first.

5. Always stack items so that the descriptive labels face outwards.

6. Make sure you always comply with any specific storage instructions (such as 'this way up' or 'keep away from direct heat').

7. Keep all potentially hazardous items in their containers, e.g. scissors and drawing pins in boxes.

8. Store any inflammable liquids on the floor with the label clearly visible.

9. Use a safety kick stool to reach high shelves.

10. Update each stock record once the item has been checked against the quantity ordered/delivery note. Notify finance immediately of any discrepancies.

11. If, for any reason, stored stock is accidentally damaged refer the matter to the senior administrator. Do not adjust the stock record without specific authorisation.

PROCEDURES IN BUSINESS

The importance of procedures for stock control becomes obvious when you know that more than £3,100 million is spent by British businesses on stationery each year. According to research, about 15 per cent of this is wasted, stolen or never used. This works out at about £126 for every employee.

To help to save money, many companies are reviewing their procedures as well as their list of suppliers and are buying more and more goods online. This has obvious benefits. Only authorised staff have passwords to enable them to prepare an order, and all orders can then be collated daily and electronically sent to the finance or purchasing department for approval. Only after approval has been given will the order be accepted and processed by the online supplier. This has many benefits, because individual departments can prepare their own orders but the total quantity and amount can be checked carefully and the usage of each department quickly analysed.

Strict procedures are also in force in relation to the type of goods which can be ordered, how goods should be checked and delivery notes matched against the online orders.

To find out more about online suppliers follow the links from www.heinemann.co.uk/hotlinks.

OVER TO YOU!

1. Find out the exact procedure you will have to follow to do each of the following activities:
   a) Maintaining the stock records and keeping them up-to-date when you issue stock or a new delivery arrives.
   b) Issuing new stock against a requisition.
   c) Checking current stock levels for certain items.
   d) Completing a purchase requisition or an order form.
   e) Checking a delivery of stock.
   f) Storing supplies appropriately and safely.

2. For each of the above procedures, explain its purpose in your own words.

3. Many stock control problems are covered by procedures, but not all of them. On some occasions you need to refer to the procedures whilst on others you might have to use your common sense.

   Whilst you are controlling stock the following problems occur. In each case decide:
   a) whether there is likely to be a procedure you should check to find out what to do, or whether you should use your own initiative
   b) what the procedure – or your supervisor – would tell you to do in each case.

   Check your answers with your tutor.

i) There are only four lever arch files in the stock cupboard because you are awaiting a delivery and someone wants all of them.

ii) For the third time, your supplier has returned your order for cartridges for the laser printer marked 'out of stock'.

iii) A stapler booked in two months ago has just been issued and the recipient has returned it because it won't work.

iv) You need to update the stock card for file folders but can't find it when you look in the index box.

v) You receive two more boxes of pens than you ordered.

vi) You make a mistake on the stock card when you are calculating the balance and put the wrong number.

vii) Although your stock card shows that you should have 40 rulers in stock, during a stock check you can find only 10.

viii) You accidentally knock correction fluid over five document wallets and now they are unusable.

ix) You discover some unwrapped paper has been left near the window and has discoloured.

x) You wanted 500 economy pockets but did not realise each unit was a box of 200. You have now received 500 boxes!

▼FOLLOWING PROCEDURES FOR PROCESSING INCOMING AND OUTGOING POST

The Royal Mail handles over 70 million items of mail every day, most of which is received and sent by businesses. This doesn't include all the other items handled by private couriers or private delivery services. Therefore you can see that a large organisation may receive and send thousands of items each day. Even in the smallest firm, however, the post is very important, as many business transactions will rely upon communications sent and received by mail.

For this reason, there are procedures for dealing with the incoming and outgoing post in every company. In a large organisation there will be a central mailroom with trained staff and, quite probably, a considerable amount of equipment to help them. Within each department the administrators will be responsible for collecting the mail from the mailroom and distributing it to their own staff twice a day, as well as taking the post they have prepared for dispatch to the mailroom each afternoon. In a small firm, the task of processing the post may be given to one or two staff to do as part of their overall duties.

Therefore the procedures for handling the post within an organisation will vary, usually depending upon its size and the quantity of post handled each day. There are often different procedures for mailroom staff and departmental staff. In this section, the example procedures assume you are working in a relatively small business where you are responsible for all the main aspects of processing the post each day. Note that you would have to adapt these if you worked for an organisation which handles far more items and so operates rather differently.

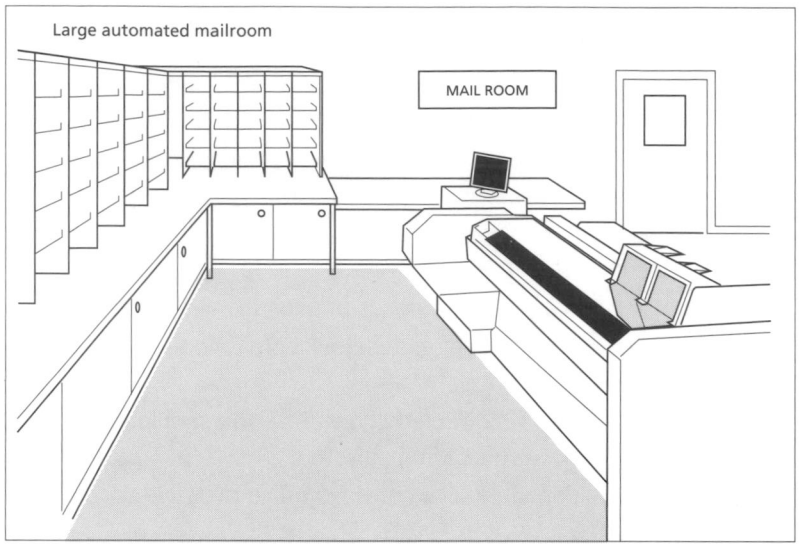

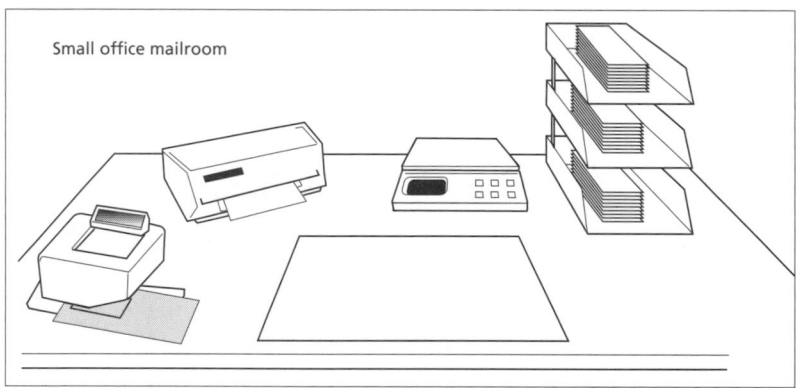

▲ A large organisation will have an automated central mailroom whereas in a small organisation the mailroom will be quite different

Procedures for processing incoming mail

Incoming mail must always be distributed as early as possible in the working day, because it is likely to contain important and urgent items. Many staff like to check their post as quickly as possible, in case the information they receive affects their planned activities. For this reason, opening and distributing the post is usually given top priority each morning.

The first task is to pre-sort the mail into different categories. A list of these is given in the table on page 371, together with the normal action you would be expected to take.

Different types of incoming mail items

Item	Action to take
Urgent mail – marked with Special Delivery sticker, or marked URGENT or delivered by courier	You will have to sign for many of these items. Open them *first* and keep separate from routine items. Record in incoming mail log*. If the item is delivered during the day, process and distribute it immediately.
Recorded Delivery items – marked with special sticker	Sign for item and record in incoming mail log*.
Mail marked Personal or Private and Confidential	Do not open. If the recipient is away and the item is also marked Urgent, tell your supervisor.
First class mail	Open after processing urgent items.
Second class mail	Open after processing first class mail.
Circulars, booklets, journals which must be seen by several staff	Attach a circulation slip and send to the first person on the list, if this is the company policy.
Cheques and postal orders	Attach securely to attached paperwork and record in incoming mail log*.
Parcels and packages	Sign for as 'received but contents not checked'. Open only if instructed to do so by named recipient then open carefully to prevent damage and check contents.
Wrongly delivered mail	Repost unopened. Add any additional postal instructions to envelope e.g. 'not known at this address'.

* Not all organisations operate an incoming mail log for recording post. See page 372.

The other main points to note are given below.

▷ The post is usually opened in priority order, i.e. urgent and special items first, then first class then second class. This is very important if there is a lot of post and you are short of time, because it means that you have dealt with the main items.

▷ You may have to sort and distribute internal items (from one department to another) as well as those received from outside the firm. You treat these in exactly the same way as external items, especially if they are marked 'urgent' or 'confidential'.

Once you know what to do with the different categories of mail, the procedure will tell you how to process it.

Example procedure for processing incoming mail

1 All mail must be opened and pre-sorted on arrival, apart from Personal or Private and Confidential items.

2 All mail, apart from financial or legal documents, must be date-stamped.

3 All enclosures must be checked and clipped to the main document. Any omission must be noted on the document and initialled.

4 All mail must be placed in the labelled baskets in priority order, so that urgent and special items are on the top, then first class post and finally second class post and circulars.

5 All envelopes must be retained for 24 hours in case of queries.

6 Any suspicious packages or items must be reported immediately to the nearest supervisor or manager. There are separate procedures for dealing with these items.

Do bear in mind that the procedure above can vary in several ways.

▶ It may be your job to distribute the mail to recipients rather than put it into baskets for collection. In this case, you will need to know what to do if someone is away because they are on holiday or ill. It is not enough simply to dump their post on their empty desk!

▶ A few organisations deliver the post to recipients unopened, to save time. The disadvantage is that the contents then aren't date-stamped. Most companies prefer to do this in case there are any later queries about when it was received.

▶ Many organisations circulate items which must be seen by several staff but which obviously can't be photocopied, such as a magazine or journal, whereas others send them to a named manager or department. If you have to circulate something, you simply attach a slip which lists the names of people who must see it and sent it to the first person. An example is shown below.

CIRCULATION SLIP

Name	Date received	Date passed on
Philip Conway		
Karen Davidson		
Sonia Milewski		
Jamila Mirza		
Andrew Slater		
Sarah Woods		

Please return to: Fiona Rooney

▲ A circulation slip

▶ Procedures for handling suspicious packages vary, depending upon the organisation. If security is paramount, then all incoming mail may even be scanned on arrival in machines similar to those used at airports. In other mailrooms there may simply be a poster telling staff what to do if they receive a parcel or letter which looks 'odd', for example because it is not addressed to a known individual, has an unusual postmark or is discoloured on the packaging. In this case, staff are instructed not to touch or move the parcel or use the telephone, as some devices are activated by telephone signals. The parcel should be placed on a table away from windows and doors, everyone should leave the room and lock the door and report their concerns immediately.

Recording incoming post

Some organisations don't record incoming post at all, while others record only urgent and special items which had to be signed for on receipt. Some also record incoming cheques as they are received, although today this task is often carried out after the cheques have been sent to the finance department.

If records are kept, these may be in a book in the mailroom or on a computer. An example of the type of headings you may find is shown below.

Record of incoming mail

Special items record

Date	Name of recipient	Name of sender	Type of item
1 March	William Kent	Jan Palowski	Special delivery
1 March	Susan Pearson	Bryant & Webb	Recorded delivery
2 March	Hasan Demir	Kenton Graphics	Courier delivery
2 March	Simon Finlay	Lisa Olah	Special delivery

Record of money received

Remittances record

Date	Name	Amount £	Account Number	Comments
1 March	Ben Parkinson	248.10	290839	
1 March	Nadine Taylor	22.50	103892	
1 March	Junaid Ali	105.70	308991	
1 March	Emma Reid	50.60	109829	Cheque not signed

Using equipment to process incoming post

The main two items used to process incoming post are:

▶ a **letter opening machine**, which automatically makes a slit in the envelope, very close to the edge, so that the contents aren't damaged. You simply stack the envelopes correctly in the hopper and then pass these through the machine.

▶ a **date stamp** which records the date the item was received, in case there are any queries later. When you are date-stamping the post, make sure you never obscure any written text on a page – the usual place is at the very top or at the bottom of the document. Check, too, the type of items which must not be date-stamped for any reason.

Obviously, in an organisation which handles thousands of items a day you will find far more sophisticated machines in operation. For example, a large credit card company will have mail opening equipment that automatically opens each envelope, removes the contents, stacks them and may even process the cheques received at the same time.

Following procedures for processing outgoing post

Outgoing post, also, falls into different categories. There will be some urgent items, some of which are valuable or fragile, a few parcels – and many routine items. All need processing correctly and promptly for dispatch the same day. A large organisation will have its mail collected in the late afternoon; in a small firm it is more likely to be taken to the nearest post box or post office. In either case, the mail must be ready by a specific deadline.

The type of items you may have to deal with are shown in the table opposite. Again the procedures will tell you how to process it.

Example procedure for processing outgoing post

1 Check all letters have been signed and the enclosures are attached.

2 If an envelope or label has been prepared, check the name and address match that on the letter. Otherwise, use a window envelope making certain that the name and address of the recipient shows clearly in the window.

3 Seal the envelope. Today many organisations use self-seal or 'peel and seal' envelopes.

4 Pack any parcels or packages securely. All parcels and packages must be addressed using the company label which clearly states the name and address of the sender.

5 Pre-sort outgoing post into separate categories, i.e. special items, overseas mail, routine items, parcels.

6 Weigh and calculate the postage for each item of mail. If necessary write the postage amount *in pencil* on the envelope or package.

7 All routine items must be sent by second class mail unless they are specifically marked to be sent first class.

8 Complete any forms required for special mail items, such as Special Delivery and Recorded Delivery.

9 Process each item through the franking machine, checking that the postage set is correct. Frank an adhesive label for all items which cannot be processed through the machine and attach firmly.

Different types of outgoing mail items

Item	Action to take
Urgent and valuable items – usually sent by Special Delivery	Complete Special Delivery sticker according to instructions before processing. Add Special Delivery fee to normal amount of postage.
Important documents – usually sent by Recorded Delivery	Complete Recorded Delivery sticker according to to instructions before processing. Postage will depend whether item is to be sent first or second class, then add Recorded Delivery fee.
Routine letters and documents	Weigh all items containing more than two sheets of paper to calculate postage. All routine items are normally sent second class, unless they are specially marked on the envelope to be sent by first class post.
Reply paid or Freepost envelopes	Separate these from other items so that they are not franked in error.
Personal staff mail	Most organisations do not allow this to be franked. It must have stamps on before being accepted and is then grouped with the Freepost items.
Overseas mail	Urgent items can be sent by Swiftair for an additional fee. All items must be weighed and calculated based on the country they are being sent to. In some cases a customs declaration sticker must be completed. An airmail sticker is not required for European countries.
Internal mail	Usually sorted and placed direct in departmental trays. Mail for branch offices is usually put in large envelopes throughout the day and are then sealed to save the cost of posting separate items.
Parcels	Contents must be securely wrapped and protected using bubblewrap or similar. Spaces within a box must also be filled with packaging material (e.g. polystyrene chips or shredded paper waste). Box must be fastened securely with packaging tape and both recipient's name/address and sender's name/address clearly shown. Box must be weighed on parcel scales to calculate postage. Put a FRAGILE sticker on if appropriate.
Small fragile items and bulky packages	Small fragile items and heavy documents are usually dispatched in padded bags for security. The top can be stapled for additional protection but any staples must be covered with tape before posting.

As before, the procedure may vary in several ways.

▶ In some organisations, the contents of letters are checked within each department and all mail is sealed before it is sent to the mailroom for processing.

▶ Departments may also have the task of packing any parcels or packages before they are sent to the mailroom.

▶ There is often a specific instruction that senders of special mail must mark the service they require clearly on the envelope or package.

▶ The actual process to follow to weigh and frank the post will depend upon the equipment available, as you will see below.

▶ In some organisations, special items of outgoing post are recorded in a log. This will be similar to the record shown on page 373, only this time the sender's name will be recorded first and the recipient's address will also be included.

▶ All organisations need to track the amount of money spent on postage. In the past this was recorded in a special log and this still may be the case when stamps are used. There is no need to do this if a franking machine is used, because a record is provided through the cost of the postage units which must be purchased for the machine.

Using equipment to process outgoing post

The main items of equipment you will use are described below.

▶ **A postage scale.** Many organisations use electronic scales for standard items of post. These incorporate a chip which has been pre-programmed with current postal rates. You simply select either first or second class, overseas rates and any special fee services such as Recorded or Special Delivery, and the scale weighs the item and displays the amount of postage required.

These scales are too small to weigh heavy or bulky items, so larger postage scales must be used. In this case you must work out the postage yourself. You will also have to do this if you use the old type of manual scales. In this case, follow the procedure shown below.

Calculating postage using manual scales

Procedure to follow

1 Place the letter or parcel on the platform of the scales.

2 Read off the weight and note it in pencil on the envelope or package.

3 Refer to the postal rate charge chart supplied by the Royal Mail and read off the standard charge for that weight. Note that weights are always 'up to' so that each weight band shows the maximum that is allowed at that charge.

4 Add on any charges for special services.

5 Use stamps or frank the item for the total value.

▶ **A franking machine**. These are used by most organisations as they are much quicker and more convenient than using stamps and there is greater security. The franking impression or label can include an advertisement for the organisation and this also operates as a return address if the item is undeliverable.

Franking machines vary from quite basic models to highly sophisticated equipment which also incorporates electronic scales – so that each item is automatically weighed and franked by the machine as it passes through. Many will also seal envelopes automatically and most automatically change the date themselves. Whichever type you use, you need to establish a few basic points before you start, for example:

- the position of the hopper or feeder which holds the mail prior to processing

- whether the machine can accept mail of different thicknesses or whether you have to pre-sort the items in any way (such as smaller envelopes on the top)

- which way up to place the envelopes (normally address side up with the address oriented so that you can read it)

- how to print a label for packages and parcels

- how to stop the machine quickly in an emergency

- what to do if you make a mistake or have a problem.

You then have the choice whether to process items singly or automatically. You should choose the first for special items where you constantly need to change the postage amount. Select the second for large batches of standard items, e.g. first or second class.

There are not many things to go wrong on a franking machine. The mailroom operator is usually responsible for ensuring that there are sufficient postage units in the machine and that the ink and water (if there is a sealer) are replenished when necessary. However, it is possible to make a silly mistake and frank an item with the wrong amount. This isn't a disaster unless you under-frank an envelope and post it, because the recipient then has to collect it from the nearest Royal Mail depot and pay a surcharge (currently 80p plus the cost of the shortfall). This is not the best way to impress a customer! For that reason you need to be alert when you are franking and know what to do if you make an error.

- If you *under-frank* an envelope, then – if there is space – you can frank a label for the shortfall and stick this on as well. Alternatively, keep it safely and use it on the next envelope or parcel which has the same amount due.

- If you *over-frank* an item (or cannot use an under-franked item) then give the envelope or label to your supervisor. This is because it is normally possible to obtain a refund for any wrongly franked, unused envelopes or labels. Then you will have to put the contents in a new envelope and this time do the job correctly!

▶ **Folding and inserting machines** A highly mechanised mailroom will have a series of equipment linked together which may be operated by computer. In this case the first machine may print the labels from information stored in the computer database and attach these to the envelopes. The next will fold all the enclosures and put them into the envelopes which are then passed through a sealing unit, weighed and franked – all automatically. This is the type of system used by businesses that send out thousands of items of mail every day such as banks and insurance companies.

Smaller organisations may have a more basic version of a folding and inserting machine on which enclosures are stacked at one side, on different trays, and the pre-prepared envelopes on the other. The machines feed one of each item towards the envelopes, fold them, insert them and then seal the envelope. They are quite simple to operate providing you stack the enclosures and the envelopes according to instructions.

▶ **Miscellaneous items**. These may include marking stamps (to save having to write 'first class' or 'urgent' on different items), labels for special post, special stickers (e.g. *Fragile* or *This way up*), scissors, string holders and trolleys for heavy batches of post.

PROCEDURES IN BUSINESS

Many businesses have changed their mailroom procedures so they can generate new business through sending out direct mailshots, often known as database marketing. In most households this has another name – junk mail. According to the Direct Mail Information Service the total number of addressed junk mail items rose from 2.3 billion in 1990 to 5.23 billion in 2002 and the total amount spent on sending junk mail was nearly £2.4 billion.

Although many people complain about junk mail arriving through their letterbox every day, these mailshots resulted in £25.1 billion of new business – which makes it worthwhile for the companies. Consumers who seriously object can register with the Mailing Preference Service to have their name and address removed from non-customer mailing lists used by organisations.

Obviously a highly automated mailroom is required to deal with large quantities of outgoing mail – not just direct mail but also invoices and other routine documents if these need to be processed by the thousand. New types of equipment and processes are regularly featured by the Mailroom Innovations group of companies at displays around the country. You can find out more about the latest ideas and equipment, as well as how to reduce the amount of junk mail you receive, by following the links at www.heinemann.co.uk/hotlinks.

▲ Junk mail is now big business

Working safely

Needless to say, you must take due care for your own health and care and that of other people when you are processing mail. This means remembering the following safety points.

▶ Using all equipment in accordance with instructions.

▶ Never moving any equipment or tampering with it in any way.

▶ Not lifting or moving heavy parcels or items on your own.

▶ Not leaving parcels where people can fall over them.

▶ Passing scissors to people with the handles first.

OVER TO YOU!

1. Find out the exact procedures in operation in your own mailroom for each of the following activities:
   a) using the letter opening machine
   b) processing and distributing incoming post
   c) preparing different items of outgoing post for dispatch
   d) keeping any records of incoming and/or outgoing postal items
   e) using the postal scales to calculate the postage amount required
   f) using the franking machine.

2. For each of these procedures, explain the main purpose in your own words.

3. Many mailroom problems are covered by procedures, but not all of them. This is because no one who writes procedures can think of every difficulty that could occur. On some occasions you need to refer to the procedures, whilst on others you might have to use your common sense.

   Whilst you are processing the post, the following problems occur. In each case decide:
   a) whether there is likely to be a procedure you should check, to find out what to do, or whether you should use your own initiative
   b) what the procedure – or your supervisor – would tell you to do in each case.

   Check your answers with your tutor.
   i)   By mistake, you open an envelope marked *Personal* and extract the contents.
   ii) You receive two envelopes for someone marked *Urgent* but you know that person is away on holiday at the moment.
   iii) You have to insert three letters into window envelopes but no matter how you fold them you can't get the address to show properly, because it has been typed in the wrong place on each one.
   iv) You have received a catalogue which must be seen by six people.
   v)   You have received a letter addressed to Mr K. Smith – and there are three people with that name in your organisation.
   vi) The latest time by which the post must be prepared for dispatch is 4 pm and you know there is too much mail to process in the time you have left.
   vii) The roll of labels runs out in the franking machine.

viii) You under-frank a label for a parcel in error.

ix) You over-frank an envelope in error.

x) You have to weigh a package to be sent overseas and can't find out how much it will cost on the chart.

4 Practise folding A4 paper so that it will fit neatly into a DL envelope with three folds only. Then practise folding a sheet of letter-headed paper with a typed address on the top so that it will show clearly in a window envelope. Bear in mind that folding documents neatly and with the minimum number of creases takes skill but gives a much better impression of your organisation when the customer opens the mail!

▼ REVIEW THE WAYS IN WHICH PROCEDURES ARE IMPLEMENTED AND THEIR EFFECTIVENESS

This unit has covered a wide variety of office-based procedures. You have seen how these can vary between organisations depending upon many factors – from their size, to their working practices and according to the type or model of equipment that you have to use.

However, when you start work you are not supposed to know all these procedures on your first day or learn them off by heart. There will be various ways in which you can check the exact procedures to use and refer to them when you need them. You will also be trained to use those that are particularly important or relevant to your own job. This section looks at the different ways you will learn about procedures at work.

Whilst procedures are important they may not be perfect or they may go out-of-date. Therefore it is usual to check routinely that those who are using them can do so without any problems. There are several reasons why users may have difficulties and why the procedures may need to be improved. In this final section you will learn about these and find out how to evaluate procedures yourself to judge their effectiveness.

The ways in which procedures are supported and promoted

There are several ways in which you can find out about the procedures that exist and refer back to them when you need to.

▶ **Procedure manuals**. Some organisations keep special procedure manuals or handbooks for staff which cover all the procedures relating to relevant aspects of work. There may be separate manuals, for example, for staff who work in a specific area – such as the mailroom or stock control – to guide them through the particular tasks they have to do. These manuals are normally revised at regular intervals, so the first point to check is that you are referring to the most recent version.

Alternative information sources are the manuals which are issued with items of equipment. These include the procedures to follow and a 'trouble shooting' section to help you if you have a problem. Every office will keep manuals for main items of equipment, such as the fax machine, photocopier and printer so that users can refer to them as and when required.

▶ **Training**. During induction, all staff receive training in relation to health and safety procedures (see Unit 3, page 292). Anyone who is responsible for a specific item of equipment, such as a photocopier or franking machine, will usually receive some basic training by the supplier when the equipment is first installed. This person may then be responsible for training other people who have to undertake routine operations.

A variation is a **mentor**. This is someone who will show you what to do and be on hand to help if you encounter any difficulties or do not understand something. A mentor is normally a more experienced colleague who works in the same office or department.

▶ **Tracking documents.** These are designed to guide users through a procedure. They are most commonly used when the steps in a procedure are performed by different people in different locations. The tracking document lists each step, and each person following the procedure identifies the steps he or she has carried out. An example is shown below. In this case, the tracking document has been designed to make sure that the correct procedure is followed before any invoice is passed for payment. It therefore lists all the items that have to be checked. This document will be attached to the invoice and passed to the various people responsible at each stage for their signature. It would then be sent back to the accounts department who complete the final checks and will pay the invoice.

ACCOUNT VERIFICATION FORM		
Item to be checked	**Status**	**Verified by**
Goods received as per order		
Invoice details correct as per quotation/order		
For completion by accounts department:		
Invoice calculations correct .... (Signed)		
Payment approved .... (Signed)		

▶ **Timescales**   Some departmental procedures include a deadline that must be observed by anyone following the procedure. Examples include:

– processing the outgoing post by the time the mail is scheduled for collection

– answering the telephone within a stated number of rings

– delivering fax messages to recipients within a stated time

– acknowledging all complaints within so many days

– issuing stock items within so many hours from the receipt of a completed stationery requisition

– completing a stock take within a fixed time period.

▶ **Internal communications**. This method is frequently used for simple procedures or to inform users about changes to existing procedures. A memo is likely to be sent if users must keep the information and update their procedure manual. An email will be sent for more minor updates and when information needs to be circulated rapidly, e.g. a minor change to the logging-in procedure on the computer system.

Identifying possible difficulties in following procedures

There are many reasons why a procedure may not work, in which case there is no point in having it. A procedure certainly won't work if it is written by someone who doesn't know much about the task and then everyone is simply told to 'do it'. Therefore a key aim of anyone who writes a procedure must be to make sure that it is effective. This means it can be followed easily, it helps people to work more efficiently, and it achieves its main purpose.

The main reasons why people experience difficulties are given below.

▶ **Unclear procedures**. Many people have never got beyond the first, basic stage of using their video recorder because they simply cannot understand what they have to do to carry out the more complicated operations. The same can be said about many computer help screens, too! As you probably know yourself, if you can't get beyond the first few words without getting confused, you simply think of another way of doing something – or don't bother.

▶ **Others not knowing the procedures**. Unless people are told what to do (and sometimes reminded at regular intervals!) they are highly unlikely to follow the correct procedure. In this case, they will simply guess. This can cause chaos for other people as records may not be kept correctly or equipment not used properly. This can happen, for example, in an organisation where many staff have open access to the photocopier. If there are a large number of staff, some of whom work only on a casual basis, then it is unlikely all of them will have received the proper training. This can lead to many problems – and even machine breakdowns – which can seriously inconvenience other users.

▶ **Procedure breaking down**. There are many reasons why a procedure may break down. For example:

– It may be too ambitious. A procedure which stated that a college administrator has to telephone every student who is absent is fine if ten students are away but will break down if one hundred are missing on the same day.

– It may be badly written or miss out key steps so that, no matter how you try, you can't obtain the desired result. As an example, try the procedure on page 16 of this book (customising your spell-checker) without step two – which is how it was originally printed in an article!

- It may rely on one person to coordinate it and break down if this person isn't available or is too busy to give it enough attention. For example, if a procedure stated that all new computer users must register with a certain person at computer services, this procedure would break down every time that person was away.

- It may involve too many people and so become impossible to control. This is why, for example, the overall responsibility for ordering stock is normally limited to just a few people.

▶ **No tracking systems**. Tracking and monitoring a procedure helps to check it is working and proves to users that there is a good reason for doing it. A common procedure in your college is for your tutors to complete a register for each class. If it didn't matter whether they were filled in or not, because no one ever did anything with this information, then before too long every tutor would stop completing them. Instead, all tutors know that the information in their registers is recorded and monitored all the time and, if they didn't complete it, they would have to explain why. Similarly, if you forgot to update stock records, you would soon have to give a good reason, because stock-taking and ordering would then become a nightmare. If, however, you found that you were filling in records that no one ever checked or needed, it would be only human nature if you stopped bothering with them after a time.

PROCEDURES IN BUSINESS

Some organisations have made it their business to track whether other people are following procedures. They have become successful by realising that, unless people are tracked and monitored, they rarely continue doing things – even when they want to!

A good example is Weight Watchers and other slimming clubs. They know that no matter how many people vow to diet (a type of procedure), they often fall by the wayside after a while and give up. Going to a weekly class where their weight is recorded helps to keep them on target. So Weight Watchers has made its money from tracking the weight loss of its members and keeping them motivated.

Another example is your dentist. Although it may seem like common sense to have regular dental check-ups, because problems can be remedied more easily, the main reason why there are likely to be fewer problems is because patients who go regularly are more likely to follow the recommended procedures for cleaning their teeth. They know their dentist will be checking up on them at regular intervals!

The government is also aware that people become lax if they are not regularly checked, which is the reason why tax returns have to be submitted regularly, people claiming job seekers allowance have to report regularly and there are annual MOT tests – to prevent people driving unroadworthy vehicles.

The government also insists that your attendance at college is tracked. You might like to think about whether it would be any different if this wasn't done!

▲ A tutor's register is a type of procedure to track students' attendance

Identification of possible improvements

Once you realise what can go wrong with procedures, it becomes much easier to identify possible improvements. In each case, the improvement you suggest should link to the type of difficulty you have identified, as you will see in the table opposite.

Evaluating the effectiveness of procedures when completing tasks

For the final part of your assessment you have to evaluate procedures yourself. This means you have to think critically about the procedures you have used and give your own opinion about whether they were effective or not. This should be based on evidence relating to the procedure itself and the outcome, and not be influenced by your mood that day!

Learning how to evaluate procedures is important because the only way procedures will ever be improved is through feedback from users. Without feedback, the person who wrote the procedure may be sitting smugly in an office thinking everything is perfect, whilst in the office alongside everyone is saying how stupid it is. A more professional approach is to suggest improvements based on clear evidence that it isn't working properly – which is what this section is all about.

If you are worried about evaluating procedures, console yourself with the fact you have probably been doing this informally for years. How many times have you had to do something and thought it was pointless or decided that it could be done in a much better or easier way? Most people think this almost every day when they visit a shop with long queues, have to fill in a long form with irrelevant information or can't make head or tail of what a written instruction really means.

Difficulties with procedures and identifying improvements

Difficulty	Suggested improvement
A procedure is too long or is difficult to understand.	Shorten or simplify it so that it is more 'user-friendly'.
A procedure is out-of-date (e.g. applies to old equipment or methods of working).	Update or revise the procedure.
A procedure isn't known by everyone.	Review the way in which the procedure is communicated or how staff are trained.
The procedure takes too long to do.	Either shorten the procedure or split up the task among more people.
A procedure doesn't work because it is too reliant on one person.	Change the procedure so that there are more options if this person is away.
A procedure doesn't work because even when it is followed it doesn't achieve the desired result.	Revise the procedure and test it to make sure it works.
A procedure doesn't work because too many people are involved, many of whom don't follow it properly.	Revise the procedure and/or reduce the number of users and/or improve the training.
A procedure is unnecessary because the records you need to complete are never used.	Review the records kept and assess if these are necessary and then revise the procedure to bring it up-to-date.
A procedure doesn't work because, although many people don't follow it, nothing is done about this.	Check whether the procedure is stil necessary. If so, improve the tracking and monitoring systems.

For your assessment, you must write a clear review which addresses all the key points and makes suggestions which would *work*, given the procedure you are following. For example, suggesting that all the staff in the organisation go on a five-day training course to learn to refill the paper tray in the photocopier is both impractical and unnecessary. Recommending that a poster is placed above the machine which illustrates the procedure clearly is far more sensible and appropriate.

To help, a checklist of the main items to consider is given on page 386.

If you think about the procedure you have followed and complete the checklist whilst your experience is still fresh in your mind, this will help you to prepare for writing your review.

Checklist for evaluating a procedure

The procedure was:	Yes/No
Easy to understand	
– each step was clear	
– each step was in the right order	
– illustrated when appropriate	
Up-to-date	
– it related to the equipment you were using	
– it related to the working methods you had to follow	
– it included current telephone numbers/contact names	
Helpful	
– it explained how to carry out tasks	
– it explained what to do if there was a problem	
– it covered all the likely problems	
Efficient	
– it helped you to do the task more quickly	
– it helped to prevent wastage	
Well supported	
– it was easy to find the procedure	
– the procedure was in a manual/clearly documented	
– there was appropriate training	
Effective	
– other people knew it and followed it too	
– there were no unexpected problems	
– it achieved its purpose and helped you to do the job efficiently	

Writing your review

Your review can be typed or written, but should take about one A4 page if you type it. Start with an appropriate heading, for example **Review of procedures for processing incoming and outgoing post**. You then need to write a brief introduction to explain the tasks you have carried out, and continue by reviewing the procedures you have followed under four headings:

▶ **Two ways in which the procedure is supported and promoted within the organisation**

In this section you need to identify where anyone undertaking the task can find out about the procedures. For example, there may be a user manual, notices, posters, or special training during which some procedures are explained verbally.

▶ **Any difficulties faced in following the procedure**

This is where you list any difficulties you encountered. Be careful to focus on difficulties relating to the *procedure*. Any problems you faced using the equipment (such as the fax machine running out of paper) are not relevant unless you referred to the procedure for help and found that you couldn't understand it or that no help was given.

▶ **At least one improvement to the procedure to increase its effectiveness**

If you had problems finding or understanding a procedure, then explain how it could be improved. For example, you might think it would be better if there was a diagram or illustration or if there was more training or guidance for new users.

▶ **The overall effectiveness of the procedure based on my experience of it**

In this section you should describe the extent to which you feel the procedures you used helped you to do your work.

An example of a review is shown below to help you. Ruksana enjoyed her experience controlling stock but this hasn't prevented her from suggesting one or two improvements.

Review of procedures used for controlling stock

I was responsible for controlling stock when I worked in the administration office for two weeks. I had to check that the requisitions were completed properly and authorised by a manager, select the correct stock for distribution, and update the stock cards. I made out two orders for new stock and, when this was delivered, checked it carefully and stored it. I then entered the new stock levels on the stock cards.

▶ **Two ways in which the procedures is supported and promoted within the organisation**

Before I started I was taken through the process several times by my supervisor. She also stressed I could ask her if I had any problems. I was also given a printed manual, which included the procedures for checking requisitions, updating stock cards and making out orders. There is a notice in the stock cupboard which summarises the procedures for storing stock properly.

▶ **Any difficulties faced in following the procedure**

I didn't have any difficulties because all the steps were clear and included the action to take if I had any difficulties. It was helpful that these were documented because I could refer to them all the time and look at the illustrations of the completed forms.

My only problem was that staff could interrupt me to bring a requisition and ask for individual items of stock. I also had problems because one person had completed some stock cards in pencil and I couldn't read the figures clearly.

▶ **At least one improvement to the procedure to increase its effectiveness**

I think the stock control procedure would be improved if staff could only obtain stock on demand in an emergency and the rest of the time they were issued with stock twice a day.

I also think the procedure should say that people completing stock cards must use a pen.

▶ **The overall effectiveness of the procedure based on my experience of it**

Overall, I think the procedures were very effective because I quickly learned to do the job properly. When I unpacked a broken hole punch I referred to the procedures, which told me exactly what to do. I was also able to refer to them whenever I had forgotten what to do, which was very useful.

1 Nicola and Bernadette have both been working in the college office. Nicola has been filing documents and retrieving information and was asked to archive some old files following the procedure on page 331. The senior administrator went through the procedure with her verbally and gave her a document that listed the procedure. She then left her to do the task. Although Nicola understood what to do, she had problems interpreting 'when a file has reached the end of its natural cycle' because she didn't know enough to decide this and had to keep going back to the senior administrator to check. This caused difficulties later in the day when the senior administrator left to go to a meeting and Nicola had to wait for her return. Nicola used the shredder to destroy some old documents and, when a large report jammed, she referred to the handbook, which clearly explained how to release the paper properly.

Bernadette helped to process the post using the procedures on page 372 and 374. She didn't have any problems opening and sorting the mail and enjoyed helping to process the outgoing post. She found the posters on the wall of the mailroom very helpful, especially the one about using the postage scales. She also referred to other notices that clearly explained the procedures to follow when opening and sorting the post. The staff also showed her what to do. Although Bernadette didn't have any difficulties following these she thought it would be better if there were clearer instructions on using the franking machine. The handbook was very complicated and on one occasion she franked the back of the envelopes by mistake.

Write a review, using the correct headings, to cover both their experiences and check your work with your tutor.

2 a) Choose one task you have undertaken and identify at least *two* procedures you have followed. Describe exactly how these are supported and promoted in terms of manuals, documentation and training.

b) For the procedures you have identified, state any difficulties you experienced. (If you didn't have any, then say so.)

c) Identify at least one improvement that would help to make the procedures more effective.

d) State whether you think the procedures, overall, are effective or not and give a reason for your opinion. Use the checklist on page 386 to help you.

Index

A

accidents, reporting 285
administration
– contribution of 229
– department 208
– importance of effective 226–229
– range of tasks in a company 227, 228
advertisements, *see* promotional material
agendas 39
– conventions 39
– format of 39, 40
aims and objectives of businesses 192–197
analysing, extracting and adapting information
9, 29, 48
apostrophe, use of 26, 27, 52
appraisals 265
articles 57, 58
– conventions 57
– format of 57, 60
– tone and style 58
assertiveness 119
assessment information 2, 76, 77, 121, 170, 310,
311, 387, 388

B

board of directors 220
body language 130, 144
business documents, A–Z 3
business letters 17–20
– conventions 17
– format of 17, 18
– tone and style 19
business organisations
– development of 185–197
– structures of 199–217
– roles within 219–225
– types of 171–184
business relationships, *see* working
relationships

C

centralised services 215, 216
charities 177–179
Commission for Racial Equality 305
communicating changes to plans 250
communications
– accuracy and clarity 152
– between departments and groups 216, 217
– body language 130, 144
– customers 130, 135–153
– diplomacy and tact 106
– face-to-face 101, 103
– importance of 141, 258
– language and tone 106
– manner/style of address 105, 136
– methods of 101
– solving problems with 147, 148
– in teams 100–108
– telephone 102
– tone and manner 149, 150
– verbal skills 101, 142, 143
– written 1–73, 104
companies
– private 171, 175–176
– public 171, 176–177
complaints, *see* customers
Copyright Licensing Agency 349
confidentiality
– and customers 138, 139, 152
– and planning 236
– and storing and retrieving information 332, 333
– and teamwork 93
contract of employment 294, 297
culture, of companies 196
customers
– accuracy and clarity with 152
– answering queries 157
– body language 130
– communications with 130–153
– complaints 162
– confidentiality 138, 139, 152
– customer service 132
– dealing with complaints 137, 138, 155, 156
– interactions with 141
– internal and external 128
– liability 159
– listening skills 144, 146
– manner and attitude towards 130
– meeting requirements of 164–166
– personal presentation and 129
– positive image to 128–132
– problems 158
– procedures for communicating with 135–139
– procedures for resolving difficulties with
153–159

– providing attention to 135
– questioning skills 144, 145
– recording information about 160–163, 165
– solving communication problems with 147
– special requirements of 153, 154
– styles of address with 136
– tone and manner with 149, 150
– verbal and non-verbal communication skills
    142, 143
– working with 128
customer service
– department 208, 209
– effectiveness of and benefits 132
– standards 135

D

Data Protection Act 140, 163, 333
deadlines 85, 94, 235
– difficulties meeting 251
decentralised services 215, 216
desk, organisation of 243, 244
development of business organisations
– costs of 186
– impacts of 189, 190
– liability 186
– mergers and takeovers 189
– reasons for 185
– specialisation/diversification 187, 188
diaries 90, 238
– electronic 239
Disability Discrimination Act 1995 303
Disability Rights Commission 305
disciplinary procedures 301
discrimination and the law 302
dismissal 300–302
displacement activity 257
distractions, dealing with 255, 256
distribution 206, 207
diversification 187, 188

E

efficiency, factors that impact on 253–259
electronic filing 322
emails 4–8
– conventions 5
– format of 4
– perils of 105
– tone and style 6
employment and equal opportunities legislation
    299, 306
English, use of 7, 14, 21, 26, 37, 42, 54, 58, 64, 69
equal opportunities 302–305
Equal Opportunities Commission 305

Equal Pay Act 1970 304
equipment, position of 273, 274

F

fax machines
– basic maintenance 357
– features 351, 352
– instructions and procedures for use of
    equipment 354, 355
– logging use of 356
– refilling paper in 355
– speaking before/after transmission
    356
– poor quality originals 355
– problem solving 358
fax messages 24–26
– conventions 26
– cover pages/sheets 25, 353
– format of 24, 28
– tone and style 26
feedback on own performance 261,
    262
filing 321–336
– archiving files 330
– classification methods 325–329
– confidentiality 332, 333
– creating files 330
– cross-referencing 329
– electronic 322
– equipment for 334
– good practice procedures for paper based
    systems 323, 324
– index systems 335
– retrieving information 331
– safety 335
– storage materials for 334, 335
finance and accounting 200
flat structures 223
flexibility
– contingencies 250
– during planning and monitoring
    249
– importance of 248
flow charts, and procedures 314, 315
forms 33–37
– completion of 35
– conventions 33
– designing 36
– format of 33, 34
functional areas 199–210

G

grievance procedures 300

H

harassment 303
hazards and risks 277, 278, 285
health and safety
– codes of practice 290
– display screen equipment 287
– Display Screen Equipment Regulations 1992 288
– emergency procedures 286
– first aid 286
– in an administrative environment 277–289
– Health and Safety at Work Act 1974 278, 279
– mail handling 379
– office design and layout 274, 275
– photocopying 349
– precautions 279
– preventative measures 291
– regulations 280
– reporting accidents and hazards 285
– risk assessments 284, 291
– safe working practices 278, 281
– safety committees/representatives/officers 293
– safety policy 290
– storage of stock 367
– storing and retrieving information 335
– and teams 92
– and training 292
hierarchies 223, 224
human resources 201

I

improving own performance 261–267
– obtaining feedback 261
– self-assessment 267
– setting targets 262
– reviewing work with manager 265, 266
– training 263, 265
information: analysing, extracting and adapting
    9, 29, 48
instructions, following 91, 253
interaction
– between departments and groups 216
– with customers 141
Investors in People 268
ISO quality procedures 319
IT policies 94
IT services department 209, 210

J

job descriptions 61, 63
– conventions 62
– format of 61, 63
– tone and style 62

L

leaflets, see promotional material
legal rights of employers and employees 298
letters, see business letters
limited companies 171, 175–177
local authorities 182, 183

M

mail 369–379
– circulation slips 372
– equipment 374, 376, 377
– procedures for processing incoming 370–373
– procedures for processing outgoing 374–378
– recording incoming mail/money received 373
– safety 379
– types of incoming mail items 371
– types of outgoing mail items 375
managers
– roles and responsibilities of 219–222
– levels of 221
– titles of 223
managing director 219, 220
matrix structure 214
meeting notes 41
– conventions 41
– format of 40, 46
– tone and style 41
meeting documents 39–42
– agendas 39
– meeting notes 41
memos 13, 14
– conventions 13
– format of 13, 15
– tone and style 13
messages, writing 9, 10
mission statements 192–194, 197
monitoring
– flexibility 249
– progress and reporting back 237

N

notes, taking 48
notices, see promotional material

O

objectives of organisations 194, 195
office environment and efficiency 269
office layout and design 270–275
office procedures, see procedures
organisation structures 211–215, 223–225
organising activities to suit objectives 211–217

organising the work area, *see* work area
OCR teamwork review, writing 121–126
organisations, *see* business organisations

P

partnerships 171, 173, 174
person specification 64
PEST analysis 196
photocopying 337–349
– copyright 349
– checking standard of copying 339, 340
– collating and fastening copies 346, 347
– good practice procedures 340
– logging photocopier use 341
– minimising waste 246, 347
– photocopier facilities and features 338, 339
– procedures for reporting problems 347, 348
– procedures for use of equipment 342
– refilling paper 341, 342
– safety procedures 349
– using facilities to produce copies 343–345
Plain English Campaign 17
planning
– aids 90, 238
– confidentiality 236
– deadlines 235
– flexibility 249
– importance of 231
– prioritising 235
– stages in process 232–234
– to improve own performance 263
policy of companies 196
post, *see* mail
preparing business communications 1
prioritising 90, 235
private sector 171–179, 184
problems and teamwork 85, 86, 94, 98
procedures
– flow charts 314, 315
– health and safety 286, 290–292
– teams 85
– benefits of 318
– communications with customers 135–139
– evaluating effectiveness of 384, 385
– follow to complete tasks 309–389
– identifying difficulties in following 382, 383
– identifying improvements in 384
– importance of identifying and following 258, 259
– processing incoming and outgoing post 369–379
– purpose of 315, 316
– reproducing information (photocopying) 337–349

– resolving difficulties with customers 153–159
– sending and receiving information (by fax) 350–359
– stock control 361–368
– storing and retrieving information (filing) 321–336
– steps in 313, 314
– support for and promotion of 380–382
– types of 311
– unfair dismissal 300–302
– writing a review of 387, 388
production 202
promotional material 67–69
– conventions 67
– formats of 67, 72
– tone and style 69
public corporations 180, 181
public sector 180–184
purchasing 204, 205

R

Race Relations Act 1976 (as amended) 303
reports 52–54
– conventions 53
– format of 52, 56
reproducing information, *see* photocopiers
research and development 203
resources for teams 85, 87
rights and responsibilities at work 111, 294–306
roles
– in organisations 219–225
– in teams 79, 87

S

safety, *see* Health and Safety
sales and marketing 205, 206
self-assessment 267
sending and receiving information, *see* fax machines
Sex Discrimination Act 1975 (as amended) 303
sole traders 171–173
span of control 224
specialisation 187, 188
spell-checkers 14, 52
statutory employment rights 305, 306
stock control 361–368
– completing purchase requisitions and orders 365
– computerised systems 362, 363
– maintaining stock records 361–364, 367
– procedures for issuing stock 364, 365